Course	Introduction to Information Systems
Course Number	**MGM371 / MGT371**
Professor	Gordon Lucas
	University of Toronto, Mississauga
	Management

Contents

Credits

Business Plug-Ins 179

Achieving Business Success

CHAPTER 1

Business Driven Technology

1.1. Compare management information systems (MIS) and information technology (IT).

1.2. Describe the relationships among people, information technology, and information.

1.3. Identify four different departments in a typical business and explain how technology helps them to work together.

1.4. Compare the four different types of organizational information cultures and decide which culture applies to your school.

Information Technology's Role in Business

Students frequently ask, "Why do we need to study information technology?" The answer is simple: Information technology is everywhere in business. Understanding information technology provides great insight to anyone learning about business.

FIGURE 1.1

Technology in *BusinessWeek* and *Fortune*

It is easy to demonstrate information technology's role in business by reviewing a copy of popular business magazines such as *BusinessWeek, Fortune,* or *Fast Company.* Placing a marker (such as a Post-it Note) on each page that contains a technology-related article or advertisement indicates that information technology is everywhere in business (see Figure 1.1). These are *business* magazines, not *technology* magazines, yet they are filled with technology. Students who understand technology have an advantage in business, and gaining a detailed understanding of information technology is important to all students regardless of their area of expertise.

The magazine articles typically discuss such topics as databases, customer relationship management, web services, supply chain management, security, ethics, business intelligence, and so on. They also focus on companies such as Siebel, Oracle, Microsoft, and IBM. This text explores these topics in detail, along with reviewing the associated business opportunities and challenges.

INFORMATION TECHNOLOGY'S IMPACT ON BUSINESS OPERATIONS

Figure 1.2 highlights the business functions receiving the greatest benefit from information technology, along with the common business goals associated with information technology projects according to *CIO* magazine.

Achieving the results outlined in Figure 1.2, such as reducing costs, improving productivity, and generating growth, is not easy. Implementing a new accounting system or marketing plan is not likely to generate long-term growth or reduce costs across an entire organization. Businesses must undertake enterprisewide initiatives to achieve broad general business goals such as reducing costs. Information technology plays a critical role in deploying such initiatives by facilitating communication and increasing business intelligence. For example instant messaging and WiMAX allow people across an organization to communicate in new and innovative ways.

Understanding information technology begins with gaining an understanding of how businesses function and IT's role in creating efficiencies and effectiveness across the organization. Typical businesses operate by functional areas (often called functional silos). Each functional area undertakes a specific core business function (see Figure 1.3).

Functional areas are anything but independent in a business. In fact, functional areas are *interdependent* (see Figure 1.4). Sales must rely on information from operations to understand inventory, place orders, calculate transportation costs, and gain insight into product availability based on production schedules. For an organization to succeed, every department or functional area must work together sharing common information and not be a "silo." Information technology can enable departments to more efficiently and effectively perform their business operations.

Any individual anticipating a successful career in business whether it is in accounting, finance, human resources, or operation management must understand the basics of information technology.

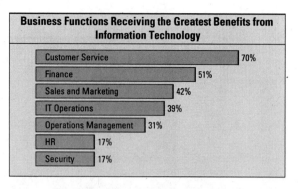

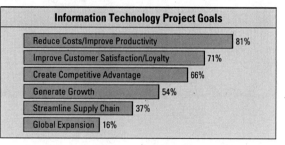

FIGURE 1.2

Business Benefits and Information Technology Project Goals

Information Technology Basics

Information technology (IT) is a field concerned with the use of technology in managing and processing information. Today, the term *information technology* has ballooned to encompass many aspects of computing and technology, and the term is more recognizable than ever. The information technology umbrella can be quite large, covering many fields that deal with the use of electronic computers and computer software to convert, store, protect, process, transmit, and retrieve information securely. Information technology can be an important enabler of business success and innovation. This is not to say that IT *equals* business success and innovation or that IT *represents* business success and innovation. Information technology is most useful when it leverages the talents of people. Information technology in and of itself is not useful unless the right people know how to use and manage it effectively.

Management information systems is a business function just as marketing, finance, operations, and human resources are business functions. Formally defined, *management information systems (MIS)* is a general name for the business function and academic discipline covering the application of people, technologies, and procedures—collectively called information systems—to solve business problems.

FIGURE 1.3

Departmental Structure of
a Typical Organization

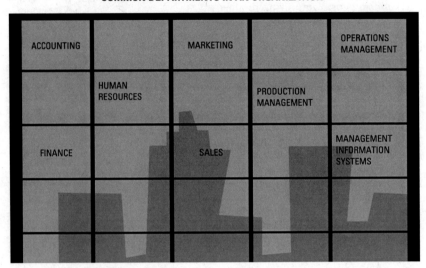

COMMON DEPARTMENTS IN AN ORGANIZATION

- **Accounting** provides quantitative information about the finances of the business including recording, measuring, and describing financial information.

- **Finance** deals with the strategic financial issues associated with increasing the value of the business, while observing applicable laws and social responsibilities.

- **Human resources (HR)** includes the policies, plans, and procedures for the effective management of employees (human resources).

- **Sales** is the function of selling a good or service and focuses on increasing customer sales, which increases company revenues.

- **Marketing** is the process associated with promoting the sale of goods or services. The marketing department supports the sales department by creating promotions that help sell the company's products.

- **Operations management** (also called **production management**) is the management of systems or processes that convert or transform resources (including human resources) into goods and services.

- **Management information systems (MIS)** is the academic discipline covering the application of people, technologies, and procedures—collectively called information systems—to solve business problems.

When beginning to learn about management information systems it is important to understand the following:

- Data, information, and business intelligence.
- IT resources.
- IT cultures.

DATA, INFORMATION, AND BUSINESS INTELLIGENCE

It is important to distinguish between data, information, and business intelligence. *Data* are raw facts that describe the characteristics of an event. Characteristics for a sales event could include the date, item number, item description, quantity ordered, customer name, and shipping details. *Information* is data converted into a meaningful and useful context. Information from sales events could include best-selling

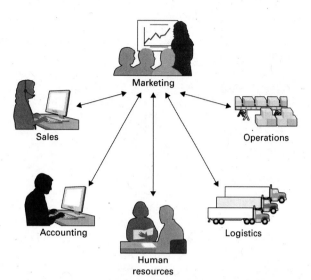

FIGURE 1.4

Marketing Working with
Other Organizational
Departments

Functional organization—Each functional area has its own systems
and communicates with every other functional area (diagram
displays Marketing communicating with all other functional areas
in the organization).

item, worst-selling item, best customer, and worst customer. ***Business intelligence***
refers to applications and technologies that are used to gather, provide access to, and
analyze data and information to support decision-making efforts. Business intelligence helps companies gain a more comprehensive knowledge of the factors affecting their business, such as metrics on sales, production, and internal operations,
which help companies make better business decisions (see Figures 1.5, 1.6, 1.7).

IT RESOURCES

The plans and goals of the IT department must align with the plans and goals of
the organization. Information technology can enable an organization to increase
efficiency in manufacturing, retain key customers, seek out new sources of supply,
and introduce effective financial management.

It is not always easy for managers to make the right choices when using IT to support (and often drive) business initiatives. Most managers understand their business initiatives well, but are often at a loss when it comes to knowing how to use

FIGURE 1.5

Data in an Excel
Spreadsheet

OrderDate	ProductName	Quantity	Unit Price	Total Sales	Unit Cost	Total Cost	Profit	Customer	SalesRep
04-Jan-10	Mozzarella cheese	41	24	984	18	738	246	The Station	Debbie Fernande
04-Jan-10	Romaine lettuce	90	15	1,350	14	1,260	90	The Station	Roberta Cross
05-Jan-10	Red onions	27	12	324	8	216	108	Bert's Bistro	Loraine Schultz
06-Jan-10	Romaine lettuce	67	15	1,005	14	938	67	Smoke House	Roberta Cross
07-Jan-10	Black olives	79	12	948	6	474	474	Flagstaff House	Loraine Schultz
07-Jan-10	Romaine lettuce	46	15	690	14	644	46	Two Bitts	Loraine Schultz
07-Jan-10	Romaine lettuce	52	15	780	14	728	52	Pierce Arrow	Roberta Cross
08-Jan-10	Red onions	39	12	468	8	312	156	Mamm'a Pasta Palace	Loraine Schultz
09-Jan-10	Romaine lettuce	66	15	990	14	924	66	The Dandelion	Loraine Schultz
10-Jan-10	Romaine lettuce	58	15	870	14	812	58	Carmens	Loraine Schultz
10-Jan-10	Pineapple	40	33	1,320	28	1,120	200	The Station	Loraine Schultz

Rows of data in an Excel spreadsheet.

FIGURE 1.6

Data Turned into
Information

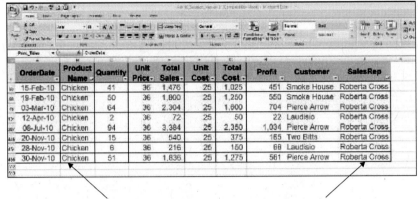

Data features, such as Autofilter, turn data into information.
This view shows all of Roberta Cross's chicken sales.

FIGURE 1.7

Information Turned into
Business Intelligence

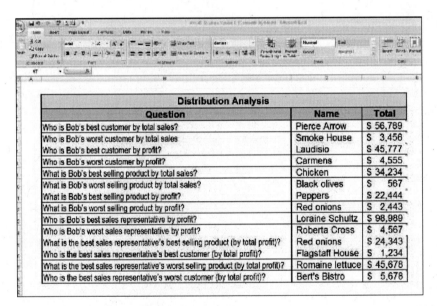

Advanced analytical tools, such as Pivot Tables, uncover business
intelligence in the data. For example, best customer, worst
customer, and best sales representative's best-selling product.

and manage IT effectively in support of those initiatives. Managers who understand what IT is, and what IT can and cannot do, are in the best position for success.

Putting It All Together

In essence,

- *People* use
- *information technology* to work with
- *information* (see Figure 1.8).

Those three key resources—people, information, and information technology (in that order of priority)—are inextricably linked. If one fails, they all fail. Most important, if one fails, then chances are the business will fail.

IT CULTURES

An organization's culture plays a large role in determining how successfully it will share information. Culture will influence the way people use information (their information behavior) and will reflect the importance that company leaders attribute to the use of information in achieving success or avoiding failure. Four common information-sharing cultures exist in organizations today: information-functional, information-sharing, information-inquiring, and information-discovery (see Figure 1.9).

An organization's IT culture can directly affect its ability to compete in the global market. If an organization operates with an information-functional culture it will have a great degree of difficulty operating. Getting products to market quickly and creating a view of its end-to-end (or entire) business from sales to billing will be a challenge. If an organization operates with an information-discovery culture it will be able to get products to market quickly and easily see a 360-degree view of its entire organization. Employees will be able to use this view to better understand the market and create new products that offer a competitive advantage.

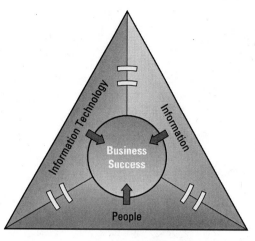

FIGURE 1.8

The Relationship among People, Information, and Information Technology

Organizational Information Cultures	
Information-Functional Culture	Employees use information as a means of exercising influence or power over others. For example, a manager in sales refuses to share information with marketing. This causes marketing to need the sales manager's input each time a new sales strategy is developed.
Information-Sharing Culture	Employees across departments trust each other to use information (especially about problems and failures) to improve performance.
Information-Inquiring Culture	Employees across departments search for information to better understand the future and align themselves with current trends and new directions.
Information-Discovery Culture	Employees across departments are open to new insights about crises and radical changes and seek ways to create competitive advantages.

FIGURE 1.9

Different Information Cultures Found in Organizations

OPENING CASE STUDY QUESTIONS

1. Explain how Apple achieved business success through the use of information, information technology, and people.

2. Describe the types of information employees at an Apple store require and compare it to the types of information the executives at Apple's corporate headquarters require. Are there any links between these two types of information?

3. Identify the type of information culture that would have the greatest negative impact on Apple's operations.

Chapter One Case: The World Is Flat—Thomas Friedman

In his book, *The World is Flat,* Thomas Friedman describes the unplanned cascade of technological and social shifts that effectively leveled the economic world, and "accidentally made Beijing, Bangalore, and Bethesda next-door neighbors." Chances are good that Bhavya in Bangalore will read your next X-ray, or as Friedman learned firsthand, "Grandma Betty in her bathrobe" will make your JetBlue plane reservation from her Salt Lake City home.

Friedman believes this is Globalization 3.0. "In Globalization 1.0, which began around 1492, the world went from size large to size medium. In Globalization 2.0, the era that introduced us to multinational companies, it went from size medium to size small. And then around 2000 came Globalization 3.0, in which the world went from being small to tiny. There is a difference between being able to make long-distance phone calls cheaper on the Internet and walking around Riyadh with a PDA where you can have all of Google in your pocket. It is a difference in degree that's so enormous it becomes a difference in kind," Friedman states. Figure 1.10 displays Friedman's list of "flatteners."

Friedman says these flatteners converged around the year 2000 and "created a flat world: a global, Web-enabled platform for multiple forms of sharing knowledge and work, irrespective of time, distance, geography, and increasingly, language." At the very moment this platform emerged, three huge economies materialized—those of India, China, and the former Soviet Union—"and 3 billion people who were out of the game, walked onto the playing field." A final convergence may determine the fate of the United States in this chapter of globalization. A "political perfect storm," as Friedman describes it—the dot-com bust, the attacks of 9/11, and the Enron scandal—"distract us completely as a country." Just when we need to face the fact of globalization and the need to compete in a new world, "we're looking totally elsewhere."

Friedman believes that the next great breakthrough in bioscience could come from a 5-year-old who downloads the human genome in Egypt. Bill Gates's view is similar: "Twenty years ago, would you rather have been a B-student in Poughkeepsie or a genius in Shanghai?

FIGURE 1.10

Thomas Friedman's 10 Forces That Flattened the World

1. **Fall of the Berlin Wall**	The events of November 9, 1989, tilted the worldwide balance of power toward democracies and free markets.
2. **Netscape IPO**	The August 9, 1995, offering sparked massive investment in fiber-optic cables.
3. **Work flow software**	The rise of applications from PayPal to VPNs enabled faster, closer coordination among far-flung employees.
4. **Open-sourcing**	Self-organizing communities, such as Linux, launched a collaborative revolution.
5. **Outsourcing**	Migrating business functions to India saved money *and* a Third World economy.
6. **Offshoring**	Contract manufacturing elevated China to economic prominence.
7. **Supply-chaining**	Robust networks of suppliers, retailers, and customers increased business efficiency.
8. **Insourcing**	Logistics giants took control of customer supply chains, helping mom-and-pop shops go global.
9. **Informing**	Power searching allowed everyone to use the Internet as a "personal supply chain of knowledge."
10. **Wireless**	Wireless technologies pumped up collaboration, making it mobile and personal.

Twenty years ago you'd rather be a B-student in Poughkeepsie. Today, it is not even close. You'd much prefer to be the genius in Shanghai because you can now export your talents anywhere in the world."

Questions

1. Do you agree or disagree with Friedman's assessment that the world is flat? Be sure to justify your answer.
2. What are the potential impacts of a flat world for a student performing a job search?
3. What can students do to prepare themselves for competing in a flat world?
4. Identify a current flattener not mentioned on Friedman's list.

CHAPTER 2   Identifying Competitive Advantages

2.1. Explain why competitive advantages are typically temporary.

2.2. List and describe each of the five forces in Porter's Five Forces Model.

2.3. Compare Porter's three generic strategies.

2.4. Describe the relationship between business processes and value chains.

Identifying Competitive Advantages

To survive and thrive, an organization must create a competitive advantage. A *competitive advantage* is a product or service that an organization's customers place a greater value on than similar offerings from a competitor. Unfortunately, competitive advantages are typically temporary because competitors often seek ways to duplicate the competitive advantage. In turn, organizations must develop a strategy based on a new competitive advantage.

When an organization is the first to market with a competitive advantage, it gains a first-mover advantage. The *first-mover advantage* occurs when an organization can significantly impact its market share by being first to market with a competitive advantage. FedEx created a first-mover advantage several years ago when it developed its customer self-service software allowing people and organizations to request a package pick-up, print mailing slips, and track packages online. Other parcel delivery services quickly followed with their own versions of the software. Today, customer self-service on the Internet is a standard for doing business in the parcel delivery industry.

As organizations develop their competitive advantages, they must pay close attention to their competition through environmental scanning. *Environmental scanning* is the acquisition and analysis of events and trends in the environment external to an organization. Information technology has the opportunity to play an important role in environmental scanning. For example, Frito-Lay, a premier provider of snack foods such as Cracker Jacks and Cheetos, does not just send its representatives into grocery stores to stock shelves—they carry handheld computers and record the product offerings, inventory, and even product locations of competitors. Frito-Lay uses this information to gain business intelligence on everything from how well competing products are selling to the strategic placement of its own products.

Organizations use three common tools to analyze and develop competitive advantages: (1) the Five Forces Model, (2) the three generic strategies, and (3) value chains.

The Five Forces Model—Evaluating Business Segments

For a business to prosper it must be able to quickly respond to all forms of competition from its rivals. To remain competitive businesses face decisions such as offering new products, entering new markets, and even competing in new industries

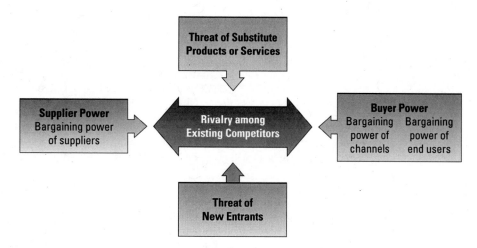

FIGURE 2.1

Porter's Five Forces Model

or industry segments. Michael Porter, a university professor at Harvard Business School, identified four competitive forces that can hurt potential sales:

1. Knowledgeable customers can force down prices by pitting rivals against each another.
2. Influential suppliers can drive down profits by charging higher prices for supplies.
3. New market entrants can steal potential investment capital.
4. Substitute products can steal customers.

To combat these competitive forces Porter developed the Five Forces Model, which is a useful tool to aid in understanding competition and its implications for business strategy. Understanding Porter's five forces can help a company identify potential opportunities and create a competitive advantage while deterring potential rivals. The **Five Forces Model** helps determine the relative attractiveness of an industry and includes the following five forces (see Figure 2.1).

1. Buyer power
2. Supplier power
3. Threat of substitute products or services
4. Threat of new entrants
5. Rivalry among existing competitors

BUYER POWER

Buyer power is assessed by analyzing the ability of buyers to directly impact the price they are willing to pay for an item. Factors used to assess buyer power include number of customers, size of orders, differences between competitors, sensitivity of price, and availability of substitute products. If buyer power is high they can force a company and its competitors to compete on price, which typically drives prices down. One way to reduce buyer power is by using switching costs. **Switching costs** are costs that can make customers reluctant to switch to another product or service. A switching cost need not have an associated monetary cost. For example, switching doctors is difficult because the new doctor will not have the patient's history and the relationship with the patient. This is a great example of using a switching cost to reduce buyer power, as switching doctors has an associated intangible cost.

Another way a company can reduce buyer power—and create a competitive advantage—is to expand and improve services so it is harder for customers to leave. One common tool companies use to reduce buyer power is a loyalty program. *Loyalty programs* reward customers based on the amount of business they do with a particular organization. The travel industry is famous for its loyalty programs such as frequent-flyer programs for airlines and frequent-stayer programs for hotels. Keeping track of the activities and accounts of many thousands or millions of customers covered by loyalty programs is not practical without large-scale IT systems. Loyalty programs are a good example of using IT to reduce buyer power. Because of the rewards (e.g., free airline tickets, upgrades, or hotel stays) travelers receive, they are more likely to be loyal to or give most of their business to a single organization.

SUPPLIER POWER

A *supply chain* consists of all parties involved, directly or indirectly, in the procurement of a product or raw material. In a typical supply chain, an organization will probably be both a supplier (to customers) and a customer (of other supplier organizations) as illustrated in Figure 2.2. *Supplier power* is assessed by the suppliers' ability to directly impact the price they are charging for supplies (including materials, labor, and services). Factors used to assess supplier power include number of suppliers, size of suppliers, uniqueness of services, and availability of substitute products. If supplier power is high the supplier can directly influence the industry by:

- Charging higher prices
- Limiting quality or services
- Shifting costs to industry participants

Typically, when a supplier raises prices the buyers will pass on the increase in price to their customers by raising prices on the end-product. When supplier power is high, buyers lose revenue because they cannot pass on the raw material price increase to their customers. For example, if Microsoft (supplier with high power) raises the price of its operating system it will decrease the profitability of its buyers (PC manufacturers such as Dell, Gateway, HP). The PC market is fierce and customers frequently purchase PCs based on price. If Microsoft increases the price of operating systems and the PC manufacturers cannot raise prices without jeopardizing sales, then the PC manufacturers have no choice—they must pay more for raw materials while selling their end-products at the same price thereby shrinking their profits. One tactic a company can use to decrease the power of its suppliers is to use standardized parts so it can easily switch suppliers.

THREAT OF SUBSTITUTE PRODUCTS OR SERVICES

The *threat of substitute products or services* is high when there are many alternatives to a product or service and low when there are few alternatives from which to choose. For example, there are many substitute products in the airline industry. Buyers have numerous substitute products for transportation including automobiles, trains, and boats. Technology has even created substitute products to the airline industry including videoconferencing and virtual meetings. Many individuals use collaboration meeting software such as WebEx instead of traveling.

FIGURE 2.2

An Organization within the Supply Chain

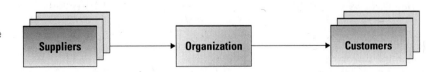

Ideally, an organization would like to be in a market in which there are few substitutes for the products or services it offers. Polaroid had this unique competitive advantage for many years until it forgot to continuously scan the competitive environment and soon went bankrupt when people began taking pictures with everything from their video cameras to their cell phones. A company can reduce the threat of substitute products by offering added-value through wider product availability. Soft-drink manufacturers reduced the threat of substitute products by introducing product availability through vending machines, gas stations, and convenience stores, which dramatically increased the availability of soft drinks relative to other beverages. Companies can also offer various add-on services making the substitute product less of a threat. For example, cellular phones could also include GPS and digital video capabilities making the landline phone less of a substitute.

THREAT OF NEW ENTRANTS

The ***threat of new entrants*** is high when it is easy for new competitors to enter a market and low when there are significant entry barriers to entering a market. An ***entry barrier*** is a product or service feature that customers have come to expect from organizations in a particular industry and must be offered by an entering organization to compete and survive. For example, a new bank must offer its customers an array of IT-enabled services, including ATMs, online bill paying, and online account monitoring. These are significant barriers to entering the banking market. At one time, the first bank to offer such services gained a valuable first-mover advantage, but only temporarily, as other banking competitors developed their own IT systems.

RIVALRY AMONG EXISTING COMPETITORS

Rivalry among existing competitors is high when competition is fierce in a market and low when competition is more complacent. Although competition is always more intense in some industries than in others, the overall trend is toward increased competition in almost every industry. The retail grocery industry is intensively competitive. While Kroger, Safeway, and Albertson's in the United States compete in many different ways, essentially they try to beat or match the competition on price. Most implement loyalty programs to provide customers special discounts while the store gathers valuable information on purchasing habits. In the future, expect to see grocery stores using wireless technologies to track customer movement throughout the store and match it to products purchased to determine purchasing sequences.

    Product differentiation occurs when a company develops unique differences in its products with the intent to influence demand. Companies can use product differentiation to reduce rivalry. For example, there are many companies that sell books and videos on the Internet. Amazon differentiates its products by using customer profiling. When a customer visits Amazon.com repeatedly, Amazon begins to offer products tailored to that particular customer based on the customer's profile. In this way Amazon has reduced its rivals' power by offering its customers a differentiated product.

USING THE FIVE FORCES MODEL TO ANALYZE THE AIRLINE INDUSTRY

Taking a look at all five of the competitive forces can provide a company with a comprehensive picture of its industry including business strategies it can implement to remain competitive. A company that was contemplating entering the airline industry could use the five forces model to quickly understand that this might be a risky move because it is an unprofitable industry as all of the five forces are strong.

- **Buyer power:** Buyer power is high as customers have many airlines to choose from and typically make purchases based on price, not carrier.
- **Supplier power:** Supplier power is high as there are limited plane and engine manufacturers to choose from and unionized workforces squeeze the airline's profitability.
- **Threat of substitute products or services:** Threat of substitute products is high as there are numerous transportation alternatives including automobiles, trains, and boats. There are even substitutes to travel such as video conferencing and virtual meetings.
- **Threat of new entrants:** Threat of new entrants is high as new airlines are continuously entering the market including the new sky taxies which offer low-cost on-demand air taxi service.
- **Rivalry among existing competitors:** Rivalry in the airline industry is high—just search Travelocity.com and see how many choices are offered. For this reason airlines are forced to compete on price.

The Three Generic Strategies—Creating a Business Focus

Once the relative attractiveness of an industry is determined and an organization decides to enter that market, it must formulate a strategy for entering the new market. An organization can follow Porter's three generic strategies when entering a new market: (1) broad cost leadership, (2) broad differentiation, or (3) a focused strategy. Broad strategies reach a large market segment, while focused strategies target a niche market. A focused strategy concentrates on either cost leadership or differentiation. Trying to be all things to all people, however, is a recipe for disaster, since it is difficult to project a consistent image to the entire marketplace. Porter suggests that an organization is wise to adopt only one of the three generic strategies. (See Figure 2.3.)

To illustrate the use of the three generic strategies, consider Figure 2.4. The matrix shown demonstrates the relationships among strategies (cost leadership versus differentiation) and market segmentation (broad versus focused).

FIGURE 2.3

Porter's Three Generic Strategies

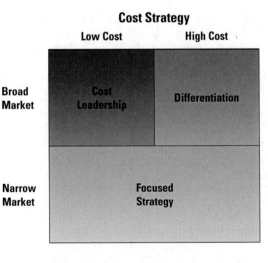

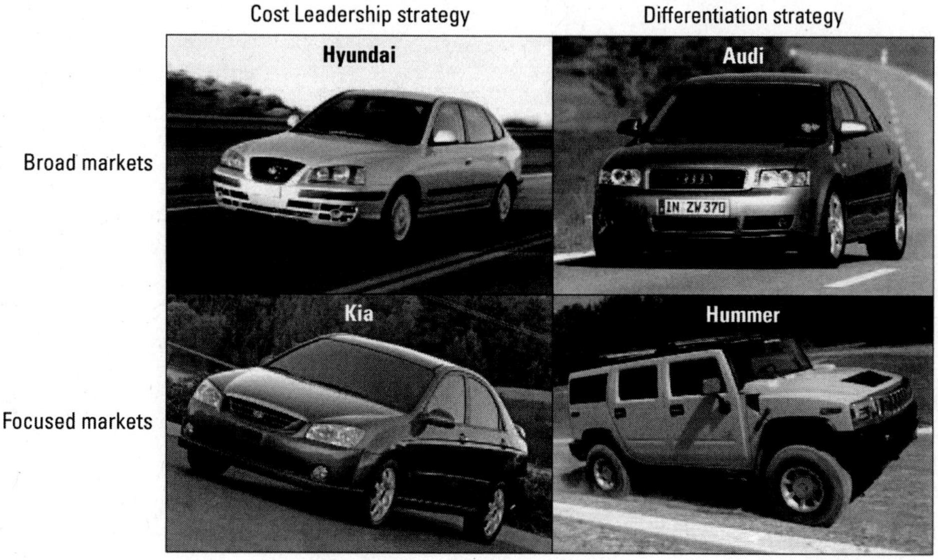

FIGURE 2.4

Three Generic Strategies
in the Auto Industry

- **Hyundai** is following a broad cost leadership strategy. Hyundai offers low-cost vehicles, in each particular model stratification, that appeal to a large audience.
- **Audi** is pursuing a broad differentiation strategy with its Quattro models available at several price points. Audi's differentiation is safety, and it prices its various Quattro models (higher than Hyundai) to reach a large, stratified audience.
- **Kia** has a more focused cost leadership strategy. Kia mainly offers low-cost vehicles in the lower levels of model stratification.
- **Hummer** offers the most focused differentiation strategy of any in the industry (including Mercedes-Benz).

Value Chain Analysis—Targeting Business Processes

Once an organization enters a new market using one of Porter's three generic strategies, it must understand, accept, and successfully execute its business strategy. Every aspect of the organization contributes to the success (or failure) of the chosen strategy. The business processes of the organization and the value chain they create play an integral role in strategy execution. Figure 2.5 combines Porter's Five Forces and his three generic strategies creating business strategies for each segment.

VALUE CREATION

A **business process** is a standardized set of activities that accomplish a specific task, such as processing a customer's order. To evaluate the effectiveness of its business processes, an organization can use Michael Porter's value chain approach. An organization creates value by performing a series of activities that Porter identified as the value chain. The **value chain** approach views an organization as a series of processes, each of which adds value to the product or service for each

Generic Strategies			
Industry Force	**Cost Leadership**	**Differentiation**	**Focused**
Entry Barriers	Ability to cut price in retaliation deters potential entrants.	Customer loyalty can discourage potential entrants.	Focusing develops core competencies that can act as an entry barrier.
Buyer Power	Ability to offer lower price to powerful buyers.	Large buyers have less power to negotiate because of few close alternatives.	Large buyers have less power to negotiate because of few alternatives.
Supplier Power	Better insulated from powerful suppliers.	Better able to pass on supplier price increases to customers.	Suppliers have power because of low volumes, but a differentiation-focused firm is better able to pass on supplier price increases.
Threat of Substitutes	Can use low price to defend against substitutes.	Customers become attached to differentiating attributes, reducing threat of substitutes.	Specialized products and core competency protect against substitutes.
Rivalry	Better able to compete on price.	Brand loyalty to keep customers from rivals.	Rivals cannot meet differentiation-focused customer needs.

FIGURE 2.5

Generic Strategies and
Industry Forces

customer. To create a competitive advantage, the value chain must enable the organization to provide unique value to its customers. In addition to the firm's own value-creating activities, the firm operates in a value system of vertical activities including those of upstream suppliers and downstream channel members. To achieve a competitive advantage, the firm must perform one or more value-creating activities in a way that creates more overall value than do competitors. Added value is created through lower costs or superior benefits to the consumer (differentiation).

Organizations can add value by offering lower prices or by competing in a distinctive way. Examining the organization as a value chain (actually numerous distinct but inseparable value chains) leads to the identification of the important activities that add value for customers and then finding IT systems that support those activities. Figure 2.6 depicts a value chain. Primary value activities, shown at the bottom of the graph, acquire raw materials and manufacture, deliver, market, sell, and provide after-sales services. Support value activities, along the top of

FIGURE 2.6

A Graphical Depiction of a
Value Chain

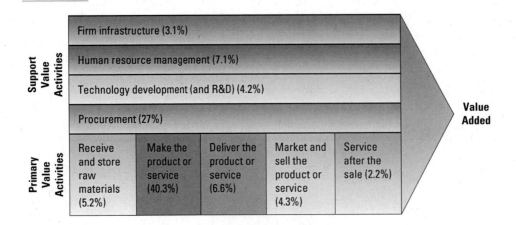

the graph, such as firm infrastructure, human resource management, technology development, and procurement, support the primary value activities.

The goal here is to survey the customers and ask them the extent to which they believe each activity adds value to the product or service. This generates a quantifiable metric, displayed in percentages in Figure 2.6, for how each activity adds value (or reduces value). The competitive advantage decision then is to (1) target high value-adding activities to further enhance their value, (2) target low value-adding activities to increase their value, or (3) perform some combination of the two.

Organizations should attempt to use information technology to add value to both primary and support value activities. One example of a primary value activity facilitated by IT is the development of a marketing campaign management system that could target marketing campaigns more efficiently, thereby reducing marketing costs. The system would also help the organization better pinpoint target market needs, thereby increasing sales. One example of a support value activity facilitated by IT is the development of a human resources system that could more efficiently reward employees based on performance. The system could also identify employees who are at risk of leaving their jobs, allowing the organization to find additional challenges or opportunities that would help retain these employees and thus reduce turnover costs.

Value chain analysis is a highly useful tool in that it provides hard and fast numbers for evaluating the activities that add value to products and services. An organization can find additional value by analyzing and constructing its value chain in terms of Porter's Five Forces (see Figure 2.7). For example, if an organization wants to decrease its buyers' or customers' power it can construct its value chain activity of "service after the sale" by offering high levels of quality customer service.

FIGURE 2.7

The Value Chain and Porter's Five Forces

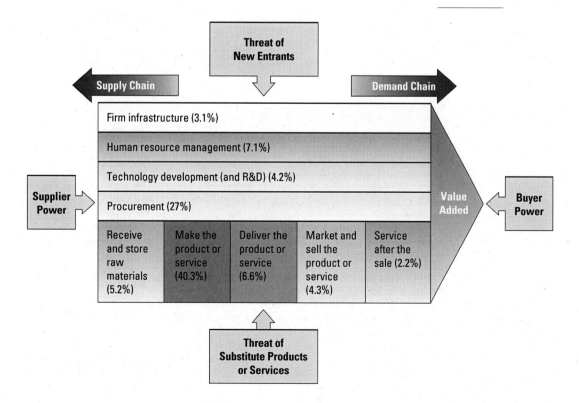

This will increase the switching costs for its customers, thereby decreasing their power. Analyzing and constructing its support value activities can help an organization decrease the threat of new entrants. Analyzing and constructing its primary value activities can help an organization decrease the threat of substitute products or services.

A company can implement its selected strategy by means of programs, budgets, and procedures. Implementation involves organization of the firm's resources and motivation of the employees to achieve objectives. How the company implements its chosen strategy can have a significant impact on its success. In a large company, the personnel implementing the strategy are usually different from those formulating the strategy. For this reason, proper communication of the strategy is critical. Failure can result if the strategy is misunderstood or if lower-level managers resist its implementation because they do not understand the process for selecting the particular strategy.

An organization must continually adapt to its competitive environment, which can cause its business strategy to change. To remain successful, an organization should use Porter's Five Forces, the three generic strategies, and value chain analysis to adopt new business strategies.

OPENING CASE STUDY QUESTIONS

1. How can Apple use environmental scanning to gain business intelligence?
2. Using Porter's Five Forces Model, analyze Apple's buyer power and supplier power.
3. Which of the three generic strategies is Apple following?
4. Which of Porter's Five Forces did Apple address through the introduction of the iPhone and customer developed iPhone applications?

Chapter Two Case: *BusinessWeek* Interview with Michael Porter

The Harvard professor and popular author explains the "location paradox" and talks about the competitive challenges facing the United States. Ever since his 1990 book *The Competitive Advantage of Nations,* Harvard Business School professor Michael Porter has been regarded as a leading authority on the economic development of nations, regions, and cities. Both as an academic and consultant, Porter is best known for his work on the importance of developing a specialty in industrial clusters—high concentrations of companies in a sector such as semiconductors, cars, or textiles. In an interview with Senior Writer Pete Engardio, Porter explains why he believes globalization has actually made industry clusters and local advantages even more important, rather than weakened them.

If globalization means that work, technology, and money can now move anywhere over the Internet, does the physical location of an industry still really matter?
"I call it the location paradox. If you think of globalization, your first reaction is to think that location doesn't matter anymore. There are no barriers to investment. But the paradox is that location still matters. The U.S. is still the most important space in the world, for example, and regions have tremendous specialization. Anything that can be easily accessed from a distance no longer is a competitive advantage. But the more there are no barriers, the more things are mobile, the more decisive location becomes. This point has tripped up a lot of really smart people.

As a result, the bottom half of U.S. locations are facing more stress. Many cities used to have a natural advantage just because they were in the U.S. But that is not such an advantage anymore. We are finding a tendency for the rich regions to get richer."

How has globalization affected the idea of regional clusters?
"Now that globalization continues to power forward, what has happened is that clusters must become more specialized in individual locations. The global economy is speeding up the process by which clusters get more focused. There is a footwear cluster in Italy, for example, where they still produce very advanced products. The design, marketing, and technology still are in Italy. But much of the production has shifted to Romania, where the Italians have developed another cluster. All of the production companies actually are Italian-owned. Taiwan has done the same by shifting production to China. The innovation is in Taiwan, but its companies are moving aspects of their cluster that don't need to be in Taiwan."

What are the big differences in the way communities approach development today compared to 1990, when you wrote *The Competitive Advantage of Nations?*
"There has been tremendous change in the last 15 or 20 years. Before *Competitive Advantage* was published, the dominant view was that you need to get costs down, offer incentives, and have a development department that hunts for investment. I think the level of sophistication has risen at the state and local level. They now understand that competitiveness does not just mean low costs.

Another big change from 20 years ago is that the notion of industry clusters is now pretty much ubiquitous. Many regions now look at development in these terms, and have identified hundreds and hundreds of different clusters. I think that the fact that productivity growth has risen dramatically shows that economic development has been a big success over the past few years."

If every community is developing the same industry clusters, how do they stand out?
"I think it's very important to understand that the bar has risen substantially. Everything matters now. The schools matter. The roads matter. You have to understand this is a marathon. Also, you can't try to build clusters across the board and be into everything. You have to build on your strengths."

Many local officials in the U.S. talk a lot about collaboration among universities, companies, and governments across an entire region. Is this new?
"There is a growing recognition that the interaction between one region or metropolitan area and its neighbors is important. The overlap between clusters is very important in stimulating growth. Isolated clusters are less powerful than integrated clusters. That's because new clusters often grow out of old clusters. I also think there is more recognition that you need a lot of cross-company collaboration in a region. Companies realize they have a lot of shared issues. Meanwhile, universities used to be seen as standalone institutions. Now, more regional economies see universities as players and are integrating them into industrial clusters."

Does the U.S. have a competitiveness problem?
"I think the U.S. is facing some very serious challenges. But the most important drivers of competitiveness are not national. They are regional and local. National policies and circumstances explain about 20 percent to 25 percent of why a regional economy is doing well. What really matters is where the skills and highly competitive institutions are based. Some of these assets take a very long time to build. But competitiveness essentially is in the hands of regions."

Questions

1. In today's global business environment, does the physical location of a business matter?
2. Why is collaboration among universities important?
3. Is there a competitiveness problem in the United States?
4. What are the big differences in the way communities approach development today compared to 1990, when Porter wrote *The Competitive Advantage of Nations?*

3

Strategic Initiatives for Implementing Competitive Advantages

LEARNING OUTCOMES

3.1. List and describe the four basic components of supply chain management.

3.2. Explain customer relationship management systems and how they can help organizations understand their customers.

3.3. Summarize the importance of enterprise resource planning systems.

3.4. Identify how an organization can use business process reengineering to improve its business.

Strategic Initiatives

Trek, a leader in bicycle products and accessories, gained more than 30 percent of the worldwide market by streamlining operations through the implementation of several IT systems. According to Jeff Stang, director of IT and operational accounting, the most significant improvement realized from the new systems was the ability to obtain key management information to drive business decisions in line with the company's strategic goals. Other system results included a highly successful website developed for the 1,400 Trek dealers where they could enter orders directly, check stock availability, and view accounts receivable and credit summaries. Tonja Green, Trek channel manager for North America, stated, "We wanted to give our dealers an easier and quicker way to enter their orders and get information. Every week the number of web orders increases by 25 to 30 percent due to the new system."

This chapter introduces high-profile strategic initiatives that an organization can undertake to help it gain competitive advantages and business efficiencies—supply chain management, customer relationship management, business process reengineering, and enterprise resource planning. Each of these strategic initiatives is covered in detail throughout this text. This chapter provides a brief introduction only.

Supply Chain Management

To understand a supply chain, consider a customer purchasing a Trek bike from a dealer. On one end, the supply chain has the customer placing an order for the bike with the dealer. The dealer purchases the bike from the manufacturer, Trek. Trek purchases raw materials such as packaging material, metal, and accessories from many different suppliers to make the bike. The supply chain for Trek encompasses every activity and party involved in the process of fulfilling the order from the customer for the new bike.

Supply chain management (SCM) involves the management of information flows between and among stages in a supply chain to maximize total supply chain effectiveness and profitability. The four basic components of supply chain management are:

1. **Supply chain strategy**—the strategy for managing all the resources required to meet customer demand for all products and services.
2. **Supply chain partners**—the partners chosen to deliver finished products, raw materials, and services including pricing, delivery, and payment processes along with partner relationship monitoring metrics.
3. **Supply chain operation**—the schedule for production activities including testing, packaging, and preparation for delivery. Measurements for this component include productivity and quality.
4. **Supply chain logistics**—the product delivery processes and elements including orders, warehouses, carriers, defective product returns, and invoicing.

Dozens of steps are required to achieve and carry out each of the above components. SCM software can enable an organization to generate efficiencies within these steps by automating and improving the information flows throughout and among the different supply chain components.

Wal-Mart and Procter & Gamble (P&G) implemented a tremendously successful SCM system. The system linked Wal-Mart's distribution centers directly to P&G's manufacturing centers. Every time a Wal-Mart customer purchases a P&G product, the system sends a message directly to the factory alerting P&G to restock the product. The system also sends an automatic alert to P&G whenever a product is running low at one of Wal-Mart's distribution centers. This real-time information allows P&G to efficiently make and deliver products to Wal-Mart without having to maintain large inventories in its warehouses. The system also generates invoices and receives payments automatically. The SCM system saves time, reduces inventory, and decreases order-processing costs for P&G. P&G passes on these savings to Wal-Mart in the form of discounted prices.

Figure 3.1 diagrams the stages of the SCM system for a customer purchasing a product from Wal-Mart. The diagram demonstrates how the supply chain is dynamic and involves the constant flow of information between the different parties. For example, the customer generates order information by purchasing a product from Wal-Mart. Wal-Mart supplies the order information to its warehouse or distributor. The warehouse or distributor transfers the order information to the manufacturer, who provides pricing and availability information to the store and replenishes the product to the store. Payment funds among the various partners are transferred electronically.

FIGURE 3.1

Supply Chain for a Product Purchased from Wal-Mart

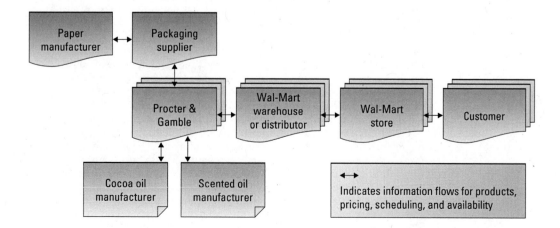

FIGURE 3.2

Effective and Efficient Supply Chain Management's Effect on Porter's Five Forces

Effective and efficient supply chain management systems can enable an organization to:

- Decrease the power of its buyers.
- Increase its own supplier power.
- Increase switching costs to reduce the threat of substitute products or services.
- Create entry barriers thereby reducing the threat of new entrants.
- Increase efficiencies while seeking a competitive advantage through cost leadership (see Figure 3.2).

Customer Relationship Management

Today, most competitors are simply a mouse-click away. This intense marketplace has forced organizations to switch from being sales focused to being customer focused.

Charles Schwab recouped the cost of a multimillion-dollar customer relationship management system in less than two years. The system, developed by Siebel, allows the brokerage firm to trace each interaction with a customer or prospective customer and then provide services (retirement planning, for instance) to each customer's needs and interests. The system gives Schwab a better and more complete view of its customers, which it can use to determine which customers are serious investors and which ones are not. Automated deposits from paychecks, for example, are a sign of a serious investor, while stagnant balances signal a nonserious investor. Once Schwab is able to make this determination, the firm allocates its resources accordingly, saving money by not investing time or resources in subsidizing nonserious investors.

Customer relationship management (CRM) involves managing all aspects of a customer's relationship with an organization to increase customer loyalty and retention and an organization's profitability. CRM allows an organization to gain insights into customers' shopping and buying behaviors in order to develop and implement enterprisewide strategies. Kaiser Permanente undertook a CRM strategy to improve and prolong the lives of diabetics. After compiling CRM information on 84,000 of its diabetic patients among its 2.4 million northern California members, Kaiser determined that only 15 to 20 percent of its diabetic patients were getting their eyes checked routinely. (Diabetes is the leading cause of blindness.) As a result, Kaiser is now enforcing more rigorous eye-screening programs for diabetics and creating support groups for obesity and stress (two more factors that make diabetes even worse). This CRM-based "preventive medicine" approach is saving Kaiser considerable sums of money and saving the eyesight of diabetic patients.

Figure 3.3 provides an overview of a typical CRM system. Customers contact an organization through various means including call centers, web access, email, faxes, and direct sales. A single customer may access an organization multiple times through many different channels. The CRM system tracks every communication between the customer and the organization and provides access to CRM information within different systems from accounting to order fulfillment. Understanding all customer communications allows the organization to communicate effectively with each customer. It gives the organization a detailed understanding

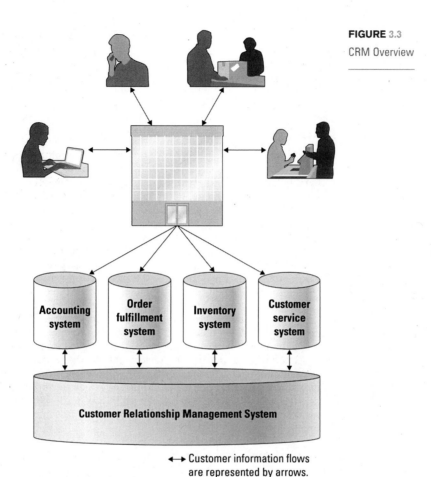

FIGURE 3.3

CRM Overview

Accounting system

Order fulfillment system

Inventory system

Customer service system

Customer Relationship Management System

⟷ Customer information flows are represented by arrows.

of each customer's products and services record regardless of the customer's preferred communication channel. For example, a customer service representative can easily view detailed account information and history through a CRM system when providing information to a customer such as expected delivery dates, complementary product information, and customer payment and billing information.

CRM STRATEGY

Eddie Bauer ships 110 million catalogs a year, maintains two websites, and has over 600 retail stores. The company collects information through customer transactions and analyzes the information to determine the best way to market to each individual customer. Eddie Bauer discovered that customers who shop across all three of its distribution channels—catalogs, websites, and stores—spend up to five times more than customers who shop through only one channel.

Michael Boyd, director of CRM at Eddie Bauer, stated, "Our experience tells us that CRM is in no way, shape, or form a software application. Fundamentally, it is a business strategy to try to optimize profitability, revenue, and satisfaction at an individual customer level. Everything in an organization, every single process, every single application, is a tool that can be used to serve the CRM goal."

It is important to realize that CRM is not just technology, but also a strategy that an organization must embrace on an enterprise level. Although there are many technical components of CRM, it is actually a process and business goal simply enhanced by technology. Implementing a CRM system can help an organization identify customers and design specific marketing campaigns tailored to each customer, thereby increasing customer spending. A CRM system also allows an organization to treat customers as individuals, gaining important insights into their buying preferences and behaviors and leading to increased sales, greater profitability, and higher rates of customer loyalty.

Business Process Reengineering

A ***business process*** is a standardized set of activities that accomplish a specific task, such as processing a customer's order. ***Business process reengineering (BPR)*** is the analysis and redesign of workflow within and between enterprises. The concept of BPR traces its origins to management theories developed as early as the 19th century. The purpose of BPR is to make all business process the best-in-class. Frederick Taylor suggested in the 1880s that managers could discover the best processes for performing work and reengineer the processes to optimize productivity. BPR echoes the classical belief that there is one best way to conduct tasks. In Taylor's time, technology did not allow large companies to design processes in a cross-functional or cross-departmental manner. Specialization was the state-of-the-art method to improve efficiency given the technology of the time.

BPR reached its heyday in the early 1990s when Michael Hammer and James Champy published their best-selling book, *Reengineering the Corporation*. The authors promoted the idea that radical redesign and reorganization of an enterprise (wiping the slate clean) sometimes was necessary to lower costs and increase quality of service and that information technology was the key enabler for that radical change. Hammer and Champy believed that the workflow design in most large corporations was based on invalid assumptions about technology, people, and organizational goals. They suggested seven principles of reengineering to streamline the work process and thereby achieve significant improvement in quality, time management, and cost (see Figure 3.4).

FINDING OPPORTUNITY USING BPR

Companies frequently strive to improve their business processes by performing tasks faster, cheaper, and better. Figure 3.5 displays different ways to travel the same road. A company could improve the way that it travels the road by moving from foot to horse and then from horse to car. However, true BPR would look at taking a different path. A company could forget about traveling on the same old road and use an airplane to get to its final destination. Companies often follow the same indirect path for doing business, not realizing there might be a different, faster, and more direct way of doing business.

Creating value for the customer is the leading factor for instituting BPR, and information technology often plays an important enabling role. Radical and fundamentally

FIGURE 3.4

Seven Principles of Business Process Reengineering

Seven Principles of Business Process Reengineering
1 Organize around outcomes, not tasks.
2 Identify all the organization's processes and prioritize them in order of redesign urgency.
3 Integrate information processing work into the real work that produces the information.
4 Treat geographically dispersed resources as though they were centralized.
5 Link parallel activities in the workflow instead of just integrating their results.
6 Put the decision point where the work is performed, and build control into the process.
7 Capture information once and at the source.

new business processes enabled Progressive Insurance to slash the claims settlement from 31 days to four hours. Typically, car insurance companies follow this standard claims resolution process: The customer gets into an accident, has the car towed, and finds a ride home. The customer then calls the insurance company to begin the claims process, which usually takes over a month (see Figure 3.6).

Progressive Insurance improved service to its customers by offering a mobile claims process. When a customer has a car accident he or she calls in the claim on the spot. The Progressive claims adjustor comes to the accident and performs a mobile claims process, surveying the scene and taking digital photographs. The adjustor then offers the customer on-site payment, towing services, and a ride home (see Figure 3.6).

A true BPR effort does more for a company than simply improve it by performing a process better, faster, and cheaper. Progressive Insurance's BPR effort redefined best practices for its entire industry. Figure 3.7 displays the different types of change an organization can achieve, along with the magnitude of change and the potential business benefit.

FIGURE 3.5

Better, Faster, Cheaper or BPR

PITFALLS OF BPR

One hazard of BPR is that the company becomes so wrapped up in fighting its own demons that it fails to keep up with its competitors in offering new products or services. While American Express tackled a comprehensive reengineering of its credit card business, MasterCard and Visa introduced a new product—the corporate procurement card. American Express lagged a full year behind before offering its customers the same service.

Enterprise Resource Planning

Today's business leaders need significant amounts of information to be readily accessible with real-time views into their businesses so that decisions can be made when they need to be, without the added time of tracking data and generating reports. *Enterprise resource planning (ERP)* integrates all departments and functions throughout an organization into a single IT system (or integrated set of IT systems) so that employees can make decisions by viewing enterprisewide information on all business operations.

Many organizations fail to maintain consistency across business operations. If a single department, such as sales, decides to implement a new system without considering the other departments, inconsistencies can occur throughout the company. Not all systems are built to talk to each other and share data, and if sales

FIGURE 3.6

Auto Insurance Claims Processes

Company A: Claims Resolution Process

Progressive Insurance: Claims Resolution Process

Resolution Cycle Time: 3–8 weeks

Resolution Cycle Time: 30 min–3 hours

FIGURE 3.7

The Benefits and Magnitude of Change

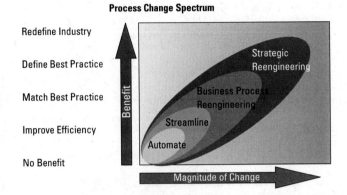

suddenly implements a new system that marketing and accounting cannot use or is inconsistent in the way it handles information, the company's operations become siloed. Figure 3.8 displays sample data from a sales database, and Figure 3.9 displays samples from an accounting database. Notice the differences in data formats, numbers, and identifiers. Correlating this data would be difficult, and the inconsistencies would cause numerous reporting errors from an enterprisewide perspective.

Los Angeles is a city of 3.5 million, with 44,000 city employees, and a budget of $4 billion. Yet a few years ago each department conducted its own purchasing. That meant 2,000 people in 600 city buildings and 60 warehouses were ordering material. Some 120,000 purchase orders (POs) and 50,000 checks per year went to more than 7,000 vendors. Inefficiency was rampant.

"There was a lack of financial responsibility in the old system, and people could run up unauthorized expenditures," said Bob Jensen, the city's ERP project manager. Each department maintained its own inventories on different systems. Expense-item mismatches piled up. One department purchased one way, others preferred a different approach. Mainframe-based systems were isolated. The city

FIGURE 3.8

Sales Information Sample

	OrderDate	ProductName	Quantity	Unit Price	Unit Cost	Customer ID	SalesRep ID
2	Monday, January 04, 2010	Mozzarella cheese	41.5	$ 24.15	$ 15.35	AC45	EX-107
3	Monday, January 04, 2010	Romaine lettuce	90.65	$ 15.06	$ 14.04	AC45	EX-109
4	Tuesday, January 05, 2010	Red onions	27.15	$ 12.08	$ 10.32	AC07	EX 104
5	Wednesday, January 06, 2010	Romaine lettuce	87.25	$ 15.16	$ 10.54	AC08	FX-109
6	Thursday, January 07, 2010	Black olives	79.28	$ 12.18	$ 9.56	AC44	EX-104
7	Thursday, January 07, 2010	Romaine lettuce	46.52	$ 15.24	$ 11.54	AC32	EX-104
8	Thursday, January 07, 2010	Romaine lettuce	52.5	$ 15.26	$ 11.12	AC04	EX-109
9	Friday, January 08, 2010	Red onions	39.5	$ 12.55	$ 9.51	AC103	EX 104
10	Saturday, January 09, 2010	Romaine lettuce	[illegible]	$ 16.98	$ 9.50	AC4	EX 104
11	Sunday, January 10, 2010	Romaine lettuce	58.28	$ 16.87	$ 9.50	AC174	FX-104
12	Sunday, January 10, 2010	Pineapple	40.15	$ 33.54	$ 22.12	AC45	EX-104
13	Monday, January 11, 2010	Pineapple	71.56	$ 33.56	$ 22.05	AC4	EX-104
14	Thursday, January 14, 2010	Romaine lettuce	18.25	$ 15.00	$ 10.25	AC174	EX-104
15	Thursday, January 14, 2010	Romaine lettuce	28.15	$ 15.26	$ 10.54	AC44	EX 107
16	Friday, January 15, 2010	Pepperoni	[illegible]	$ 16.24	$ 10.24	AC91	FX-109
17	Friday, January 15, 2010	Parmesan cheese	14.26	$ 8.05	$ 4.00	AC08	FX-104
18	Saturday, January 16, 2010	Parmesan cheese	72.15	$ 8.50	$ 4.00	AC103	EX-109
19	Monday, January 18, 2010	Parmesan cheese	41.5	$ 24.15	$ 15.35	AC45	EX-107
20	Monday, January 18, 2010	Romaine lettuce	90.65	$ 15.06	$ 14.04	AC45	EX-109
21	Wednesday, January 20, 2010	Tomatoes	27.15	$ 12.08	$ 10.32	AC07	EX 104
22	Thursday, January 21, 2010	Peppers	87.25	$ 15.16	$ 10.54	AC08	FX-109
23	Thursday, January 21, 2010	Mozzarella cheese	79.28	$ 12.18	$ 9.56	AC44	EX-104
24	Saturday, January 23, 2010	Black olives	46.52	$ 15.24	$ 11.54	AC32	EX-104
25	Sunday, January 24, 2010	Mozzarella cheese	52.5	$ 15.26	$ 11.12	AC04	EX-109
26	Tuesday, January 26, 2010	Romaine lettuce	39.5	$ 12.56	$ 9.51	AC103	EX 104
27	Wednesday, January 27, 2010	Parmesan cheese	[illegible]	$ 16.98	$ 9.50	AC4	EX 104
28	Thursday, January 28, 2010	Peppers	58.28	$ 16.87	$ 9.50	AC174	FX-104
29	Thursday, January 28, 2010	Mozzarella cheese	40.15	$ 33.54	$ 22.12	AC45	EX-104
30	Friday, January 29, 2010	Tomatoes	71.56	$ 33.56	$ 22.05	AC4	EX-104
31	Friday, January 29, 2010	Peppers	18.25	$ 15.00	$ 10.25	AC174	EX-104

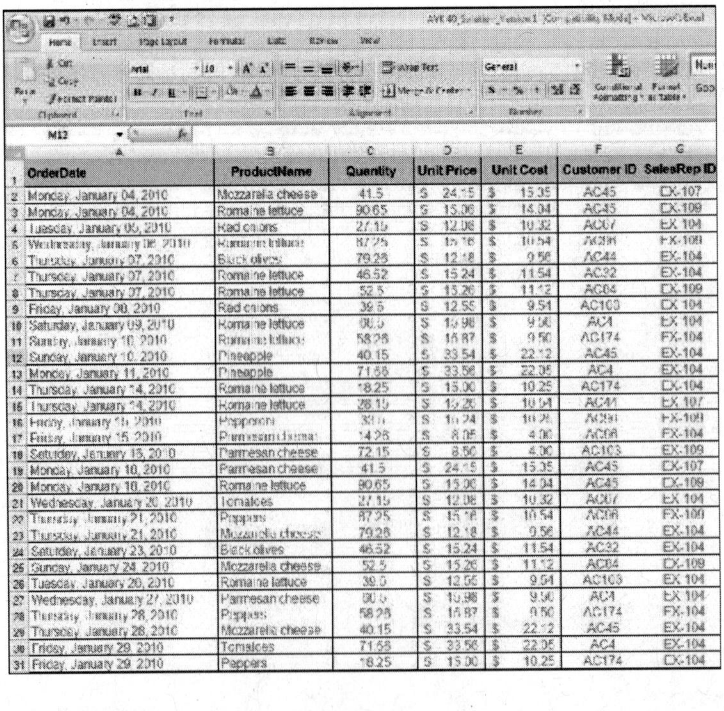

FIGURE 3.9

Accounting Information Sample

chose an ERP system as part of a $22 million project to integrate purchasing and financial reporting across the entire city. The project resulted in cutting the check processing staff in half, processing POs faster than ever, reducing the number of workers in warehousing by 40 positions, decreasing inventories from $50 million to $15 million, and providing a single point of contact for each vendor. In addition, $5 million a year has been saved in contract consolidation.

Figure 3.10 shows how an ERP system takes data from across the enterprise, consolidates and correlates the data, and generates enterprisewide organizational reports. Original ERP implementations promised to capture all information onto one true "enterprise" system, with the ability to touch all the business processes within the organization. Unfortunately, ERP solutions have fallen short of these promises, and typical implementations have penetrated only 15 to 20 percent of the organization. The issue ERP intends to solve is that knowledge within a majority of organizations currently resides in silos that are maintained by a select few, without the ability to be shared across the organization, causing inconsistency across business operations. ·

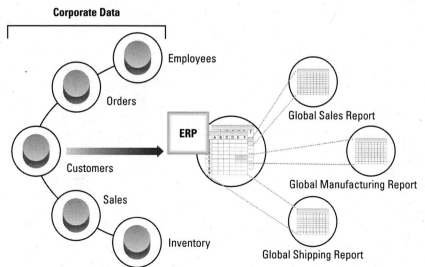

Corporate Data

Employees

Orders

Customers

Sales

Inventory

ERP

Global Sales Report

Global Manufacturing Report

Global Shipping Report

FIGURE 3.10

Enterprise Resource Planning System

Chapter Three Case: Got Milk? It's Good for You— Unless It Is Contaminated!

Dong Lizhong, a farmer and migrant worker dairy farmer in China, bet that being a dairy farmer was his golden ticket out of a factory job. Unfortunately, a contamination crisis shattered his dairy business when babies mysteriously started developing kidney stones from contaminated baby formula. A chemical called melamine—an additive used to make plastic—was discovered in the milk supply of China's third-largest dairy producer. Tragically, four infants died from the contamination and at least 53,000 fell ill. According to the official Xinhua news agency, officials knew about problems with the milk for months before informing the public.

China's four largest dairy organizations, accounting for nearly half the country's milk market, pulled their goods off shelves. More than 20 countries, including France, India, and South Korea, banned not only dairy products from China, but also candies, cookies, and chocolates. "This is a disastrous setback. I estimate that it will take one or two years to rebuild confidence in dairy products," says Luo Yunbo, dean of the College of Food Science and Nutritional Engineering at China Agricultural University.

The local milk-collection station in Dong Lizhong's village has discontinued purchasing milk. Farmers are continuing to milk their cows, but they now drink the milk themselves or "feed the cabbages"—pour the milk in their cabbage fields. Dong estimates that he has already lost $1,461, or a quarter of his annual income last year, in expenses to feed corn and fresh grass to his 20 dairy cows. "Unless someone starts buying milk, we're going to see a lot of cows being slaughtered very soon," states Dong.

Cutting Corners

Chinese do not traditionally drink milk. However, as the country has grown more affluent over the past few decades, the domestic dairy industry has skyrocketed. China's two largest dairy companies have greatly benefited from this new trend: China Mengniu Dairy and Inner Mongolia Yili Industrial Group. Simultaneously, numerous entrepreneurs—from dairy farmers to milk-collection station owners to milk distributors—have jumped into the supply chain of dairy products to make their fortunes. Due to the fierce competition within China's dairy industry a few companies decided to cut corners to reduce costs, regardless of the consequences.

As Mengniu and Yili expanded at breathtaking speed, they found themselves in the unique position where supply could not keep up with demand. According to KPMG, China consumes 25 million tons of milk yearly, putting its dairy market ahead of France and Germany. In their quest for more raw milk, Mengniu and Yili have expanded outside their base in the northern province of Inner Mongolia and set up milk production facilities in other parts of China. Not surprisingly, most of the quality problems in milk have been found in dairy farms in Hebei and Inner Mongolia provinces, where the competition for raw milk supplies has been the fiercest.

Most dairy farmers in Hebei province traditionally sold their milk to milk-collection stations established by local heavyweight Sanlu. In recent years, new privately owned milk-collection stations to buy raw milk for Mengniu and Yili started popping up next to existing stations. These new entrants captured raw milk supplies by offering dairy farmers slightly higher prices. "This competition broke the rules. As milk buyers fought over milk supplies, their standards for quality fell," says Roger Liu, vice-chairman of American Dairy (ADY), a Heilongjiang province-based powdered milk company.

Additives to Boost Protein

Many of the milking stations do not have the equipment to test milk for additives. At the Nanxincheng station, 16 households bring their dairy cows in the area to be milked in the red brick farmhouse. The farmers hook up the cows up to a milking machine, which pumps the milk directly into a big vat. "They didn't test the milk here. They sent it to Sanlu for testing," says Du Yanjun, a government inspector posted to monitor the Nanxincheng station after the contamination crisis broke.

The milk is collected from the stations and shipped by middlemen to big dairy companies like Sanlu, which do their own testing and grading. It now appears that unscrupulous middlemen commonly add melamine into the raw milk to increase protein levels in their milk samples, so their milk will be graded higher. Ingesting melamine can cause kidney stones or kidney failure, especially in infants.

Matthew Estes, president and CEO of BabyCare, had looked into switching from Australian and New Zealand sources of milk for the company's infant-formula business in China. Baby-Care did extensive testing of possible suppliers and realized it could not locate a suitable supplier in China. "We couldn't the find quality that met our standards. We chose to not sell rather than take the risk," he says.

Going to Jail

A Chinese court sentenced two of the primary middlemen to death and a dairy boss to life in prison for their roles in the milk contamination scandal. The swift trial and harsh sentences show Beijing's resolve in tackling the country's stubborn food safety problems and an eagerness by the communist leadership to move past the embarrassing scandal.

Going to Starbucks

Starbucks Corp. has launched a new brand of coffee grown by farmers in China and says it hopes to bring the blend to stores all over the world. The Seattle-based company, which has been closing stores in the U.S. to cut costs, says its new blend is made in China's southwestern province of Yunnan, bordering Vietnam, Laos and Myanmar. "Our intention is to work with the officials and the farmers in Yunnan province to bring Chinese coffee not (only) to China, but Chinese coffee to the world," Martin Coles, president of Starbucks Coffee International, told the Associated Press. "Ultimately I'd love to see our coffees from China featured on the shelves of every one of our stores in 49 countries around the world," he said. A launch date for foreign distribution hasn't been announced and will depend on how soon farmers can grow enough beans to ensure local and overseas supply.

The company has been working for three years with farmers and officials in the province before the launch, and the coffee will initially combine Arabica beans from Latin America and the Asia-Pacific with local Yunnan beans. But Coles said they hope to develop a source of superpremium Arabica coffee from the province, expanding it to new brand offerings in China, and then internationally. The new blend will be called "South of the Clouds," the meaning of Yunnan in Chinese.

Questions

1. Explain why the supply chain can dramatically impact a company's base performance.
2. List all of the products that could possibly be affected by a problem in the U.S. milk supply chain.
3. How can a CRM system help communicate issues in the supply chain?
4. How could BPR help uncover issues in a company's supply chain?
5. What are the pros and cons for Starbucks of outsourcing the growing of its coffee beans to Chinese farmers?

CHAPTER

4

Measuring the Success of Strategic Initiatives

LEARNING OUTCOMES

4.1. Compare efficiency IT metrics and effectiveness IT metrics.

4.2. List and describe five common types of efficiency IT metrics.

4.3. List and describe four types of effectiveness IT metrics.

4.4. Explain customer metrics and their importance to an organization.

Measuring Information Technology's Success

IT has become an important part of organizations' strategy, competitive advantage, and profitability. There is management pressure to build systems faster, better, and at minimum cost. The return on investment that an organization can achieve from the money it spends on IT has come under increased scrutiny from senior business executives and directors. Consequently, IT now has to operate like other parts of the organization, being aware of its performance and its contribution to the organization's success and opportunities for improvement. So what is it that managers need to know about measuring the success of information technology?

The first thing managers need to understand about IT success is that it is incredibly difficult to measure. Determining the return on investment (ROI) of new computer equipment is difficult. For example, what is the ROI of a fire extinguisher? If the fire extinguisher is never used, the return on the investment is low. If the extinguisher puts out a fire that could destroy the entire building, then its ROI is high. This is similar to IT systems. If a company implements a $5,000 firewall to virus attacks on the computer systems and it never stops a virus, the company lost $5,000. If the firewall stops viruses that could have cost the company millions of dollars, then the ROI of that firewall is significantly greater than $5,000. A few questions banking executives recently raised regarding their IT systems include:

- Is the internal IT operation performing satisfactorily?
- Should the company outsource some or all of the IT operations?
- How is the outsourcing company performing?
- What are the risk factors to consider in an IT project?
- What questions should be asked to ensure an IT project proposal is realistic?
- What are the characteristics of a healthy project?
- Which factors are most critical to measure to ensure the project achieves success?

Peter Drucker, a famous management guru, once stated that if you cannot measure it, you cannot manage it. Managers need to ask themselves how they are going to manage IT projects if they cannot find a way to measure the projects.

IT professionals know how to install and maintain information systems. Business professionals know how to run a successful business. But how does a company decide if an information system helps make a business successful?

The answer lies in the metrics. Designing metrics requires an expertise that neither IT nor business professionals usually possess. Metrics are about neither technology nor business strategy. The questions that arise in metrics design are almost philosophical: How do you define success? How do you apply quantifiable measures to business processes, especially qualitative ones like customer service? What kind of information best reflects progress, or the lack of it?

Key performance indicators (KPIs) are the measures that are tied to business drivers. Metrics are the detailed measures that feed those KPIs. Performance metrics fall into a nebulous area of business intelligence that is neither technology- nor business-centered, but this area requires input from both IT and business professionals to find success. Cisco Systems implemented a cross-departmental council to create metrics for improving business process operations. The council developed metrics to evaluate the efficiency of Cisco's online order processing and discovered that due to errors, more than 70 percent of online orders required manual input and were unable to be automatically routed to manufacturing. By changing the process and adding new information systems, within six months the company doubled the percentage of orders that went directly to manufacturing.

Efficiency and Effectiveness

Organizations spend enormous sums of money on IT to compete in today's fast-paced business environment. Some organizations spend up to 50 percent of their total capital expenditures on IT. To justify these expenditures, an organization must measure the payoff of these investments, their impact on business performance, and the overall business value gained.

Efficiency and effectiveness metrics are two primary types of IT metrics. *Efficiency IT metrics* measure the performance of the IT system itself including throughput, speed, and availability. *Effectiveness IT metrics* measure the impact IT has on business processes and activities including customer satisfaction, conversion rates, and sell-through increases. Peter Drucker offers a helpful distinction between efficiency and effectiveness. Drucker states that managers "Do things right" and/or "Do the right things." Doing things right addresses efficiency—getting the most from each resource. Doing the right things addresses effectiveness—setting the right goals and objectives and ensuring they are accomplished.

Effectiveness focuses on how well an organization is achieving its goals and objectives, while efficiency focuses on the extent to which an organization is using its resources in an optimal way. The two—efficiency and effectiveness—are definitely interrelated. However, success in one area does not necessarily imply success in the other.

Benchmarking—Baseline Metrics

Regardless of what is measured, how it is measured, and whether it is for the sake of efficiency or effectiveness, there must be *benchmarks,* or baseline values the system seeks to attain. *Benchmarking* is a process of continuously measuring system results, comparing those results to optimal system performance (benchmark values), and identifying steps and procedures to improve system performance.

Efficiency	Effectiveness
1. United States (3.11)	1. Canada
2. Australia (2.60)	2. Singapore
3. New Zealand (2.59)	3. United States
4. Singapore (2.58)	4. Denmark
5. Norway (2.55)	5. Australia
6. Canada (2.52)	6. Finland
7. United Kingdom (2.52)	7. Hong Kong
8. Netherlands (2.51)	8. United Kingdom
9. Denmark (2.47)	9. Germany
10. Germany (2.46)	10. Ireland

FIGURE 4.1

Comparing Efficiency IT and Effectiveness IT Metrics for Egovernment Initiatives

Consider egovernment worldwide as an illustration of benchmarking efficiency IT metrics and effectiveness IT metrics (see survey results in Figure 4.1). From an effectiveness point of view, Canada ranks number one in terms of egovernment satisfaction of its citizens. (The United States ranks third.) The survey, sponsored by Accenture, also included such attributes as CRM practices, customer-service vision, approaches to offering egovernment services through multiple-service delivery channels, and initiatives for identifying services for individual citizen segments. These are all benchmarks at which Canada's government excels.

In contrast, the *United Nations Division for Public Economics and Public Administration* ranks Canada sixth in terms of efficiency IT metrics. (It ranked the United States first.) This particular ranking based purely on efficiency IT metrics includes benchmarks such as the number of computers per 100 citizens, the number of Internet hosts per 10,000 citizens, the percentage of the citizen population online, and several other factors. Therefore, while Canada lags behind in IT efficiency, it is the premier egovernment provider in terms of effectiveness.

Governments hoping to increase their egovernment presence would benchmark themselves against these sorts of efficiency and effectiveness metrics. There is a high degree of correlation between egovernment efficiency and effectiveness, although it is not absolute.

The Interrelationships of Efficiency and Effectiveness IT Metrics

Efficiency IT metrics focus on the technology itself. Figure 4.2 highlights the most common types of efficiency IT metrics.

While these efficiency metrics are important to monitor, they do not always guarantee effectiveness. Effectiveness IT metrics are determined according to an organization's goals, strategies, and objectives. Here, it becomes important to consider the strategy an organization is using, such as a broad cost leadership strategy (Wal-Mart, for example), as well as specific goals and objectives such as increasing new customers by 10 percent or reducing new-product development

FIGURE 4.2

Common Types of Efficiency IT Metrics

Efficiency IT Metrics	
Throughput	The amount of information that can travel through a system at any point.
Transaction speed	The amount of time a system takes to perform a transaction.
System availability	The number of hours a system is available for users.
Information accuracy	The extent to which a system generates the correct results when executing the same transaction numerous times.
Web traffic	Includes a host of benchmarks such as the number of page views, the number of unique visitors, and the average time spent viewing a web page.
Response time	The time it takes to respond to user interactions such as a mouse click.

Effectiveness IT Metrics	
Usability	The ease with which people perform transactions and/or find information. A popular usability metric on the Internet is degrees of freedom, which measures the number of clicks required to find desired information.
Customer satisfaction	Measured by such benchmarks as satisfaction surveys, percentage of existing customers retained, and increases in revenue dollars per customer.
Conversion rates	The number of customers an organization "touches" for the first time and persuades to purchase its products or services. This is a popular metric for evaluating the effectiveness of banner, pop-up, and pop-under ads on the Internet.
Financial	Such as return on investment (the earning power of an organization's assets), cost-benefit analysis (the comparison of projected revenues and costs including development, maintenance, fixed, and variable), and break-even analysis (the point at which constant revenues equal ongoing costs).

FIGURE 4.3

Common Types of Effectiveness IT Metrics

cycle times to six months. Broad, general effectiveness metrics are outlined in Figure 4.3.

In the private sector, eBay constantly benchmarks its information technology efficiency and effectiveness. Maintaining constant website availability and optimal throughput performance is critical to eBay's success. Jupiter Media Metrix ranked eBay as the website with the highest visitor volume (efficiency) for the fourth year in a row, with an 80 percent growth from the previous year. The eBay site averaged 8 million unique visitors during each week of the holiday season that year with daily peaks exceeding 12 million visitors. To ensure constant availability and reliability of its systems, eBay implemented ProactiveNet, a performance measurement and management-tracking tool. The tool allows eBay to monitor its environment against baseline benchmarks, which helps the eBay team keep tight control of its systems. The new system has resulted in improved system availability with a 150 percent increase in productivity as measured by system uptime.

Be sure to consider the issue of security while determining efficiency and effectiveness IT metrics. When an organization offers its customers the ability to purchase products over the Internet it must implement the appropriate security—such as encryption and Secure Sockets Layers (SSLs; denoted by the lock symbol in the lower right corner of a browser window and/or the "s" in https). It is actually inefficient for an organization to implement security measures for Internet-based transactions as compared to processing nonsecure transactions. However, an organization will probably have a difficult time attracting new customers and increasing web-based revenue if it does not implement the necessary security measures. Purely from an efficiency IT metric point of view, security generates some inefficiency. From an organization's business strategy point of view, however, security should lead to increases in effectiveness metrics.

Figure 4.4 depicts the interrelationships between efficiency and effectiveness. Ideally, an organization should operate in the upper right-hand corner of the graph, realizing both significant increases in efficiency and effectiveness.

FIGURE 4.4

The Interrelationships between Efficiency and Effectiveness

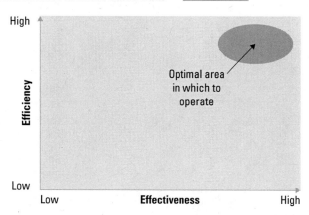

However, operating in the upper left-hand corner (minimal effectiveness with increased efficiency) or the lower right-hand corner (significant effectiveness with minimal efficiency) may be in line with an organization's particular strategies. In general, operating in the lower left-hand corner (minimal efficiency and minimal effectiveness) is not ideal for the operation of any organization.

Metrics for Strategic Initiatives

What is a metric? A metric is nothing more than a standard measure to assess performance in a particular area. Metrics are at the heart of a good, customer-focused management system and any program directed at continuous improvement. A focus on customers and performance standards shows up in the form of metrics that assess the ability to meet customers' needs and business objectives.

Business leaders want to monitor key metrics in real time to actively track the health of their business. Most business professionals are familiar with financial metrics. Different financial ratios are used to evaluate a company's performance. Companies can gain additional insight into their performance by comparing financial ratios against other companies in their industry. A few of the more common financial ratios include:

- Internal rate of return (IRR)—the rate at which the net present value of an investment equals zero.
- Return on investment (ROI)—indicates the earning power of a project and is measured by dividing the benefits of a project by the investment.
- Payback method—number of years to recoup the cost of an initiative based on projected annual net cash flow.
- Break-even analysis—determines the volume of business required to make a profit at the current prices charged for the products or services. For example, if a promotional mailing costs $1,000 and each item generates $50 in revenue, the company must generate 20 sales to break even and cover the cost of the mailing. The break-even point is the point at which revenues equal costs. The point is located by performing a break-even analysis. All sales over the break-even point produce profits; any drop in sales below that point will produce losses (see Figure 4.5).

Most managers are familiar with financial metrics but unfamiliar with information system metrics. The following metrics will help managers measure and manage their strategic initiatives:

FIGURE 4.5

Break-Even Analysis

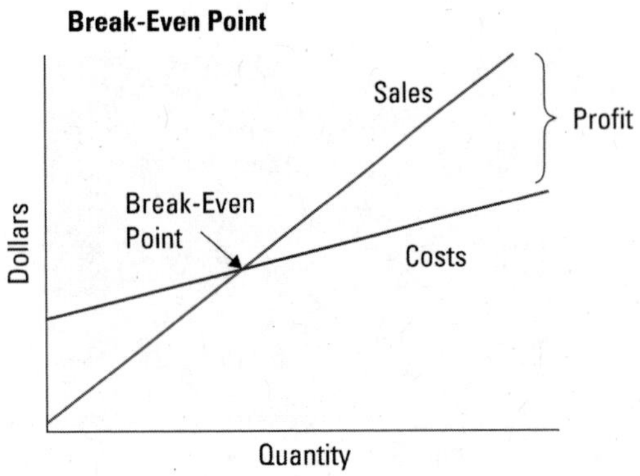

- Website metrics.
- Supply chain management (SCM) metrics.
- Customer relationship management (CRM) metrics.
- Business process reengineering (BPR) metrics.
- Enterprise resource planning (ERP) metrics.

Break-Even Point

WEBSITE METRICS

Most companies measure the traffic on a website as the primary determinant of the website's success. However, heavy website traffic does not necessarily indicate large sales. Many organizations with lots of website traffic have minimal sales. A company can use web traffic analysis or web analytics to determine the revenue generated, the number of new customers acquired, any reductions in customer service calls, and

Website Metrics

- **Abandoned registrations:** Number of visitors who start the process of completing a registration page and then abandon the activity.

- **Abandoned shopping carts:** Number of visitors who create a shopping cart and start shopping and then abandon the activity before paying for the merchandise.

- **Click-through:** Count of the number of people who visit a site, click on an ad, and are taken to the site of the advertiser.

- **Conversion rate:** Percentage of potential customers who visit a site and actually buy something.

- **Cost-per-thousand (CPM):** Sales dollars generated per dollar of advertising. This is commonly used to make the case for spending money to appear on a search engine.

- **Page exposures:** Average number of page exposures to an individual visitor.

- **Total hits:** Number of visits to a website, many of which may be by the same visitor.

- **Unique visitors:** Number of unique visitors to a site in a given time. This is commonly used by Nielsen/Net ratings to rank the most popular websites.

FIGURE 4.6

Website Metrics

Supply Chain Management Metrics

- **Back order:** An unfilled customer order. A back order is demand (immediate or past due) against an item whose current stock level is insufficient to satisfy demand.

- **Customer order promised cycle time:** The anticipated or agreed upon cycle time of a purchase order. It is a gap between the purchase order creation date and the requested delivery date.

- **Customer order actual cycle time:** The average time it takes to actually fill a customer's purchase order. This measure can be viewed on an order or an order line level.

- **Inventory replenishment cycle time:** Measure of the manufacturing cycle time plus the time included to deploy the product to the appropriate distribution center.

- **Inventory turns (inventory turnover):** The number of times that a company's inventory cycles or turns over per year. It is one of the most commonly used supply chain metrics.

FIGURE 4.7

Supply Chain Management Metrics

so on. The Yankee Group reports that 66 percent of companies determine website success solely by measuring the amount of traffic. New customer acquisition ranked second on the list at 34 percent, and revenue generation ranked third at 23 percent. Figure 4.6 displays a few metrics managers should be familiar with to help measure website success along with an organization's strategic initiatives. A web-centric metric is a measure of the success of web and ebusiness initiatives. Of the hundreds of web-centric metrics available, some are general to almost any web or ebusiness initiative and others are dependent on the particular initiative.

SUPPLY CHAIN MANAGEMENT (SCM) METRICS

Supply chain management metrics can help an organization understand how it's operating over a given time period. Supply chain measurements can cover many areas including procurement, production, distribution, warehousing, inventory, transportation, and customer service. However, a good performance in one part of the supply chain is not sufficient. A supply chain is only as strong as its weakest link. The solution is to measure all key areas of the supply chain. Figure 4.7 displays common supply chain management metrics.

FIGURE 4.8

CRM Metrics

Sales Metrics	Service Metrics	Marketing Metrics
■ Number of prospective customers	■ Cases closed same day	■ Number of marketing campaigns
■ Number of new customers	■ Number of cases handled by agent	■ New customer retention rates
■ Number of retained customers	■ Number of service calls	■ Number of responses by marketing campaign
■ Number of open leads	■ Average number of service requests by type	■ Number of purchases by marketing campaign
■ Number of sales calls	■ Average time to resolution	■ Revenue generated by marketing campaign
■ Number of sales calls per lead	■ Average number of service calls per day	■ Cost per interaction by marketing campaign
■ Amount of new revenue	■ Percentage compliance with service-level agreement	■ Number of new customers acquired by marketing campaign
■ Amount of recurring revenue	■ Percentage of service renewals	■ Customer retention rate
■ Number of proposals given	■ Customer satisfaction level	■ Number of new leads by product

CUSTOMER RELATIONSHIP MANAGEMENT (CRM) METRICS

Wondering what CRM metrics to track and monitor using reporting and real-time performance dashboards? Best practice is no more than seven (plus or minus two) metrics out of the hundreds possible should be used at any given management level. Figure 4.8 displays common CRM metrics tracked by organizations.

BUSINESS PROCESS REENGINEERING (BPR) AND ENTERPRISE RESOURCE PLANNING (ERP) METRICS

Business process reengineering and enterprise resource planning are large, organizationwide initiatives. Measuring these types of strategic initiatives is extremely difficult. One of the best methods is the balanced scorecard. This approach to strategic management was developed in the early 1990s by Drs. Robert Kaplan of the Harvard Business School and David Norton. Addressing some of the weaknesses and vagueness of previous measurement techniques, the balanced scorecard approach provides a clear prescription as to what companies should measure in order to balance the financial perspective.

The *balanced scorecard* is a management system, in addition to a measurement system, that enables organizations to clarify their vision and strategy and translate them into action. It provides feedback around both the internal business processes and external outcomes in order to continuously improve strategic performance and results. When fully deployed, the balanced scorecard transforms strategic planning from an academic exercise into the nerve center of an enterprise. Kaplan and Norton describe the innovation of the balanced scorecard as follows:

> The balanced scorecard retains traditional financial measures. But financial measures tell the story of past events, an adequate story for industrial age companies for which

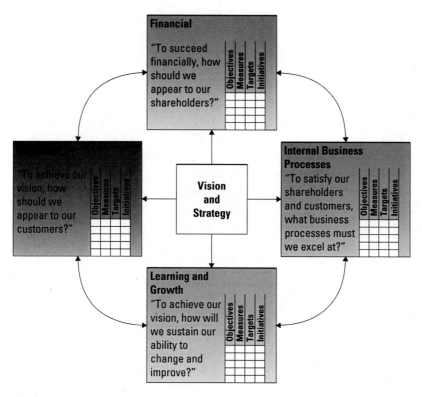

FIGURE 4.9

The Four Primary
Perspectives of the
Balanced Scorecard

investments in long-term capabilities and customer relationships were not critical for success. These financial measures are inadequate, however, for guiding and evaluating the journey that information age companies must make to create future value through investment in customers, suppliers, employees, processes, technology, and innovation. (Kaplan, Robert, Norton, David, "The BSC: Translating Strategy into Action" (Vintage Books: 1998))

The balanced scorecard views the organization from four perspectives, and users should develop metrics, collect data, and analyze their business relative to each of these perspectives:

- The learning and growth perspective.
- The internal business process perspective.
- The customer perspective.
- The financial perspective (see Figure 4.9).

Recall that companies cannot manage what they cannot measure. Therefore, metrics must be developed based on the priorities of the strategic plan, which provides the key business drivers and criteria for metrics that managers most desire to watch.

One warning regarding metrics—do not go crazy. The trick is to find a few key metrics to track that provide significant insight. Remember to tie metrics to other financial and business objectives in the firm. The key is to get good insight without becoming a slave to metrics. The rule of thumb is to develop seven key metrics, plus or minus two.

Chapter Four Case: How Do You Value Friendster?

Jonathan Abrams is keeping quiet about how he is going to generate revenue from his website, Friendster, which specializes in social networking. Abrams was a 33-year-old Canadian software developer whose experiences included being laid off by Netscape and then moving from one start-up to another. Abrams was unemployed, not doing well financially, and certainly not looking to start another business, when he developed the idea for Friendster. He quickly coded a working prototype and watched in amazement as his website took off.

The buzz around social networking start-ups has been on the rise. A number of high-end venture capital (VC) firms, including Sequoia and Mayfield, have invested more than $40 million into social networking start-ups such as LinkedIn, Spoke, and Tribe Networks. Friendster received over $13 million in venture capital from Kleiner, Perkins, Caufield, Byers, and Benchmark Capital, which reportedly valued the company at $53 million—a startling figure for a company that had yet to generate even a single dime in revenue.

A year after making its public debut, Friendster was one of the largest social networking websites, attracting over 5 million users and receiving more than 50,000 page views per day. The question is how do efficiency metrics, such as web traffic and page views, turn into cash flow? Everyone is wondering how Friendster is going to begin generating revenue.

The majority of Abrams's competitors make their money by extracting fees from their subscribers. Friendster is going to continue to let its subscribers meet for free but plans to charge them for premium services such as the ability to customize their profile page. The company also has plans to extend beyond social networking to an array of value-added services such as friend-based job referrals and classmate searches. Abrams is also looking into using his high-traffic website to tap into the growing Internet advertising market.

Abrams does not appear concerned about generating revenue or about potential competition. He states, "Match.com has been around eight years, has 12 million users, and has spent many millions of dollars on advertising to get them. We're a year old, we've spent zero dollars on advertising, and in a year or less, we'll be bigger than them—it's a given."

The future of Friendster is uncertain. Google offered to buy Friendster for $30 million even though there are signs, both statistical and anecdotal, that Friendster's popularity may have peaked.

Questions

1. How could you use efficiency IT metrics to help place a value on Friendster?
2. How could you use effectiveness IT metrics to help place a value on Friendster?
3. Explain how a venture capital company can value Friendster at $53 million when the company has yet to generate any revenue.
4. Explain why Google would be interested in buying Friendster for $30 million when the company has yet to generate any revenue.
5. Google purchased You-Tube for $1.65 billion. Do you think this was a smart investment? Why or why not?

CHAPTER 5

Organizational Structures That Support Strategic Initiatives

LEARNING OUTCOMES

5.1. Compare the responsibilities of a chief information officer (CIO), chief technology officer (CTO), chief privacy officer (CPO), chief security officer (CSO), and chief knowledge officer (CKO).

5.2. Explain the gap between IT people and business people and the primary reason this gap exists.

5.3. Define the relationship between security and ethics.

Organizational Structures

Employees across the organization must work closely together to develop strategic initiatives that create competitive advantages. Understanding the basic structure of a typical IT department including titles, roles, and responsibilities will help an organization build a cohesive enterprisewide team.

IT Roles and Responsibilities

Information technology is a relatively new functional area, having been around formally in most organizations only for about 40 years. Job titles, roles, and responsibilities often differ dramatically from organization to organization. Nonetheless, clear trends are developing toward elevating some IT positions within an organization to the strategic level.

Most organizations maintain positions such as chief executive officer (CEO), chief financial officer (CFO), and chief operations officer (COO) at the strategic level. Recently there are more IT-related strategic positions such as chief information officer (CIO), chief technology officer (CTO), chief security officer (CSO), chief privacy officer (CPO), and chief knowledge officer (CKO).

J. Greg Hanson is proud to be the first CIO of the U.S. Senate. Contrary to some perceptions, the technology found in the Senate is quite good, according to Hanson. Hanson's responsibilities include creating the Senate's technology vision, leading the IT department, and deploying the IT infrastructure. Hanson must work with everyone from the 137 network administrators to the senators themselves to ensure that everything is operating smoothly. Hanson is excited to be the first CIO of the U.S. Senate and proud of the honor and responsibility that come with the job.

The *chief information officer (CIO)* is responsible for (1) overseeing all uses of information technology and (2) ensuring the strategic alignment of IT with business goals and objectives. The CIO often reports directly to the CEO. (See Figure 5.1 for the average CIO compensation.) CIOs must possess a solid and detailed understanding of every aspect of an organization coupled with tremendous insight into the capability of IT. Broad functions of a CIO include:

1. *Manager*—ensure the delivery of all IT projects, on time and within budget.
2. *Leader*—ensure the strategic vision of IT is in line with the strategic vision of the organization.

3. *Communicator*—advocate and communicate the IT strategy by building and maintaining strong executive relationships.

Although CIO is considered a position within IT, CIOs must be concerned with more than just IT. According to a recent survey (see Figure 5.2), most CIOs ranked "enhancing customer satisfaction" ahead of their concerns for any specific aspect of IT. CIOs with the broad business view that customer satisfaction is more crucial and critical than specific aspects of IT should be applauded.

Industry	Average CIO Compensation
Wholesale/Retail/Distribution	$243,304
Finance	$210,547
Insurance	$197,697
Manufacturing	$190,250
Medical/Dental/Health Care	$171,032
Government	$118,359
Education	$ 93,750

FIGURE 5.1

Average CIO Compensation by Industry

The *chief technology officer (CTO)* is responsible for ensuring the throughput, speed, accuracy, availability, and reliability of an organization's information technology. CTOs are similar to CIOs, except that CIOs take on the additional responsibility for effectiveness of ensuring that IT is aligned with the organization's strategic initiatives. CTOs have direct responsibility for ensuring the *efficiency* of IT systems throughout the organization. Most CTOs possess well-rounded knowledge of all aspects of IT, including hardware, software, and telecommunications.

The *chief security officer (CSO)* is responsible for ensuring the security of IT systems and developing strategies and IT safeguards against attacks from hackers and viruses. The role of a CSO has been elevated in recent years because of the number of attacks from hackers and viruses. Most CSOs possess detailed knowledge of networks and telecommunications because hackers and viruses usually find their way into IT systems through networked computers.

The *chief privacy officer (CPO)* is responsible for ensuring the ethical and legal use of information within an organization. CPOs are the newest senior executive position in IT. Recently, 150 of the Fortune 500 companies added the CPO position to their list of senior executives. Many CPOs are lawyers by training, enabling them to understand the often complex legal issues surrounding the use of information.

The *chief knowledge officer (CKO)* is responsible for collecting, maintaining, and distributing the organization's knowledge. The CKO designs programs and systems that make it easy for people to reuse knowledge. These systems create repositories of organizational documents, methodologies, tools, and practices, and they establish methods for filtering the information. The CKO must continuously encourage employee contributions to keep the systems up-to-date. The CKO can contribute directly to the organization's bottom line by reducing the learning curve for new employees or employees taking on new roles.

Danny Shaw was the first CKO at Children's Hospital in Boston. His initial task was to unite information from disparate systems to enable analysis of both the efficiency and effectiveness of the hospital's care. Shaw started by building a series of small, integrated information systems that quickly demonstrated value. He then gradually built on those successes, creating a knowledge-enabled organization one layer at a time. Shaw's information systems have enabled administrative and clinical operational analyses.

FIGURE 5.2

What Concerns CIOs the Most?

Percentage	CIOs' Concerns
94%	Enhancing customer satisfaction
92	Security
89	Technology evaluation
87	Budgeting
83	Staffing
66	ROI analysis
64	Building new applications
45	Outsourcing hosting

With the election of President Barack Obama comes the appointment of the first-ever national chief technology officer (CTO). The job description, as listed on Change. gov, states that the first CTO must "ensure the safety of our networks and lead an interagency effort, working with chief technology and chief information officers of each of the federal agencies, to ensure that they use best-in-class technologies and share best practices." A federal level CTO demonstrates the ongoing growth of technology positions outside corporate America. In the future expect to see many

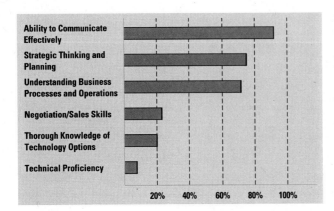

FIGURE 5.3

Skills Pivotal for Success in Executive IT Roles

more technology positions in government and nonprofit organizations.

All the above IT positions and responsibilities are critical to an organization's success. While many organizations may not have a different individual for each of these positions, they must have leaders taking responsibility for all these areas of concern. The individuals responsible for enterprisewide IT and IT-related issues must provide guidance and support to the organization's employees. Figure 5.3 displays the personal skills pivotal for success in an executive IT role.

The Gap between Business Personnel and IT Personnel

One of the greatest challenges today is effective communication between business personnel and IT personnel. Business personnel possess expertise in functional areas such as marketing, accounting, sales, and so forth. IT personnel have the technological expertise. Unfortunately, a communications gap often exists between the two. Business personnel have their own vocabularies based on their experience and expertise. IT personnel have their own vocabularies consisting of acronyms and technical terms. Effective communication between business and IT personnel should be a two-way street with each side making the effort to better understand the other (including through written and oral communication).

IMPROVING COMMUNICATIONS

Business personnel must seek to increase their understanding of IT. Although they do not need to know every technical detail, it will benefit their careers to understand what they can and cannot accomplish using IT. Business managers and leaders should read business-oriented IT magazines, such as *InformationWeek* and *CIO*, to increase their IT knowledge.

At the same time, an organization must develop strategies for integrating its IT personnel into the various business functions. Too often, IT personnel are left out of strategy meetings because of the belief they do not understand the business so they will not add any value. That is a dangerous position to take. IT personnel must understand the business if the organization is going to determine which technologies can benefit (or hurt) the business. With a little effort to communicate, IT personnel, by providing information on the functionality available in CRM systems, might add tremendous value to a meeting about how to improve customer service. Working together, business and IT personnel have the potential to create customer-service competitive advantages.

It is the responsibility of the CIO to ensure effective communications between business and IT personnel. While the CIO assumes the responsibility on an enterprisewide level, it is also each employee's responsibility to communicate effectively on a personal level.

Organizational Fundamentals—Ethics and Security

Ethics and security are two fundamental building blocks that organizations must base their businesses on. Such events as the Enron and Bernie Madoff scandals along with 9/11 have shed new light on the meaning of ethics and security. When the behavior of a few individuals can destroy billion-dollar organizations because of a lapse in ethics or security, the value of highly ethical and highly secure organizations should be evident. Review the Ethics and Security plug-ins to gain a detailed understanding of these topics. Due to the importance of these topics, they will be readdressed throughout this text.

Ethics

Ian Clarke, the inventor of a file-swapping service called Freenet, decided to leave the United States for the United Kingdom, where copyright laws are more lenient. Wayne Rosso, the inventor of a file-sharing service called Grokster, left the United States for Spain, again saying goodbye to tough U.S. copyright protections. File sharing encourages a legal network of shared thinking that can improve drug research, software development, and flow of information. The United States copyright laws, designed decades before the Internet was invented, make file sharing and many other Internet technologies illegal.

The ethical issues surrounding copyright infringement and intellectual property rights are consuming the ebusiness world. Advances in technology make it easier and easier for people to copy everything from music to pictures. Technology poses new challenges for our *ethics*—the principles and standards that guide our behavior toward other people. Review Figure 5.4 for an overview of concepts, terms, and ethical issues stemming from advances in technology.

In today's electronic world, privacy has become a major ethical issue. *Privacy* is the right to be left alone when you want to be, to have control over your own personal possessions, and to not be observed without your consent. Some of the most problematic decisions organizations face lie in the murky and turbulent waters of privacy. The burden comes from the knowledge that each time employees make a decision regarding issues of privacy, the outcome could sink the company some day.

The Securities and Exchange Commission (SEC) began inquiries into Enron's accounting practices on October 22, 2001. David Duncan, the Arthur Andersen partner in charge of Enron, instructed his team to begin destroying paper and electronic Enron-related records on October 23, 2001. Kimberly Latham, a subordinate to Duncan, sent instructions on October 24, 2001, to her entire team to follow Duncan's orders and even compiled a list of computer files to delete. Arthur Andersen blames Duncan for destroying thousands of Enron-related documents. Duncan blames the Arthur Andersen attorney, Nancy Temple, for sending him a memo instructing him to destroy files. Temple blames Arthur Andersen's document deletion policies.

Regardless of who is to blame, the bigger issue is that the destruction of files after a federal investigation has begun is both unethical and illegal. A direct corporate order to destroy information currently under federal investigation poses a dilemma for any professional. Comply, and you participate in potentially criminal activities; refuse, and you might find yourself looking for a new job.

Privacy is one of the biggest ethical issues facing organizations today. Trust between companies, customers, partners, and suppliers is the support structure of

Intellectual property	Intangible creative work that is embodied in physical form.
Copyright	The legal protection afforded an expression of an idea, such as a song, video game, and some types of proprietary documents.
Fair use doctrine	In certain situations, it is legal to use copyrighted material.
Pirated software	The unauthorized use, duplication, distribution, or sale of copyrighted software.
Counterfeit software	Software that is manufactured to look like the real thing and sold as such.

FIGURE 5.4

Issues Affected by Technology Advances

FIGURE 5.5

Primary Reasons Privacy
Issues Reduce Trust for
Ebusiness

1.	Loss of personal privacy is a top concern for Americans in the 21st century.
2.	Among Internet users, 37 percent would be "a lot" more inclined to purchase a product on a website that had a privacy policy.
3.	Privacy/security is the number one factor that would convert Internet researchers into Internet buyers.

the ebusiness world. One of the main ingredients in trust is privacy. Widespread fear about privacy continues to be one of the biggest barriers to the growth of ebusiness. People are concerned their privacy will be violated as a consequence of interactions on the web. Unless an organization can effectively address this issue of privacy, its customers, partners, and suppliers may lose trust in the organization, which hurts its business. Figure 5.5 displays the results from a *CIO* survey as to how privacy issues reduce trust for ebusiness.

Security—How Much Will Downtime Cost Your Business?

The old business axiom "time is money" needs to be updated to more accurately reflect the crucial interdependence between IT and business processes. To reflect the times, the phrase should be "uptime is money." The leading cause of downtime is a software failure followed by human error, according to Infonetics research. Unplanned downtime can strike at any time from any number of causes, ranging from tornadoes to sink overflows to network failures to power outages. Although natural disasters may appear to be the most devastating causes of IT outages, they are hardly the most frequent or biggest threats to uptime. Figure 5.6 highlights sources of unplanned downtime.

FIGURE 5.6

Sources of Unplanned
Downtime

Sources of Unplanned Downtime		
Bomb threat	Hacker	Snowstorm
Burst pipe	Hail	Sprinkler malfunction
Chemical spill	Hurricane	Static electricity
Construction	Ice storm	Strike
Corrupted data	Insects	Terrorism
Earthquake	Lightning	Theft
Electrical short	Network failure	Tornado
Epidemic	Plane crash	Train derailment
Equipment failure	Frozen pipe	Smoke damage
Evacuation	Power outage	Vandalism
Explosion	Power surge	Vehicle crash
Fire	Rodents	Virus
Flood	Sabotage	Water damage (various)
Fraud	Shredded data	Wind

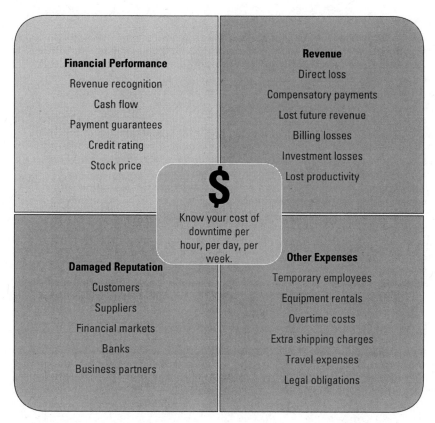

FIGURE 5.7

The Cost of Downtime

According to Gartner Group, on average, enterprises lose $108,000 of revenue every hour their IT infrastructure is down. Figure 5.7 displays the four categories of costs associated with downtime, according to the Gartner Group. A few questions companies should ask when determining the cost of downtime include:

- How many transactions can the company afford to lose without significantly impacting business?
- Does the company depend upon one or more mission-critical applications to conduct business?
- How much revenue will the company lose for every hour a critical application is unavailable?
- What is the productivity cost associated with each hour of downtime?
- How will collaborative business processes with partners, suppliers, and customers be affected by an unexpected IT outage?
- What is the total cost of lost productivity and lost revenue during unplanned downtime?

The reliability and resilience of IT systems have never been more essential for success as businesses cope with the forces of globalization, 24 × 7 operations, government and trade regulations, and overextended IT budgets and resources. Any unexpected IT downtime in today's business environment has the potential to cause both short- and long-term costs with far-reaching consequences. Understanding information security's role in a business is critical to keeping downtime to a minimum and uptime to a maximum.

PROTECTING INTELLECTUAL ASSETS

Smoking is not just bad for a person's health; it seems that it is also bad for company security, according to a new study. With companies banning smoking inside their offices, smokers are forced outside—usually to specific smoking areas in the back of the building. The doors leading out to them are a major security hole, according to a study undertaken by NTA Monitor Ltd., a U.K.-based Internet security tester.

NTA's tester was able to easily get inside a corporate building through a back door that was left open so smokers could easily and quickly get out and then back in, according to the company. Once inside, the tester asked an employee to take him to a meeting room, claiming that the IT department had sent him. Even without a pass, he reportedly gained access unchallenged and was then able to connect his laptop to the company's network.

Organizational information is intellectual capital. Just as organizations protect their assets—keeping their money in an insured bank or providing a safe working environment for employees—they must also protect their intellectual capital. An organization's intellectual capital includes everything from its patents to its transactional and analytical information. With security breaches on the rise and computer hackers everywhere, an organization must put in place strong security measures to survive.

The Health Insurance Portability and Accountability Act (HIPAA) protects the privacy and security of personal health records and has the potential to impact every business in the United States. HIPAA affects all companies that use electronic data interchange (EDI) to communicate personal health records. HIPAA requires health care organizations to develop, implement, and maintain appropriate security measures when sending electronic health information. Most important, these organizations must document and keep current records detailing how they are performing security measures for all transmissions of health information. On April 21, 2005, security rules for HIPAA became enforceable by law.

According to recent Gartner polls, less than 10 percent of all health care organizations have begun to implement the security policies and procedures required by HIPAA. The Health Information Management Society estimates that 70 percent of all health care providers failed to meet the April 2005 deadline for privacy rule compliance. Health care organizations need to start taking HIPAA regulations seriously since noncompliance can result in substantial fines and even imprisonment.

Beyond the health care industry, all businesses must understand the importance of information security, even if it is not enforceable by law. **Information security** is a broad term encompassing the protection of information from accidental or intentional misuse by persons inside or outside an organization. With current advances in technologies and business strategies such as CRM, organizations are able to determine valuable information—such as who are the top 20 percent of their customers who produce 80 percent of their revenues. Most organizations view this type of information as valuable intellectual capital, and they are implementing security measures to prevent the information from walking out the door or falling into the wrong hands.

Adding to the complexity of information security is the fact that organizations must enable employees, customers, and partners to access all sorts of information electronically to be successful. Doing business electronically automatically creates tremendous information security risks for organizations. There are many technical aspects of security, but the biggest information security issue is not technical, but human. Most information security breaches result from people misusing an organization's information either intentionally or inadvertently. For example, many individuals freely give up their passwords or leave them on sticky notes next to their computers, leaving the door wide open to intruders.

Figure 5.8 displays the typical size of an organization's information security budget relative to the organization's overall IT budget from the CSI/FBI Computer Crime and Security Survey. Forty-six percent of respondents indicated that their

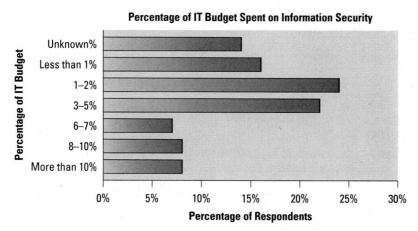

Percentage of IT Budget Spent on Information Security

FIGURE 5.8

Organizational Spending
on Information Security

organization spent between 1 and 5 percent of the total IT budget on security. Only 16 percent indicated that their organization spent less than 1 percent of the IT budget on security.

Figure 5.9 displays the spending per employee on computer security broken down by both public and private industries. The highest average computer security investment per employee was found in the transportation industry.

Security is perhaps the most fundamental and critical of all the technologies/ disciplines an organization must have squarely in place to execute its business strategy. Without solid security processes and procedures, none of the other technologies can develop business advantages.

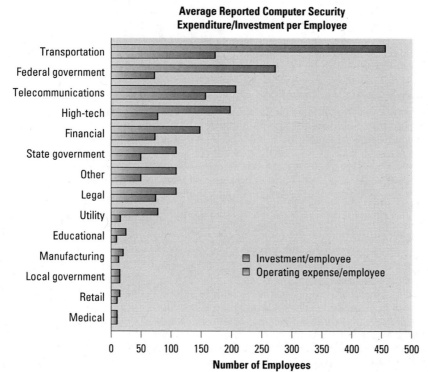

Average Reported Computer Security Expenditure/Investment per Employee

FIGURE 5.9

Computer Security
Expenditures/Investments
by Industry

1. Predict what might have happened to Apple if its top executives had not supported investments in IT.

2. Explain why it would be unethical for Apple to allow its customers to download free music from iTunes.

3. Evaluate the effects on Apple's business if it failed to secure its customer information and all of it was accidentally posted to an anonymous website.

4. Explain why Apple should have a CIO, CTO, CPO, CSO, and CKO.

Chapter Five Case: Executive Dilemmas in the Information Age

The vast array of business initiatives from supply chain management, to customer relationship management, business process reengineering, and enterprise resource planning makes it clear that information technology has evolved beyond the role of mere infrastructure to the support of business strategy. Today, in more and more industries, IT is a business strategy and is quickly becoming a survival issue.

Board and executive team agendas are increasingly peppered with, or even hijacked by, a growing range of IT issues from compliance to ethics and security. In most companies today, computers are key business tools. They generate, process, and store the majority of critical business information. Executives must understand how IT can affect a business by successfully addressing a wide range of needs—from large electronic discovery projects to the online review of document collections by geographically dispersed teams. A few examples of executive IT issues follow.

Stolen Proprietary Information

A computer company investigated to determine if an executive who accepted a job with a competitor stole proprietary information. The hard drive from the executive's laptop and desktop machine were forensically imaged. The analysis established that the night before the executive left, he downloaded all of the company's process specifications and distributor agreements, which he then zipped and emailed to the competitor. Additionally, reconstruction of deleted files located emails between the executive and the competitor discussing his intent to provide the proprietary information if he was offered additional options in the new company.

Sexual Harassment

A woman employed by a large defense contractor accused her supervisor of sexual harassment. The woman was fired from her job for poor performance and subsequently sued her ex-boss and the former employer.

A computer company was retained by the plaintiff's attorneys to investigate allegations of the former supervisor's harassing behavior. After making a forensic image backup of the ex-boss's hard drive, the forensic company was able to recover deleted electronic messages that showed the ex-boss had a history of propositioning women under his supervision for "special favors." A situation that might have been mired in a "he said/she said" controversy was quickly resolved; the woman got her job back, and the real culprit was terminated.

Stolen Trade Secrets

The board of directors of a technical research company demoted the company's founder and CEO. The executive, disgruntled because of his demotion, was later terminated. It was subsequently determined that the executive had planned to quit about the same time he was fired and establish a competitive company. Upon his termination, the executive took home two computers; he returned them to the company four days later, along with another company computer that he had previously used at home. Suspicious that critical information had been taken, the company's attorneys sent the computers to a computer forensic company for examination.

After making a forensic image backup of the hard drives, the forensic analysis identified a file directory that had been deleted during the aforementioned four-day period that had the same name as the competing company the executive had established. A specific search of the deleted files in this directory identified the executive's "to do list" file. This file indicated the executive planned to copy the company's database (valued at $100 million) for his personal use. Another item specified the executive was to "learn how to destroy evidence on a computer."

The computer forensic company's examination also proved that the executive had been communicating with other competing companies to establish alliances, in violation of the executive's nondisclosure agreement with the company. It was also shown that numerous key company files were located on removable computer storage media that had not been turned over by the executive to the company.

Questions

1. Explain why understanding technology, especially in the areas of security and ethics, is important for a CEO. How do a CEO's actions affect the organizational culture?

2. Identify why executives in nontechnological industries need to worry about technology and its potential business ramifications.

3. Describe why continuously learning about technology allows an executive to better analyze threats and opportunities.

4. Identify three things that a CTO, CPO, or CSO could do to prevent the above issues.

Exploring Business Intelligence

CHAPTER **6**

Valuing Organizational Information

LEARNING OUTCOMES

6.1. Describe the broad levels, formats, and granularities of information.

6.2. Differentiate between transactional and analytical information.

6.3. List, describe, and provide an example of each of the five characteristics of high quality information.

6.4. Assess the impact of low quality information on an organization and the benefits of high quality information on an organization.

Organizational Information

Google recently reported a 200 percent increase in sales of its new Enterprise Search Appliance tool. Companies use the tool within an enterprise information portal (EIP) to search corporate information for answers to customer questions and to fulfill sales orders. Hundreds of Google's customers are already using the tool— Xerox, Hitachi Data Systems, Nextel Communications, Procter & Gamble, Discovery Communications, Cisco Systems, Boeing. The ability to search, analyze, and comprehend information is vital for any organization's success. The incredible 200 percent growth in sales of Google's Search Appliance tool is a strong indicator that organizations are coveting technologies that help organize and provide access to information.

Information is everywhere in an organization. When addressing a significant business issue, employees must be able to obtain and analyze all the relevant information so they can make the best decision possible. Organizational information comes at different levels and in different formats and "granularities." *Information granularity* refers to the extent of detail within the information (fine and detailed or coarse and abstract). Employees must be able to correlate the different levels, formats, and granularities of information when making decisions. For example, if employees are using a supply chain management system to make decisions, they might find that their suppliers send information in different formats and granularity at different levels. One supplier might send detailed information in a spreadsheet, another supplier might send summary information in a Word document, and still another might send aggregate information from a database. Employees will need to compare these different types of information for what they commonly reveal to make strategic SCM decisions. Figure 6.1 displays types of information found in organizations.

Successfully collecting, compiling, sorting, and finally analyzing information from multiple levels, in varied formats, exhibiting different granularity can provide tremendous insight into how an organization is performing. Taking a hard look at organizational information can yield exciting and unexpected results such as potential new markets, new ways of reaching customers, and even new ways of doing business.

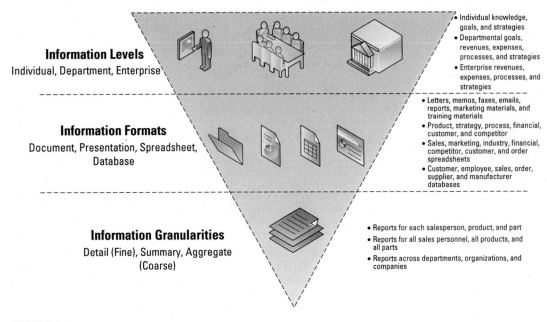

Information Levels
Individual, Department, Enterprise

- Individual knowledge, goals, and strategies
- Departmental goals, revenues, expenses, processes, and strategies
- Enterprise revenues, expenses, processes, and strategies

Information Formats
Document, Presentation, Spreadsheet, Database

- Letters, memos, faxes, emails, reports, marketing materials, and training materials
- Product, strategy, process, financial, customer, and competitor
- Sales, marketing, industry, financial, competitor, customer, and order spreadsheets
- Customer, employee, sales, order, supplier, and manufacturer databases

Information Granularities
Detail (Fine), Summary, Aggregate (Coarse)

- Reports for each salesperson, product, and part
- Reports for all sales personnel, all products, and all parts
- Reports across departments, organizations, and companies

FIGURE 6.1

Levels, Formats, and Granularities of Organizational Information

Samsung Electronics took a detailed look at over 10,000 reports from its resellers to identify "lost deals" or orders lost to competitors. The analysis yielded the enlightening result that 80 percent of lost sales occurred in a single business unit, the health care industry. Furthermore, Samsung was able to identify that 40 percent of its lost sales in the health care industry were going to one particular competitor. Before performing the analysis, Samsung was heading into its market blind. Armed with this valuable information, Samsung is changing its selling strategy in the health care industry by implementing a new strategy to work more closely with hardware vendors to win back lost sales.

Not all companies are successful at managing information. Staples, the office-supplies superstore, opened its first store in 1986 with state-of-the-art technology. The company experienced rapid growth and soon found itself overwhelmed with the resulting volumes of information. The state-of-the-art technology quickly became obsolete, and the company was unable to obtain any insight into its massive volumes of information. A simple query such as identifying the customers who purchased a computer, but not software or peripherals, took hours. Some queries required several days to complete and by the time the managers received answers to their queries it was too late for action.

After understanding the different levels, formats, and granularities of information, it is important to look at a few additional characteristics that help determine the value of information. These characteristics are type (transactional and analytical), timeliness, and quality.

The Value of Transactional and Analytical Information

Transactional information encompasses all of the information contained within a single business process or unit of work, and its primary purpose is to support the performing of daily operational tasks. Examples of transactional information are withdrawing cash from an ATM, making an airline reservation, or purchasing stocks. Organizations capture and store transactional information in databases, and they use it when performing operational tasks and repetitive decisions such as analyzing daily sales reports and production schedules to determine how much inventory to carry.

Analytical information encompasses all organizational information, and its primary purpose is to support the performing of managerial analysis tasks. Analytical information includes transactional information along with other information such as market and industry information. Examples of analytical information are trends, sales, product statistics, and future growth projections. Analytical information is used when making important ad hoc decisions such as whether the organization should build a new manufacturing plant or hire additional sales personnel. Figure 6.2 displays different types of transactional and analytical information.

The Value of Timely Information

The need for timely information can change for each business decision. Some decisions require weekly or monthly information while other decisions require daily information. Timeliness is an aspect of information that depends on the situation. In some industries, information that is a few days or weeks old can be relevant while in other industries information that is a few minutes old can be almost worthless. Some organizations, such as 911 centers, stock traders, and banks, require consolidated, up-to-the-second information, 24 hours a day, seven days a week. Other organizations, such as insurance and construction companies, require only daily or even weekly information.

Real-time information means immediate, up-to-date information. *Real-time systems* provide real-time information in response to query requests. Many organizations use real-time systems to exploit key corporate transactional information. In a survey of 700 IT executives by Evans Data Corp., 48 percent of respondents said they were already analyzing information in or near real-time, and another 25 percent reported plans to add real-time systems.

The growing demand for real-time information stems from organizations' need to make faster and more effective decisions, keep smaller inventories, operate more efficiently, and track performance more carefully. But timeliness is relative. Organizations need fresh, timely information to make good decisions. Information also needs to be timely in the sense that it meets employees' needs—but no more. If employees can absorb information only on an hourly or daily basis, there is no need to gather real-time information in smaller increments. For example, MBIA Insurance Corp. uses overnight updates to feed its real-time systems. Employees use this information to make daily risk decisions for mortgages, insurance policies, and

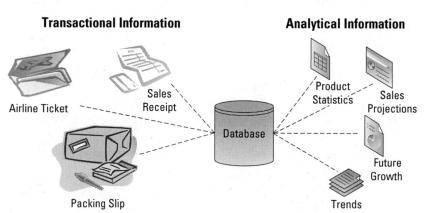

Transactional Information

Airline Ticket   Sales Receipt   Database

Packing Slip

Analytical Information

Product Statistics   Sales Projections

Future Growth

Trends

FIGURE 6.2

Transactional versus Analytical Information

other services. The company found that overnight updates were sufficient, as long as users could gain immediate access to the information they needed to make business decisions during the day.

Most people request real-time information without understanding one of the biggest pitfalls associated with real-time information—continual change. Imagine the following scenario: Three managers meet at the end of the day to discuss a business problem. Each manager has gathered information at different times during the day to create a picture of the situation. Each manager's picture may be different because of this time discrepancy. Their views on the business problem may not match since the information they are basing their analysis on is continually changing. This approach may not speed up decision making, and may actually slow it down.

The timeliness of the information required must be evaluated for each business decision. Organizations do not want to find themselves using real-time information to make a bad decision faster.

The Value of Quality Information

Westpac Financial Services (WFS), one of the four major banks in Australia, serves millions of customers from its many core systems, each with its own database. The databases maintain information and provide users with easy access to the stored information. Unfortunately, the company failed to develop information-capturing standards, which led to inconsistent organizational information. For example, one system had a field to capture email addresses while another system did not. Duplicate customer information among the different systems was another major issue, and the company continually found itself sending conflicting or competing messages to customers from different operations of the bank. A customer could also have multiple accounts within the company, one representing a life insurance policy and one representing a credit card. WFS had no way to identify that the two different customer accounts were for the same customer.

WFS had to solve its information quality problems immediately if it was to remain competitive. The company purchased NADIS (Name & Address Data Integrity Software), a software solution that filters customer information, highlighting missing, inaccurate, and redundant information. Customer service ratings are on the rise for WFS now that the company can operate its business with a single and comprehensive view of each one of its customers.

Business decisions are only as good as the quality of the information used to make the decisions. Figure 6.3 reviews five characteristics common to high quality information: accuracy, completeness, consistency, uniqueness, and timeliness. Figure 6.4 highlights several issues with low quality information including:

1. The first issue is *missing* information. The customer's first name is missing. (See #1 in Figure 6.4.)

FIGURE 6.3

Five Common Characteristics of High Quality Information

Accuracy	Are all the values correct? For example, is the name spelled correctly? Is the dollar amount recorded properly?
Completeness	Are any of the values missing? For example, is the address complete including street, city, state, and zip code?
Consistency	Is aggregate or summary information in agreement with detailed information? For example, do all total fields equal the true total of the individual fields?
Uniqueness	Is each transaction, entity, and event represented only once in the information? For example, are there any duplicate customers?
Timeliness	Is the information current with respect to the business requirements? For example, is information updated weekly, daily, or hourly?

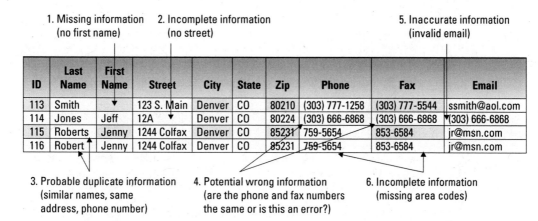

1. Missing information (no first name) 2. Incomplete information (no street) 5. Inaccurate information (invalid email)

ID	Last Name	First Name	Street	City	State	Zip	Phone	Fax	Email
113	Smith	▼	123 S. Main	Denver	CO	80210	(303) 777-1258	(303) 777-5544	ssmith@aol.com
114	Jones	Jeff	12A ▼	Denver	CO	80224	(303) 666-6868	(303) 666-6868	▼(303) 666-6868
115	Roberts	Jenny	1244 Colfax	Denver	CO	85231	759-5654	853-6584	jr@msn.com
116	Robert	Jenny	1244 Colfax	Denver	CO	85231	759-5654	853-6584	jr@msn.com

3. Probable duplicate information (similar names, same address, phone number)   4. Potential wrong information (are the phone and fax numbers the same or is this an error?)   6. Incomplete information (missing area codes)

FIGURE 6.4

Low Quality Information Example

2. The second issue is *incomplete* information since the street address contains only a number and not a street name.

3. The third issue is a probable *duplication* of information since the only slight difference between the two customers is the spelling of the last name. Similar street addresses and phone numbers make this likely.

4. The fourth issue is potential *wrong* information because the customer's phone and fax numbers are the same. Some customers might have the same number for phone and fax line, but the fact that the customer also has this number in the email address field is suspicious.

5. The fifth issue is definitely an example of *inaccurate* information since a phone number is located in the email address field.

6. The sixth issue is *incomplete* information since there is not a valid area code for the phone and fax numbers.

Recognizing how low quality information issues occur will allow organizations to begin to correct them. The four primary sources of low quality information are:

1. Online customers intentionally enter inaccurate information to protect their privacy.

2. Different systems have different information entry standards and formats.

3. Call center operators enter abbreviated or erroneous information by accident or to save time.

4. Third-party and external information contains inconsistencies, inaccuracies, and errors.

Addressing the above sources of information inaccuracies will significantly improve the quality of organizational information and the value that can be extracted from the information.

UNDERSTANDING THE COSTS OF POOR INFORMATION

Using the wrong information can lead to making the wrong decision. Making the wrong decision can cost time, money, and even reputations. Every business decision is only as good as the information used to make the decision. Bad information can cause serious business ramifications such as:

- Inability to accurately track customers, which directly affects strategic initiatives such as CRM and SCM.

- Difficulty identifying the organization's most valuable customers.

- Inability to identify selling opportunities and wasted revenue from marketing to nonexisting customers and nondeliverable mail.
- Difficulty tracking revenue because of inaccurate invoices.
- Inability to build strong relationships with customers—which increases buyer power.

UNDERSTANDING THE BENEFITS OF GOOD INFORMATION

High quality information can significantly improve the chances of making a good decision and directly increase an organization's bottom line. Lillian Vernon Corp., a catalog company, used web analytics to discover that men preferred to shop at Lillian Vernon's website instead of looking through its paper catalog. Based on this information, the company began placing male products more prominently on its website and soon realized a 15 percent growth in sales to men.

Another company discovered that Phoenix, Arizona, is not a good place to sell golf clubs, even with its high number of golf courses. An analysis revealed that typical golfers in Phoenix are either tourists or conventioneers. These golfers usually bring their clubs with them while visiting Phoenix. The analysis further revealed that two of the best places to sell golf clubs in the United States are Rochester, New York, and Detroit, Michigan.

There are numerous examples of companies that have used their high quality information to make solid strategic business decisions. High quality information does not automatically guarantee that every decision made is going to be a good one, since people ultimately make decisions. But such information ensures that the basis of the decisions is accurate. The success of the organization depends on appreciating and leveraging the true value of timely and high quality information.

OPENING CASE STUDY QUESTIONS

1. Determine if an entry in Wikipedia is an example of transactional information or analytical information.
2. Describe the impact to Wikipedia if the information contained in its database is of low quality.
3. Review the five common characteristics of high quality information and rank them in order of importance to Wikipedia.
4. Explain how Wikipedia is resolving the issue of poor information.

Chapter Six Case: Political Microtargeting: What Data Crunchers Did for Obama

In his Presidential Inauguration speech President Barack Obama spoke a word rarely expressed—*data*—referencing indicators of economic and other crises. It is not surprising that the word *data* was spoken in his inauguration speech as capturing and analyzing data has been crucial to Obama's rise to power. Throughout Obama's historic campaign he used the Internet not only for social networking and fund raising, but also to identify potential swing voters. Obama's team carefully monitored contested states and congressional districts, since one to two thousand voters could prove decisive—meaning the focus was on only a tiny fraction of the voting public. Both political parties hired technology wizards to help sift through the mountains of consumer and demographic details to recognize these important voters.

Ten "Tribes"

Spotlight Analysis, a Democratic consultancy, used political microtargeting to analyze neighborhood details, family sizes, and spending patterns to categorize every American of voting age—175 million of us—into 10 "values tribes." Individual tribe members do not necessarily share the same race, religion, or income bracket, but they have common mind-sets about political issues: God, community, responsibility, opportunity. Spotlight identified a particular morally guided (but not necessarily religious) tribe of some 14 million voters that it dubbed "Barn Raisers." Barn Raisers comprise many races, religions, and ethnic groups and around 40 percent of Barn Raisers favor Democrats and 27 percent favor Republicans. Barn Raisers are slightly less likely to have a college education than Spotlight's other swing groups. They are active in community organizations, ambivalent about government, and care deeply about "playing by the rules" and "keeping promises," to use Spotlight's definitions. Spotlight believed that the Barn Raisers held the key to the race between Obama and his Republican challenger, Arizona Senator John McCain.

Not typically seen outside of such corporate American icons as Google, Amazon, and eBay, political microtargeting, which depends on data, databases, and data analysis techniques, is turning political parties into sophisticated, intelligent, methodical machines. In nanoseconds, computers sort 175 million voters into segments and quickly calculate the potential that each individual voter has to swing from red or purple to blue or vice versa.

For some, political microtargeting signals the dehumanization of politics. For others, this type of sophisticated analysis is a highly efficient way of pinpointing potential voters. For example, analyzing a voter in Richmond, Virginia, traditionally simply identifies the number of school-age children, type of car, zip code, magazine subscriptions, and mortgage balance. But data crunching could even indicate if the voter has dogs or cats. (Cat owners lean slightly for Democrats, dog owners trend Republican.) After the analysis the voter is placed into a political tribe and analyzers can draw conclusions about the issues that matter to this particular voter. Is that so horrible?

Behavioral Grouping

For generations, governments lacked the means to study individual behaviors and simply placed all citizens into enormous groupings such as Hispanics, Jews, union members, hunters, soccer moms, etc. With the use of sophisticated databases and data analysis techniques companies such as Spotlight can group individuals based more on specific behavior and choices, and less on the names, colors, and clans that mark us from birth.

When Spotlight first embarked on its research the company interviewed thousands of voters the old-fashioned way. At first, the Barn Raisers did not seem significant and the tribe represented about 9 percent of the electorate. However, when Spotlight's analysts dug deeper, they discovered that Barn Raisers stood at the epicenter of America's political swing. In 2004, 90 percent of them voted for President Bush, but then the group's political leanings shifted, with 64 percent of them saying they voted for Democrats in the 2006 election. Spotlight surveys showed that political scandals, tax-funded boondoggles like Alaska's Bridge to Nowhere, and the botched job on Hurricane Katrina sent them packing.

Suddenly, Spotlight identified millions of potential swing voters. The challenge then became locating the swing voters by states. For this, the company analyzed the demographics and buying patterns of the Barn Raisers they surveyed personally. Then it began correlating data from the numerous commercially available databases with matching profiles. By Spotlight's count, this approach nailed Barn Raisers three times out of four. So Democrats could bet that at least three-quarters of them would be likely to welcome an appeal stressing honesty and fair play.

Still Swing Voters

It is still undetermined to what extent Spotlight's strategy worked and the company has not correlated the Barn Raisers to their actual votes. However, it is reasonable to presume that amid that sea of humanity stretched out before Obama on Washington's Mall on January 20, at least some were moved by microtargeted appeals. And if Obama and his team fail to honor their mathematically honed vows, the Barn Raisers may abandon them in droves. They are swing voters, after all.

Questions

1. Describe the difference between transactional and analytical information and determine which types Spotlight used to identify its 10 tribes.
2. Explain the importance of high quality information for political microtargeting.
3. Review the five common characteristics of high quality information and rank them in order of importance for political microtargeting.
4. In terms of political microtargeting explain the following sentence: It is never possible to have all of the information required to make a 100 percent accurate prediction.
5. Do you agree that political microtargeting signals the dehumanization of politics?

CHAPTER 7

Storing Organizational Information—Databases

7.1. Define the fundamental concepts of the relational database model.

7.2. Evaluate the advantages of the relational database model.

7.3. Compare relational integrity constraints and business-critical integrity constraints.

7.4. Describe the benefits of a data-driven website.

7.5. Describe the two primary methods for integrating information across multiple databases.

Storing Organizational Information

Organizational information is stored in a database. Applications and programs, such as supply chain management systems, and customer relationship management systems, access the data in the database so the program can consult it to answer queries. The records retrieved in answer to questions become information that can be used to make decisions. The computer program used to manage and query a database is known as a database management system (DBMS). The properties and design of database systems are included in the study of information science.

The central concept of a database is that of a collection of records, or pieces of information. Typically, a given database has a structural description of the type of facts held in that database: This description is known as a *schema*. The schema describes the objects that are represented in the database and the relationships among them. There are a number of different ways of organizing a schema, that is, of modeling the database structure: These are known as database models (or data models). The most commonly used model today is the relational model, which represents all information in the form of multiple related tables each consisting of rows and columns. This model represents relationships by the use of values common to more than one table. Other models, such as the hierarchical model, and the network model, use a more explicit representation of relationships.

Many professionals consider a collection of data to constitute a database only if it has certain properties, for example, if the data are managed to ensure integrity and quality, if it allows shared access by a community of users, if it has a schema, or if it supports a query language. However, there is no definition of these properties that is universally agreed upon.

Relational Database Fundamentals

There are many different models for organizing information in a database, including the hierarchical database, network database, and the most prevalent—the relational database model. Broadly defined, a **database** maintains information about various types of objects (inventory), events (transactions), people (employees), and places (warehouses). In a **hierarchical database model,** information is organized into a tree-like structure that allows repeating information using parent/child relationships in such a way that it cannot have too many relationships. Hierarchical structures were widely used in the first mainframe database management systems. However, owing to their restrictions, hierarchical structures often cannot be used to relate to structures that exist in the real world. The **network database model** is a flexible way of representing objects and their relationships. Where the hierarchical model structures data as a tree of records, with each record having one parent record and many children, the network model allows each record to have multiple parent and child records, forming a lattice structure. The **relational database model** is a type of database that stores information in the form of logically related two-dimensional tables. This text focuses on the relational database model.

Consider how the Coca-Cola Bottling Company of Egypt (TCCBCE) implemented an inventory-tracking database to improve order accuracy by 27 percent, decrease order response time by 66 percent, and increase sales by 20 percent. With over 7,400 employees, TCCBCE owns and operates 11 bottling plants and 29 sales and distribution centers, making it one of the largest companies in Egypt.

Traditionally, the company sent distribution trucks to each customer's premises to take orders and deliver stock. Many problems were associated with this process including numerous information entry errors, which caused order-fulfillment time to take an average of three days. To remedy the situation, Coca-Cola decided to create presales teams equipped with handheld devices to visit customers and take orders electronically. On returning to the office, the teams synchronized orders with the company's inventory-tracking database to ensure automated processing and rapid dispatch of accurate orders to customers.

ENTITIES AND ATTRIBUTES

Figure 7.1 illustrates the primary concepts of the relational database model—entities, entity classes, attributes, keys, and relationships. An **entity** in the relational database model is a person, place, thing, transaction, or event about which information is stored. A table in the relational database model is a collection of similar entities. The tables of interest in Figure 7.1 are *CUSTOMER, ORDER, ORDER LINE, PRODUCT,* and *DISTRIBUTOR.* Notice that each entity class (the collection of similar entities) is stored in a different two-dimensional table. **Attributes,** also called fields or columns, are characteristics or properties of an entity class. In Figure 7.1 the attributes for *CUSTOMER* include *Customer ID, Customer Name, Contact Name,* and *Phone.* Attributes for *PRODUCT* include *Product ID, Product Description,* and *Price.* Each specific entity in an entity class (e.g., Dave's Sub Shop in the *CUSTOMER* table) occupies one row in its respective table. The columns in the table contain the attributes.

KEYS AND RELATIONSHIPS

To manage and organize various entity classes within the relational database model, developers must identify primary keys and foreign keys and use them to create logical relationships. A **primary key** is a field (or group of fields) that uniquely identifies a given entity in a table. In *CUSTOMER,* the *Customer ID* uniquely identifies each entity (customer) in the table and is the primary key. Primary keys are important because they provide a way of distinguishing each entity in a table.

FIGURE 7.1

Potential Relational Database for Coca-Cola Bottling Company of Egypt (TCCBCE)

Order Number: 34562

Coca-Cola Bottling Company of Egypt
Sample Sales Order

Customer:	Dave's Sub Shop	Date:	8/6/2008

Quantity	Product	Price	Amount
100	Vanilla Coke	$0.55	$55

Distributor Fee $12.95
Order Total $67.95

CUSTOMER

Customer ID	*Customer Name*	*Contact Name*	*Phone*
23	Dave's Sub Shop	David Logan	(555)333-4545
43	Pizza Palace	Debbie Fernandez	(555)345-5432
765	T's Fun Zone	Tom Repicci	(555)565-6655

ORDER

Order ID	*Order Date*	*Customer ID*	*Distributor ID*	*Distributor Fee*	*Total Due*
34561	7/4/2008	23	DEN8001	$22.00	$145.75
34562	8/6/2008	23	DEN8001	$12.95	$67.95
34563	6/5/2008	765	NY9001	$29.50	$249.50

ORDER LINE

Order ID	*Line Item*	*Product ID*	*Quantity*
34561	1	12345AA	75
34561	2	12346BB	50
34561	3	12347CC	100
34562	1	12349EE	100
34563	1	12345AA	100
34563	2	12346BB	100
34563	3	12347CC	50
34563	4	12348DD	50
34563	5	12349EE	100

DISTRIBUTOR

Distributor ID	*Distributor Name*
DEN8001	Hawkins Shipping
CHI3001	ABC Trucking
NY9001	Van Distributors

PRODUCT

Product ID	*Product Description*	*Price*
12345AA	Coca-Cola	$0.55
12346BB	Diet Coke	$0.55
12347CC	Sprite	$0.55
12348DD	Diet Sprite	$0.55
12349EE	Vanilla Coke	$0.55

A *foreign key* in the relational database model is a primary key of one table that appears as an attribute in another table and acts to provide a logical relationship between the two tables. Consider Hawkins Shipping, one of the distributors appearing in the *DISTRIBUTOR* table. Its primary key, *Distributor ID,* is DEN8001. Notice that *Distributor ID* also appears as an attribute in the ORDER table. This establishes the fact that Hawkins Shipping (*Distributor ID* DEN8001) was responsible for delivering orders 34561 and 34562 to the appropriate customer(s). Therefore, *Distributor ID* in the *ORDER* table creates a logical relationship (who shipped what order) between *ORDER* and *DISTRIBUTOR*.

Relational Database Advantages

From a business perspective, database information offers many advantages, including:

- Increased flexibility.
- Increased scalability and performance.
- Reduced information redundancy.
- Increased information integrity (quality).
- Increased information security.

INCREASED FLEXIBILITY

Databases tend to mirror business structures, and a good database can handle changes quickly and easily, just as any good business needs to be able to handle changes quickly and easily. Equally important, databases provide flexibility in allowing each user to access the information in whatever way best suits his or her needs. The distinction between logical and physical views is important in understanding flexible database user views. The *physical view* of information deals with the physical storage of information on a storage device such as a hard disk. The *logical view* of information focuses on how users logically access information to meet their particular business needs. This separation of logical and physical views is what allows each user to access database information differently. That is, while a database has only one physical view, it can easily support multiple logical views. In the previous database illustration, for example, users could perform a query to determine which distributors delivered shipments to Pizza Palace last week. At the same time, another person could perform some sort of statistical analysis to determine the frequency at which Sprite and Diet Coke appear on the same order. These represent two very different logical views, but both views use the same physical view.

Consider another example—a mail-order business. One user might want a CRM report presented in alphabetical format, in which case last name should appear before first name. Another user, working with a catalog mailing system, would want customer names appearing as first name and then last name. Both are easily achievable, but different logical views of the same physical information.

INCREASED SCALABILITY AND PERFORMANCE

The official website of The American Family Immigration History Center, www.ellisisland.org, generated over 2.5 billion hits in its first year of operation. The site offers easy access to immigration information about people who entered America through the Port of New York and Ellis Island between 1892 and 1924. The database contains over 25 million passenger names correlated to 3.5 million images of ships' manifests.

Only a database could "scale" to handle the massive volumes of information and the large numbers of users required for the successful launch of the Ellis Island website. *Scalability* refers to how well a system can adapt to increased demands. *Performance* measures how quickly a system performs a certain process or transaction. Some organizations must be able to support hundreds or thousands of online users including employees, partners, customers, and suppliers, who all want to access and share information. Databases today scale to exceptional levels, allowing all types of users and programs to perform information-processing and information-searching tasks.

REDUCED INFORMATION REDUNDANCY

Redundancy is the duplication of information, or storing the same information in multiple places. Redundant information occurs because organizations frequently capture and store the same information in multiple locations. The primary problem with redundant information is that it is often inconsistent, which makes it difficult to determine which values are the most current or most accurate. Not having correct information is confusing and frustrating for employees and disruptive to an organization. One primary goal of a database is to eliminate information redundancy by recording each piece of information in only one place in the database. Eliminating information redundancy saves space, makes performing information updates easier, and improves information quality.

INCREASED INFORMATION INTEGRITY (QUALITY)

Information integrity is a measure of the quality of information. Within a database environment, *integrity constraints* are rules that help ensure the quality of information. Integrity constraints can be defined and built into the database design. The database (more appropriately, the database management system, which is discussed below) ensures that users can never violate these constraints. There are two types of integrity constraints: (1) relational integrity constraints and (2) business-critical integrity constraints.

Relational integrity constraints are rules that enforce basic and fundamental information-based constraints. For example, an operational integrity constraint would not allow someone to create an order for a nonexistent customer, provide a markup percentage that was negative, or order zero pounds of raw materials from a supplier. *Business-critical integrity constraints* enforce business rules vital to an organization's success and often require more insight and knowledge than relational integrity constraints. Consider a supplier of fresh produce to large grocery chains such as Kroger. The supplier might implement a business-critical integrity constraint stating that no product returns are accepted after 15 days past delivery. That would make sense because of the chance of spoilage of the produce. These types of integrity constraints tend to mirror the very rules by which an organization achieves success.

The specification and enforcement of integrity constraints produce higher quality information that will provide better support for business decisions. Organizations that establish specific procedures for developing integrity constraints typically see a decline in information error rates and an increase in the use of organizational information.

INCREASED INFORMATION SECURITY

Information is an organizational asset. Like any asset, the organization must protect its information from unauthorized users or misuse. As systems become increasingly complex and more available over the Internet, security becomes an even bigger issue. Databases offer many security features including passwords, access levels, and access controls. Passwords provide authentication of the user who is gaining access to the system. Access levels determine who has access to the different types of information, and access controls determine what type of access they have to the information. For example, customer service representatives might need read-only access to customer order information so they can answer customer order inquiries; they might not have or need the authority to change or delete order information. Managers might require access to employee files, but they should have access only to their own employees' files, not the employee files for the entire company. Various security features of databases can ensure that individuals have only certain types of access to certain types of information.

Databases can increase personal security as well as information security. The Chicago Police Department (CPD) has relied on a crime-fighting system called Citizen and Law Enforcement Analysis and Reporting (CLEAR). CLEAR electronically streamlines the way detectives enter and access critical information to help them solve crimes, analyze crime patterns, and ultimately promote security in a proactive manner. The CPD enters 650,000 new criminal cases and 500,000 new arrests into CLEAR each year.

Database Management Systems

Ford's European plant manufactures more than 5,000 vehicles a day and sells them in over 100 countries worldwide. Every component of every model must conform to complex European standards, including passenger safety standards and pedestrian and environmental protection standards. These standards govern each stage of Ford's manufacturing process from design to final production. The company needs to obtain many thousands of different approvals each year to comply with the standards. Overlooking just one means the company cannot sell the finished vehicle, which brings the production line to a standstill and could potentially cost Ford up to 1 million euros per day. Ford built the Homologation Timing System (HTS), based on a relational database, to help it track and analyze these standards. The reliability and high performance of the HTS have helped Ford substantially reduce its compliance risk.

A database management system is used to access information from a database. A ***database management system (DBMS)*** is software through which users and application programs interact with a database. The user sends requests to the DBMS and the DBMS performs the actual manipulation of the information in the database. There are two primary ways that users can interact with a DBMS: (1) directly and (2) indirectly, as displayed in Figure 7.2. In either case, users access the DBMS and the DBMS accesses the database.

FIGURE 7.2

Interacting Directly and Indirectly with a Database through a DBMS

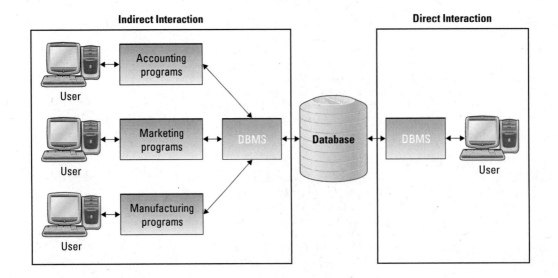

DATA-DRIVEN WEBSITES

The pages on a website must change according to what a site visitor is interested in browsing. Consider for example, a company selling sports cars. A database is created with information on each of the currently available cars (e.g., make, model, engine details, year, a photograph, etc.). A visitor to the website clicks on Porsche, for example, enters the price range he or she is interested in, and hits "Go." The visitor is presented with information on available cars within the price range and an invitation to purchase or request more information from the company. Via a secure administration area on the website, the company has the ability to modify, add, or remove cars to the database.

A ***data-driven website*** is an interactive website kept constantly updated and relevant to the needs of its customers through the use of a database. Data-driven websites are especially useful when the site offers a great deal of information, products, or services. Website visitors are frequently angered if they are buried under an avalanche of information when searching a website. A data-driven website invites visitors to select and view what they are interested in by inserting a query. The website analyzes the query and then custom builds a web page in real-time that satisfies the query. Figure 7.3 displays a Wikipedia user querying business intelligence and the database sending back the appropriate web page that satisfies the user's request.

Data-Driven Website Business Advantages

When building a website, ask two primary questions to determine if the website needs a database:

1. How often will the content change?
2. Who will be making the content changes?

FIGURE 7.3

Wikipedia—Data-Driven Website

① Search Query　　③ Results

② Database

Data-Driven Website Advantages
■ Development: Allows the website owner to make changes any time—all without having to rely on a developer or knowing HTML programming. A well-structured, data-driven website enables updating with little or no training.
■ Content management: A static website requires a programmer to make updates. This adds an unnecessary layer between the business and its web content, which can lead to misunderstandings and slow turnarounds for desired changes.
■ Future expandability: Having a data-driven website enables the site to grow faster than would be possible with a static site. Changing the layout, displays, and functionality of the site (adding more features and sections) is easier with a data-driven solution.
■ Minimizing human error: Even the most competent programmer charged with the task of maintaining many pages will overlook things and make mistakes. This will lead to bugs and inconsistencies that can be time consuming and expensive to track down and fix. Unfortunately, users who come across these bugs will likely become irritated and may leave the site. A well-designed, data-driven website will have "error trapping" mechanisms to ensure that required information is filled out correctly and that content is entered and displayed in its correct format.
■ Cutting production and update costs: A data-driven website can be updated and "published" by any competent data-entry or administrative person. In addition to being convenient and more affordable, changes and updates will take a fraction of the time that they would with a static site. While training a competent programmer can take months or even years, training a data-entry person can be done in 30 to 60 minutes.
■ More efficient: By their very nature, computers are excellent at keeping volumes of information intact. With a data-driven solution, the system keeps track of the templates, so users do not have to. Global changes to layout, navigation, or site structure would need to be programmed only once, in one place, and the site itself will take care of propagating those changes to the appropriate pages and areas. A data-driven infrastructure will improve the reliability and stability of a website, while greatly reducing the chance of "breaking" some part of the site when adding new areas.
■ Improved stability: Any programmer who has to update a website from "static" templates must be very organized to keep track of all the source files. If a programmer leaves unexpectedly, it could involve re-creating existing work if those source files cannot be found. Plus, if there were any changes to the templates, the new programmer must be careful to use only the latest version. With a data-driven website, there is peace of mind, knowing the content is never lost—even if your programmer is.

FIGURE 7.4

Data-Driven Website Advantages

For a general informational website with static information, it is best to build a "static" website—one that a developer can update on an as-needed basis, perhaps a few times a year. A static website is less expensive to produce and typically meets business needs.

For a website with continually changing information—press releases, new product information, updated pricing, etc.—it is best to build a data-driven website. Figure 7.4 displays the many advantages associated with a data-driven website.

Data-Driven Business Intelligence

Companies can gain business intelligence by viewing the data accessed and analyzed from their website. Figure 7.5 displays how running queries or using analytical tools, such as a Pivot Table, on the database that is attached to the website can offer insight into the business, such as items browsed, frequent requests, items bought together, etc.

Integrating Information among Multiple Databases

Until the 1990s, each department in the United Kingdom's Ministry of Defense (MOD) and Army headquarters had its own systems, each system had its own database, and sharing information among the departments was difficult. Manually

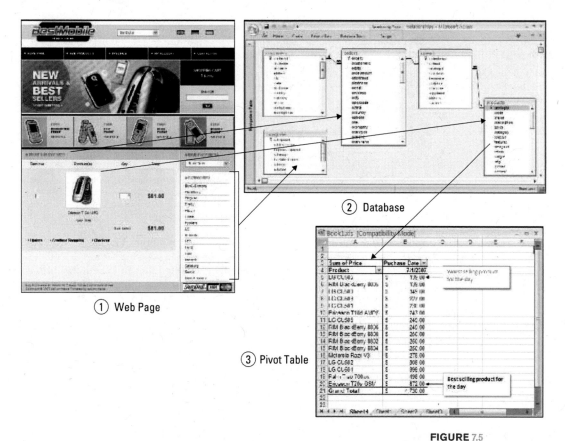

① Web Page

② Database

③ Pivot Table

FIGURE 7.5

BI in a Data-Driven Website

inputting the same information multiple times into the different systems was also time consuming and inefficient. In many cases, management could not even compile the information it required to answer questions and make decisions.

The Army solved the problem by integrating its systems, or building connections between its many databases. These integrations allow the Army's multiple systems to automatically communicate by passing information between the databases, eliminating the need for manual information entry into multiple systems because after entering the information once, the integrations send the information immediately to all other databases. The integrations not only enable the different departments to share information, but have also dramatically increased the quality of the information. The Army can now generate reports detailing its state of readiness and other vital issues, nearly impossible tasks before building the integrations among the separate systems.

An ***integration*** allows separate systems to communicate directly with each other. Similar to the UK's Army, an organization will probably maintain multiple systems, with each system having its own database. Without integrations, an organization will (1) spend considerable time entering the same information in multiple systems and (2) suffer from the low quality and inconsistency typically embedded in redundant information. While most integrations do not completely eliminate redundant information, they can ensure the consistency of it across multiple systems.

FIGURE 7.6

A Forward and Backward Customer Information Integration Example

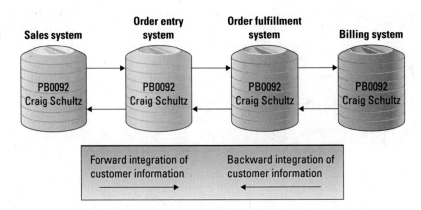

An organization can choose from two integration methods. The first is to create forward and backward integrations that link processes (and their underlying databases) in the value chain. A ***forward integration*** takes information entered into a given system and sends it automatically to all downstream systems and processes. A ***backward integration*** takes information entered into a given system and sends it automatically to all upstream systems and processes.

Figure 7.6 demonstrates how this method works across the systems or processes of sales, order entry, order fulfillment, and billing. In the order entry system, for example, an employee can update the information for a customer. That information, via the integrations, would be sent upstream to the sales system and downstream to the order fulfillment and billing systems.

Ideally, an organization wants to build both forward and backward integrations, which provide the flexibility to create, update, and delete information in any of the systems. However, integrations are expensive and difficult to build and maintain and most organizations build only forward integrations (sales through billing in Figure 7.6). Building only forward integrations implies that a change in the initial system (sales) will result in changes occurring in all the other systems. Integration of information is not possible for any changes occurring outside the initial system, which again can result in inconsistent organizational information. To address this issue, organizations can enforce business rules that all systems, other than the initial system, have read-only access to the integrated information. This will require users to change information in the initial system only, which will always trigger the integration and ensure that organizational information does not get out of sync.

The second integration method builds a central repository for a particular type of information. Figure 7.7 provides an example of customer information integrated using this method across four different systems in an organization. Users can create, update, and delete customer information only in the central customer information database. As users perform these tasks on the central customer information database, integrations automatically send the

FIGURE 7.7

Integrating Customer Information among Databases

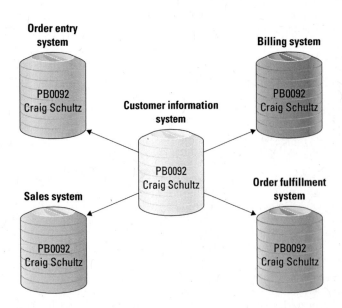

new and/or updated customer information to the other systems. The other systems limit users to read-only access of the customer information stored in them. Again, this method does not eliminate redundancy—but it does ensure consistency of the information among multiple systems.

OPENING CASE STUDY QUESTIONS

1. Identify the different types of entity classes that might be stored in Wikipedia's database.

2. Explain why database technology is so important to Wikipedia's business model.

3. Explain the difference between logical and physical views and why logical views are important to Wikipedia's customers.

Chapter Seven Case: Keeper of the Keys

More than 145,000 consumers nationwide were placed at risk by a data theft at database giant ChoicePoint. Criminals tricked the company by posing as legitimate businesses to gain access to the various ChoicePoint databases, which contain a treasure trove of consumer data, including names, addresses, Social Security numbers, credit reports, and other information. At least 50 suspicious accounts had been opened in the name of nonexistent debt collectors, insurance agencies, and other companies, according to the company.

Without a doubt, databases are one of the most important IT tools that organizations use today. Databases contain large repositories of detailed data. When a transaction occurs, a sale, for example, a database stores every detail of the transaction including customer name, customer address, credit card number, products purchased, discounts received, and so on.

Organizations must carefully manage their databases. This management function includes properly organizing the information in these repositories in the most efficient way, ensuring that no erroneous information ever enters the databases, and—most important—protecting the information from thieves and hackers.

Information is a valuable commodity, and, sadly, this makes it a target for theft. Organizations store large amounts of customer information including Social Security numbers, credit card numbers, and bank account numbers—just think of the information stored at eBay, Amazon, or the IRS. When someone steals personal information (not necessarily by taking it from the person, but rather stealing it from a company), that person becomes a victim of identity theft. Consider this short list of organizations that have lost information and the huge numbers of customers affected.

- Bank of America: 1.2 million customers.
- CardSystems: 40 million customers.
- Citigroup: 3.9 million customers.
- DSW Shoe Warehouse: 1.4 million customers.
- TJX Companies: 45.6 million customers.
- Wachovia: 676,000 customers.

Adding up the numbers, over 90 million people had their personal information either stolen or lost through organizations.

Business Accountability in Data Security

Companies may soon face stiff penalties for wayward data security practices. Massachusetts is considering legislation that would require companies to pay for any costs associated with a data breach of their IT systems. This move to protect customer data in Massachusetts comes at a fitting time, as two prominent retailers in the area, TJX Companies and Stop & Shop, wrestle with the aftermath of significant breaches that have exposed some of their customers to fraud.

Much of the expense associated with stopping fraudulent activity, such as canceling or reissuing credit or debit cards, stopping payment, and refunding customers, has been absorbed by the banks issuing credit or debit cards to the victims. The merchant banks that allow businesses such as TJX and Stop & Shop stores to accept credit and debit card transactions are penalized with fines from Visa, MasterCard, and other credit card organizations if the merchants they work with are found to violate the payment card industry's data security standards.

But the businesses who have had customer data stolen have largely suffered only from the costs to offer customers free credit-monitoring services and to repair a tarnished public image. In the case of popular retailers, this tarnish is easily polished away when juicy sales incentives are offered to get customers back.

Massachusetts House Bill 213, sponsored by Rep. Michael Costello, proposes to amend the Commonwealth's general laws to include a section that would require any corporation or other commercial entity whose sensitive customer information is stolen to notify customers about the data breach and also make companies liable to card-issuing banks for the costs those banks incur because of the breach and any subsequent fraudulent activity. This would include making businesses cover the costs to cancel or reissue cards, stop payments or block transactions with respect to any such account, open or reopen an account, and issue any refund or credit made to any customer of the bank as a result of unauthorized transactions.

The Massachusetts legislation is a key step in compelling companies to invest in better data security. Passage of this bill would put Massachusetts ahead of other states in terms of protecting customer data and spreading out the penalties so that both financial institutions and retailers have incentives to improve security. Security vendors are likely to be watching Massachusetts very closely, as the bill also would create an urgent need for companies doing business in that state to invest in ways to improve their ability to protect customer data. If the companies will not do this on their own, then holding them accountable for their customers' financial losses may be just what is needed to stop the next data breach from occurring.

Questions

1. How many organizations have your personal information, including your Social Security number, bank account numbers, and credit card numbers?

2. What information is stored at your college? Is there a chance your information could be hacked and stolen from your college?

3. What can you do to protect yourself from identity theft?

4. Do you agree or disagree with changing laws to hold the company where the data theft occurred accountable? Why or why not?

5. What impact would holding the company liable where the data theft occurred have on large organizations?

6. What impact would holding the company liable where the data theft occurred have on small businesses?

CHAPTER 8

Accessing Organizat Information—Data Warehouse

8.1. Describe the roles and purposes of data warehouses and data marts in an organization.

8.2. Compare the multidimensional nature of data warehouses (and data marts) with the two-dimensional nature of databases.

8.3. Identify the importance of ensuring the cleanliness of information throughout an organization.

8.4. Explain the relationship between business intelligence and a data warehouse.

Accessing Organizational Information

Applebee's Neighborhood Grill & Bar posts annual sales in excess of $3.2 billion and is actively using information from its data warehouse to increase sales and cut costs. The company gathers daily information for the previous day's sales into its data warehouse from 1,500 restaurants located in 49 states and seven countries. Understanding regional preferences, such as patrons in Texas preferring steaks more than patrons in New England, allows the company to meet its corporate strategy of being a neighborhood grill appealing to local tastes. The company has found tremendous value in its data warehouse by being able to make business decisions about customers' regional needs. The company also uses data warehouse information to perform the following:

- Base labor budgets on actual number of guests served per hour.
- Develop promotional sale item analysis to help avoid losses from overstocking or understocking inventory.
- Determine theoretical and actual costs of food and the use of ingredients.

History of Data Warehousing

In the 1990s as organizations began to need more timely information about their business, they found that traditional operational information systems were too cumbersome to provide relevant data efficiently and quickly. Operational systems typically include accounting, order entry, customer service, and sales and are not appropriate for business analysis for the following reasons:

- Information from other operational applications is not included.
- Operational systems are not integrated, or not available in one place.
- Operational information is mainly current—does not include the history that is required to make good decisions.
- Operational information frequently has quality issues (errors)—the information needs to be cleansed.

- Without information history, it is difficult to tell how and why things change over time.
- Operational systems are not designed for analysis and decision support.

During the latter half of the 20th century, the numbers and types of databases increased. Many large businesses found themselves with information scattered across multiple platforms and variations of technology, making it almost impossible for any one individual to use information from multiple sources. Completing reporting requests across operational systems could take days or weeks using antiquated reporting tools that were designed to execute the business rather than run the business. From this idea, the data warehouse was born as a place where relevant information could be held for completing strategic reports for management. The key here is the word *strategic* as most executives were less concerned with the day-to-day operations than they were with a more overall look at the model and business functions.

A key idea within data warehousing is to take data from multiple platforms/technologies (as varied as spreadsheets, databases, and word files) and place them in a common location that uses a common querying tool. In this way operational databases could be held on whatever system was most efficient for the operational business, while the reporting/strategic information could be held in a common location using a common language. Data warehouses take this a step further by giving the information itself commonality by defining what each term means and keeping it standard. An example of this would be gender, which can be referred to in many ways (Male, Female, M/F, 1/0), but should be standardized on a data warehouse with one common way of referring to each sex (M/F).

This design makes decision support more readily available without affecting day-to-day operations. One aspect of a data warehouse that should be stressed is that it is *not* a location for *all* of a business's information, but rather a location for information that is interesting, or information that will assist decision makers in making strategic decisions relative to the organization's overall mission.

Data warehousing is about extending the transformation of data into information. Data warehouses offer strategic level, external, integrated, and historical information so businesses can make projections, identify trends, and decide key business issues. The data warehouse collects and stores integrated sets of historical information from multiple operational systems and feeds them to one or more data marts. It may also provide end-user access to support enterprisewide views of information.

Data Warehouse Fundamentals

A *data warehouse* is a logical collection of information—gathered from many different operational databases—that supports business analysis activities and decision-making tasks. The primary purpose of a data warehouse is to aggregate information throughout an organization into a single repository in such a way that employees can make decisions and undertake business analysis activities. Therefore, while databases store the details of all transactions (for instance, the sale of a product) and events (hiring a new employee), data warehouses store that same information but in an aggregated form more suited to supporting decision-making tasks. Aggregation, in this instance, can include totals, counts, averages, and the like. Because of this sort of aggregation, data warehouses support only analytical processing.

The data warehouse modeled in Figure 8.1 compiles information from internal databases or transactional/operational databases and external databases through *extraction, transformation, and loading (ETL),* which is a process that extracts information from internal and external databases, transforms the information using a common set of enterprise definitions, and loads the information into a data warehouse. The data warehouse then sends subsets of the information to data marts. A *data mart* contains a subset of data warehouse information. To distinguish between

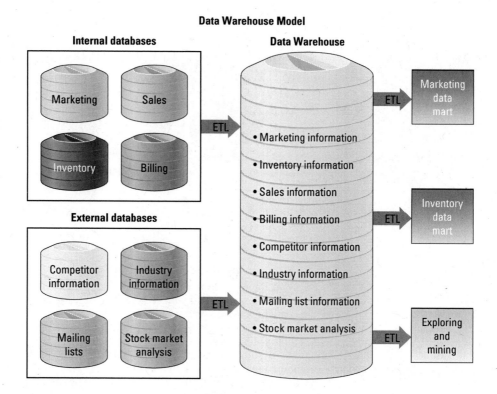

Data Warehouse Model

FIGURE 8.1

Model of a Typical Data Warehouse

data warehouses and data marts, think of data warehouses as having a more organizational focus and data marts as having focused information subsets particular to the needs of a given business unit such as finance or production and operations.

Lands' End created an organizationwide data warehouse so all its employees could access organizational information. Lands' End soon found out that there could be "too much of a good thing." Many of its employees would not use the data warehouse because it was simply too big, too complicated, and had too much irrelevant information. Lands' End knew there was valuable information in its data warehouse, and it had to find a way for its employees to easily access the information. Data marts were the perfect solution to the company's information overload problem. Once the employees began using the data marts, they were ecstatic at the wealth of information. Data marts were a huge success for Lands' End.

MULTIDIMENSIONAL ANALYSIS AND DATA MINING

A relational database contains information in a series of two-dimensional tables. In a data warehouse and data mart, information is multidimensional, meaning it contains layers of columns and rows. For this reason, most data warehouses and data marts are *multidimensional databases*. A *dimension* is a particular attribute of information. Each layer in a data warehouse or data mart represents information according to an additional dimension. A ***cube*** is the common term for the representation of multidimensional information. Figure 8.2 displays a cube (cube *a*) that represents store information (the layers), product information (the rows), and promotion information (the columns).

Once a cube of information is created, users can begin to slice and dice the cube to drill down into the information. The second cube (cube *b*) in Figure 8.2 displays a slice representing promotion II information for all products, at all stores. The third

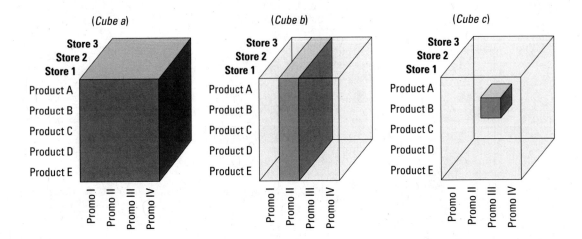

(Cube a) (Cube b) (Cube c)

FIGURE 8.2

A Cube of Information for Performing a Multidimensional Analysis on Three Different Stores, for Five Different Products, and Four Different Promotions

cube (cube *c*) in Figure 8.2 displays only information for promotion III, product B, at store 2. By using multidimensional analysis, users can analyze information in a number of different ways and with any number of different dimensions. For example, users might want to add dimensions of information to a current analysis including product category, region, and even forecasted versus actual weather. The true value of a data warehouse is its ability to provide multidimensional analysis that allows users to gain insights into their information.

Data warehouses and data marts are ideal for off-loading some of the querying against a database. For example, querying a database to obtain an average of sales for product B at store 2 while promotion III is under way might create a considerable processing burden for a database, essentially slowing down the time it takes another person to enter a new sale into the same database. If an organization performs numerous queries against a database (or multiple databases), aggregating that information into a data warehouse could be beneficial.

Data mining is the process of analyzing data to extract information not offered by the raw data alone. For example, Ruf Strategic Solutions helps organizations employ statistical approaches within a large data warehouse to identify customer segments that display common traits. Marketers can then target these segments with specially designed products and promotions.

Data mining can also begin at a summary information level (coarse granularity) and progress through increasing levels of detail (drilling down), or the reverse (drilling up). To perform data mining, users need data-mining tools. **Data-mining tools** use a variety of techniques to find patterns and relationships in large volumes of information and infer rules from them that predict future behavior and guide decision making. Data-mining tools for data warehouses and data marts include query tools, reporting tools, multidimensional analysis tools, statistical tools, and intelligent agents.

Sega of America, one of the largest publishers of video games, uses a data warehouse and statistical tools to distribute its annual advertising budget of more than $50 million. With its data warehouse, product line specialists and marketing strategists "drill" into trends of each retail store chain. Their goal is to find buying trends that help them determine which advertising strategies are working best and how to reallocate advertising resources by media, territory, and time.

INFORMATION CLEANSING OR SCRUBBING

Maintaining quality information in a data warehouse or data mart is extremely important. The Data Warehousing Institute estimates that low quality information costs U.S. businesses $600 billion annually. That number may seem high, but it is not. If an organization is using a data warehouse or data mart to allocate dollars across advertising strategies (such as in the case of Sega of America), low quality information will definitely have a negative impact on its ability to make the right decision.

To increase the quality of organizational information and thus the effectiveness of decision making, businesses must formulate a strategy to keep information clean. This is the concept of information cleansing or scrubbing. **_Information cleansing or scrubbing_** is a process that weeds out and fixes or discards inconsistent, incorrect, or incomplete information.

Specialized software tools use sophisticated algorithms to parse, standardize, correct, match, and consolidate data warehouse information. This is vitally important because data warehouses often contain information from several different databases, some of which can be external to the organization. In a data warehouse, information cleansing occurs first during the ETL process and second on the information once it is in the data warehouse. Companies can choose information cleansing software from several different vendors including Oracle, SAS, Ascential Software, and Group 1 Software. Ideally, scrubbed information is error free and consistent.

Dr Pepper/Seven Up, Inc., was able to integrate its myriad databases in a data warehouse (and subsequently data marts) in less than two months, giving the company access to consolidated, clean information. Approximately 600 people in the company regularly use the data marts to analyze and track beverage sales across multiple dimensions, including various distribution routes such as bottle/can sales, fountain food-service sales, premier distributor sales, and chain and national accounts. The company is now performing in-depth analysis of up-to-date sales information that is clean and error free.

Looking at customer information highlights why information cleansing is necessary. Customer information exists in several operational systems. In each system all details of this customer information could change from the customer ID to contact information (see Figure 8.3). Determining which contact information is accurate and correct for this customer depends on the business process that is being executed.

Figure 8.4 displays a customer name entered differently in multiple operational systems. Information cleansing allows an organization to fix these types of inconsistencies and cleans the information in the data warehouse. Figure 8.5 displays the typical events that occur during information cleansing.

Achieving perfect information is almost impossible. The more complete and accurate an organization wants its information to be, the more it costs (see Figure 8.6). The trade-off for perfect information lies in accuracy versus completeness. Accurate information means it is correct, while complete information means there are no blanks. A birth date of 2/31/10 is an example of complete but inaccurate information

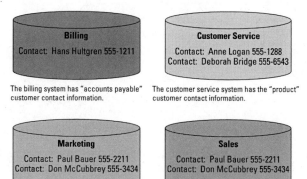

FIGURE 8.3

Contact Information in Operational Systems

The billing system has "accounts payable" customer contact information.

The customer service system has the "product" customer contact information.

The marketing and sales system has "decision maker" customer contact information.

FIGURE 8.4

Standardizing Customer
Name from Operational
Systems

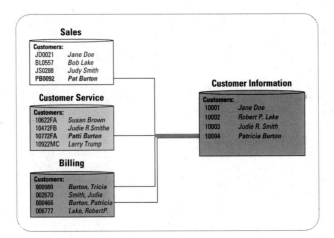

FIGURE 8.5

Information Cleansing
Activities

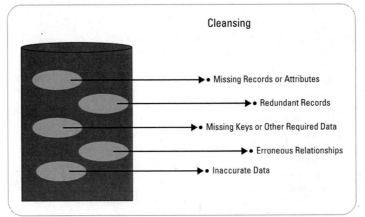

FIGURE 8.6

Accurate and Complete
Information

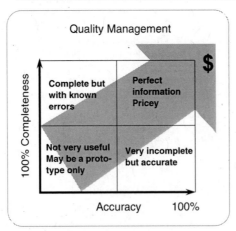

(February 31 does not exist). An address containing Denver, Colorado, without a ZIP code is an example of incomplete information that is accurate. For their information, most organizations determine a percentage high enough to make good decisions at a reasonable cost, such as 85 percent accurate and 65 percent complete.

Business Intelligence

Business intelligence (BI) refers to applications and technologies that are used to gather, provide access to, and analyze data and information to support decision-making efforts. An early reference to business intelligence occurs in Sun Tzu's book titled *The Art of War*. Sun Tzu claims that to succeed in war, one should have full knowledge of one's own strengths and weaknesses and full knowledge of the enemy's strengths and weaknesses. Lack of either one might result in defeat. A certain school of thought draws parallels between the challenges in business and those of war, specifically:

- Collecting information.
- Discerning patterns and meaning in the information.
- Responding to the resultant information.

Before the start of the information age in the late 20th century, businesses sometimes collected information from nonautomated sources. Businesses then lacked the computing resources to properly analyze the information and often made commercial decisions based primarily on intuition.

As businesses started automating more and more systems, more and more information became available. However, collection remained a challenge due to a lack of infrastructure for information exchange or to incompatibilities between systems. Reports sometimes took months to generate. Such reports allowed informed long-term strategic decision making. However, short-term tactical decision making continued to rely on intuition.

In modern businesses, increasing standards, automation, and technologies have led to vast amounts of available information. Data warehouse technologies have set up repositories to store this information. Improved ETL has increased the speedy collecting of information. Business intelligence has now become the art of sifting through large amounts of data, extracting information, and turning that information into actionable knowledge.

ENABLING BUSINESS INTELLIGENCE

Competitive organizations accumulate business intelligence to gain sustainable competitive advantage, and they may regard such intelligence as a valuable core competence in some instances. The principal BI enablers are technology, people, and corporate culture.

Technology

Even the smallest company with BI software can do sophisticated analyses today that were unavailable to the largest organizations a generation ago. The largest companies today can create enterprisewide BI systems that compute and monitor metrics on virtually every variable important for managing the company. How is this possible? The answer is technology—the most significant enabler of business intelligence.

People

Understanding the role of people in BI allows organizations to systematically create insight and turn these insights into actions. Organizations can improve their decision making by having the right people making the decisions. This usually means a manager who is in the field and close to the customer rather than an analyst rich in data but poor in experience. In recent years "business intelligence for the masses" has been an important trend, and many organizations have made great strides in providing sophisticated yet simple analytical tools and information to a much larger user population than was previously possible.

Culture

A key responsibility of executives is to shape and manage corporate culture. The extent to which the BI attitude flourishes in an organization depends in large part on the organization's culture. Perhaps the most important step an organization can take to encourage BI is to measure the performance of the organization against a set of key indicators. The actions of publishing what the organization thinks are the most important indicators, measuring these indicators, and analyzing the results to guide improvement display a strong commitment to BI throughout the organization.

OPENING CASE STUDY QUESTIONS

1. Determine how Wikipedia could use a data warehouse to improve its business operations.

2. Explain why Wikipedia must cleanse or scrub the information in its data warehouse.

3. Explain how a company could use information from Wikipedia to gain business intelligence.

Chapter Eight Case: Mining the Data Warehouse

According to a Merrill Lynch survey in 2006, business intelligence software and data-mining tools were at the top of CIOs' technology spending list. Following are a few examples of how companies are using data warehousing and data-mining tools to gain valuable business intelligence.

Ben & Jerry's

These days, when we all scream for ice cream, Ben & Jerry's cuts through the din by using integrated query, reporting, and online analytical processing technology from BI software vendor Business Objects. Through an Oracle database and with BI from Business Objects, Ben & Jerry's tracks the ingredients and life of each pint. If a consumer calls in with a complaint, the consumer affairs staff matches the pint with which supplier's milk, eggs, cherries, or whatever did not meet the organization's near-obsession with quality.

The BI tools let Ben & Jerry's officials access, analyze, and act on customer information collected by the sales, finance, purchasing, and quality-assurance departments. The company can determine what milk customers prefer in the making of the ice cream. The technology helped Ben & Jerry's track more than 12,500 consumer contacts in 2005. The information ranged from comments about the ingredients used in ice cream to queries about social causes supported by the company.

California Pizza Kitchen

California Pizza Kitchen (CPK) is a leading casual dining chain in the premium pizza segment with a recognized consumer brand and an established, loyal customer base. Founded in 1985, there are currently more than 130 full-service restaurants in over 26 states, the District of Columbia, and five foreign countries.

Before implementing its BI tool, Cognos, CPK used spreadsheets to plan and track its financial statements and line items. The finance team had difficulty managing the volumes of data, complex calculations, and constant changes to the spreadsheets. It took several weeks of two people working full time to obtain one version of the financial statements and future forecast. In addition, the team was limited by the software's inability to link cells and calculations across multiple spreadsheets, so updating other areas of corporate records became a time-consuming task. With Cognos, quarterly forecasting cycles have been reduced from eight days to two days. The finance team can now spend more time reviewing the results rather than collecting and entering the data.

Noodles & Company

Noodles & Company has more than 70 restaurants throughout Colorado, Illinois, Maryland, Michigan, Minnesota, Texas, Utah, Virginia, and Wisconsin. The company recently purchased Cognos BI tools to help implement reporting standards and communicate real-time operational information to field management throughout the United States.

Before implementing the first phase of the Cognos solution, IT and finance professionals spent days compiling report requests from numerous departments including sales and marketing, human resources, and real estate. Since completing phase one, operational Cognos reports are being accessed on a daily basis through the Noodles & Company website. This provides users with a single, 360-degree view of the business and consistent reporting throughout the enterprise.

Noodles & Company users benefit from the flexible query and reporting capabilities, allowing them to see patterns in the data to leverage new business opportunities. Cognos tools can pull information directly from a broad array of relational, operational, and other systems.

Questions

1. Explain how Ben & Jerry's is using business intelligence tools to remain successful and competitive in a saturated market.
2. Identify why information cleansing is critical to California Pizza Kitchen's business intelligence tool's success.
3. Illustrate why 100 percent accurate and complete information is impossible for Noodles & Company to obtain.
4. Describe how each of the companies above is using BI to gain a competitive advantage.

⚝ UNIT SUMMARY

The five common characteristics of quality information include accuracy, completeness, consistency, uniqueness, and timeliness. The costs to an organization of having low quality information can be enormous and could result in revenue losses and ultimately business failure. Databases maintain information about various types of objects, events, people, and places and help to alleviate many of the problems associated with low quality information such as redundancy, integrity, and security.

A data warehouse is a logical collection of information—gathered from many different operational databases—that supports business analysis activities and decision-making tasks. Data marts contain a subset of data warehouse information. Organizations gain tremendous insight into their business by mining the information contained in data warehouses and data marts.

Understanding the value of information is key to business success. Employees must be able to optimally access and analyze organizational information. The more knowledge employees have concerning how the organization stores, maintains, provides access to, and protects information the better prepared they will be when they need to use that information to make critical business decisions.

⚝ KEY TERMS

Analytical information, 79
Attribute, 86
Backward integration, 94
Business Intelligence (BI), 103
Business-critical integrity constraint, 89
Cube, 99
Database, 86
Database management system (DBMS), 90
Data-driven website, 91
Data mart, 98
Data mining, 100
Data-mining tools, 100

Data warehouse, 98
Entity, 86
Extraction, transformation, and loading (ETL), 98
Foreign key, 88
Forward integration, 94
Hierarchical database model, 86
Information cleansing or scrubbing, 101
Information granularity, 77
Information integrity, 89
Integration, 93
Integrity constraint, 89

Logical view, 88
Network database model, 86
Performance, 89
Physical view, 88
Primary key, 86
Real-time information, 79
Real-time system, 79
Redundancy, 89
Relational database model, 86
Relational integrity constraint, 89
Scalability, 89
Transactional information, 78

⭐ UNIT CLOSING CASE ONE

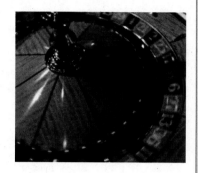

Harrah's—Gambling Big on Technology

The large investment made by Harrah's Entertainment Inc. in its information technology strategy has been tremendously successful. The results of Harrah's investment include:

- 10 percent annual increase in customer visits.
- 33 percent increase in gross market revenue.
- Yearly profits of over $208 million.
- Highest three-year ROI (return on investment) in the industry.
- A network that links over 42,000 gaming machines in 26 casinos across 12 states.
- Rated number six of the 100 best places to work in IT for 2003 by *ComputerWorld* magazine.
- Recipient of 2000 Leadership in Data Warehousing Award from the Data Warehousing Institute (TDWI), the premier association for data warehousing.

The casino industry is highly competitive. Bill Harrah was a man ahead of his time when he opened his first bingo parlor in 1937 with the commitment of getting to know each one of his customers. In 1984, Phil Satre, president and CEO of Harrah's, continued a commitment to customers. In search of its competitive advantage, Harrah's invested in an enterprisewide technology infrastructure to maintain Bill Harrah's original conviction: "Serve your customers well and they will be loyal."

Harrah's Commitment to Customers

Harrah's recently implemented its patented Total Rewards™ program to help build strong relationships with its customers. The program rewards customers for their loyalty by tracking their gaming habits across its 26 properties and currently maintains information on over 19 million customers, information the company uses to analyze, predict, and maximize each customer's value.

One major reason for the company's success is Harrah's implementation of a service-oriented strategy. Total Rewards allows Harrah's to give every customer the appropriate amount of personal attention, whether it's leaving sweets in the hotel room or offering free meals. Total Rewards works by providing each customer with an account and a corresponding card that the player swipes each time he or she plays a casino game. The program collects information on the amount of time the customers gamble, their total winnings and losses, and their betting strategies. Customers earn points based on the amount of time they spend gambling, which they can then exchange for comps such as free dinners, hotel rooms, tickets to shows, and even cash.

Total Rewards helps employees determine which level of service to provide each customer. When a customer makes a reservation at Harrah's, the service representative taking the call can view the customer's detailed information including the customer's loyalty level, games typically played, past winnings and losses, and potential net worth. If the service representative notices that the customer has a Diamond loyalty level, for example, the service representative knows that customer should never have to wait in line and should always receive free upgrades to the most expensive rooms.

"Almost everything we do in marketing and decision making is influenced by technology," says Gary Loveman, Harrah's chief operating officer. "The prevailing wisdom in this business is that the attractiveness of property drives customers. Our approach is different. We stimulate demand by knowing our customers. For example, if one of our customers always vacations at Harrah's in April, they will receive a promotion in February redeemable for a free weekend in April."

Gaining Business Intelligence with a Data Warehouse

Over 90 million customers visit Harrah's each year, and tracking a customer base larger than the population of Australia is a challenge. To tackle it, Harrah's began developing a system called WINet (Winner's Information Network). WINet links all Harrah's properties, allowing the company to collect and share customer information on an enterprisewide basis. WINet collects customer information from all the company transactions, game machines, and hotel management and reservations systems and places the information in a central data warehouse. Information in the data warehouse includes both customer and gaming information recorded in hourly increments. The marketing department uses the data warehouse to analyze customer information for patterns and insights, which allows it to create individualized marketing programs for each customer based on spending habits. Most important, the data warehouse allows the company to make business decisions based on information, not intuition.

Casinos traditionally treat customers as though they belong to a single property, typically the place the customer most frequently visits. Harrah's was the first casino to realize the potential of rewarding customers for visiting more than one property. Today, Harrah's has found that customers who visit more than one of its properties represent the fastest growing revenue segment. In the first two years of the Total Rewards program, the company received a $100 million increase in revenue from customers who gambled at more than one casino.

Harrah's also uses business intelligence to determine gaming machine performance. Using the data warehouse, Harrah's examines the performance and cost structure of each individual gaming machine. The company can quickly identify games that do not deliver optimal operational performance and can make a decision to move or replace the games. The capability to assess the performance of each individual slot machine has provided Harrah's with savings in the tens of millions of dollars. CIO Tim Stanley stated, "As we leverage more data from our data warehouse and increase the use and sophistication of our decision science analytical tools, we expect to have many new ways to improve customer loyalty and satisfaction, drive greater revenues, and decrease our costs as part of our ongoing focus on achieving sustainable profitability and success."

Information Security and Privacy

Some customers have concerns about Harrah's information collection strategy since they want to keep their gambling information private. The good news for these customers is that casinos are actually required to be more mindful of privacy concerns than most companies. For example, casinos cannot send marketing material to any underage persons. To adhere to strict government regulations, casinos must ensure that the correct information security and restrictions are in place. Many other companies actually make a great deal of money by selling customer information. Harrah's will not be joining in this trend since its customer information is one of its primary competitive advantages.

The Future of Harrah's

Harrah's current systems support approximately $140,000 in revenue per hour (that's almost $25 million weekly). In the future, Harrah's hopes to become device-independent by allowing employees to access the company's data warehouse via PDAs, handheld computers, and even cell phones. "Managing relationships with customers is incredibly important to the health of our business," Stanley says. "We will apply whatever technology we can to do that."

Questions

1. Identify the effects poor information might have on Harrah's service-oriented business strategy.
2. Summarize how Harrah's uses database technologies to implement its service-oriented strategy.
3. Harrah's was one of the first casino companies to find value in offering rewards to customers who visit multiple Harrah's locations. Describe the effects on the company if it did not build any integrations among the databases located at each of its casinos.
4. Estimate the potential impact to Harrah's business if there is a security breach in its customer information.
5. Explain the business effects if Harrah's fails to use data-mining tools to gather business intelligence.
6. Identify three different types of data marts Harrah's might want to build to help it analyze its operational performance.
7. Predict what might occur if Harrah's fails to clean or scrub its information before loading it into its data warehouse.
8. How could Harrah's use data mining to increase revenue?

✶ UNIT CLOSING CASE TWO

Searching for Revenue—Google

Google founders Sergey Brin and Larry Page recently made *Forbes* magazine's list of world billionaires. The company is famous for its highly successful search engine.

How Google Works

Figure Unit 2.1 displays the life of an average Google query. The web server sends the query to the index servers. The content inside the index server is similar to the index at the back of a book—it tells which pages contain the words that match any particular query term.

Then the query travels to the document servers, which actually retrieve the stored documents and generate snippets to describe each search result. Finally, the search engine returns the results to the user. All these activities occur within a fraction of a second.

Google consists of three distinct parts:

1. The web crawler, known as Googlebot, finds and retrieves web pages and passes them to the Google indexer. Googlebot functions much like a web browser. It sends a request for a web page to a web server, downloads the entire page, and then hands it off to Google's indexer. Googlebot can request thousands of different web pages simultaneously.
2. The indexer indexes every word on each page and stores the resulting index of words in a huge database. This index is sorted alphabetically by search term, with each index entry

FIGURE UNIT 2.1

How Google Works

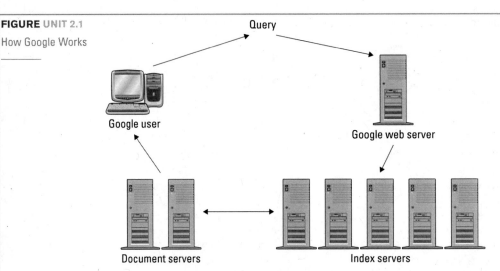

Query

Google user

Google web server

Document servers

Index servers

storing a list of documents in which the term appears and the location within the text where it occurs. Indexing the full text of web pages allows Google to go beyond simply matching single search terms. Google gives more priority to pages that have search terms near each other and in the same order as the query. Google can also match multi-word phrases and sentences.

3. The query processor compares the search query to the index and recommends the documents that it considers most relevant. Google considers over a hundred factors in determining which documents are most relevant to a query, including the popularity of the page, the position and size of the search terms within the page, and the proximity of the search terms to one another. The query processor has several parts, including the user interface (search box), the "engine" that evaluates queries and matches them to relevant documents, and the results formatter.

Selling Words

Google's primary line of business is its search engine; however, the company does not generate revenue from people using its site to search the Internet. It generates revenue from the marketers and advertisers that are paying to place their ads on the site.

Around 200 million times each day, people from all over the world access Google to perform searches. AdWords, a part of the Google site, allows advertisers to bid on common search terms. The advertisers simply enter in the keywords they want to bid on and the maximum amounts they want to pay per click, per day. Google then determines a price and a search ranking for those keywords based on how much other advertisers are willing to pay for the same terms. Pricing for keywords can range from 5 cents to $3 a click. A general search term like "tropical vacation" costs less than a more specific term like "Hawaiian vacation." Whoever bids the most for a term appears in a sponsored advertisement link either at the top or along the side of the search-results page.

Paid search is the ultimate in targeted advertising because consumers type in exactly what they want. One of the primary advantages of paid search web programs such as AdWords is that customers do not find it annoying, as is the problem with some forms of web advertising such as banner ads and pop-up ads. According to the Interactive Advertising Bureau, overall industry revenues from paid search surpassed banner ads in the third quarter of 2003.

"A big percentage of queries we get are commercial in nature," confirms Salar Kamangar, Google's director of product management. "It is a marketplace where the advertisers tell us about themselves by telling us how much each lead is worth. They have an incentive to bid how much they really want to pay, because if they underbid, their competitors will get more traffic."

Kamangar came up with the AdWords concept and oversees that part of the business today. AdWords, which launched in 2005, accounts for the vast majority of Google's annual revenue and the company has over 150,000 advertisers in its paid-search program, up from zero in 2002.

Expanding Google

Google has a secret weapon working for its research and development department—hackers. Hackers actually develop many of the new and unique ways to expand Google. The company elicits hacker ideas through its application program interface (API), a large piece of the Google code. The API enables developers to build applications around the Google search engine. By making the API freely available, Google has inspired a community of programmers that are extending Google's capabilities. "It's working," states Nelson Minar, who runs the API effort. "We get clever hacks, educational uses, and wacky stuff. We love to see people do creative things with our product." A few of the successful user-developed applications include:

- **Banana Slug**—www.bananaslug.com. For customers who hit a dead end with Google search, the site adds a random word to search text that generates surprising results.
- **Cookin' with Google**—www.researchbuzz.org. Enter the ingredients that are in the fridge and the site returns potential recipes for those ingredients.
- **Google Alert**—www.googlealert.com. Google Alert automatically searches the web for information on a topic and returns the results by email.
- **RateMyProfessors.com**—www.ratemyprofessors.com. The goal of this site was to create a place where students could rank their teachers. However, too many jokesters typing in false professor names such as "Professor Harry Leg" and "Professor Ima Dog" left the information on the site questionable. The developers turned to the Google API to create an automatic verification tool. If Google finds enough mentions in conjunction with a professor or university then it considers the information valid and posts it to the website.

Stopping Google

As part of its Google Print Library Project, the company is working to scan all or parts of the book collections of the University of Michigan, Harvard University, Stanford University, the New York Public Library, and Oxford University. It intends to make those texts searchable on Google and to sell advertisements on the web pages.

The Authors Guild filed a lawsuit against Google, alleging that its scanning and digitizing of library books constitutes a massive copyright infringement. "This is a plain and brazen violation of copyright law," Nick Taylor, president of the New York-based Authors Guild, said in a statement about the lawsuit, which is seeking class-action status. "It's not up to Google or anyone other than the authors, the rightful owners of these copyrights, to decide whether and how their works will be copied."

In response, Google defended the program in a company blog posting. "We regret that this group chose to sue us over a program that will make millions of books more discoverable to the world—especially since any copyright holder can exclude their books from the program," wrote Susan Wojcicki, vice president of product management. "Google respects copyright. The use we make of all the books we scan through the Library Project is fully consistent with both the fair use doctrine under U.S. copyright law and the principles underlying copyright law itself, which allow everything from parodies to excerpts in book reviews."

Questions

1. Determine if Google's search results are examples of transactional or analytical information.
2. Describe the impact on Google's business if the search information it presented to its customers was of low quality.

3. Explain how the website RateMyProfessors.com solved its problem of poor information.
4. Identify how Google might use a data warehouse to improve its business.
5. Explain why Google would need to cleanse the information in its data warehouse.
6. Identify a data mart that Google's marketing and sales department might use to track and analyze its AdWords revenue.

★ MAKING BUSINESS DECISIONS

1. Improving Information Quality

HangUps Corporation designs and distributes closet organization structures. The company operates five different systems: order entry, sales, inventory management, shipping, and billing. The company has severe information quality issues including missing, inaccurate, redundant, and incomplete information. The company wants to implement a data warehouse containing information from the five different systems to help maintain a single customer view, drive business decisions, and perform multidimensional analysis. Identify how the organization can improve its information quality when it begins designing and building its data warehouse.

2. Information Timeliness

Information timeliness is a major consideration for all organizations. Organizations need to decide the frequency of backups and the frequency of updates to a data warehouse. In a team, describe the timeliness requirements for backups and updates to a data warehouse for

- Weather tracking systems.
- Car dealership inventories.
- Vehicle tire sales forecasts.
- Interest rates.
- Restaurant inventories.
- Grocery store inventories.

3. Entities and Attributes

Martex Inc. is a manufacturer of athletic equipment and its primary lines of business include running, tennis, golf, swimming, basketball, and aerobics equipment. Martex currently supplies four primary vendors including Sam's Sports, Total Effort, The Underline, and Maximum Workout. Martex wants to build a database to help it organize its products. In a group, identify the different types of entity classes and the related attributes that Martex will want to consider when designing the database.

4. Integrating Information

You are currently working for the Public Transportation Department of Chatfield. The department controls all forms of public transportation including buses, subways, and trains. Each department has about 300 employees and maintains its own accounting, inventory, purchasing, and human resource systems. Generating reports across departments is a difficult task and usually involves gathering and correlating the information from the many different systems. It typically takes about two weeks to generate the quarterly balance sheets and profit and loss statements. Your team has been asked to compile a report recommending what the Public Transportation Department of Chatfield can do to alleviate its information and system issues. Be sure that your report addresses the various reasons departmental reports are presently difficult to obtain as well as how you plan to solve this problem.

5. Explaining Relational Databases

You have been hired by Vision, a start-up recreational equipment company. Your manager, Holly Henningson, is unfamiliar with databases and their associated business value. Holly has asked you to create a report detailing the basics of databases. Holly would also like you to provide a detailed explanation of relational databases along with their associated business advantages.

 APPLY YOUR KNOWLEDGE

1. Determining Information Quality Issues

Real People is a magazine geared toward working individuals that provides articles and advice on everything from car maintenance to family planning. *Real People* is currently experiencing problems with its magazine distribution list. Over 30 percent of the magazines mailed are returned because of incorrect address information, and each month it receives numerous calls from angry customers complaining that they have not yet received their magazines. Below is a sample of *Real People*'s customer information. Create a report detailing all of the issues with the information, potential causes of the information issues, and solutions the company can follow to correct the situation.

ID	First Name	Middle Name	Last Name	Street	City	State	ZIP Code
433	M	J	Jones	13 Denver	Denver	CO	87654
434	Margaret	J	Jones	13 First Ave.	Denver	CO	87654
434	Brian	F	Hoover	Lake Ave.	Columbus	OH	87654
435	Nick	H	Schweitzer	65 Apple Lane	San Francisco	OH	65664
436	Richard	A		567 55th St.	New York	CA	98763
437	Alana	B	Smith	121 Tenny Dr.	Buffalo	NY	142234
438	Trevor	D	Darrian	90 Fresrdestil	Dallas	TX	74532

2. Mining the Data Warehouse

Alana Smith is a senior buyer for a large wholesaler that sells different types of arts and crafts to greeting card stores such as Hallmark. Alana's latest marketing strategy is to send all of her customers a new line of hand-made picture frames from Russia. Alana's data support her decision for the new line. Her analysis predicts that the frames should sell an average of 10 to 15 per store, per day. Alana is excited about the new line and is positive it will be a success.

One month later Alana learns that the frames are selling 50 percent below expectations and averaging between five and eight frames sold daily in each store. Alana decides to access the company's data warehouse to determine why sales are below expectations. Identify several different dimensions of data that Alana will want to analyze to help her decide what is causing the problems with the picture frame sales.

3. Cleansing Information

You are working for BI, a start-up business intelligence consulting company. You have a new client that is interested in hiring BI to clean up its information. To determine how good your work is, the client would like your analysis of the following spreadsheet.

CUST ID	First Name	Last Name	Address	City	State	ZIP	Phone	Last Order Date
233620	Christopher	Lee	12421 W Olympic Blvd	Los Angeles	CA	75080-1100	(972)680-7848	4/18/2002
233621	Bruce	Brandwen	268 W 44th St	New York	PA	10036-3906	(212)471-6077	5/3/2002
233622	Glr	Johnson	4100 E Dry Creek Rd	Littleton	CO	80122-3729	(303)712-5461	5/6/2002
233623	Dave	Owens	466 Commerce Rd	Staunton	VA	24401-4432	(540)851-0362	3/19/2002
233624	John	Coulbourn	124 Action St	Maynard	MA	1754	(978)987-0100	4/24/2002
233629	Dan	Gagliardo	2875 Union Rd	Cheektowaga	NY	14227-1461	(716)558-8191	5/4/2002
23362	Damanceee	Allen	1633 Broadway	New York	NY	10019-6708	(212)708-1576	
233630	Michael	Peretz	235 E 45th St	New York	NY	10017-3305	(212)210-1340 (608)238-9690	4/30/2002
233631	Jody	Veeder	440 Science Dr	Madison	WI	53711-1064	X227	3/27/2002
233632	Michael	Kehrer	3015 SSE Loop 323	Tyler	TX	75701	(903)579-3229	4/28/
233633	Erin	Yoon	3500 Carillon Pt	Kirkland	WA	98033-7354	(425)897-7221	3/25/2002
233634	Madeline	Shefferly	4100 E Dry Creek Rd	Littleton	CO	80122-3729	(303)486-3949	3/33/2002
233635	Steven	Conduit	1332 Enterprise Dr	West Chester	PA	19380-5970	(610)692-5900	4/27/2002
233636	Joseph	Kovach	1332 Enterprise Dr	West Chester	PA	19380-5970	(610)692-5900	4/28/2002
233637	Richard	Jordan	1700 N	Philadelphia	PA	19131-4728	(215)581-6770	3/19/2002
233638	Scott	Mikolajczyk	1655 Crofton Blvd	Crofton	MD	21114-1387	(410)729-8155	4/28/2002
233639	Susan	Shragg	1875 Century Park E	Los Angeles	CA	90067-2501	(310)785-0511	4/29/2002
233640	Rob	Ponto	29777 Telegraph Rd	Southfield	MI	48034-1303	(810)204-4724	5/5/2002
233642	Lauren	Butler	1211 Avenue Of The Americas	New York	NY	10036-8701	(212)852-7494	4/22/2002
233643	Christopher	Lee	12421 W Olympic Blvd	Los Angeles	CA	90064-1022	(310)689-2577	3/25/2002
233644	Michelle	Decker	6922 Hollywood Blvd	Hollywood	CA	90028-6117	(323)817-4655	5/8/2002
233647	Natalia	Galeano	1211 Avenue Of The Americas	New York	NY	10036-8701	(646)728-6911	4/23/2002
233648	Bobbie	Orchard	4201 Congress St	Charlotte	NC	28209-4617	(704)557-2444	5/11/2002
233650	Ben	Konfino	1111 Stewart Ave	Bethpage	NY	11714-3533	(516)803-1406	3/19/2002
233651	Lenee	Santana	1050 Techwood Dr NW	Atlanta	GA	30318-KKRR	(404)885-2000	3/22/2002
233652	Lauren	Monks	7700 Wisconsin Ave	Bethesda	MD	20814-3578	(301)771-4772	3/19/2005
233653	Mark	Woolley	10950 Washington Blvd	Culver City	CA	90232-4026	(310)202-2900	4/20/2002
233654	Stan	Matthews	1235 W St NE	Washington	DC	20018-1107	(202)608-2000	3/25/2002

4. Different Dimensions

The focus of data warehousing is to extend the transformation of data into information. Data warehouses offer strategic level, external, integrated, and historical information so businesses can make projections, identify trends, and make key business decisions. The data warehouse collects and stores integrated sets of historical information from multiple operational systems and feeds them to one or more data marts. It may also provide end-user access to support enterprisewide views of information.

Project Focus

You are currently working on a marketing team for a large corporation that sells jewelry around the world. Your boss has asked you to look at the following dimensions of data to determine which ones you want in your data mart for performing sales and market analysis (see Figure AYK.1). As a team, categorize the different dimensions ranking them from 1 to 5, with 1 indicating that the dimension offers the highest value and must be in your data mart and 5 indicating that the dimension offers the lowest value and does not need to be in your data mart.

5. Understanding Search

Pretend that you are a search engine. Choose a topic to query. It can be anything such as your favorite book, movie, band, or sports team. Search your topic on Google, pick three or four pages from the results, and print them out. On each printout, find the individual words

FIGURE AYK.1

Data Warehouse Data

Dimension	Value (1–5)	Dimension	Value (1–5)
Product number		Season	
Store location		Promotion	
Customer net worth		Payment method	
Number of sales personnel		Commission policy	
Customer eating habits		Manufacturer	
Store hours		Traffic report	
Salesperson ID		Customer language	
Product style		Weather	
Order date		Customer gender	
Product quantity		Local tax information	
Ship date		Local cultural demographics	
Current interest rate		Stock market closing	
Product cost		Customer religious affiliation	
Customer's political affiliation		Reason for purchase	
Local market analysis		Employee dress code policy	
Order time		Customer age	
Customer spending habits		Employee vacation policy	
Product price		Employee benefits	
Exchange rates		Current tariff information	
Product gross margin			

from your query (such as "Boston Red Sox" or "The Godfather") and use a highlighter to mark each word with color. Do that for each of the documents that you print out. Now tape those documents on a wall, step back a few feet, and review your documents. If you did not know what the rest of a page said and could only judge by the colored words, which document do you think would be most relevant? Is there anything that would make a document look more relevant? Is it better to have the words be in a large heading or to occur several times in a smaller font? Do you prefer it if the words are at the top or the bottom of the page? How often do the words need to appear? Come up with two or three things you would look for to see if a document matched a query well. This exercise mimics search engine processes and should help you understand why a search engine returns certain results over others.

★ BUSINESS DRIVEN BEST SELLERS

Business @ The Speed of Thought. **By Bill Gates (Grand Central Publishing, 1999).**

Business @ The Speed of Thought was written by Bill Gates to inspire you to demand—and get—more from technology, enabling you and your company to respond faster to your customers, adapt to changing business demands, and prosper in the digital economy. "How you gather, manage, and use information will determine whether you win or lose" is Bill Gates's simple message. *Business @ The Speed of Thought* is not a technical book. It shows how business and technology are now inextricably linked. Each chapter is structured around a business or management issue, showing how digital processes can dramatically improve your results.

Why Smart Executives Fail. **By Sydney Finkelstein. (Penguin Putnam, 2003).**

In *Why Smart Executives Fail,* Sydney Finkelstein, a professor of management at Dartmouth's Tuck School of Business, explains why leadership fails and how company leaders can get back on track. This book shows examples from GM, Mattel, Motorola, Rite Aid, Webvan, and other companies as well as the results of six years of research on the issue of leadership failure. Finkelstein explains that the causes of failed management are surprisingly few, and they are not ineptitude or greed. Even the brightest executives fail because:

- They choose not to cope with innovation, change, and management.
- They misread the competition.
- They brilliantly fulfill the wrong vision.
- They cling to an inaccurate view of reality.
- They ignore vital information.
- They identify too closely with the company.

Streamlining Business Operations

CHAPTER 10 Extending the
Organization—Supply
Chain Management

10.1. List and describe the components of a typical supply chain.

10.2. Define the relationship between decision making
and supply chain management.

10.3. Describe the four changes resulting from
advances in IT that are driving supply chains.

10.4. Summarize the best practices for implementing
a successful supply chain management system.

Supply Chain Management

Companies that excel in supply chain operations perform better in almost every
financial measure of success, according to a report from Boston-based AMR Research
Inc. When supply chain excellence improves operations, companies experience a
5 percent higher profit margin, 15 percent less inventory, 17 percent stronger "perfect order" ratings, and 35 percent shorter cycle times than their competitors. "The
basis of competition for winning companies in today's economy is supply chain
superiority," says Kevin O'Marah, vice president of research at AMR Research.
"These companies understand that value chain performance translates to productivity and market-share leadership. They also understand that supply chain leadership means more than just low costs and efficiency; it requires a superior ability to
shape and respond to shifts in demand with innovative products and services."

Basics of Supply Chain

The average company spends nearly half of every dollar that it earns on production
needs—goods and services it needs from external suppliers to keep producing. A
supply chain consists of all parties involved, directly or indirectly, in the procurement of a product or raw material. *Supply chain management (SCM)* involves the
management of information flows between and among stages in a supply chain to
maximize total supply chain effectiveness and profitability.

In the past, companies focused primarily on manufacturing and quality improvements within their four walls; now their efforts extend beyond those walls to
influence the entire supply chain including customers, customers' customers, suppliers, and suppliers' suppliers. Today's supply chain is a complex web of suppliers,
assemblers, logistic firms, sales/marketing channels, and other business partners
linked primarily through information networks and contractual relationships. SCM
systems enhance and manage the relationships. The supply chain has three main
links (see Figure 10.1):

1. Materials flow from suppliers and their upstream suppliers at all levels.

2. Transformation of materials into semi-finished and finished products, or the
   organization's own production processes.

3. Distribution of products to customers and their downstream customers at all
   levels.

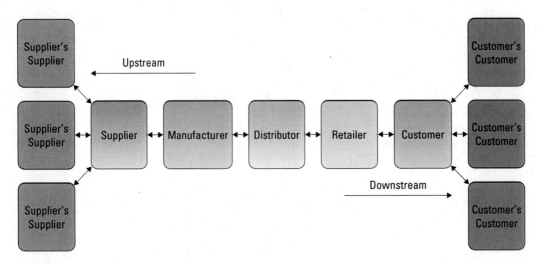

FIGURE 10.1

A Typical Supply Chain

Organizations must embrace technologies that can effectively manage and oversee their supply chains. SCM is becoming increasingly important in creating organizational efficiencies and competitive advantages. Best Buy checks inventory levels at each of its 750 stores in North America as often as every half-hour with its SCM system, taking much of the guesswork out of inventory replenishment. Supply chain management improves ways for companies to find the raw components they need to make a product or service, manufacture that product or service, and deliver it to customers. Figure 10.2 highlights the five basic components for supply chain management.

Technology advances in the five SCM components have significantly improved companies' forecasting and business operations in the last few years. Businesses today have access to modeling and simulation tools, algorithms, and applications that can combine information from multiple sources to build forecasts for days, weeks, and months in advance. Better forecasts for tomorrow result in better preparedness today.

Mattel Inc. spent several years investing heavily in software and processes that simplify its supply chain, cut costs, and shorten cycle times. Using supply chain management strategies the company cut weeks out of the time it takes to design, produce, and ship everything from Barbies to Hot Wheels. Mattel installed optimization software that measures, tweaks, and validates the operations of its seven distribution centers, seven manufacturing plants, and other facilities that make up its vast worldwide supply chain. Mattel improved forecasting from monthly to weekly. The company no longer produces more inventory than stores require and delivers inventory upon request. Mattel's supply chain moves quickly to make precise forecasts that help the company meet demand.

Information Technology's Role in the Supply Chain

As companies evolve into extended organizations, the roles of supply chain participants are changing. It is now common for suppliers to be involved in product development and for distributors to act as consultants in brand marketing. The notion of virtually seamless information links within and between organizations is an essential element of integrated supply chains.

Information technology's primary role in SCM is creating the integrations or tight process and information linkages between functions within a firm—such as

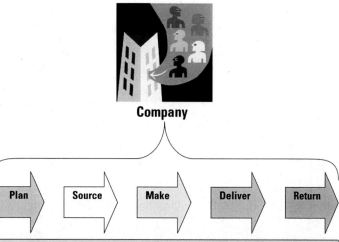

FIGURE 10.2

The Five Basic Supply
Chain Management
Components

THE FIVE BASIC SUPPLY CHAIN MANAGEMENT COMPONENTS
1. **Plan** – This is the strategic portion of supply chain management. A company must have a plan for managing all the resources that go toward meeting customer demand for products or services. A big piece of planning is developing a set of metrics to monitor the supply chain so that it is efficient, costs less, and delivers high quality and value to customers.
2. **Source** – Companies must carefully choose reliable suppliers that will deliver goods and services required for making products. Companies must also develop a set of pricing, delivery, and payment processes with suppliers and create metrics for monitoring and improving the relationships.
3. **Make** – This is the step where companies manufacture their products or services. This can include scheduling the activities necessary for production, testing, packaging, and preparing for delivery. This is by far the most metric-intensive portion of the supply chain, measuring quality levels, production output, and worker productivity.
4. **Deliver** – This step is commonly referred to as logistics. *Logistics* is the set of processes that plans for and controls the efficient and effective transportation and storage of supplies from suppliers to customers. During this step, companies must be able to receive orders from customers, fulfill the orders via a network of warehouses, pick transportation companies to deliver the products, and implement a billing and invoicing system to facilitate payments.
5. **Return** – This is typically the most problematic step in the supply chain. Companies must create a network for receiving defective and excess products and support customers who have problems with delivered products.

marketing, sales, finance, manufacturing, and distribution—and between firms, which allow the smooth, synchronized flow of both information and product between customers, suppliers, and transportation providers across the supply chain. Information technology integrates planning, decision-making processes, business operating processes, and information sharing for business performance management (see Figure 10.3). Considerable evidence shows that this type of supply chain integration results in superior supply chain capabilities and profits.

FIGURE 10.3

The Integrated Supply
Chain

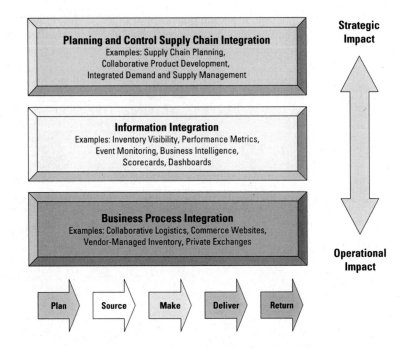

Planning and Control Supply Chain Integration
Examples: Supply Chain Planning,
Collaborative Product Development,
Integrated Demand and Supply Management

Information Integration
Examples: Inventory Visibility, Performance Metrics,
Event Monitoring, Business Intelligence,
Scorecards, Dashboards

Business Process Integration
Examples: Collaborative Logistics, Commerce Websites,
Vendor-Managed Inventory, Private Exchanges

Strategic
Impact

Operational
Impact

Plan Source Make Deliver Return

Adaptec, Inc., of California manufactures semiconductors and markets them to the world's leading PC, server, and end-user markets through more than 115 distributors and thousands of value-added resellers worldwide. Adaptec designs and manufactures products at various third-party locations around the world. The company uses supply chain integration software over the Internet to synchronize planning. Adaptec personnel at the company's geographically dispersed locations communicate in real time and exchange designs, test results, and production and shipment information. Internet-based supply chain collaboration software helped the company reduce inventory levels and lead times.

Although people have been talking about the integrated supply chain for a long time, it has only been recently that advances in information technology have made it possible to bring the idea to life and truly integrate the supply chain. Visibility, consumer behavior, competition, and speed are a few of the changes resulting from information technology advances that are driving supply chains (see Figure 10.4).

FIGURE 10.4

Factors Driving Supply
Chain Management

VISIBILITY

Supply chain visibility is the ability to view all areas up and down the supply chain. Changing supply chains requires a comprehensive strategy buoyed by information technology. Organizations can use technology tools that help them integrate upstream and downstream, with both customers and suppliers.

To make a supply chain work most effectively, organizations must create visibility in real time. Organizations must know about customer events triggered downstream, but so must their suppliers and their suppliers' suppliers. Without this information, partners throughout the supply chain can experience a bullwhip effect, in which disruptions intensify throughout the chain. The *bullwhip effect* occurs when distorted product demand information passes from one entity to the next throughout the supply chain. The misinformation regarding a slight rise in demand for a product could cause different members in the supply chain to stockpile inventory. These changes ripple throughout the supply chain, magnifying the issue and creating excess inventory and costs.

Today, information technology allows additional visibility in the supply chain. Electronic information flows allow managers to view their suppliers' and customers' supply chains. Some organizations have completely changed the dynamics of their industries because of the competitive advantage gained from high visibility in the supply chain. Dell is the obvious example. The company's ability to get product to the customer and the impact of the economics have clearly changed the nature of competition and caused others to emulate this model.

CONSUMER BEHAVIOR

The behavior of customers has changed the way businesses compete. Customers will leave if a company does not continually meet their expectations. They are more demanding because they have information readily available, they know exactly what they want, and they know when and how they want it. **Demand planning software** generates demand forecasts using statistical tools and forecasting techniques. Companies can respond faster and more effectively to consumer demands through supply chain enhancements such as demand planning software. Once an organization understands customer demand and its effect on the supply chain it can begin to estimate the impact that its supply chain will have on its customers and ultimately the organization's performance. The payoff for a successful demand planning strategy can be tremendous. A study by Peter J. Metz, executive director of the MIT Center for ebusiness, found that companies have achieved impressive bottom-line results from managing demand in their supply chains, averaging a 50 percent reduction in inventory and a 40 percent increase in timely deliveries.

COMPETITION

Supply chain management software can be broken down into (1) supply chain planning software and (2) supply chain execution software—both increase a company's ability to compete. **Supply chain planning (SCP) software** uses advanced mathematical algorithms to improve the flow and efficiency of the supply chain while reducing inventory. SCP depends entirely on information for its accuracy. An organization cannot expect the SCP output to be accurate unless correct and up-to-date information regarding customer orders, sales information, manufacturing capacity, and delivery capability is entered into the system.

An organization's supply chain encompasses the facilities where raw materials, intermediate products, and finished goods are acquired, transformed, stored, and sold. These facilities are connected by transportation links, where materials and products flow. Ideally, the supply chain consists of multiple organizations that function as efficiently and effectively as a single organization, with full information visibility. **Supply chain execution (SCE) software** automates the different steps and stages of the supply chain. This could be as simple as electronically routing orders from a manufacturer to a supplier. Figure 10.5 details how SCP and SCE software correlate to the supply chain.

General Motors, Ford, and DaimlerChrysler made history when the three automotive giants began working together to create a unified supply chain planning/execution system that all three companies and their suppliers could leverage. The combined automotive giants' purchasing power is tremendous with GM spending $85 billion per year, Ford spending $80 billion per year, and DaimlerChrysler spending $73 billion per year. The ultimate goal is to process automotive production from ordering materials and forecasting demand to making cars directly to consumer specifications through the web. The automotive giants understand the impact strategic supply chain planning and execution can have on their competition.

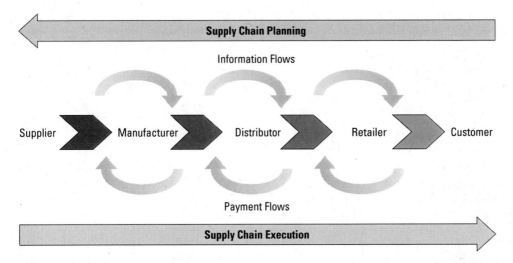

FIGURE 10.5

Supply Chain Planning and
Supply Chain Execution:
Software's Correlation to
the Supply Chain

SPEED

During the past decade, competition has focused on speed. New forms of servers, telecommunications, wireless applications, and software are enabling companies to perform activities that were once never thought possible. These systems raise the accuracy, frequency, and speed of communication between suppliers and customers, as well as between internal users. Another aspect of speed is the company's ability to satisfy continually changing customer requirements efficiently, accurately, and quickly. Timely and accurate information is more critical to businesses than ever before. Figure 10.6 displays the three factors fostering this change.

Supply Chain Management Success Factors

To succeed in today's competitive markets, companies must align their supply chains with the demands of the markets they serve. Supply chain performance is now a distinct competitive advantage for companies proficient in the SCM area. Perdue Farms excels at decision making based on its supply chain management system. Perdue Farms moves roughly 1 million turkeys, each within 24 hours of processing, to reach holiday tables across the nation yearly. The task is no longer as complicated as it was before Perdue Farms invested $20 million in SCM technology. SCM makes Perdue more adept at delivering the right number of turkeys, to the right customers, at the right time.

FIGURE 10.6

Three Factors Fostering
Speed

To achieve success such as reducing operating costs, improving asset productivity, and compressing order cycle time, an organization should follow the seven principles of supply chain management outlined in Figure 10.7.

These seven principles run counter to previous built-in functional thinking of how companies organize, operate, and serve customers. Old concepts of supply chains are typified by discrete manufacturing, linear structure, and a focus on buy-sell transactions ("I buy from my suppliers, I sell to my customers"). Because the traditional supply chain is spread out linearly, some suppliers are removed from the end customer. Collaboration adds the value of visibility for these companies. They benefit by knowing

Factors Fostering Supply Chain Speed
1. Pleasing customers has become something of a corporate obsession. Serving the customer in the best, most efficient, and most effective manner has become critical, and information about issues such as order status, product availability, delivery schedules, and invoices has become a necessary part of the total customer service experience.
2. Information is crucial to managers' abilities to reduce inventory and human resource requirements to a competitive level.
3. Information flows are essential to strategic planning for and deployment of resources.

Seven Principles of Supply Chain Management
1. Segment customers by service needs, regardless of industry, and then tailor services to those particular segments.
2. Customize the logistics network and focus intensively on the service requirements and on the profitability of the preidentified customer segments.
3. Listen to signals of market demand and plan accordingly. Planning must span the entire chain to detect signals of changing demand.
4. Differentiate products closer to the customer, since companies can no longer afford to hold inventory to compensate for poor demand forecasting.
5. Strategically manage sources of supply, by working with key suppliers to reduce overall costs of owning materials and services.
6. Develop a supply chain information technology strategy that supports different levels of decision making and provides a clear view (visibility) of the flow of products, services, and information.
7. Adopt performance evaluation measures that apply to every link in the supply chain and measure true profitability at every stage.

FIGURE 10.7

Seven Principles of Supply Chain Management

immediately what is being transacted at the customer end of the supply chain (the end customer's activities are visible to them). Instead of waiting days or weeks (or months) for the information to flow upstream through the supply chain, with all the potential pitfalls of erroneous or missing information, suppliers can react in near real-time to fluctuations in end-customer demand.

Dell Inc. offers one of the best examples of an extremely successful SCM system. Dell's highly efficient build-to-order business model enables it to deliver customized computer systems quickly. As part of the company's continual effort to improve its supply chain processes, Dell deploys supply chain tools to provide global views of forecasted product demand and materials requirements, as well as improved factory scheduling and inventory management.

Organizations should study industry best practices to improve their chances of successful implementation of SCM systems. The following are keys to SCM success.

MAKE THE SALE TO SUPPLIERS

The hardest part of any SCM system is its complexity because a large part of the system extends beyond the company's walls. Not only will the people in the organization need to change the way they work, but also the people from each supplier that is added to the network must change. Be sure suppliers are on board with the benefits that the SCM system will provide.

WEAN EMPLOYEES OFF TRADITIONAL BUSINESS PRACTICES

Operations people typically deal with phone calls, faxes, and orders scrawled on paper and will most likely want to keep it that way. Unfortunately, an organization cannot disconnect the telephones and fax machines just because it is implementing a supply chain management system. If the organization cannot convince people that using the software will be worth their time, they will easily find ways to work around it, which will quickly decrease the chances of success for the SCM system.

ENSURE THE SCM SYSTEM SUPPORTS THE ORGANIZATIONAL GOALS

It is important to select SCM software that gives organizations an advantage in the areas most crucial to their business success. If the organizational goals support highly efficient strategies, be sure the supply chain design has the same goals.

DEPLOY IN INCREMENTAL PHASES AND MEASURE AND COMMUNICATE SUCCESS

Design the deployment of the SCM system in incremental phases. For instance, instead of installing a complete supply chain management system across the company and all suppliers at once, start by getting it working with a few key suppliers, and then move on to the other suppliers. Along the way, make sure each step is adding value through improvements in the supply chain's performance. While a big-picture perspective is vital to SCM success, the incremental approach means the SCM system should be implemented in digestible bites, and also measured for success one step at a time.

BE FUTURE ORIENTED

The supply chain design must anticipate the future state of the business. Because the SCM system likely will last for many more years than originally planned, managers need to explore how flexible the systems will be when (not if) changes are required in the future. The key is to be certain that the software will meet future needs, not only current needs.

SCM Success Stories

Figure 10.8 depicts the top reasons more and more executives are turning to SCM to manage their extended enterprises. Figure 10.9 lists several companies using supply chain management to drive operations.

Apple Computer initially distributed its business operations over 16 legacy applications. Apple quickly realized that it needed a new business model centered around an integrated supply chain to drive performance efficiencies. Apple devised an implementation strategy that focused on specific SCM functions—finance, sales, distribution, and manufacturing—that would most significantly help its business. The company decided to deploy leading-edge functionality with a new business model that provided:

- Build-to-order and configure-to-order manufacturing capabilities.
- Web-enabled configure-to-order order entry and order status for customers buying directly from Apple at Apple.com.
- Real-time credit card authorization.
- Available-to-promise and rules-based allocations.
- Integration to advanced planning systems.

FIGURE 10.8

Top Reasons Executives Use SCM to Manage Extended Enterprises

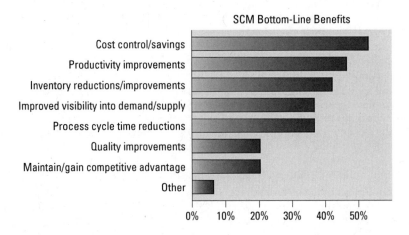

SCM Bottom-Line Benefits

Since its SCM system went live, Apple has experienced substantial benefits in many areas including measurable improvements in its manufacturing processes, a decrease by 60 percent in its build-to-order and configure-to-order cycle times, and the ability to process more than 6,000 orders daily.

Companies Using Supply Chain to Drive Operations	
Dell	Business grows 17 percent per year with a $40 billion revenue base.
Nokia	Supply chain best practices are turning ideas into profitable businesses.
Procter & Gamble	Consumer-driven supply chain is the defining architecture for large consumer companies. Best practices in product innovation and supply chain effectiveness are tops.
IBM	Hardware supply chain product-development processes overhauled to the tune of 70 percent better, faster, and cheaper.
Wal-Mart Stores	Everyday low prices define the customer demand driving Wal-Mart's partner integrated supply chain.
Toyota Motor	Lean is one of the top three best practices associated with benchmarked supply chain excellence.
The Home Depot	Cutting-edge supply chain management improved logistics and innovative services.
Best Buy	SCM has radically thinned inventories and delivered enviable business positions.
Marks & Spencer	A pioneer in the use of radio frequency identification (RFID) in stores, Marks & Spencer manages to grow and stay lean.

FIGURE 10.9

Companies Using Supply Chain Management Technologies to Drive Operations

OPENING CASE STUDY QUESTIONS

1. Would you need supply chain management systems in a virtual world such as Second Life? Why or why not?

2. How could a real company augment its supply chain management system through Second Life?

3. If you were an apparel company, such as Nike or REI, what would your virtual SCM system look like? Create a drawing of this system and be sure to include all upstream and downstream participants.

Chapter Ten Case: RFID—Future Tracking the Supply Chain

One of the hottest new technologies in the supply chain is a radio frequency identification (RFID) tag. These tags are tiny and can carry large amounts of data tracking everything from price to temperature. Supply chains around the globe are being revamped with RFID tags. However, some people might be taking the ability to track the supply chain with RFID tags a bit too far.

Tracking People

The elementary school that required students to wear RFID tags to track their movements ended the program because the company that developed the technology pulled out. "I'm disappointed; that's about all I can say at this point," stated Ernie Graham, the superintendent and principal of Brittan Elementary School. "I think I let my staff down."

Students were required to wear identification cards around their necks with their picture, name, and grade and a wireless transmitter that beamed ID numbers to a teacher's handheld computer when the children passed under an antenna posted above a classroom door. The school instituted the system, without parental input, to simplify attendance-taking and potentially reduce vandalism and improve student safety. "I'm happy for now that kids are not being tagged, but I'm still fighting to keep it out of our school system," said parent Dawn Cantrall, who filed a complaint with the American Civil Liberties Union. "It has to stop here."

While many parents criticized the tags for violating privacy and possibly endangering children's health, some parents supported the plan. "Technology scares some people; it's a fear of the unknown," parent Mary Brower said. "Any kind of new technology has the potential for misuse, but I feel confident the school is not going to misuse it."

Tracking Children

Children's sleepwear with radio frequency identification tags sewn into the seams hit stores in early 2006. Made by Lauren Scott California, the nightgowns and pajamas will be one of the first commercial RFID-tagged clothing lines sold in the United States. The PJs are designed to keep kids safe from abductions, says proprietor Lauren Scott, who licensed the RFID technology from SmartWear Technologies Inc., a maker of personal security systems. Readers positioned in doorways and windows throughout a house scan tags within a 30-foot radius and trigger an alarm when boundaries are breached.

A pamphlet attached to the garment informs customers that the sleepwear is designed to help prevent child abductions. It directs parents to a website that explains how to activate and encode the RFID tag with a unique digital identification number. The site also provides information on a $500 home-installed system that consists of RFID readers and a low-frequency encoder that connects through a USB port to a computer. Parents can sign up to include data about their children, including photos, in the SmartWear database. That information can be shared with law enforcement agencies or the Amber Alert system if a child disappears.

SmartWear has several other projects in the works including an extended-range RFID tag that can transmit signals up to 600 feet. The tag could be inserted into law enforcement and military uniforms or outerwear, such as ski jackets, and used to find a missing or lost person or to recover and identify a body.

Plastic RFID

A typical RFID tag costs 40 cents, making price a barrier for many potential applications. Start-up OrganicID is creating a plastic RFID tag that it expects will reduce the price to a penny or less. CEO Klaus Dimmler hopes to market the plastic tags, which will operate in the 13.56-MHz range, by 2008.

Questions

1. What are some advantages and disadvantages of tagging students with RFID tags?
2. What are some advantages and disadvantages of tagging children's pajamas with RFID tags?
3. Do you agree or disagree that tagging students with RFID tags is a violation of privacy rights? Explain why.
4. Do you agree or disagree that tagging children's pajamas with RFID tags is a violation of privacy rights? Explain why.
5. Describe the relationship between privacy rights and RFID.
6. Determine a way that schools could use RFID tags without violating privacy rights.

11

Building a Customer-centric Organization—Customer Relationship Management

LEARNING OUTCOMES

11.1. Compare operational and analytical customer relationship management.

11.2. Identify the primary forces driving the explosive growth of customer relationship management.

11.3. Define the relationship between decision making and analytical customer relationship management.

11.4. Summarize the best practices for implementing a successful customer relationship management system.

Customer Relationship Management (CRM)

After 1-800-Flowers.com achieved operational excellence in the late 1990s, it turned to building customer intimacy to continue to improve profits and business growth. The company turned brand loyalty into brand relationships by using the vast amounts of information it collected to better understand customers' needs and expectations. The floral delivery company adopted SAS Enterprise Miner to analyze the information in its CRM systems. Enterprise Miner sifts through information to reveal trends, explain outcomes, and predict results so that businesses can increase response rates and quickly identify their profitable customers. With the help of Enterprise Miner, 1-800-Flowers.com is continuing to thrive, with 27 percent annual increases in revenue.

CRM is a business philosophy based on the premise that those organizations that understand the needs of individual customers are best positioned to achieve sustainable competitive advantage in the future. Many aspects of CRM are not new to organizations; CRM is simply performing current business better. Placing customers at the forefront of all thinking and decision making requires significant operational and technology changes, however.

A customer strategy starts with understanding who the company's customers are and how the company can meet strategic goals. *The New York Times* understands this and has spent the past decade researching core customers to find similarities among groups of readers in cities outside the New York metropolitan area. Its goal is to understand how to appeal to those groups and make *The New York Times* a national newspaper, expanding its circulation and the "reach" it offers to advertisers. *The New York Times* is growing in a relatively flat publishing market and has achieved a customer retention rate of 94 percent in an industry that averages roughly 60 percent.

As the business world increasingly shifts from product focus to customer focus, most organizations recognize that treating existing customers well is the best source of profitable and sustainable revenue growth. In the age of ebusiness, however, an organization is challenged more than ever before to truly satisfy its customers. CRM will allow an organization to:

- Provide better customer service.
- Make call centers more efficient.

- Cross-sell products more effectively.
- Help sales staff close deals faster.
- Simplify marketing and sales processes.
- Discover new customers.
- Increase customer revenues.

The National Basketball Association's New York Knicks are becoming better than ever at communicating with their fans. Thanks to a CRM solution, the New York Knicks' management now knows which season-ticket holders like which players, what kind of merchandise they buy, and where they buy it. Management is finally able to send out fully integrated email campaigns that do not overlap with other marketing efforts.

Recency, Frequency, and Monetary Value

An organization can find its most valuable customers by using a formula that industry insiders call RFM—recency, frequency, and monetary value. In other words, an organization must track:

- How recently a customer purchased items (recency).
- How frequently a customer purchases items (frequency).
- How much a customer spends on each purchase (monetary value).

Once a company has gathered this initial customer relationship management (CRM) information, it can compile it to identify patterns and create marketing campaigns, sales promotions, and services to increase business. For example, if Ms. Smith buys only at the height of the season, then the company should send her a special offer during the off-season. If Mr. Jones always buys software but never computers, then the company should offer him free software with the purchase of a new computer.

CRM technologies can help organizations track RFM and answer tough questions such as who are their best customers and which of their products are the most profitable. This chapter details the different operational and analytical CRM technologies an organization can use to strengthen its customer relationships and increase revenues.

The Evolution of CRM

Knowing the customer, especially knowing the profitability of individual customers, is highly lucrative in the financial services industry. Its high transactional nature has always afforded the financial services industry more access to customer information than other industries have, but it has embraced CRM technologies only recently.

Barclays Bank is a leading financial services company operating in more than 70 countries. In the United Kingdom, Barclays has over 10 million personal customers and about 9.3 million credit cards in circulation, and it serves 500,000 small-business customers. Barclays decided to invest in CRM technologies to help gain valuable insights into its business and customers.

With its new CRM system, Barclays' managers are better able to predict the financial behavior of individual customers and assess whether a customer is likely to pay back a loan in full and within the agreed upon time period. This helps Barclays manage its profitability with greater precision because it can charge its customers a more appropriate rate of interest based on the results of the customer's risk assessment. Barclays also uses a sophisticated customer segmentation system to identify groups of profitable customers, both on a corporate and a personal level, which it can then target for new financial products. One of the most valuable pieces of

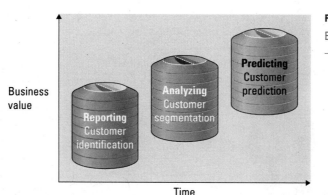

FIGURE 11.1

Evolution of CRM

information Barclays discovered was that about 50 percent of its customers are not profitable and that less than 30 percent of its customers provide 90 percent of its profits.

There are three phases in the evolution of CRM: (1) reporting, (2) analyzing, and (3) predicting (see Figure 11.1). CRM reporting technologies help organizations identify their customers across other applications. CRM analysis technologies help organizations segment their customers into categories such as best and worst customers. CRM predicting technologies help organizations make predictions regarding customer behavior such as which customers are at risk of leaving.

Both operational and analytical CRM technologies can assist in customer reporting (identification), customer analysis (segmentation), and customer prediction. Figure 11.2 highlights a few of the important questions an organization can answer using CRM technologies.

The Ugly Side of CRM: Why CRM Matters More Now than Ever Before

Business 2.0 ranked "You—the customer" as number one in the top 50 people who matter most in business. It has long been said that the customer is always right, but for a long time companies never really meant it. Now, companies have no choice as the power of the customer grows exponentially as the Internet grows. You—or

FIGURE 11.2

Reporting, Analyzing, and Predicting Examples

REPORTING "Asking What Happened"	ANALYZING "Asking Why It Happened"	PREDICTING "Asking What Will Happen"
What is the total revenue by customer?	Why did sales not meet forecasts?	What customers are at risk of leaving?
How many units did we manufacture?	Why was production so low?	What products will the customer buy?
Where did we sell the most products?	Why did we not sell as many units as last year?	Who are the best candidates for a mailing?
What were total sales by product?	Who are our customers?	What is the best way to reach the customer?
How many customers did we serve?	Why was customer revenue so high?	What is the lifetime profitability of a customer?
What are our inventory levels?	Why are inventory levels so low?	What transactions might be fraudulent?

FIGURE 11.3

The Power of You—
Websites Demonstrating
the Power of an Individual

rather, the collaborative intelligence of tens of millions of people, the networked you—continually create and filter new forms of content, anointing the useful, the relevant, and the amusing and rejecting the rest. You do it on websites like Amazon, Flickr, and YouTube, via podcasts and SMS polling, and on millions of self-published blogs. In every case, you have become an integral part of the action as a member of the aggregated, interactive, self-organizing, auto-entertaining audience. But the "You Revolution" goes well beyond user-generated content. Companies as diverse as Delta Air Lines and T-Mobile are turning to you to create their ad slogans. Procter & Gamble and Lego are incorporating your ideas into new products. You constructed open-source software and are its customer and its caretaker. None of this should be a surprise, since it was you—your crazy passions and hobbies and obsessions—that built out the web in the first place. And somewhere out there, you are building web 3.0. We do not yet know what that is, but one thing is for sure: It will matter. Figure 11.3 displays a few examples of the power of the people.

Customer Relationship Management's Explosive Growth

Brother International Corporation experienced skyrocketing growth in its sales of multifunction centers, fax machines, printers, and labeling systems in the late 1990s. Along with skyrocketing sales growth came a tremendous increase in customer service calls. When Brother failed to answer the phone fast enough, product returns started to increase. The company responded by increasing call center capacity, and the rate of returns began to drop. However, Dennis Upton, CIO of Brother International, observed that all the company was doing was answering the phone. He quickly realized that the company was losing a world of valuable market intelligence (business intelligence) about existing customers from all those telephone calls. The company decided to deploy SAP's CRM solution. The 1.8 million calls Brother handled dropped to 1.57 million, which reduced call center staff from 180 agents to 160 agents. Since customer demographic information is now stored and displayed on the agent's screen based on the incoming telephone number, the company has reduced call duration by an average of one minute, saving the company $600,000 per year.

In the context of increasing business competition and mature markets, it is easier than ever for informed and demanding customers to defect since they are just a click away from migrating to an alternative. When customers buy on the Internet, they see, and they steer, entire value chains. The Internet is a "looking glass," a two-way mirror, and its field of vision is the entire value chain. While the Internet cannot totally replace the phone and face-to-face communication with customers, it can strengthen these interactions and all customer touch points. Customer web interactions become conversations, interactive dialogs with shared knowledge, not just business transactions. Web-based customer care can actually become the focal point of customer relationship management and provide breakthrough benefits for both the enterprise and its customers, substantially reducing costs while improving service.

According to an AMR Research survey of more than 500 businesses in 14 key vertical markets, half of all current CRM spending is by manufacturers. Current users are allocating 20 percent of their IT budgets to CRM solutions. Those who have not invested in CRM may soon come on board: Of the respondents in the study who are not currently using CRM, roughly one-third plan to implement these types of technology solutions within the next year. Figure 11.4 displays the top CRM business drivers.

FIGURE 11.4

CRM Business Drivers

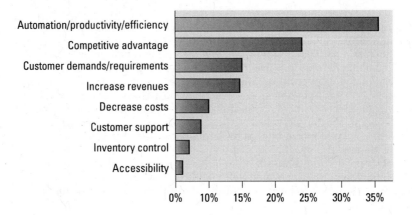

Using Analytical CRM to Enhance Decisions

Joe Guyaux knows the best way to win customers is to improve service. Under his leadership and with the help of Siebel CRM, the PNC retail banking team increased new consumer checking customers by 19 percent in 2003. Over two years, PNC retained 21 percent more of its consumer checking households as well as improved customer satisfaction by 9 percent.

The two primary components of a CRM strategy are operational CRM and analytical CRM. **Operational CRM** supports traditional transactional processing for day-to-day front-office operations or systems that deal directly with the customers. **Analytical CRM** supports back-office operations and strategic analysis and includes all systems that do not deal directly with the customers. The primary difference between operational CRM and analytical CRM is the direct interaction between the organization and its customers. See Figure 11.5 for an overview of operational CRM and analytical CRM.

Maturing analytical CRM and behavioral modeling technologies are helping numerous organizations move beyond "legacy benefits" like enhanced customer service and retention to systems that can truly improve business profitability. Unlike operational CRM that automates call centers and sales forces with the aim

FIGURE 11.5

Operational CRM and
Analytical CRM

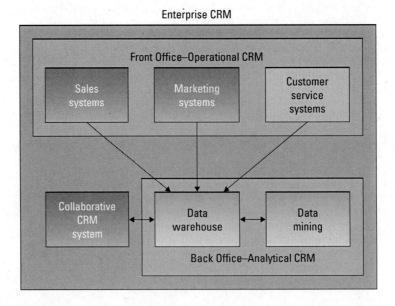

of enhancing customer transactions, analytical CRM solutions are designed to dig deep into a company's historical customer information and expose patterns of behavior on which a company can capitalize. Analytical CRM is primarily used to enhance and support decision making and works by identifying patterns in customer information collected from the various operational CRM systems.

For many organizations, the power of analytical CRM solutions provides tremendous managerial opportunities. Depending on the specific solution, analytical CRM tools can slice-and-dice customer information to create made-to-order views of customer value, spending, product affinities, percentile profiles, and segmentations. Modeling tools can identify opportunities for cross-selling, up-selling, and expanding customer relationships.

Personalization occurs when a website can know enough about a person's likes and dislikes that it can fashion offers that are more likely to appeal to that person. Many organizations are now utilizing CRM to create customer rules and templates that marketers can use to personalize customer messages.

The information produced by analytical CRM solutions can help companies make decisions about how to handle customers based on the value of each and every one. Analytical CRM can help make decisions as to which customers are worth investing in, which should be serviced at an average level, and which should not be invested in at all.

Customer Relationship Management Success Factors

CRM solutions make organizational business processes more intelligent. This is achieved by understanding customer behavior and preferences, then realigning product and service offerings and related communications to make sure they are synchronized with customer needs and preferences. If an organization is implementing a CRM system, it should study the industry best practices to help ensure a successful implementation (see Figure 11.6).

FIGURE 11.6

CRM Implementation Strategies

CRM Implementation Strategies
1. **Clearly Communicate the CRM Strategy**—Boise Office Solutions spent $25 million implementing a successful CRM system. One primary reason for the system's success was that Boise started with a clear business objective for the system: to provide customers with greater economic value. Only after establishing the business objective did Boise Office Solutions invest in CRM technology to help meet the goal. Ensuring that all departments and employees understand exactly what CRM means and how it will add value to the organization is critical. Research by Gartner Dataquest indicates that enterprises that attain success with CRM have interested and committed senior executives who set goals for what CRM should achieve, match CRM strategies with corporate objectives, and tie the measurement process to both goals and strategies.
2. **Define Information Needs and Flows**—People who perform successful CRM implementations have a clear understanding of how information flows in and out of their organization. Chances are information comes into the organization in many different forms over many different touchpoints.
3. **Build an Integrated View of the Customer**—Essential to a CRM strategy is choosing the correct CRM system that can support organizational requirements. The system must have the corresponding functional breadth and depth to support strategic goals. Remember to take into account the system's infrastructure including ease of integration to current systems, discussed in greater detail later in this unit.
4. **Implement in Iterations**—Implement the CRM system in manageable pieces—in other words avoid the "big bang" implementation approach. It is easier to manage, measure, and track the design, building, and deployment of the CRM system when it is delivered in pieces. Most important, this allows the organization to find out early if the implementation is headed for failure and thus either kill the project and save wasted resources or change direction to a more successful path.
5. **Scalability for Organizational Growth**—Make certain that the CRM system meets the organization's future needs as well as its current needs. Estimating future needs is by far one of the hardest parts of any project. Understanding how the organization is going to grow, predicting how technology is going to change, and anticipating how customers are going to evolve are very difficult challenges. Taking the time to answer some tough questions up front will ensure the organization grows into, instead of out of, its CRM system.

CRM is critical to business success. It is the key competitive strategy to stay focused on customer needs and to integrate a customer-centric approach throughout an organization. CRM can acquire enterprisewide knowledge about customers and improve the business processes that deliver value to an organization's customers, suppliers, and employees. Using the analytical capabilities of CRM can help a company anticipate customer needs and proactively serve customers in ways that build relationships, create loyalty, and enhance bottom lines.

OPENING CASE STUDY QUESTIONS

1. Why is it important for any company to use CRM strategies to manage customer information?
2. How are CRM strategies in Second Life different from CRM strategies in the real world?
3. If the virtual world is the first point of contact between a company and its customers, how might that transform the entire shopping experience?
4. How could companies use Second Life to connect with customers that would be difficult or too expensive in the real world?

Chapter Eleven Case: Can You Find Your Customers?

Entrepreneurship is all about finding niche markets, which arise from an untapped potential in a corner of an existing market ignored by major companies. Finding customers for a specialized or niche business is no longer an arduous manual task. Somewhere there is a list of names that will allow a business, no matter how "niche," to locate its specific target customers.

Vinod Gupta was working for a recreational vehicle (RV) manufacturer in Omaha, Nebraska, in 1972. One day his boss requested a list of all the RV dealers in the country. Of course, at this time no such list existed. Gupta decided to create one. Gupta ordered every Yellow Pages phone book in the country, 4,500 total, took them home to his garage, and started manually sorting through each book one-by-one, compiling the RV list that his boss coveted. After providing the list Gupta told his boss he could have it for free if he could also sell it to other RV manufacturers. Gupta's boss agreed, and his company—infoUSA, Inc.—was launched.

Today infoUSA no longer sells lists on yellow pieces of paper, but maintains one of the nation's largest databases, including 14 million businesses and 220 million consumers. Over 4 million customers access this resource. More than 90 percent are entrepreneurial companies and have only one or two employees. These small businesses account for 60 percent of infoUSA's annual revenue of $311 million.

The point is that entrepreneurial businesses that want to thrive in specialty markets can use databases for reaching customers. While this resource does not do the whole job, it can and should comprise the core of a marketing program which also includes publicity, word-of-mouth recommendations, or "buzz," savvy geographical placement of the company's physical outlets, such as retail stores and offices, and, if affordable, advertising.

Slicing and Dicing

Put another way, databases, which slice-and-dice lists to pinpoint just the right prospects for products or services, enable entrepreneurs to find the proverbial needle in the haystack. An entrepreneur might target a market of only 200 companies or a select universe of individuals who might have use for a specific product or service—such as feminist-oriented prayer books for Lutheran women ministers in their 20s, or seeds for gardeners who grow vegetables native to Sicily, or, like one of infoUSA's own customers, jelly beans for companies with employee coffee-break rooms.

Databases have the ability to take the legwork out of locating specialized customers and make the job as easy as one, two, three. According to infoUSA, to use databases effectively, company owners must take three distinct steps:

Step 1: Know Your Customers

"In any business, there is no substitute for retaining existing customers. Make these people happy, and they become the base from which you add others. As a niche marketer, you have at least an idea who might want what you have to sell, even if those prospects aren't yet actually buying. Get to know these people. Understand what they are looking for. Consider what they like and don't like about your product or service."

Step 2: Analyze Your Customers

"Your current customers or clients have all of the information you need to find other customers. Analyze them to find common characteristics. If you are selling to businesses, consider revenue and number of employees. If you are selling to consumers, focus on demographics, such as age, as well as income levels. Armed with this information about your customers, you are ready to make use of a database to look for new ones."

Step 3: Find New Customers Just Like Your Existing Customers

"In a niche business, you find new customers by cloning your existing customers. Once you know and understand your current customers, you can determine the types of businesses or customers to target."

"An online brokerage, for example, was seeking to build its business further and needed a list of names of people 'with a propensity to invest' just like its current clients. Our company used proprietary modeling to provide a set of names of individuals from throughout the U.S. with the required level of income."

"You should buy a database-generated list only if you have analyzed your current customers. In addition, you should wait to buy until you are ready to use the list, because lists do have a short shelf life—about 30 to 60 days if you are selling to consumers and six to nine months if you are selling to businesses. Indeed, about 70 percent of infoUSA's entire database changes over annually."

No Magic Bullet

The magic of databases is that there is no magic. Every entrepreneur has a product or service to sell. The trick is to match what you are selling with people who are buying. Used effectively, databases serve as the resource for making that happen. Do not make the mistake of expecting a database to perform the entire job of securing customers for products or services. An entrepreneur must be ever vigilant about prospecting—and not only when business is slow. Entrepreneurs must encourage sales representatives to call on customers even when business is booming and they do not require their revenues to keep the company afloat. Once customers are secured, make servicing them a top priority.

Questions

1. Explain how technology has dramatically impacted the efficiency and effectiveness of finding customers.

2. Explain the two different types of CRM systems and explain how a company can use infoUSA's database for creating a CRM strategy.

3. Describe three ways a new small business can extend its customer reach by performing CRM functions from an infoUSA database.

4. infoUSA discussed three distinct steps company owners must take to use databases effectively. Rank these steps in order of importance to a CRM strategy.

12

Integrating the Organization from End to End—Enterprise Resource Planning

12.1. Describe the role information plays in enterprise resource planning systems.

12.2. Identify the primary forces driving the explosive growth of enterprise resource planning systems.

12.3. Explain the business value of integrating supply chain management, customer relationship management, and enterprise resource planning systems.

Enterprise Resource Planning (ERP)

Enterprise resource planning systems serve as the organization's backbone in providing fundamental decision-making support. In the past, departments made decisions independent of each other. ERP systems provide a foundation for collaboration between departments, enabling people in different business areas to communicate. ERP systems have been widely adopted in large organizations to store critical knowledge used to make the decisions that drive performance.

To be competitive, organizations must always strive for excellence in every business process enterprisewide, a daunting challenge if the organization has multisite operations worldwide. To obtain operational efficiencies, lower costs, improve supplier and customer relations, and increase revenues and market share, all units of the organization must work together harmoniously toward congruent goals. An ERP system will help an organization achieve this.

One company that has blazed a trail with ERP is Atlanta-based United Parcel Service of America, Inc. (UPS). UPS has developed a number of web-based applications that track information such as recipient signatures, addresses, time in transit, and other shipping information. These services run on an SAP foundation that UPS customers can connect to using real-time ERP information obtained from the UPS website. Currently, 6.2 million tracking requests pass through the company's website each day. By automating the information delivery process, UPS has dramatically reduced the demand on its customer service representatives. Just as important, UPS has improved relationships with its business partners—in effect integrating its business with theirs—by making it easier for consumers to find delivery information without leaving the website of the merchant.

The heart of an ERP system is a central database that collects information from and feeds information into all the ERP system's individual application components (called modules), supporting diverse business functions such as accounting, manufacturing, marketing, and human resources. When a user enters or updates information in one module, it is immediately and automatically updated throughout the entire system, as illustrated in Figure 12.1.

ERP automates business processes such as order fulfillment—taking an order from a customer, shipping the purchase, and then billing for it. With an ERP system, when a customer service representative takes an order from a customer, he or she has all the information necessary to complete the order (the customer's credit rating and order history, the company's inventory levels, and the delivery schedule).

FIGURE 12.1

ERP Integration Data Flow

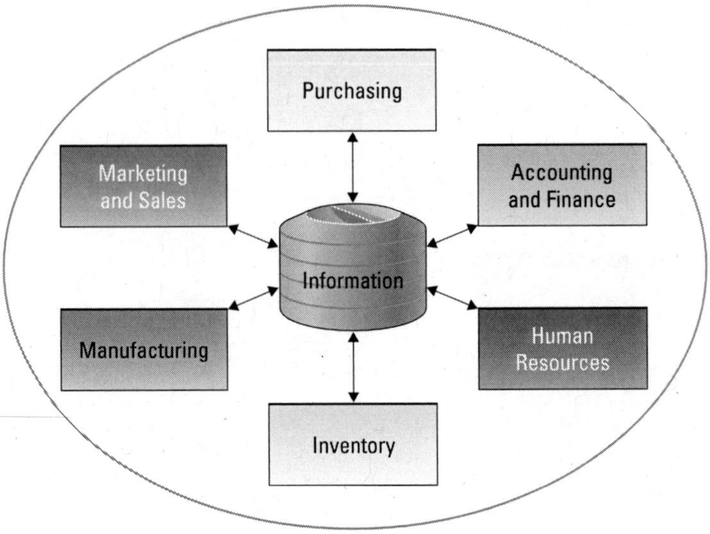

Everyone else in the company sees the same information and has access to the database that holds the customer's new order. When one department finishes with the order, it is automatically routed via the ERP system to the next department. To find out where the order is at any point, a user need only log in to the ERP system and track it down, as illustrated in Figure 12.2. The order process moves like a bolt of lightning through the organization, and customers get their orders faster and with fewer errors than ever before. ERP can apply that same magic to the other major business processes, such as employee benefits or financial reporting.

Bringing the Organization Together

In most organizations, information has traditionally been isolated within specific departments, whether on an individual database, in a file cabinet, or on an employee's PC. ERP enables employees across the organization to share information across

FIGURE 12.2

ERP Process Flow

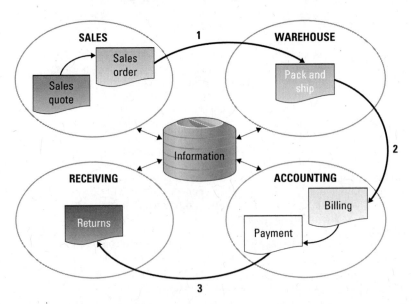

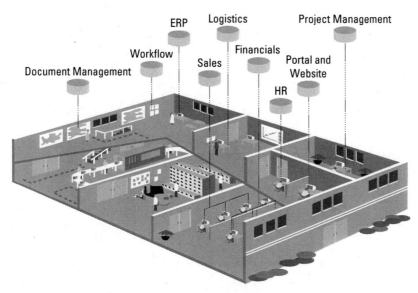

FIGURE 12.3

The Organization before ERP

a single, centralized database. With extended portal capabilities, an organization can also involve its suppliers and customers to participate in the workflow process, allowing ERP to penetrate the entire value chain, and help the organization achieve greater operational efficiency (see Figures 12.3 and 12.4).

The Evolution of ERP

Originally, ERP solutions were developed to deliver automation across multiple units of an organization, to help facilitate the manufacturing process and address issues such as raw materials, inventory, order entry, and distribution. However,

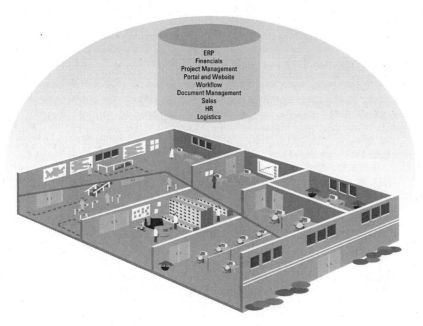

FIGURE 12.4

ERP—Bringing the Organization Together

FIGURE 12.5

The Evolution of ERP

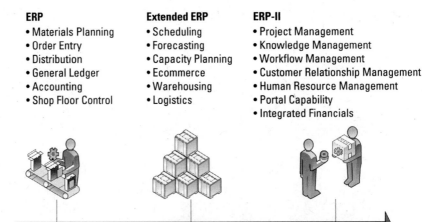

ERP
- Materials Planning
- Order Entry
- Distribution
- General Ledger
- Accounting
- Shop Floor Control

Extended ERP
- Scheduling
- Forecasting
- Capacity Planning
- Ecommerce
- Warehousing
- Logistics

ERP-II
- Project Management
- Knowledge Management
- Workflow Management
- Customer Relationship Management
- Human Resource Management
- Portal Capability
- Integrated Financials

1990   2000   Present

ERP was unable to extend to other functional areas of the company such as sales, marketing, and shipping. It could not tie in any CRM capabilities that would allow organizations to capture customer-specific information, nor did it work with websites or portals used for customer service or order fulfillment. Call center or quality assurance staff could not tap into the ERP solution, nor could ERP handle document management, such as cataloging contracts and purchase orders.

ERP has grown over the years to become part of the extended enterprise. From its beginning as a tool for materials planning, it has extended to warehousing, distribution, and order entry. With its next evolution, ERP expands to the front office including CRM. Now administrative, sales, marketing, and human resources staff can share a tool that is truly enterprisewide. To compete on a functional level today, companies must adopt an enterprisewide approach to ERP that utilizes the Internet and connects to every facet of the value chain. Figure 12.5 shows how ERP has grown since the 1990s to accommodate the needs of the entire organization.

FIGURE 12.6

SCM Market Overview

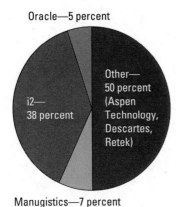

Oracle—5 percent

i2—38 percent

Manugistics—7 percent

Other—50 percent (Aspen Technology, Descartes, Retek)

Integrating SCM, CRM, and ERP

Applications such as SCM, CRM, and ERP are the backbone of ebusiness. Integration of these applications is the key to success for many companies. Integration allows the unlocking of information to make it available to any user, anywhere, anytime. Originally, there were three top ERP vendors—PeopleSoft, Oracle, and SAP. In December 2004, Oracle purchased PeopleSoft for $10 billion, leaving two main competitors in the ERP market—Oracle and SAP.

Most organizations today have no choice but to piece their SCM, CRM, and ERP applications together since no one vendor can respond to every organizational need; hence, customers purchase applications from multiple vendors. Oracle and SAP both offer CRM and SCM components. However, these modules are not as functional or flexible as the modules offered by industry leaders of SCM and CRM such as Siebel and i2 Technologies, as depicted in Figures 12.6 and 12.7. As a result, organizations face the challenge of integrating their systems. For example, a single organization might choose its CRM components from Siebel, SCM components from i2, and financial components and HR management components from Oracle. Figure 12.8 displays the general audience and purpose for each of these applications that have to be integrated.

From its roots in the California Gold Rush era, San Francisco–based Del Monte Foods has grown to become the nation's largest producer and distributor of premium quality processed fruits, vegetables, and tomato products. With annual sales of over $3 billion, Del Monte is also one of the country's largest producers, distributors, and marketers of private-label food and pet products with a powerful portfolio of brands including Del Monte, StarKist, Nature's Goodness, 9Lives, and Kibbles 'n Bits.

Del Monte's acquisition of StarKist, Nature's Goodness, 9Lives, and Kibbles 'n Bits from the H. J. Heinz Company required an integration between Del Monte's and H. J. Heinz's business processes. Del Monte needed to overhaul its IT infrastructure, migrating from multiple platforms including UNIX and mainframe systems and consolidating applications centrally on a single system. The work required integration of business processes across manufacturing, financial, supply chain, decision support, and transactional reporting areas.

The revamp of Del Monte's architecture stemmed from a strategic decision. Del Monte decided to implement an ERP system to support its entire U.S. operations, with headquarters in San Francisco, operations in Pittsburgh, and distribution centers and manufacturing facilities across the country. The company concluded that the only way it could unite its global operations and open its system to its customers, which are mainly large retailers, was through the use of an ERP system. Among other key factors was the need to embrace an ebusiness strategy. The challenge facing Del Monte was to select an ERP system to merge multiple systems quickly and cost effectively. If financial and customer service targets were to be achieved, Del Monte needed to integrate new businesses that more than doubled

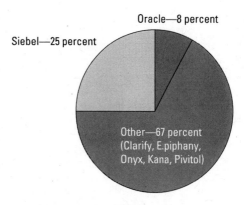

FIGURE 12.7

CRM Market Overview

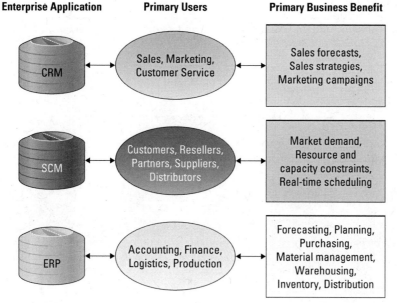

FIGURE 12.8

Primary Users and Business Benefits of Strategic Initiatives the size of the company. Since implementing the ERP system, customers and trading partners are now provided with a single, consistent, and integrated view of the company.

Integration Tools

Effectively managing the transformation to an integrated enterprise will be critical to the success of the 21st century organization. The key is the integration of the disparate IT applications. An integrated enterprise infuses support areas, such as finance and human resources, with a strong customer orientation. Integrations are achieved using *middleware*—several different types of software that sit in the middle of and provide connectivity between two or more software applications. Middleware translates information between disparate systems. ***Enterprise application integration (EAI) middleware*** represents a new approach to middleware by packaging together commonly used functionality, such as providing prebuilt links to popular enterprise applications, which reduces the time necessary to develop solutions that integrate applications from multiple vendors. A few leading vendors of EAI middleware include Active Software, Vitria Technology, and Extricity. Figure 12.9 displays the data points where these applications integrate and illustrates the underlying premise of architecture infrastructure design.

Companies run on interdependent applications, such as SCM, CRM, and ERP. If one application performs poorly, the entire customer value delivery system is affected. For example, no matter how great a company is at CRM, if its SCM system does not work and the customer never receives the finished product, the company will lose that customer. The world-class enterprises of tomorrow must be built on the foundation of world-class applications implemented today.

Coca-Cola's business model is a common one among well-known franchisers. Coca-Cola gets the majority of its $18 billion in annual revenue from franchise fees it earns from bottlers all over the world. Bottlers, along with the franchise, license Coke's secret recipe and many others including recipes for Odwalla, Nestea, Minute Maid, and Sprite. Now Coca-Cola hopes that bottlers will also buy into adopting common business practices using a service-oriented architecture ERP system.

The target platform chosen by Coca-Cola is mySAP enterprise resource planning (ERP) by SAP. If it works, Coca-Cola and its bottlers stand to make and save a lot of money, and SAP will be able to position itself as one of the dominant ERP

FIGURE 12.9

Integrations between SCM, CRM, and ERP Applications

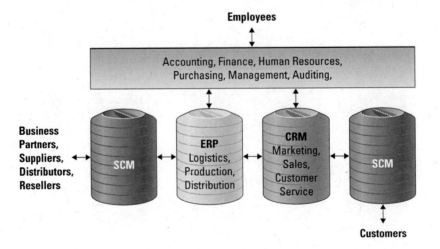

players. Already, Coca-Cola and many of its bottlers use versions of SAP for finance, manufacturing, and a number of administrative functions. But Coca-Cola wants everyone to move to a "services" architecture environment.

Coca-Cola hopes that this services standardization will make its supply chain more efficient and reduce costs. In explaining why a services approach is so vitally important, Jean-Michel Ares, CIO of Coca-Cola, stated, "That will allow bottlers to converge one step at a time, one process area at a time, one module at a time, at a time that's right for the bottler. We can march across the bottling world incrementally."

Enterprise Resource Planning's Explosive Growth

Cisco Systems Inc., a $22 billion producer of computer-network equipment, is using an ERP system to create a consolidated trial balance sheet and a consolidated income statement within a half day of a fiscal quarter's close, compared with two weeks more than five years ago when Cisco was a $4 billion company. What's more, during those years, the time devoted to transaction processing has fallen from 65 percent to 35 percent, and finance group expenses, as a percentage of the total company revenues, have fallen from 2 percent to 1.3 percent. All that has occurred even as Cisco added people to its finance department to keep pace with the company's growth. The ERP system gives Cisco executives a look at revenues, expenses, margins, and profits every day of every month.

Business in the 21st century is complex, fluid, and customer-centric. It requires stringent, yet flexible processes and communications systems that extend globally and respond instantaneously. The processes and systems must be integrated. No part of the enterprise can escape the pressure to deliver measurable results. Here are a few reasons ERP solutions have proven to be such a powerful force:

- ERP is a logical solution to the mess of incompatible applications that had sprung up in most businesses.
- ERP addresses the need for global information sharing and reporting.
- ERP is used to avoid the pain and expense of fixing legacy systems.

To qualify as a true ERP solution, the system not only must integrate various organization processes, but also must be:

- **Flexible**—An ERP system should be flexible in order to respond to the changing needs of an enterprise.
- **Modular and open**—An ERP system has to have an open system architecture, meaning that any module can be interfaced with or detached whenever required without affecting the other modules. The system should support multiple hardware platforms for organizations that have a heterogeneous collection of systems. It must also support third-party add-on components.
- **Comprehensive**—An ERP system should be able to support a variety of organizational functions and must be suitable for a wide range of business organizations.
- **Beyond the company**—An ERP system must not be confined to organizational boundaries but rather support online connectivity to business partners or customers.

ERP as a business concept resounds as a powerful internal information management nirvana: Everyone involved in sourcing, producing, and delivering the company's product works with the same information, which eliminates redundancies, cuts wasted time, and removes misinformation.

OPENING CASE STUDY QUESTIONS

1. If you operated a business entirely on Second Life would you require an ERP system? Why or why not?

2. How would an ERP system be used in Second Life to support a global organization?

Chapter Twelve Case: Shell Canada Fuels Productivity with ERP

Shell Canada is one of the nation's largest integrated petroleum companies and is a leading manufacturer, distributor, and marketer of refined petroleum products. The company, headquartered in Calgary, produces natural gas, natural gas liquids, and bitumen. Shell Canada is also the country's largest producer of sulphur. There is a Canada-wide network of 1,809 Shell-branded retail gasoline stations and convenience food stores from coast-to-coast.

To run such a complex and vast business operation successfully, the company relies heavily on the use of a mission-critical enterprise resource planning (ERP) system. The use of such a system is a necessity in helping the company integrate and manage its daily operations— operations that span from wells and mines, to processing plants, to oil trucks and gas pumps.

For example, the ERP system has helped the company immensely in terms of reducing and streamlining the highly manual process of third-party contractors submitting repair information and invoices. On average, there are between 2,500 and 4,000 service orders handled by these contractors per month on a nationwide basis.

Before implementation of the ERP system, contractors had to send Shell Canada monthly summarized invoices that listed maintenance calls the contractors made at various Shell gasoline stations. Each one of these invoices would take a contractor between 8 and 20 hours to prepare. Collectively, the contractors would submit somewhere between 50 and 100 invoices every month to Shell Canada. This involved each invoice being reviewed by the appropriate territory manager and then forwarded to the head office for payment processing. This alone consumed another 16 to 30 hours of labor per month. At the head office, another 200 hours of work was performed by data entry clerks who had to manually enter batch invoice data into the payment system.

And this would be the amount of time needed if things went smoothly! More hours of labor were required to decipher and correct errors if any mistakes were introduced from all the manual invoice generation and data reentry involved. Often errors concerning one line item on an invoice would deter payment of the whole invoice. This irritated the contractors and did not help foster healthy contractor relationships.

To make matters worse, despite the hours involved and the amount of human data-handling required, detailed information about the service repairs that contractors did was often not entered into the payment system. And if it was entered, the information was not timely—it was often weeks or even months old by the time it made it into the payment processing system. As a result, Shell was not collecting sufficient information about what repairs were being done, what had caused the problem, and how it had been resolved.

Fortunately, the ERP solution solved these inadequacies by providing an integrated web-based service order, invoicing, and payment submission system. With this tool, third-party contractors can enter service orders directly into Shell's ERP system via the web. When this is done, the contractors can also enter detailed information about the work that was performed—sometimes even attaching photos and drawings to help describe the work that was done. With the ERP system, it takes only a few minutes for a contractor to enter details about a service order. Further, this information can be transmitted through a wireless PDA to the appropriate Shell manager for immediate approval—shaving off more time in unnecessary delays.

Another bonus of the ERP system is that the contractor's monthly summarized invoices can now be generated automatically and fed directly into the ERP system's account payables application for processing. No rekeying of data required! Even better, if there is an issue or concern with one invoice item, the other items on the invoice can still be processed for payment.

Shell Canada's ERP system also handles other operational tasks. For example, the system can help speed up maintenance and repair operations at the company's refineries. With the ERP system in place, rather than trying to utilize a variety of disparate internal systems to access blueprints, schematics, spare parts lists, and other tools and information, workers at the refineries can now use the ERP system to access these things directly from a centralized database.

An added benefit of the ERP system is its ease of use. Past systems used by refinery workers were complex and difficult to search for information. The ERP system in place now has a portal-like interface that allows refinery workers to access the functions and information they need to keep operations running. The web interface allows workers access to this information with one or two clicks of a mouse.

An important part of any successful ERP implementation is training end users to learn how to utilize the system and to teach them about the functions and abilities of the ERP system. Recognizing this, Shell Canada offered its personnel both formal and informal ERP training. These proved to be invaluable in teaching end users the mechanics of the system and raising awareness of the benefits of the system and the efficiencies that the ERP system could offer Shell Canada. This not only helped promote end-user acceptance of the ERP system, but also greatly increased employees' intentions to use the system in their daily work.

Shell Canada executives are pleased and optimistic about the advantages of the ERP system. With this new system, employees across the company have gained fast and easy access to the tools and information they need to conduct their daily operations.

Questions

1. How did ERP help improve business operations at Shell?
2. How important was training in helping roll out the system to Shell personnel?
3. How could extended ERP components help improve business operations at Shell?
4. What advice would you give Shell if it decided to choose a different ERP software solution?
5. How can integrating SCM, CRM, and ERP help improve business operations at Shell?

Today, organizations of various sizes are proving that systems that support decision making and opportunity seizing are essential to thriving in the highly competitive electronic world. We are living in an era when information technology is a primary tool, knowledge is a strategic asset, and decision making and problem solving are paramount skills. The tougher, larger, and more demanding a problem or opportunity is, and the faster and more competitive the environment is, the more important decision-making and problem-solving skills become. This unit discussed numerous tools and strategic initiatives that an organization can take advantage of to assist in decision making:

- Supply chain management (SCM)—managing information flows within the supply chain to maximize total supply chain effectiveness and profitability.

- Customer relationship management (CRM)—managing all aspects of customers' relationships with an organization to increase customer loyalty and retention and an organization's profitability.

- Enterprise resource planning (ERP)—integrating all departments and functions throughout an organization into a single IT system (or integrated set of IT systems) so that managers and leaders can make enterprisewide decisions by viewing enterprisewide information on all business operations.

★ KEY TERMS

Analytical CRM, 152
Artificial intelligence (AI), 131
Bullwhip effect, 140
Consolidation, 128
Decision support system (DSS), 126
Demand planning software, 141
Digital dashboard, 128
Drill-down, 128
Ebusiness, 123
Enterprise application integration (EAI) middleware, 162
Executive information system (EIS), 128
Expert system, 131

Fuzzy logic, 133
Genetic algorithm, 133
Goal-seeking analysis, 126
Intelligent agent, 133
Intelligent system, 131
Logistics, 139
Middleware, 162
Model, 124
Neural network or artificial neural network, 132
Online analytical processing (OLAP), 125
Online transaction processing (OLTP), 125
Operational CRM, 152

Personalization, 153
Sensitivity analysis, 126
Shopping bot, 133
Slice-and-dice, 128
Supply chain, 137
Supply chain execution (SCE) software, 141
Supply chain management (SCM), 137
Supply chain planning (SCP) software, 141
Supply chain visibility, 140
Transaction processing system (TPS), 125
What-if analysis, 126

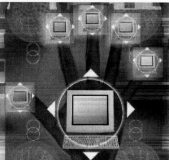

Dell's Famous Supply Chain

Speed is at the core of everything Dell does. Dell assembles nearly 80,000 computers every 24 hours. The computer manufacturer has done more than any other company when it comes to tweaking its supply chain. More than a decade ago, Dell carried 20 to 25 days of inventory in a sprawling network of warehouses. Today, Dell does not have a single warehouse and carries only two hours of inventory in its factories and a maximum of just 72 hours across its entire operation. Dell's vast, global supply chain is in constant overdrive making the company one of the fastest, most hyperefficient organizations on the planet.

Disaster Occurs

In 2002, a 10-day labor lockout shut down 29 West Coast ports extending from Los Angeles to Seattle, idled 10,000 union dockworkers, and blocked hundreds of cargo ships from unloading raw materials and finished goods. The port closings paralyzed global supply chains and ultimately cost U.S. consumers and businesses billions of dollars.

Analysts expected Dell, with its just-in-time manufacturing model, would be especially hard hit when parts failed to reach its two U.S.-based factories. Without warehouses filled with motherboards and hard drives the world's largest PC maker would simply find itself with nothing to sell within a matter of days. Dell knew all too well that its ultra-lean, high-speed business model left it vulnerable to just such a situation. "When a labor problem or an earthquake or a SARS epidemic breaks out, we've got to react quicker than anyone else," said Dick Hunter, the company's supply chain expert. "There's no other choice. We know these things are going to happen; we must move fast to fix them. We just can't tolerate any kind of delay."

Fortunately, the same culture of speed and flexibility that seems to put Dell at the mercy of disruptions also helps it deal with them. Dell was in constant, round-the-clock communication with its parts makers in Taiwan, China, and Malaysia and its U.S.-based shipping partners. Hunter dispatched a "tiger team" of 10 logistics specialists to Long Beach, California, and other ports; they worked with Dell's carrying and freight-forwarding networks to assemble a contingency plan.

When the tiger team confirmed that the closings were all but certain, Dell moved into high gear. It chartered 18 airplanes (747s) from UPS, Northwest Airlines, and China Airlines. A 747 holds the equivalent of 10 tractor-trailers—enough parts to manufacture 10,000 PCs. The bidding for the planes grew fierce, running as high as $1 million for a one-way flight from Asia to the West Coast. Dell got in the bidding early and kept costs around $500,000 per plane. Dell also worked with its Asia-based suppliers to ensure that its parts were always at the Shanghai and Taipei airports in time for its returning charters to land, reload, refuel, and take off. The company was consistently able to get its planes to the United States and back within 33 hours, which kept its costs down and its supply chain moving.

Meanwhile, Dell had people on the ground in every major harbor. In Asia, the freight specialists saw to it that Dell's parts were the last to be loaded onto each cargo ship so they would be unloaded first when the ship hit the West Coast. The biggest test came when the ports reopened and companies scrambled to sort through the backed-up mess of thousands of containers. Hunter's tiger team had anticipated this logistical nightmare. Even though Dell had PC components in hundreds of containers on 50 ships, it knew the exact moment when each component cycled through the harbor, and it was among the first to unload its parts and speed them to its factories in Austin, Texas, and Nashville, Tennessee. In the end, Dell did the impossible: It survived a 10-day supply chain blackout with roughly 72 hours of inventory without delaying a single customer order.

The aftershocks of the port closings reverberated for weeks. Many companies began to question the wisdom of running so lean in an uncertain world, and demand for warehouse space soared as they piled up buffer inventory to ensure against labor unrest, natural disasters, and terrorist attacks.

Building a "Dell-like" Supply Chain

Dell's ultimate competitive weapon is speed, which gives the technical giant's bottom line a real boost. Figure Unit 3.2 displays a five-point plan for building a fast supply chain—direct from Dell.

Questions

1. Identify a few key metrics a Dell marketing executive might want to monitor on a digital dashboard.
2. Determine how Dell can benefit from using decision support systems and executive information systems in its business.
3. Describe how Dell has influenced visibility, consumer behavior, competition, and speed though the use of IT in its supply chain.
4. Explain the seven principles of SCM in reference to Dell's business model.
5. Identify how Dell can use CRM to improve its business operations.
6. Explain how an ERP system could help Dell gain business intelligence.

FIGURE UNIT 3.2

How to Build a Dell-like Supply Chain

Dell-Like Supply Chain Plan
1. **The supply chain starts with the customer.** By cutting out retailers and selling directly to its customers, Dell is in a far better position to forecast real customer demand.
2. **Replace inventory with information.** To operate with close to zero inventory, Dell communicates constantly with its suppliers. It sends out status updates three times a day from its assembly plants; every week it updates its quarterly demand forecasts. By making communication its highest priority, Dell ensures the lowest possible inventory.
3. **If you cannot measure it, you cannot manage it.** Dell knows what works because it measures everything from days in inventory to the time it takes to build a PC. As Dell slashed those numbers, it got more efficient.
4. **Complexity slows you down.** Dell cut the number of its core PC suppliers from several hundred to about 25. It standardized critical PC components, which streamlined its manufacturing. Dell got faster by making things simpler.
5. **Create a watershed mind-set.** Dell is not content with incremental improvement; it demands massive change. Each year, it wants its Austin-based PC-assembly plant—already very fast—to improve production by 30 percent. "You don't get a big result if you do not challenge people with big goals," Dell CEO Kevin Rollins said.

★ UNIT CLOSING CASE TWO

Revving Up Sales at Harley-Davidson

Harley-Davidson produces 290,000 motorcycles and generates over $4 billion in net revenues yearly. There is a mystique associated with a Harley-Davidson motorcycle. No other motorcycle in the world has the look, feel, and sound of a Harley-Davidson, and many people consider it a two-wheeled piece of art. Demand for Harley-Davidson motorcycles outweighs supply. Some models have up to a two-year wait list. Harley-Davidson has won a number of awards including:

- Rated second in *ComputerWorld*'s Top 100 Best Places to Work in IT.
- Rated 51st in *Fortune*'s 100 Best Companies to Work For.
- Rated first in *Fortune*'s 5 Most Admired Companies in the motor vehicles industry.
- Rated first in the Top 10 Sincerest Corporations by the *Harris Interactive Report*.
- Rated second in the Top 10 Overall Corporations by the *Harris Interactive Report*.

Harley-Davidson's Focus on Technology

Harley-Davidson's commitment to technology is paying off: In 2003 it decreased production costs and inventories by $40 million as a direct result of using technology to increase production capacity. The company's technology budget of $50 million is more than 2 percent of its revenue, which is far above the manufacturing industry average. More than 50 percent of this budget is devoted to developing new technology strategies.

Harley-Davidson focuses on implementing ebusiness strategies to strengthen its market share and increase customer satisfaction. Over 80 projects were in development in 2003, and the majority of the new projects focused on sharing information, gaining business intelligence, and enhancing decision making.

Talon, Harley-Davidson's proprietary dealer management system, is one of its most successful technology initiatives. Talon handles inventory, vehicle registration, warranties, and point-of-sale transactions for all Harley-Davidson dealerships. The system performs numerous time-saving tasks such as checking dealer inventory, automatically generating parts orders, and allowing the company to review and analyze information across its global organization. Talon gives Harley-Davidson managers a 360-degree view into enterprisewide information that supports strategic goal setting and decision making throughout all levels of the organization.

Building Supplier Relationships

Harley-Davidson invests time, energy, and resources into continually improving its company-to-company strategic business initiatives such as supply chain management. The company understands and values the importance of building strong relationships with its suppliers. To develop these important relationships the company deployed Manugistics, an SCM system that allows it to do business with suppliers in a collaborative, web-based environment. The company plans to use the SCM software to better manage its flow of materials and improve collaboration activities with its key suppliers.

Building Customer Relationships

Each time a customer reaches out to the company, Harley-Davidson has an opportunity to build a trusting relationship with that particular customer. Harley-Davidson realizes that it takes more than just building and selling motorcycles to fulfill the dreams of its customers. For this reason, the company strives to deliver unforgettable experiences along with its top quality products.

Harley-Davidson sells over $500 million worth of parts and accessories to its loyal followers. Ken Ostermann, Harley-Davidson's manager of electronic commerce and communications, decided that the company could increase these sales if it could offer the products online. The dilemma facing Ostermann's online strategy was that selling jackets, saddlebags, and T-shirts directly to consumers would bypass Harley-Davidson's 650 dealers, who depend on the high-margin accessories to fuel their businesses' profits. Ostermann's solution was to build an online store, Harley-Davidson.com, which prompts customers to select a participating Harley-Davidson dealership before placing any online orders. The selected dealership is then responsible for fulfilling the order. This strategy has helped ensure that the dealers remain the focal point of customers' buying experiences.

To guarantee that every customer has a highly satisfying online buying experience, the company asks the dealers to agree to a number of standards including:

- Checking online orders twice daily.
- Shipping online orders within 24 hours.
- Responding to customer inquiries within 24 hours.

The company still monitors online customer metrics such as time taken to process orders, number of returned orders, and number of incorrect orders, ensuring that Harley-Davidson delivers on its message of prompt, excellent service consistently to all its loyal customers. The company receives over 1 million visitors a month to its online store. Customer satisfaction scores for the website moved from the extremely satisfied level to the exceptional level in a year.

Another of Harley-Davidson's customer-centric strategies is its Harley's Owners Group (HOG), established in 1983. HOG is the largest factory-sponsored motorcycle club in the world with more than 600,000 members. HOG offers a wide array of events, rides, and benefits to its members. HOG is one of the key drivers helping to build a strong sense of community among Harley-Davidson owners. Harley-Davidson has built a customer following that is extremely loyal, a difficult task to accomplish in any industry.

Harley-Davidson's Corporate Culture

Harley-Davidson employees are the engine behind its outstanding performance and the foundation of the company's overall success. Harley-Davidson believes in a strong sense of corporate ethics and values, and the company's top five core values serve as a framework for the entire corporation:

1. Tell the truth.
2. Be fair.
3. Keep your promises.
4. Respect the individual.
5. Encourage intellectual curiosity.

The company credits its core values as the primary reason it won the two prestigious awards from the *Harris Interactive Report,* one of the most respected consumer reviews for corporate sincerity, ethics, and standards. Sticking to strong ethics and values is and will continue to be a top priority for the company and its employees.

To enhance its enterprise further Harley-Davidson plans to keep taking advantage of new technologies and strategies including a web-based approach to accessing information and an enterprisewide system to consolidate procurement at its eight U.S. facilities.

Questions

1. Explain how Talon helps Harley-Davidson employees improve their decision-making capabilities.
2. Identify a few key metrics a Harley-Davidson marketing executive might want to monitor on a digital dashboard.
3. How can Harley-Davidson benefit from using decision support systems and executive information systems in its business?
4. How would Harley-Davidson's business be affected if it decided to sell accessories directly to its online customers? Include a brief discussion of the ethics involved with this decision.
5. Evaluate the HOG CRM strategy and recommend an additional benefit Harley-Davidson could provide to its HOG members to increase customer satisfaction.
6. How could Harley-Davidson's SCM system, Manugistics, improve its business operations?
7. Provide a potential illustration of Harley-Davidson's SCM system including all upstream and downstream participants.
8. Explain how an ERP system could help Harley-Davidson gain business intelligence in its operations.

★ MAKING BUSINESS DECISIONS

1. Implementing an ERP System

Blue Dog Inc. is a leading manufacturer in the high-end sunglasses industry. Blue Dog Inc. reached record revenue levels of over $250 million last year. The company is currently deciding on the possibility of implementing an ERP system to help decrease production costs and increase inventory control. Many of the executives are nervous about making such a large investment in an ERP system due to its low success rates. As a senior manager at Blue Dog Inc. you have been asked to compile a list of the potential benefits and risks associated with implementing an ERP system along with your recommendations for the steps the company can take to ensure a successful implementation.

2. DSS and EIS

Dr. Rosen runs a large dental conglomerate—Teeth Doctors—that staffs over 700 dentists in six states. Dr. Rosen is interested in purchasing a competitor called Dentix that has 150 dentists in three additional states. Before deciding whether to purchase Dentix, Dr. Rosen must consider several issues:

■ The cost of purchasing Dentix.
■ The location of the Dentix offices.
■ The current number of customers per dentist, per office, and per state.
■ The merger between the two companies.
■ The professional reputation of Dentix.
■ Other competitors.

Explain how Dr. Rosen and Teeth Doctors can benefit from the use of information systems to make an accurate business decision in regard to the potential purchase of Dentix.

3. SCM, CRM, and ERP

Jamie Ash is interested in applying for a job at a large software vendor. One of the criteria for the job is a detailed understanding of strategic initiatives such as SCM, CRM, and ERP. Jamie has no knowledge of any of these initiatives and cannot even explain what the acronyms mean. Jamie has come to you for help. She would like you to compile a summary of the three initiatives including an analysis of how the three are similar and how they are different. Jamie would also like to perform some self-training via the web so be sure to provide her with several additional links to key websites that offer detailed overviews on SCM, CRM, and ERP.

4. Customer Relationship Management Strategies

On average, it costs an organization six times more to sell to a new customer than to sell to an existing customer. As the co-owner of a medium-sized luggage distributor, you have recently been notified by your EIS systems that sales for the past three months have decreased by an average of 17 percent. The reasons for the decline in sales are numerous, including a poor economy, people's aversion to travel because of the terrorist attacks, and some negative publicity your company received regarding a defective product line. In a group, explain how implementing a CRM system can help you understand and combat the decline in sales. Be sure to justify why a CRM system is important to your business and its future growth.

5. Finding Information on Decision Support Systems

You are working on the sales team for a small catering company that maintains 75 employees and generates $1 million in revenues per year. The owner, Pam Hetz, wants to understand how she can use decision support systems to help grow her business. Pam has an initial understanding of DSS systems and is interested in learning more about what types are available, how they can be used in a small business, and the cost associated with different DSS systems. In a group, research the website www.dssresources.com and compile a presentation that discusses DSS systems in detail. Be sure to answer all Pam's questions on DSS systems in the presentation.

6. Analyzing Dell's Supply Chain Management System

Dell's supply chain strategy is legendary. Essentially, if you want to build a successful SCM system your best bet is to model your SCM system after Dell's. In a team, research Dell's supply chain management strategy on the web and create a report discussing any new SCM updates and strategies the company is using that were not discussed in this text. Be sure to include a graphical presentation of Dell's current supply chain model.

7. Gaining Business Intelligence from Strategic Initiatives

You are a new employee in the customer service department at Premier One, a large pet food distributor. The company, founded by several veterinarians, has been in business for three years and focuses on providing nutritious pet food at a low cost. The company currently has 90 employees and operates in seven states. Sales over the past three years have tripled and the manual systems currently in place are no longer sufficient to run the business. Your first task is to meet with your new team and create a presentation for the president and chief executive officer describing supply chain management, customer relationship management, and enterprise resource planning systems. The presentation should highlight the main benefits Premier One can receive from these strategic initiatives along with any additional added business value that can be gained from the systems.

1. Great Stories

With the advent of the Internet, when customers have an unpleasant customer experience, the company no longer has to worry about them telling a few friends and family; the company has to worry about them telling everyone. Internet service providers are giving consumers frustrated with how they were treated by a company another means of fighting back. Free or low-cost computer space for Internet websites is empowering consumers to tell not only their friends, but also the world about the way they have been treated. A few examples of disgruntled customer stories from the Internet include:

- **Bad Experience with Blue Marble Biking**—Tourist on biking tour is bitten by dog, requires stitches. Company is barred from hotel because of incident, and in turn it bars the tourist from any further tours.

- **Best Buy Receipt Check**—Shopper declines to show register receipt for purchase to door guard at Lakewood Best Buy, which is voluntary. Employees attempt to seize cart, stand in shopper's path, and park a truck behind shopper's car to prevent departure.

- **Enterprise Rent-A-Car Is a Failing Enterprise**—Enterprise Rent-A-Car did not honor reservations, did not have cars ready as stated, rented cars with nearly empty tanks, and charged higher prices to corporate account holders.

Project Focus

The Internet is raising the stakes for customer service. With the ability to create a website dedicated to a particular issue, a disgruntled customer can have nearly the same reach as a manufacturer. The Internet is making it more difficult for companies to ignore their customers' complaints. In a group, search the web for the most outrageous story of a disgruntled customer. A few places to start include:

- **Complain Complain (complaincomplain.net)**—provides professionally written, custom complaint letters to businesses.

- **The Complaint Department (www.thecomplaintdepartment.ca)**—a for-fee consumer complaint resolution and letter writing service.

- **The Complaint Station (www.thecomplaintstation.com)**—provides a central location to complain about issues related to companies' products, services, employment, and get rich quick scams.

- **Complaints.com Consumer Complaints (www.complaints.com)**—database of consumer complaints and consumer advocacy.

- **Baddealings.com (www.baddealings.com)**—forum and database on consumer complaints and scams on products and services.

2. Classic Car Problems

Classic Cars Inc. operates high-end automotive dealerships that offer luxury cars along with luxury service. The company is proud of its extensive inventory, top-of-the-line mechanics, and especially its exceptional service, which even includes a cappuccino bar at each dealership.

The company currently has 40 sales representatives at four locations. Each location maintains its own computer systems, and all sales representatives have their own contact management systems. This splintered approach to operations causes numerous problems including customer communication issues, pricing strategy issues, and inventory control issues. A few examples include:

- A customer shopping at one dealership can go to another dealership and receive a quote for a different price for the same car.
- Sales representatives are frequently stealing each other's customers and commissions.
- Sales representatives frequently send their customers to other dealerships to see specific cars and when the customer arrives, the car is not on the lot.
- Marketing campaigns are not designed to target specific customers; they are typically generic, such as 10 percent off a new car.
- If a sales representative quits, all of his or her customer information is lost.

Project Focus

You are working for Customer One, a small consulting company that specializes in CRM strategies. The owner of Classic Cars Inc., Tom Repicci, has hired you to help him formulate a strategy to put his company back on track. Develop a proposal for Tom detailing how a CRM system can alleviate the company's issues and create new opportunities.

3. Building Visibility

Visionary companies are building extended enterprises to best compete in the new Internet economy. An extended enterprise combines the Internet's power with new business structures and processes to eliminate old corporate boundaries and geographic restrictions. Networked supply chains create seamless paths of communication among partners, suppliers, manufacturers, retailers, and customers. Because of advances in manufacturing and distribution, the cost of developing new products and services is dropping, and time to market is speeding up. This has resulted in increasing customer demands, local and global competition, and increased pressure on the supply chain.

To stay competitive, companies must reinvent themselves so that the supply chain—sourcing and procurement, production scheduling, order fulfillment, inventory management, and customer care—is no longer a cost-based back-office exercise, but rather a flexible operation designed to effectively address today's challenges.

The Internet is proving an effective tool in transforming supply chains across all industries. Suppliers, distributors, manufacturers, and resellers now work together more closely and effectively than ever. Today's technology-driven supply chain enables customers to manage their own buying experiences, increases coordination and connectivity among supply partners, and helps reduce operating costs for every company in the chain.

Project Focus

In the past, assets were a crucial component of success in supply chain management. In today's market, however, a customer-centric orientation is key to retaining competitive advantage. Using the Internet and any other resources available, develop a strategic plan for implementing a networked, flexible supply chain management system for a start-up company of your choice. Research Netflix if you are unfamiliar with how start-up companies are changing the supply chain. Be sure that your supply chain integrates all partners—manufacturers, retailers, suppliers, carriers, and vendors—into a seamless unit and views customer relationship management as a key competitive advantage. There are several points to consider when creating your customer-centric supply chain strategy:

- Taking orders is only one part of serving customer needs.
- Businesses must fulfill the promise they make to customers by delivering products and information upon request—not when it is convenient for the company.

- Time to market is a key competitive advantage. Companies must ensure uninterrupted supply, and information about customer demands and activities is essential to this requirement.
- Cost is an important factor. Companies need to squeeze the costs from internal processes to make the final products less expensive.
- Reducing design-cycle times is critical, as this allows companies to get their products out more quickly to meet customer demand.

4. Netflix Your Business

Netflix reinvented the video rental business using supply chain technology. Netflix, established in 1998, is the largest online DVD rental service, offering flat-rate rental-by-mail to customers in the United States. Headquartered in Los Gatos, California, it has amassed a collection of 80,000 titles and over 6.8 million subscribers. Netflix has over 42 million DVDs and ships 1.6 million a day, on average, costing a reported $300 million a year in postage. On February 25, 2007, Netflix announced the delivery of its billionth DVD.

The company provides a monthly flat-fee service for the rental of DVD movies. A subscriber creates an ordered list, called a rental queue, of DVDs to rent. The DVDs are delivered individually via the United States Postal Service from an array of regional warehouses (44 in 29 states). A subscriber keeps a rented DVD as long as desired but has a limit on the number of DVDs (determined by subscription level) that can be checked out at any one time. To rent a new DVD, the subscriber mails the previous one back to Netflix in a prepaid mailing envelope. Upon receipt of the disc, Netflix ships another disc in the subscriber's rental queue.

Project Focus

Netflix's business is video rental, but it used technology to revamp the supply chain to completely disrupt the entire video rental industry. Reinvent IT is a statewide contest where college students can propose a new business that they will reinvent by revamping the supply chain (such as Netflix has done). You want to enter and win the contest. Reinvent a traditional business, such as the video rental business, using supply chain technologies.

5. Finding Shelf Space at Wal-Mart

Wal-Mart's business strategy of being a low-cost provider by managing its supply chain down to the minutiae has paid off greatly. Each week, approximately 100 million customers, or one-third of the U.S. population, visit Wal-Mart's U.S. stores. Wal-Mart is currently the world's largest retailer and the second largest corporation behind ExxonMobil. It was founded by Sam Walton in 1962 and is the largest private employer in the United States and Mexico. Wal-Mart is also the largest grocery retailer in the United States, with an estimated 20 percent of the retail grocery and consumables business, and the largest toy seller in the United States, with an estimated 45 percent of the retail toy business, having surpassed Toys "R" Us in the late 1990s.

Wal-Mart's business model is based on selling a wide variety of general merchandise at "always low prices." The reason Wal-Mart can offer such low prices is due to its innovative use of information technology tools to create its highly sophisticated supply chain. Over the past decade, Wal-Mart has famously invited its major suppliers to jointly develop powerful supply chain partnerships. These are designed to increase product flow efficiency and, consequently, Wal-Mart's profitability.

Many companies have stepped up to the challenge, starting with the well-known Wal-Mart/Procter & Gamble alliance, which incorporated vendor-managed inventory, category management, and other intercompany innovations. Wal-Mart's CFO became a key customer as P&G's objective became maximizing Wal-Mart's internal profitability. Unlike many other retailers, Wal-Mart does not charge a slotting fee to suppliers for their products to appear in the store. Alternatively, Wal-Mart focuses on selling more popular products and often pressures store managers to drop unpopular products in favor of more popular ones, as well as pressuring manufacturers to supply more popular products.

Project Focus

You are the owner of a high-end collectible toy company. You create everything from authentic sports figure replicas to famous musicians and movie characters including Babe Ruth, Hulk Hogan, Mick Jagger, Ozzy Osbourne, Alien, and the Terminator. It would be a huge win for your company if you could get your collectibles into Wal-Mart. Compile a strategic plan highlighting the steps required to approach Wal-Mart as your supply chain partner. Be sure to address the pros and cons of partnering with Wal-Mart, including the cost to revamp your current supply chain to meet Wal-Mart's tough supply chain requirements.

6. Shipping Problems

Entrepreneurship is in Alyssa Stuart's blood. Alyssa has been starting businesses since she was 10 years old, and she finally has the perfect business of custom-made furniture. Customers who visit Alyssa's shop can choose from a number of different fabrics and 50 different styles of couch and chair designs to create their custom-made furniture. Once the customer decides on a fabric pattern and furniture design, the information is sent to China where the furniture is built and shipped to the customer via the West Coast. Alyssa is excited about her business; all of her hard work has finally paid off as she has over 17,000 customers and 875 orders currently in the pipe.

Project Focus

Alyssa's business is booming. Her high quality products and outstanding customer service have created an excellent reputation for her business. But Alyssa's business is at risk of losing everything and she has come to you for help solving her supply chain issues.

Yesterday, a dockworkers' union strike began and shut down all of the West Coast shipping docks from San Francisco to Canada. Work will resume only when the union agrees to new labor contracts, which could take months. Alyssa has asked you to summarize the impact of the dock shutdown on her business and create a strategy to keep her business running, which is especially difficult since Alyssa guarantees 30-day delivery on all products or the product is free. What strategies do you recommend for Alyssa's business to continue working while her supply chain is disrupted by the dockworkers' strike?

7. Political Supply Chains

The U.S. government has crafted a deal with the United Arab Emirates (UAE) that would let a UAE-based firm, Dubai Ports World (DPW), run six major U.S. ports. If the approval is unchallenged, Dubai Ports World would run the ports of New York, New Jersey, Baltimore, New Orleans, Miami, and Philadelphia. Currently, London-based Peninsular and Oriental Steam Navigation Co. (P&O), the fourth largest port operator in the world, runs the six ports. But the $6.8 billion sale of P&O to DPW would effectively turn over North American operations to the government-owned company in Dubai.

Project Focus

Some citizens are worried that the federal government may be outsourcing U.S. port operations to a company prone to terrorist infiltration by allowing a firm from the United Arab Emirates to run port operations within the United States. You have been called in on an investigation to determine the potential effects on U.S. businesses' supply chains if these ports were shut down due to terrorist activities. The United Arab Emirates has had people involved in terrorism. In fact, some of its financial institutions laundered the money for the 9/11 terrorists. Create an argument for or against outsourcing these ports to the UAE. Be sure to detail the effect on U.S. businesses' supply chains if these ports are subjected to terrorist acts.

8. JetBlue on YouTube

JetBlue took an unusual and interesting CRM approach by using YouTube to apologize to its customers. JetBlue's founder and CEO, David Neeleman, apologized to customers via You-Tube after a very, very bad week for the airline: 1,100 flights canceled due to snow storms and thousands of irate passengers. Neeleman's unpolished, earnest delivery makes this apology worth accepting. But then again, we were not stuck on a tarmac for eight hours. With all of the new advances in technology and the many ways to reach customers, do you think using You-Tube is a smart approach? What else could JetBlue do to help gain back its customers' trust?

Project Focus

You are the founder and CEO of GoodDog, a large pet food manufacturing company. Recently, at least 16 pet deaths have been tied to tainted pet food, fortunately not manu-factured by your company. A recall of potentially deadly pet food has dog and cat owners studying their animals for even the slightest hint of illness and swamping veterinarians nationwide with calls about symptoms both real and imagined. Create a strategy for using YouTube as a vehicle to communicate with your customers as they fear for their pets' lives. Be sure to highlight the pros and cons of using YouTube as a customer communication vehicle. Are there any other new technologies you could use as a customer communica-tion vehicle that would be more effective than YouTube?

9. Second Life CRM

The virtual world of Second Life could become the first point of contact between compa-nies and customers and could transform the whole customer experience. Since it began hosting the likes of Adidas, Dell, Reuters, and Toyota, Second Life has become technology's equivalent of India or China—everyone needs an office and a strategy involving it to keep their shareholders happy. But beyond opening a shiny new building in the virtual world, what can such companies do with their virtual real estate?

Like many other big brands, PA Consulting has its own offices in Second Life and has learned that simply having an office to answer customer queries is not enough. Real peo-ple, albeit behind avatars, must be staffing the offices—in the same way having a website is not enough if there is not a call center to back it up when a would-be customer wants to speak to a human being. The consultants believe call centers could one day ask customers to follow up a phone call with them by moving the query into a virtual world.

Unlike many corporate areas in the virtual world, the National Basketball Association incorporates capabilities designed to keep fans coming back, including real-time 3-D diagrams of games as they are being played.

Project Focus

You are the executive director of CRM at StormPeak, an advanced AI company that devel-ops robots. You are in charge of overseeing the first virtual site being built in Second Life. Create a CRM strategy for doing business in a virtual world. Here are a few questions to get you started:

- How will customer relationships be different in a virtual world?
- What is your strategy for managing customer relationships in this new virtual environment?
- How will supporting Second Life customers differ from supporting traditional customers?
- How will supporting Second Life customers differ from supporting website customers?
- What customer security issues might you encounter in Second Life?
- What customer ethical issues might you encounter in Second Life?

Built to Last. By Jim Collins (Collins Business Essentials, 1994).

Drawing upon a six-year research project at the Stanford University Graduate School of Business, Jim Collins and Jerry I. Porras took 18 truly exceptional and long-lasting companies and studied each in direct comparison to one of its top competitors. They examined the companies from their very beginnings to the present day—as start-ups, as midsize companies, and as large corporations. Throughout, the authors asked: "What makes the truly exceptional companies different from the comparison companies and what were the common practices these enduringly great companies followed throughout their history?"

Filled with hundreds of specific examples and organized into a coherent framework of practical concepts that can be applied by managers and entrepreneurs at all levels, *Built to Last* provides a master blueprint for building organizations that will prosper long into the 21st century and beyond.

Good to Great. By Jim Collins (Collins Business Essentials, 2001).

Built to Last, the defining management study of the 90s showed how great companies triumph over time and how long-term sustained performance can be engineered into the DNA of an enterprise from the very beginning.

But what about the company that is not born with great DNA? How can good companies, mediocre companies, even bad companies achieve enduring greatness?

- The study: For years, this question preyed on the mind of Jim Collins. Are there companies that defy gravity and convert long-term mediocrity or worse into long-term superiority? And if so, what are the universal distinguishing characteristics that cause a company to go from good to great?

- The standards: Using tough benchmarks, Collins and his research team identified a set of elite companies that made the leap to great results and sustained those results for at least 15 years. How great? After the leap, the good-to-great companies generated cumulative stock returns that beat the general stock market by an average of seven times in 15 years, better than twice the results delivered by a composite index of the world's greatest companies, including Coca-Cola, Intel, General Electric, and Merck.

- The findings: The findings of the good-to-great study will surprise many readers and shed light on virtually every area of management strategy and practice.

- Level 5 leaders: The research team was shocked to discover the type of leadership required to achieve greatness.

- The hedgehog concept: To go from good to great requires transcending the curse of competence.

- A culture of discipline: When you combine a culture of discipline with an ethic of entrepreneurship, you get the magical alchemy of great results.

- Technology accelerators: Good-to-great companies think differently about the role of technology.

- The flywhere and the doom loop: Those who launch radical change programs and wrenching restructuring will almost certainly fail to make the leap.

The Anatomy of Buzz. By Emanuel Rosen (Doubleday, 2000).

Today's consumers are skeptical, and they suffer from information overload. The result: They'll probably ignore the expensive television and print ads your marketing team creates. So how do people decide which car to buy, or which fashions fit the image they are looking for, or what new techno-appliance is a must for their homes? The first section of this book discusses how buzz spreads and the huge social networks to which we all belong and what we know about how buzz spreads through them.

The second section identifies two factors that need to be there for buzz to spread. First, the product must be "contagious" in some way. For example, the game Trivial Pursuit was contagious because people who played it were compelled to demonstrate their knowledge to others. But contagion needs to be accelerated. That is the second factor. The marketers of this game executed a massive grassroots campaign that let people in numerous social networks get "infected" by the game and tell others.

The third part of the book describes techniques that companies have used to encourage their customers to talk: How BMW created buzz about the Z3 Roadster through a "sneak preview" in a James Bond movie. How the founders of Powerbar spread the word about their energy food by working with "network hubs" such as coaches and leading athletes.

Loyalty Rules! By Frederick F. Reichheld (Bain and Company, 2001).

Loyalty is at the heart of any company that boasts high productivity, solid profits, and sustained growth. For example, Harley-Davidson recovered from near bankruptcy by building loyal relationships with all stakeholders. And Southwest Airlines, which has never had a layoff, is the only consistently profitable major airline in the United States every year since 1973.

Frederick Reichheld, author of *Loyalty Rules!*, argues that loyalty is still the fuel that drives financial success—even, and perhaps especially, in today's volatile, high-speed economy—but that most organizations are running on empty. Why? Because leaders too often confuse profits with purpose, taking the low road to short-term gains at the expense of employees, customers, and, ultimately, investors. In a business environment that thrives on networks of mutually beneficial relationships, says Reichheld, it is the ability to build strong bonds of loyalty—not short-term profits—that has become the "acid test" of leadership.

Based on extensive research into companies from online start-ups to established institutions—including Harley-Davidson, Enterprise Rent-A-Car, Cisco Systems, Dell Computer, Intuit, and more—Reichheld reveals six bedrock principles of loyalty upon which leaders build enduring enterprises. Underscoring that success requires both understanding and measuring loyalty, he couples each principle with straightforward actions that drive measurement systems, compensation, organization, and strategy:

1. Play to win/win: Never profit at the expense of partners.
2. Be picky: Membership must be a privilege.
3. Keep it simple: Reduce complexity for speed and flexibility.
4. Reward the right results: Worthy partners deserve worthy goals.
5. Listen hard and talk straight: Insist on honest, two-way communication and learning.
6. Preach what you practice: Explain your principles, then live by them.

Providing tools for implementing the timeless principles of loyalty in a volatile economy, *Loyalty Rules!* is a practical guidebook for taking the high road in business—the only road that leads to lasting success.

Building Innovation

CHAPTER 13 Creating Innovative Organizations

13.1. Compare disruptive and sustaining technologies.
13.2. Explain how the Internet caused disruption among businesses.
13.3. Define the relationship between the Internet and the World Wide Web.

13.4. Describe the Internet's impact on information along with how these changes are affecting businesses.

Disruptive Technology

Polaroid, founded in 1937, produced the first instant camera in the late 1940s. The Polaroid camera was one of the most exciting technological advances the photography industry had ever seen. By using a Polaroid camera, customers no longer had to depend on others to develop their pictures. The technology was innovative and the product was high-end. The company eventually went public, becoming one of Wall Street's most prominent enterprises, with its stock trading above $60 in 1997. In 2002, the stock was down to 8 cents and the company declared bankruptcy.

How could a company like Polaroid, which had innovative technology and a captive customer base, go bankrupt? Perhaps company executives failed to use Porter's Five Forces to analyze the threat of substitute products or services. If they had, would they have noticed the two threats, one-hour film processing and digital cameras, that eventually stole Polaroid's market share? Would they have understood that their customers, people who want instant access to their pictures without having a third party involved, would be the first to use one-hour film processing and the first to purchase digital cameras? Could the company have found a way to compete with one-hour film processing and the digital camera to save Polaroid?

Most organizations face the same dilemma as Polaroid—the criteria an organization uses to make business decisions for its present business could possibly create issues for its future business. Essentially, what is best for the current business could ruin it in the long term. Some observers of our business environment have an ominous vision of the future—digital Darwinism. ***Digital Darwinism*** implies that organizations that cannot adapt to the new demands placed on them for surviving in the information age are doomed to extinction.

DISRUPTIVE VERSUS SUSTAINING TECHNOLOGY

A ***disruptive technology*** is a new way of doing things that initially does not meet the needs of existing customers. Disruptive technologies tend to open new markets and destroy old ones. A ***sustaining technology,*** on the other hand, produces an improved product customers are eager to buy, such as a faster car or larger hard drive. Sustaining technologies tend to provide us with better, faster, and cheaper products in established markets. Incumbent companies most often lead sustaining

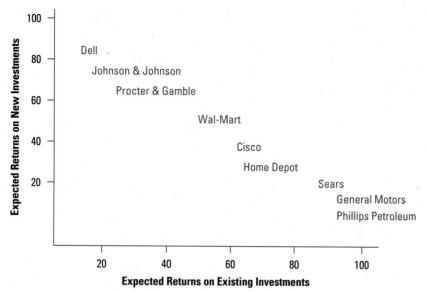

FIGURE 13.1

Disruptive and Sustaining Technologies

technology to market, but virtually never lead in markets opened by disruptive technologies. Figure 13.1 displays companies that are expecting future growth to occur from new investments (disruptive technology) and companies that are expecting future growth to occur from existing investments (sustaining technology).

Disruptive technologies typically cut into the low end of the marketplace and eventually evolve to displace high-end competitors and their reigning technologies. Sony is a perfect example of a company that entered the low end of the marketplace and eventually evolved to displace its high-end competitors. Sony started as a tiny company that built portable, battery-powered transistor radios people could carry around with them. The sound quality of Sony's transistor radios was poor because the transistor amplifiers were of lower quality than traditional vacuum tubes, which produce a better sound. But customers were willing to overlook sound quality for the convenience of portability. With the experience and revenue stream from the portables, Sony improved its technology to produce cheap, low-end transistor amplifiers that were suitable for home use and used those revenues to improve the technology further, which produced better radios.

The *Innovator's Dilemma*, a book by Clayton M. Christensen, discusses how established companies can take advantage of disruptive technologies without hindering existing relationships with customers, partners, and stakeholders. Companies like Xerox, IBM, Sears, and DEC all listened to existing customers, invested aggressively in technology, had their competitive antennae up, and still lost their market-dominant positions. Christensen states that these companies may have placed too much emphasis on satisfying customers' current needs, while neglecting to adopt new disruptive technology that will meet customers' future needs, thus causing the companies to eventually fail. Figure 13.2 highlights several companies that launched new businesses by capitalizing on disruptive technologies.

THE INTERNET—BUSINESS DISRUPTION

When the Internet was in its early days, no one had any idea how massive it would become. Computer companies did not think it would be a big deal; neither did the phone companies or cable companies. Difficult to access and operate, it seemed likely to remain an arcane tool of the Defense Department and academia. However,

FIGURE 13.2

Companies That
Capitalized on Disruptive
Technology

Company	Disruptive Technology
Charles Schwab	Online brokerage
Hewlett-Packard	Microprocessor-based computers; ink-jet printers
IBM	Minicomputers; personal computers
Intel	Low-end microprocessors
Intuit	QuickBooks software; TurboTax software; Quicken software
Microsoft	Internet-based computing; operating system software; SQL and Access database software
Oracle	Database software
Quantum	3.5-inch disks
Sony	Transistor-based consumer electronics

the Internet grew, and grew, and grew. It began with a handful of users in the mid-1960s and reached 1 billion by 2005 (see Figures 13.3 and 13.4). Estimates predict there will be more than 3 billion Internet users by 2010. Already, villages in Indonesia and India have Internet access before they have electricity.

Evolution of the Internet

During the Cold War in the mid-1960s, the U.S. military decided it needed a bomb-proof communications system, and thus the concept for the Internet was born. The system would link computers throughout the country allowing messages to get though even if a large section of the country was destroyed. In the early days, the only linked computers were at government think tanks and a few universities. The Internet was essentially an emergency military communications system operated by the Department of Defense's Advanced Research Project Agency (ARPA) and called ARPANET. Formally defined, the **Internet** is a global public network of computer networks that pass information from one to another using common

FIGURE 13.3

Internet Penetration by
World Region

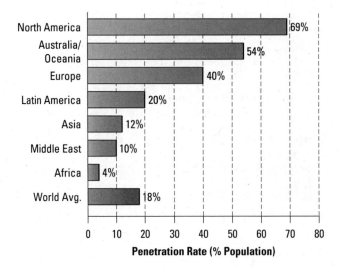

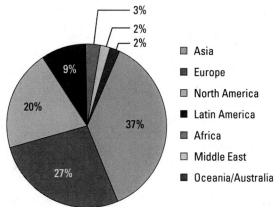

FIGURE 13.4

World Internet Users

- 3%
- 2%
- 2%
- 9%
- 20%
- 37%
- 27%

- Asia
- Europe
- North America
- Latin America
- Africa
- Middle East
- Oceania/Australia

computer protocols. ***Protocols*** are the standards that specify the format of data as well as the rules to be followed during transmission.

In time, every university in the United States that had defense-related funding installed ARPANET computers. Gradually, the Internet moved from a military pipeline to a communications tool for scientists. As more scholars came online, system administration transferred from ARPA to the National Science Foundation. Years later, businesses began using the Internet, and the administrative responsibilities were once again transferred. Today, no one party operates the Internet; however, several entities oversee the Internet and set standards including:

- Internet Engineering Task Force (IETF): The protocol engineering and development arm of the Internet.
- Internet Architecture Board (IAB): Responsible for defining the overall architecture of the Internet, providing guidance and broad direction to the IETF.
- Internet Engineering Steering Group (IESG): Responsible for technical management of IETF activities and the Internet standards process.

EVOLUTION OF THE WORLD WIDE WEB

People often interchange the terms *Internet* and the *World Wide Web,* but these terms are not synonymous. Throughout the 1960s, 1970s, and 1980s, the Internet was primarily used by the Department of Defense to support activities such as email and transferring files. The Internet was restricted to noncommercial activities, and its users included government employees, researchers, university professors, and students. The World Wide Web changed the purpose and use of the Internet.

The ***World Wide Web (WWW)*** is a global hypertext system that uses the Internet as its transport mechanism. ***Hypertext transport protocol (HTTP)*** is the Internet standard that supports the exchange of information on the WWW. By defining universal resource locators (URLs) and how they can be used to retrieve resources anywhere on the Internet, HTTP enables web authors to embed hyperlinks in web documents. HTTP defines the process by which a web client, called a browser, originates a request for information and sends it to a web server, a program designed to respond to HTTP requests and provide the desired information. In a hypertext system, users navigate by clicking a hyperlink embedded in the current document. The action displays a second document in the same or a separate browser window. The web has quickly become the ideal medium for publishing information on the Internet and serves as the platform for the electronic economy. Figure 13.5 displays the reasons for the popularity and growth in the WWW.

FIGURE 13.5

Reasons for World Wide
Web Growth

Reasons for Growth of the World Wide Web
■ The microcomputer revolution made it possible for an average person to own a computer.
■ Advancements in networking hardware, software, and media made it possible for business PCs to be inexpensively connected to larger networks.
■ Browser software such as Microsoft's Internet Explorer and Netscape Navigator gave computer users an easy-to-use graphical interface to find, download, and display web pages.
■ The speed, convenience, and low cost of email have made it an incredibly popular tool for business and personal communications.
■ Basic web pages are easy to create and extremely flexible.

The WWW remained primarily text-based until 1991 when two events occurred that would forever change the web and the amount and quality of information available (see Figure 13.6). First, Tim Berners-Lee built the first website on August 6, 1991 (http://info.cern.ch/—the site has been archived). The site provided details about the World Wide Web including how to build a browser and set up a web server. It also housed the world's first web directory, since Berners-Lee later maintained a list of other websites apart from his own.

Second, Marc Andreesen developed a new computer program called the NCSA Mosaic (National Center for Supercomputing Applications at the University of Illinois) and gave it away! The browser made it easier to access the websites that had started to appear. Soon websites contained more than just text; they also had sound and video files (see Figure 13.7). These pages, written in the hypertext markup language (HTML), have links that allow the user to quickly move from one document to another, even when the documents are stored in different computers. Web browsers read the HTML text and convert it into a web page.

By eliminating time and distance, the Internet makes it possible to perform business in ways not previously imaginable. The *digital divide* is when those with access to technology have great advantages over those without access to technology. People living in the village of Siroha, India, must bike five miles to find a telephone. For over 700 million rural people living in India, the digital divide was a way of life,

FIGURE 13.6

The Internet's Impact on
Information

Internet's Impact on Information	
Easy to compile	Searching for information on products, prices, customers, suppliers, and partners is faster and easier when using the Internet.
Increased richness	*Information richness* refers to the depth and breadth of information transferred between customers and businesses. Businesses and customers can collect and track more detailed information when using the Internet.
Increased reach	*Information reach* refers to the number of people a business can communicate with, on a global basis. Businesses can share information with numerous customers all over the world.
Improved content	A key element of the Internet is its ability to provide dynamic relevant content. Buyers need good content descriptions to make informed purchases, and sellers use content to properly market and differentiate themselves from the competition. Content and product description establish the common understanding between both parties to the transaction. As a result, the reach and richness of that content directly affects the transaction.

until recently. Media Lab Asia sells telephony and email services via a mobile Internet kiosk mounted on a bicycle, which is known as an "info-thelas." The kiosk has an onboard computer equipped with an antenna for Internet service and a specially designed all-day battery. Over 2,000 villages have purchased the kiosk for $1,200, and another 600,000 villages are interested.

WEB 2.0

The impact of Web 2.0 is just starting to become apparent. **Web 2.0** is a set of economic, social, and technology trends that collectively form the basis for the next generation of the Internet—a more mature, distinctive medium characterized by user participation, openness, and network effects. The term does not mean a new version of the WWW, but refers to changes in the ways software developers and users make use of the web as a platform. According to Tim O'Reilly, "Web 2.0 is the business revolution in the computer industry caused by the move to the Internet as platform, and an attempt to understand the rules for success on that new platform." Figure 13.8 displays O'Reilly's version of the move from Web 1.0 to Web 2.0, and Figure 13.9 displays the timeline of Web 1.0 and Web 2.0.

Web 2.0 is more than just the latest technology buzzword; it is a transformative force that is catapulting companies across all industries toward a new way of performing business. Companies that take advantage of the numerous opportunities associated with Web 2.0 can achieve the coveted first-mover advantage in their

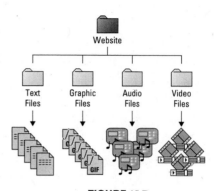

FIGURE 13.7

File Formats Offered over the WWW

	Web 1.0		Web 2.0
	Doubleclick	-->	Google Adsense
	Ofoto	-->	Flickr
	Akamai	-->	Bittorrent
	MP3.Com	-->	Napster
	Britannica Online	-->	Wikipedia
	Personal Websites	-->	Blogging
	Evite	-->	Upcoming.Org And EVDB
	Domain Name Speculation	-->	Search Engine Optimization
	Page Views	-->	Cost Per Click
	Screen Scraping	-->	Web Services
	Publishing	-->	Participation
	Content Management Systems	-->	Wikis
	Directories (Taxonomy)	-->	Tagging ("Folksonomy")
	Stickiness	-->	Syndication

FIGURE 13.8

The Move from Web 1.0 to Web 2.0

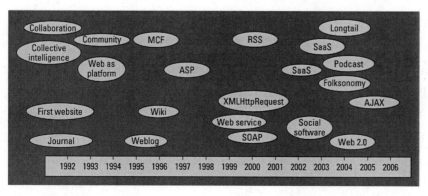

FIGURE 13.9

Timeline of Web 1.0

markets. A few reasons for this change include the following raw demographic and technological drivers:

- Over 1 billion individuals have Internet access.
- Mobile devices outnumber desktop computers by a factor of two.
- Always-on broadband connections account for over 50 percent of all U.S. Internet access.

Merging these drivers with the basic rules of social networking produces Web 2.0—the next-generation, user-driven, intelligent web. A few examples of Web 2.0 include:

- In the first quarter of 2006, MySpace.com signed up 280,000 new users each day and had the second most Internet traffic of any website.
- By the second quarter of 2006, 50 million blogs were created—new ones were added at a rate of two per second.
- In 2005, eBay conducted 8 billion web services transactions.

THE FUTURE–WEB 3.0

Web 3.0 has many different meanings and basically describes the evolution of web usage and interaction among several separate paths. Web 3.0 really transforms the web into a database, making content accessible by multiple nonbrowser applications and leveraging artificial intelligence technologies, or the semantic web. The *semantic web* is an evolving extension of the WWW in which web content can be expressed not only in natural language, but also in a format that can be read and used by software agents, thus permitting them to find, share, and integrate information more easily. It derives from W3C director Sir Tim Berners-Lee's vision of the web as a universal medium for data, information, and knowledge exchange.

OPENING CASE STUDY QUESTIONS

1. Do you believe the Ironman has used disruptive technology to change the way athletes participate in sports? Why or why not?
2. What types of Web 2.0 technologies could WTC use on the Ironman.com website?
3. What types of ethical dilemmas might WTC face in deploying real-time video over the Internet?
4. What types of security issues does WTC need to address?

Chapter Thirteen Case: Failing to Innovate

It is a sad but common tale—a dynamic company comes up with an innovative new product that utilizes cutting-edge technology in an exciting way that generates lots of hype and attention. But for some reason this new product fails to click with the masses and falls into oblivion, only to see other products gain massive success by following in its footsteps.

It's not always a case of right technology at the wrong time. Sometimes these first movers failed to build on their innovation, instead sitting on their initial achievements and letting more nimble competitors refine their idea into something more attractive and functional. And some just made too many mistakes to succeed.

Obtaining the first-mover advantage is critical to any business that wants to compete in the Internet economy. However, gaining a first-mover advantage is typically temporary, and without remaining innovative the company can soon fail. Here is a list of the top 10 first movers that flopped, according to Jim Rapoza of eWeek.

1. **Apple Newton PDA**—When it was launched in the early 90s, the Apple Newton was first lauded but later mocked because of its failings (it even had the honor of being spoofed on *The Simpsons*). But one can draw a straight line from the Newton to current products such as tablet PCs, smart phones, and the new Apple iPhone.

2. **PointCast**—In 1997, one of the hottest products found on the desktop of nearly every IT worker was PointCast, which delivered selected news items directly to the desktop. It quickly launched the "push" craze, which just as quickly imploded spectacularly. But today's RSS and news feeds all owe a debt to PointCast.

3. **Gopher Protocol**—It was so close. Launched just before the web itself, Gopher quickly became popular in universities and business. Using search technology, it worked very much like a website, but it could not compete with the web itself.

4. **VisiCalc**—Often lauded as the first killer application for the PC, the VisiCalc spreadsheet was a must-have for early PC-enabled businesses but quickly fell behind more polished spreadsheets from Lotus and Microsoft.

5. **Atari**—For those of a certain age, the word *Atari* is synonymous with video games. The pioneer in home gaming consoles failed to innovate in the face of more nimble competitors.

6. **Diamond Rio**—For $200 and with 32MB of RAM (with a SmartMedia slot for memory expansion), the Rio helped launch the MP3 revolution. That is, until white earbuds and a thing called the iPod took over.

7. **Netscape Navigator**—Netscape Navigator was essentially the web for users in the early to mid-1990s. But Netscape could not withstand the Microsoft onslaught, along with plenty of mistakes the company made itself, and now only lives on as the original basis of the Mozilla browsers.

8. **AltaVista**—Not the first search engine, but the first to use many of the natural language technologies common today and the first to gain real web popularity, AltaVista failed to keep up with technological changes.

9. **Ricochet Networks**—Nothing created geek lust like sitting next to someone who had a Ricochet card plugged into the laptop. Look, she is in a cab and accessing the Internet at ISDN speeds! But Ricochet never expanded to enough cities to be a serious player.

10. **IBM Simon Phone**—The iPhone's $499 price is nothing compared with the $900 price tag the IBM Simon had when it finally became available in 1994. But it pioneered most of the features found in today's smart phones and even beat the iPhone when it came to a buttonless touch-screen interface.

Questions

1. If these companies all had a first-mover advantage, then why did the products fail?
2. For each of the above determine if the technology used was disruptive or sustaining.
3. Choose one of the products above and determine what the company could have done to prevent the product from failing.
4. Can you name another technology product that failed? Why did it fail? What could the company have done differently for it to succeed?

CHAPTER 14 Ebusiness

14.1. Compare ecommerce and ebusiness.
14.2. Compare the four types of ebusiness models.

14.3. Describe the benefits and challenges associated with ebusiness.
14.4. Explain the differences among eshops, emalls, and online auctions.

Ebusiness

Tom Anderson and Chris DeWolf started MySpace, a social networking website that offers its members information about the independent music scene around the country representing both Internet culture and teenage culture. Musicians sign up for free MySpace home pages where they can post tour dates, songs, and lyrics. Fans sign up for their own web pages to link to favorite bands and friends. MySpace is the world's second most popular English-language website with over 100 million users.

One of the biggest benefits of the Internet is how it enables organizations to perform business with anyone, anywhere, anytime. *Ecommerce* is the buying and selling of goods and services over the Internet. Ecommerce refers only to online transactions. *Ebusiness,* derived from the term *ecommerce,* is the conducting of business on the Internet, not only buying and selling, but also serving customers and collaborating with business partners. The primary difference between ecommerce and ebusiness is that ebusiness also refers to online exchanges of information, for example, a manufacturer allowing its suppliers to monitor production schedules or a financial institution allowing its customers to review their banking, credit card, and mortgage accounts.

In the past few years, ebusiness seems to have permeated every aspect of daily life. Both individuals and organizations have embraced Internet technologies to enhance productivity, maximize convenience, and improve communications globally. From banking to shopping to entertainment, the Internet has become integral to daily life. Figure 14.1 provides examples of a few of the industries using ebusiness.

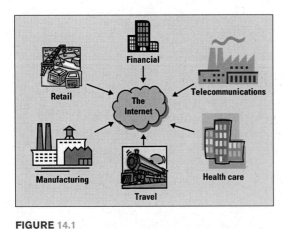

FIGURE 14.1

Overview of Several Industries Using Ebusiness

Ebusiness Models

An *ebusiness model* is an approach to conducting electronic business on the Internet. Ebusiness transactions take place between two major entities—businesses and consumers. All ebusiness activities happen within the framework of two types of

	Business	**Consumer**
Business	B2B	B2C
Consumer	C2B	C2C

Ebusiness Term	Definition
Business-to-business (B2B)	Applies to businesses buying from and selling to each other over the Internet.
Business-to-consumer (B2C)	Applies to any business that sells its products or services to consumers over the Internet.
Consumer-to-business (C2B)	Applies to any consumer that sells a product or service to a business over the Internet.
Consumer-to-consumer (C2C)	Applies to sites primarily offering goods and services to assist consumers interacting with each other over the Internet.

FIGURE 14.2

Basic Ebusiness Models

business relationships: (1) the exchange of products and services between businesses (business-to-business, or B2B) and (2) the exchange of products and services with consumers (business-to-consumer, or B2C) (see Figure 14.2).

The primary difference between B2B and B2C are the customers; B2B customers are other businesses while B2C markets to consumers. Overall, B2B relations are more complex and have higher security needs; plus B2B is the dominant ebusiness force, representing 80 percent of all online business. Figure 14.3 illustrates all the ebusiness models: business-to-business, business-to-consumer, consumer-to-consumer, and consumer-to-business.

EBags is a true ebusiness success story. It is thriving as the world's leading online provider of bags and accessories for all lifestyles. With 180 brands and over 8,000 products, eBags has sold more than 4 million bags since its launch in March 1999. It carries a complete line of premium and popular brands, including Samsonite, Jan-Sport, The North Face, Liz Claiborne, and Adidas. The company has received several awards for excellence in online retailing including the Circle of Excellence Platinum Award from Bizrate.com, Web Site of the Year from *Catalog Age* magazine, and Email Marketer of the Year from ClickZ.MessageMedia. This success can

FIGURE 14.3

Ebusiness Models

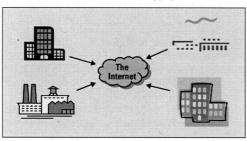

Business-to-Business (B2B)

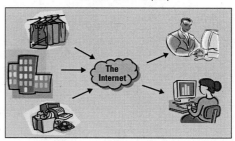

Business-to-Consumer (B2C)

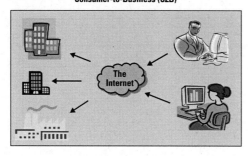

Consumer-to-Business (C2B)

Consumer-to-Consumer (C2C)

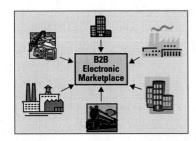

be attributed to eBags' commitment to providing each customer with superior service, 24 hours a day, 365 days a year, including convenient, real-time UPS order tracking. According to Jon Nordmark, CEO of eBags.com, "From a customer perspective, we've spent a great deal of time developing pioneering ways to guide our shoppers to the bags and accessories that enhance their lifestyles through function and fashion."

BUSINESS-TO-BUSINESS (B2B)

Business-to-business (B2B) applies to businesses buying from and selling to each other over the Internet. Online access to data, including expected shipping date, delivery date, and shipping status, provided either by the seller or a third-party provider, is widely supported by B2B models. Electronic marketplaces represent a new wave in B2B ebusiness models. ***Electronic marketplaces,*** or ***emarketplaces,*** are interactive business communities providing a central market space where multiple buyers and sellers can engage in ebusiness activities (see Figure 14.4). They present structures for conducting commercial exchange, consolidating supply chains, and creating new sales channels. Their primary goal is to increase market efficiency by tightening and automating the relationship between buyers and sellers. Existing emarketplaces allow access to various mechanisms in which to buy and sell almost anything, from services to direct materials.

BUSINESS-TO-CONSUMER (B2C)

Business-to-consumer (B2C) applies to any business that sells its products or services to consumers over the Internet. Carfax has been in the vehicle history report business for 20 years with an original customer base of used-car dealers. "The Internet was just a new way for us to reach the consumer market," Carfax President Dick Raines said. Carfax spent $20 million on print and TV ads to attract customers to its website. Customers can purchase a Carfax report for $14.95 or six days of reports for $19.95. Carfax has now launched a partnership program for small auto dealers' websites and a cash-back program offering customers 20 percent of revenues received for their referrals. "We continue to look for more and more ways to add value," Raines said. Common B2C ebusiness models include eshops and emalls.

Eshop

An ***eshop,*** sometimes referred to as an ***estore*** or ***etailer,*** is a version of a retail store where customers can shop at any hour of the day without leaving their home or office. These online stores sell and support a variety of products and services. The online businesses channeling their goods and services via the Internet only, such as Amazon.com, are called *pure plays.* The others are an extension of traditional retail outlets that sell online as well as through a traditional physical store. They are generally known as "bricks and clicks" or "clicks and mortar" organizations, such as the Gap (www.gap.com) and Best Buy (www.bestbuy.com) (see Figure 14.5).

Business Types	
Brick-and-mortar business	A business that operates in a physical store without an Internet presence.
Pure-play (virtual) business	A business that operates on the Internet only without a physical store. Examples include Amazon.com and Expedia.com.
Click-and-mortar business	A business that operates in a physical store and on the Internet. Examples include REI and Barnes and Noble.

Online Auctions	
Electronic Auction (eauction)	Sellers and buyers solicit consecutive bids from each other and prices are determined dynamically.
Forward Auction	An auction that sellers use as a selling channel to many buyers and the highest bid wins.
Reverse Auction	An auction that buyers use to purchase a product or service, selecting the seller with the lowest bid.

FIGURE 14.6

Online Auctions

Emall

An *emall* consists of a number of eshops; it serves as a gateway through which a visitor can access other eshops. An emall may be generalized or specialized depending on the products offered by the eshops it hosts. Revenues for emall operators include membership fees from participating eshops, advertising, and possibly a fee on each transaction if the emall operator also processes payments. Eshops in emalls benefit from brand reinforcement and increased traffic as visiting one shop on the emall often leads to browsing "neighboring" shops. An example of an emall is the Arizona emall www.1az1.com/shopping.

CONSUMER-TO-BUSINESS (C2B)

Consumer-to-business (C2B) applies to any consumer that sells a product or service to a business over the Internet. One example of this ebusiness model is Priceline.com where bidders (or customers) set their prices for items such as airline tickets or hotel rooms, and a seller decides whether to supply them. The demand for C2B ebusiness will increase over the next few years due to customers' desires for greater convenience and lower prices.

CONSUMER-TO-CONSUMER (C2C)

Consumer-to-consumer (C2C) applies to sites primarily offering goods and services to assist consumers interacting with each other over the Internet. The Internet's most successful C2C online auction website, eBay, links like-minded buyers and sellers for a small commission. Figure 14.6 displays the different types of online auctions.

C2C online communities, or virtual communities, interact via email groups, web-based discussion forums, or chat rooms. C2C business models are consumer-driven and opportunities are available to satisfy most consumers' needs, ranging from finding a mortgage to job hunting. They are global swap shops based on customer-centered communication. One C2C community, KazaA, allows users to download MP3 music files, enabling users to exchange files. Figure 14.7 highlights the different types of C2C communities that are thriving on the Internet.

C2C Communities
■ **Communities of interest**—People interact with each other on specific topics, such as golfing and stamp collecting.
■ **Communities of relations**—People come together to share certain life experiences, such as cancer patients, senior citizens, and car enthusiasts.
■ **Communities of fantasy**—People participate in imaginary environments, such as fantasy football teams and playing one-on-one with Michael Jordan.

FIGURE 14.7

C2C Communities

Ebusiness Benefits and Challenges

According to an NUA Internet Survey, the Internet links more than 1 billion people worldwide. Experts predict that global Internet usage will have nearly tripled between 2006 and 2010, making ebusiness a more significant factor in the global economy. As ebusiness improves, organizations will experience benefits and challenges alike. Figure 14.8 details ebusiness benefits for an organization.

The Internet is forcing organizations to refocus their information systems from the inside out. A growing number of companies are already using the Internet to streamline their business processes, procure materials, sell products, automate customer service, and create new revenue streams. Although the benefits of ebusiness systems are enticing, developing, deploying, and managing these systems is not always easy. Unfortunately, ebusiness is not something a business can just go out and buy. Figure 14.9 details the challenges facing ebusiness.

A key element of emarketplaces is their ability to provide not only transaction capabilities but also dynamic, relevant content to trading partners. The original ebusiness websites provided shopping cart capabilities built around product catalogs. As a result of the complex emarketplace that must support existing business processes and systems, content is becoming even more critical for emarketplaces. Buyers need good content description to make informed purchases, and sellers use content to properly market and differentiate themselves from the competition. Content and product description establish the common understanding between both parties to the transaction. As a result, the accessibility, usability, accuracy, and richness of that content directly affect the transaction. Figure 14.10 displays the different benefits and challenges of various emarketplace revenue models.

Mashups

A *web mashup* is a website or web application that uses content from more than one source to create a completely new service. The term is typically used in the context of music; putting Jay-Z lyrics over a Radiohead song makes something old become new. The web version of a mashup allows users to mix map data, photos, video, news feeds, blog entries and so on. Content used in mashups is typically sourced from an *application programming interface (API),* which is a set of routines, protocols, and tools for building software applications. A good API makes

FIGURE 14.8

Ebusiness Benefits

Ebusiness Benefits	
Highly Accessible	Businesses can operate 24 hours a day, 7 days a week, 365 days a year.
Increased Customer Loyalty	Additional channels to contact, respond to, and access customers helps contribute to customer loyalty.
Improved Information Content	In the past, customers had to order catalogs or travel to a physical facility before they could compare price and product attributes. Electronic catalogs and web pages present customers with updated information in real time about goods, services, and prices.
Increased Convenience	Ebusiness automates and improves many of the activities that make up a buying experience.
Increased Global Reach	Businesses, both small and large, can reach new markets.
Decreased Cost	The cost of conducting business on the Internet is substantially less than traditional forms of business communication.

Ebusiness Challenges	
Protecting Consumers	Consumers must be protected against unsolicited goods and communication, illegal or harmful goods, insufficient information about goods or their suppliers, invasion of privacy, and cyberfraud.
Leveraging Existing Systems	Most companies already use information technology to conduct business in non-Internet environments, such as marketing, order management, billing, inventory, distribution, and customer service. The Internet represents an alternative and complementary way to do business, but it is imperative that ebusiness systems integrate existing systems in a manner that avoids duplicating functionality and maintains usability, performance, and reliability.
Increasing Liability	Ebusiness exposes suppliers to unknown liabilities because Internet commerce law is vaguely defined and differs from country to country. The Internet and its use in ebusiness have raised many ethical, social, and political issues, such as identity theft and information manipulation.
Providing Security	The Internet provides universal access, but companies must protect their assets against accidental or malicious misuse. System security, however, must not create prohibitive complexity or reduce flexibility. Customer information also needs to be protected from internal and external misuse. Privacy systems should safeguard the personal information critical to building sites that satisfy customer and business needs. A serious deficiency arises from the use of the Internet as a marketing means. Sixty percent of Internet users do not trust the Internet as a payment channel. Making purchases via the Internet is considered unsafe by many. This issue affects both the business and the consumer. However, with encryption and the development of secure websites, security is becoming less of a constraint for ebusinesses.
Adhering to Taxation Rules	The Internet is not yet subject to the same level of taxation as traditional businesses. While taxation should not discourage consumers from using electronic purchasing channels, it should not favor Internet purchases over store purchases either. Instead, a tax policy should provide a level playing field for traditional retail businesses, mail-order companies, and Internet-based merchants. The Internet marketplace is rapidly expanding, yet it remains mostly free from traditional forms of taxation. In one recent study, uncollected state and local sales taxes from ebusiness were projected to exceed $60 billion in 2008.

FIGURE 14.9

Ebusiness Challenges

it easier to develop a program by providing all the building blocks. A programmer puts the blocks together. Most operating environments, such as Microsoft Windows, provide an API so that programmers can write applications consistent with the operating environment. Many people experimenting with mashups are using Microsoft, Google, eBay, Amazon, Flickr, and Yahoo APIs, which has led to the creation of mashup editors. ***Mashup editors*** are WSYIWYGs (What You See Is What You Get) for mashups. They provide a visual interface to build a mashup, often allowing the user to drag and drop data points into a web application.

Whoever thought technology could help sell bananas? Dole Organic now places three-digit farm codes on each banana and creates a mashup using Google Earth and its banana database. Socially and environmentally conscious buyers can plug the numbers into Dole's website and look at a bio of the farm where the bananas were raised. The site tells the story of the farm and its surrounding community, lists its organic certifications, posts some photos, and offers a link to satellite images of the farm in Google Earth. Customers can personally monitor the production and treatment of their fruit from the tree to the grocer. The process assures customers

Revenue Models	Advantages	Limitations
Transaction fees	■ Can be directly tied to savings (both process and price savings) ■ Important revenue source when high level of liquidity (transaction volume) is reached	■ If process savings are not completely visible, use of the system is discouraged (incentive to move transactions offline) ■ Transaction fees likely to decrease with time
License fees	■ Creates incentives to do many transactions ■ Customization and back-end integration leads to lock-in of participants	■ Up-front fee is a barrier to entry for participants ■ Price differentiation is complicated
Subscription fees	■ Creates incentives to do transactions ■ Price can be differentiated ■ Possibility to build additional revenue from new user groups	■ Fixed fee is a barrier to entry for participants
Fees for value-added services	■ Service offering can be differentiated ■ Price can be differentiated ■ Possibility to build additional revenue from established and new user groups (third parties)	■ Cumbersome process for customers to continually evaluate new services
Advertising fees	■ Well-targeted advertisements can be perceived as value-added content by trading participants ■ Easy to implement	■ Limited revenue potential ■ Overdone or poorly targeted advertisements can be disturbing elements on the website

FIGURE 14.10

The Benefits and Challenges of Various Emarketplace Revenue Models

that their bananas have been raised to proper organic standards on an environmentally friendly, holistically minded plantation. Other interesting mashups include:

- **1001 Secret Fishing Holes:** Over a thousand fishing spots in national parks, wildlife refuges, lakes, campgrounds, historic trails, etc. (Google Maps API).
- **25 Best Companies to Work For:** Map of the 100 best U.S. companies to work for as rated by *Fortune* magazine (Google Maps API).
- **Album Covers:** Uses the Amazon API and an Ajax-style user interface to retrieve CD/DVD covers from the Amazon catalog (Amazon eCommerce API).
- **Gawker:** A handy mashup for keeping up with celebrity sightings in New York City. Readers are encouraged to email as soon as the celeb is spotted (Google Maps API).
- **Gigul8tor:** Provides a data entry page where bands can enter information about upcoming gigs and venues. Gigul8tor displays a list of possible locations depending on the venue engine and enters event information right into Eventful in an interface designed just for bands. It shows how different user interfaces could be built in front of Eventful with mashup techniques.
- **GBlinker:** A Google pin wired to a serial port so it flashes when email arrives.
- **OpenKapow:** Offers a platform for creating web-based APIs, feeds, and HTML snippets from any website, taking mashup possibilities way beyond the more than 300 APIs offered on ProgrammableWeb.
- **The Hype Machine:** Combines blog posts from a set of curated music blogs with Amazon sales data and upcoming events. The Hype Machine tracks songs and discussion posted on the best blogs about music. It integrates with iTunes to take customers right from the web page to the track they are interested in. If the customer prefers buying through Amazon, The Hype Machine figures out what CD page to display.

- **Zillow:** Sophisticated home valuation tools with 65 million listings and extensive data on comparables (Microsoft Virtual Earth API).
- **ProgrammableWeb:** The favorite community website of mashup developers provides comprehensive listings of APIs available on the web and includes forums where developers can discuss how to best use them.

OPENING CASE STUDY QUESTIONS

1. Identify the type of ebusiness model WTC is using for the Ironman and explain why it has been so successful.

2. What advantages would WTC have in opening up an Ironman emarketplace?

3. What would be an example of WTC using a mashup for the Ironman?

Chapter Fourteen Case: eBiz

Amazing things are happening on the Internet, things nobody would believe. Here are two stories that demonstrate how innovation, creativity, and a great idea can turn the Internet into a cash cow.

A Million Dollar Homepage

The Million Dollar Homepage is a website conceived by Alex Tew, a 21-year-old student from Cricklade, Wiltshire, England, to help raise money for his university education. Launched on August 26, 2005, the website is said to have generated a gross income of $1,037,100 and has a current Google PageRank of 7.

The index page of the site consists of a 1000 by 1000 pixel grid (1 million pixels), on which he sells image-based links for $1 per pixel, in minimum 10 by 10 blocks. A person who buys one or more of these pixel blocks can design a tiny image that will be displayed on the block, decide which URL the block will link to, and write a slogan that appears when the cursor hovers over the link. The aim of the site was to sell all of the pixels in the image, thus generating $1 million of income for the creator, which seems to have been accomplished. On January 1, 2006, the final 1,000 pixels left were put up for auction on eBay. The auction closed on January 11 with the winning bid of $38,100. This brought the final tally to $1,037,100 in gross income. See the Million Dollar Homepage on the next page.

One Red Paperclip

The website One Red Paperclip was created by Kyle MacDonald, a Canadian blogger who bartered his way from a single paper clip to a house in a series of trades spanning almost one year. MacDonald began with one red paper clip on July 14, 2005. By July 5, 2006, a chain of bartering had ultimately led to trading a movie role for a two-story farmhouse in Kipling, Saskatchewan. On July 7, 2006—almost exactly one year after MacDonald began his experiment—the deed to the house was signed. In September, at the housewarming party where 12 of the 14 traders were present, he proposed to his girlfriend and she accepted. The wedding ring was made from the original red paper clip he got back from the first woman to have agreed to trade with him.

Following is the timeline, based on the website and as summarized by the BBC:

- On July 14, 2005, MacDonald went to Vancouver and traded the paper clip for a fish-shaped pen.

- MacDonald then traded the pen the same day for a hand-sculpted doorknob from Seattle, Washington, which he nicknamed Knob-T.

- On July 25, 2005, MacDonald traveled to Amherst, Massachusetts, with a friend to trade the Knob-T for a Coleman camp stove (with fuel).

- On September 24, 2005, he went to San Clemente, California, and traded the camp stove for a Honda generator, from a U.S. Marine.

- On November 16, 2005, MacDonald made a second (and successful) attempt (after having the generator confiscated by the New York City Fire Department) in Maspeth, Queens, to trade the generator for an "instant party": an empty keg, an IOU for filling the keg with the beer of the holder's choice, and a neon Budweiser sign.

- On December 8, 2005, he traded the "instant party" to Quebec comedian and radio personality Michel Barrette for a Ski-doo snowmobile.

- Within a week of that, MacDonald traded the snowmobile for a two-person trip to Yahk, British Columbia, in February 2006.

- On or about January 7, 2006, the second person on the trip to Yahk traded MacDonald a cube van for the privilege.

- On or about February 22, 2006, he traded the cube van for a recording contract with Metal Works in Toronto.

- On or about April 11, 2006, MacDonald traded the recording contract to Jody Gnant for a year's rent in Phoenix, Arizona.

- On or about April 26, 2006, he traded the one year's rent in Phoenix, Arizona, for one afternoon with Alice Cooper.
- On or about May 26, 2006, MacDonald traded the one afternoon with Alice Cooper for a KISS motorized snow globe.
- On or about June 2, 2006, he traded the KISS motorized snow globe to Corbin Bernsen for a role in the film *Donna on Demand*.
- On or about July 5, 2006, MacDonald traded the movie role for a two-story farmhouse in Kipling, Saskatchewan.

Questions

1. How else can you use the Internet to raise money?
2. What types of businesses could benefit from trading on the Internet?
3. Can you think of any other disruptive or nontraditional ways that you could use the Internet?

Transforming Organizations

CHAPTER 17

Building Software to Support an Agile Organization

LEARNING OUTCOMES

17.1. Identify the business benefits associated with successful software development.

17.2. Describe the seven phases of the systems development life cycle.

17.3. Summarize the different software development methodologies.

17.4. Define the relationship between the systems development life cycle and software development.

17.5. Compare the waterfall methodology and the agile methodology.

17.6 Explain why software problems are business problems.

The Crucial Role of Software

Every type of organization in business today, from farming to pharmaceutical to franchising, is affected by technology and the software developed to operate, improve, or innovate it. Companies are impacted by software solutions that enable them to improve their cost structure, manage people better, and develop and deliver new products to market. These organizational improvements help companies sustain their competitive advantage and position in the marketplace. They can solve complex problems, dislodge competitors, or create exciting opportunities to pursue. Organizations must learn and mature in their ability to identify, build, and implement systems to remain competitive.

Essentially, software built correctly can support nimble organizations and can transform as the organization and its business transforms. Software that effectively meets employee needs will help an organization become more productive and enhance decision making. Software that does not meet employee needs might have a damaging effect on productivity and can even cause a business to fail. Employee involvement along with using the right implementation methodology when developing software is critical to the success of an organization.

Developing Software

Nike's SCM system failure, which spun out of control to the tune of $400 million, is legendary. Nike blamed the system failure on its SCM vendor, i2 Technologies. Nike states that i2 Technologies' demand and supply planning module created serious inventory problems. The i2 deployment, part of a multimillion-dollar ebusiness upgrade, caused Nike CEO Philip Knight to famously say, "This is what we get for our $400 million?" The SCM vendor saw its stock plummet with the Nike disaster, along with its reputation. Katrina Roche, i2's chief marketing officer, asserted that Nike failed to use the vendor's implementation methodology and templates, which contributed to the problem.

Software development problems often lead to high-profile disasters. Hershey's glitch in its ERP implementation made the front page of *The Wall Street Journal* and cost the company millions. Hershey said computer problems with its SAP software system created a backlog of orders, causing slower deliveries, and resulting in lower earnings. Statistics released in 2006 by the National Research Council show that U.S. companies spent $250 billion in 2005 to repair damage caused by software defects.

If software does not work, the organization will not work. Traditional business risk models typically ignored software development, largely because most organizations considered the impact from software and software development on the business to be minor. In the digital age, however, software success, or failure, can lead directly to business success, or failure. Almost every large organization in the world relies on software, either to drive its business operations or to make its products work. As organizations' reliance on software grows, so do the business-related consequences of software successes and failures as displayed in Figure 17.1.

The lucrative advantages of successful software implementations provide significant incentives to manage software development risks. However, according to the Chaos report from the Standish Group, a Massachusetts-based consultancy, more than half the software development projects undertaken in the United States come in late or over budget and the majority of successful projects maintain fewer features and functions than originally specified. Organizations also cancel around 33 percent of these projects during development. Understanding the basics of software development, or the systems development life cycle, will help organizations avoid potential software development pitfalls and ensure that software development efforts are successful.

The Systems Development Life Cycle (SDLC)

The *systems development life cycle (SDLC)* is the overall process for developing information systems from planning and analysis through implementation and maintenance. The SDLC is the foundation for all systems development methodologies, and literally hundreds of different activities are associated with each phase in

Business-Related Consequences of Software Success and Failure

Increase or decrease revenues—Organizations have the ability to directly increase profits by implementing successful IT systems. Organizations can also lose millions when software fails or key information is stolen or compromised.

Nike's poorly designed supply chain management software delayed orders, increased excess inventories, and caused earnings to fall 24 percent below expectations.

Repair or damage brand reputation—Technologies such as CRM can directly enhance a company's brand reputation. Software can also severely damage a company's reputation if it fails to work as advertised or has security vulnerabilities that affect its customers' trust.

H&R Block customers were furious when the company accidentally placed its customers' passwords and Social Security numbers on its website.

Prevent or incur liabilities—Technology such as CAT scans, MRIs, and mammograms can save lives. Faulty technology used in airplanes, automobiles, pacemakers, or nuclear reactors can cause massive damage, injury, or death.

The parent company of bankrupt pharmaceutical distributor FoxMeyer sued SAP for $500 million over ERP software failure that allegedly crippled its operations.

Increase or decrease productivity—CRM and SCM software can directly increase a company's productivity. Large losses in productivity can also occur when software malfunctions or crashes.

The Standish Group estimates that defective software code accounted for 45 percent of computer-system downtime and cost U.S. companies $100 billion in lost productivity.

FIGURE 17.1

Business-Related Consequences of Software Success and Failure

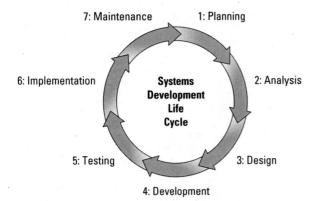

7: Maintenance   1: Planning

6: Implementation   **Systems Development Life Cycle**   2: Analysis

5: Testing   3: Design

4: Development

FIGURE 17.2

The Systems Development Life Cycle

the SDLC. Typical activities include determining budgets, gathering system requirements, and writing detailed user documentation. The activities performed during each systems development project will vary.

The SDLC begins with a business need, followed by an assessment of the functions a system must have to satisfy the need, and ends when the benefits of the system no longer outweigh its maintenance costs. This is why it is referred to as a life cycle. The SDLC has seven distinct phases: planning, analysis, design, development, testing, implementation, and maintenance (see Figure 17.2).

1. **Planning:** The *planning phase* involves establishing a high-level plan of the intended project and determining project goals. Planning is the first and most critical phase of any systems development effort an organization undertakes, regardless of whether the effort is to develop a system that allows customers to order products over the Internet, determine the best logistical structure for warehouses around the world, or develop a strategic information alliance with another organization. Organizations must carefully plan the activities (and determine why they are necessary) to be successful.

2. **Analysis:** The *analysis phase* involves analyzing end-user business requirements and refining project goals into defined functions and operations of the intended system. *Business requirements* are the detailed set of business requests that the system must meet in order to be successful. The analysis phase is obviously critical. A good start is essential and the organization must spend as much time, energy, and resources as necessary to perform a detailed, accurate analysis.

3. **Design:** The *design phase* involves describing the desired features and operations of the system including screen layouts, business rules, process diagrams, pseudo code, and other documentation.

4. **Development:** The *development phase* involves taking all of the detailed design documents from the design phase and transforming them into the actual system. In this phase the project transitions from preliminary designs to the actual physical implementation.

5. **Testing:** The *testing phase* involves bringing all the project pieces together into a special testing environment to test for errors, bugs, and interoperability and verify that the system meets all of the business requirements defined in the analysis phase.

6. **Implementation:** The *implementation phase* involves placing the system into production so users can begin to perform actual business operations with the system.

7. **Maintenance:** Maintaining the system is the final sequential phase of any systems development effort. The *maintenance phase* involves performing changes, corrections, additions, and upgrades to ensure the system continues to meet the business goals. This phase continues for the life of the system because the system must change as the business evolves and its needs change, demanding constant monitoring, supporting the new system with frequent minor changes (for example, new reports or information capturing), and reviewing the system to be sure it is moving the organization toward its strategic goals.

Traditional Software Development Methodology: Waterfall

Today, systems are so large and complex that teams of architects, analysts, developers, testers, and users must work together to create the millions of lines of custom-written code that drive enterprises. For this reason, developers have created a number of different systems development life cycle methodologies. A *methodology* is a set of policies, procedures, standards, processes, practices, tools, techniques, and tasks that people apply to technical and management challenges. It is used to manage the deployment of technology with work plans, requirements documents, and test plans. It is also used to deploy technology. A formal methodology could include coding standards, code libraries, development practices, and much more.

WATERFALL METHODOLOGY

The oldest of these, and the best known, is the waterfall methodology: a sequence of phases in which the output of each phase becomes the input for the next (see Figure 17.3). The traditional *waterfall methodology* is an activity-based process in which each phase in the SDLC is performed sequentially from planning through implementation and maintenance. The traditional waterfall method no longer serves most of today's development efforts. The success rate for software development projects that follow this approach is about 1 in 10. Paul Magin, a senior executive with Part Miner, a leading supplier of technical components, states, "Waterfall is a punishing technology. It forces people to be accurate when they simply cannot. It is dangerous and least desirable in today's development environment. It does not accommodate midcourse changes; it requires that you know exactly what you want to do on the project and a steady-state until the work is done; it requires guarantees that requirements will not change. We all know that it is nearly impossible to have all requirements up front. When you use a cascading method, you end up with cascading problems that are disastrous if not identified and corrected early in the process."

Waterfall is inflexible, expensive, and requires rigid adherence to the sequentially based steps in the process. Figure 17.4 explains some issues related to the waterfall methodology.

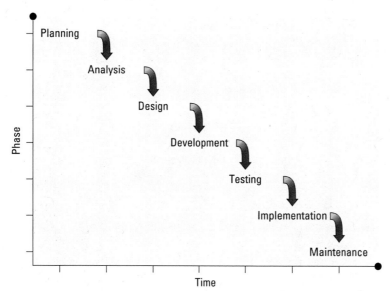

FIGURE 17.3

The Traditional Waterfall Methodology

FIGURE 17.4

Issues Related to the
Waterfall Methodology

Issues Related to the Waterfall Methodology	
The business problem	Any flaws in accurately defining and articulating the business problem in terms of what the business users actually require flow onward to the next phase.
The plan	Managing costs, resources, and time constraints is difficult in the waterfall sequence. What happens to the schedule if a programmer quits? How will a schedule delay in a specific phase impact the total cost of the project? Unexpected contingencies may sabotage the plan.
The solution	The waterfall methodology is problematic in that it assumes users can specify all business requirements in advance. Defining the appropriate IT infrastructure that is flexible, scalable, and reliable is a challenge. The final IT infrastructure solution must meet not only current but also future needs in terms of time, cost, feasibility, and flexibility. Vision is inevitably limited at the head of the waterfall.

Today's business environment is fierce. The desire and need to outsmart and out-play competitors remains intense. Given this drive for success, leaders push internal development teams and external vendors to deliver agreed-upon systems faster and cheaper so they can realize benefits as early as possible. Even so, systems remain large and complex. The traditional waterfall methodology no longer serves as an adequate systems development methodology in most cases. Because this development environment is the norm and not the exception anymore, development teams use a new breed of alternative development methods to achieve their business objectives.

Agile Software Development Methodologies

Standish Group's CHAOS research clearly shows that the smaller the project, the greater the success rate. The iterative development style is the ultimate in small projects. Basically, *iterative development* consists of a series of tiny projects. Iterative has become the foundation of multiple agile types of methodologies. Figure 17.5 displays an iterative approach.

FIGURE 17.5

The Iterative Approach

An *agile methodology* aims for customer satisfaction through early and continuous delivery of useful software components developed by an iterative process with

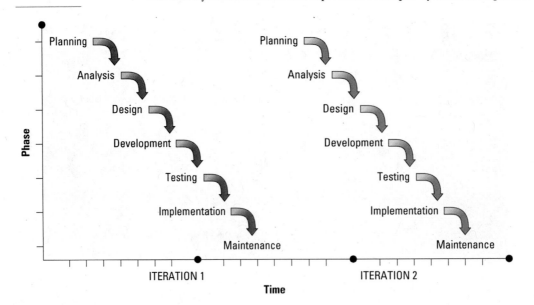

a design point that uses the bare minimum requirements. Agile is what it sounds like: fast and efficient, small and nimble, lower cost, fewer features, shorter projects. Using agile methods helps refine feasibility and supports the process for getting rapid feedback as functionality is introduced. Developers can adjust as they move along and better clarify unclear requirements.

Magin also states that the key to delivering a successful product or system is to deliver value to users as soon as possible—give them something they want and like early to create buy-in, generate enthusiasm, and, ultimately, reduce scope. Using agile methodologies helps maintain accountability and helps to establish a barometer for the satisfaction of end users. It does no good to accomplish something on time and on budget if it does not satisfy the end user. The primary forms of agile methodologies include:

- Rapid prototyping or rapid application development methodology.
- Extreme programming methodology.
- Rational unified process (RUP) methodology.
- Scrum methodology.

It is important not to get hung up on the names of the methodologies—some are proprietary brand names, others are generally accepted names. It is more important to know how these alternative methodologies are used in today's business environment and the benefits they can deliver.

RAPID APPLICATION DEVELOPMENT (RAD) METHODOLOGY

In response to the faster pace of business, rapid application development has become a popular route for accelerating systems development. *Rapid application development (RAD)* (also called *rapid prototyping*) *methodology* emphasizes extensive user involvement in the rapid and evolutionary construction of working prototypes of a system to accelerate the systems development process. Figure 17.6 displays the fundamentals of RAD.

A *prototype* is a smaller-scale representation or working model of the users' requirements or a proposed design for an information system. The prototype is an essential part of the analysis phase when using the RAD methodology.

PHH Vehicle Management Services, a Baltimore fleet-management company with over 750,000 vehicles, wanted to build an enterprise application that opened the entire vehicle information database to customers over the Internet. To build the application quickly, the company abandoned the traditional waterfall approach. Instead, a team of 30 developers began prototyping the Internet application, and the company's customers evaluated each prototype for immediate feedback. The development team released new prototypes that incorporated the customers' feedback every six weeks. The PHH Interactive Vehicle application went into production seven months after the initial work began. Over 20,000 customers, using a common browser, can now access the PHH Interactive site at any time from anywhere in the world to review their accounts, analyze billing information, and order vehicles.

EXTREME PROGRAMMING METHODOLOGY

Extreme programming (XP) methodology, like other agile methods, breaks a project into tiny phases, and developers cannot continue on to the next phase until the

Fundamentals of RAD
Focus initially on creating a prototype that looks and acts like the desired system.
Actively involve system users in the analysis, design, and development phases.
Accelerate collecting the business requirements through an interactive and iterative construction approach.

FIGURE 17.6

Fundamentals of RAD

first phase is complete. XP emphasizes the fact that the faster the communication or feedback the better the results. There are basically four parts: planning, designing, coding, and testing. Unlike other methodologies, these are not phases; they work in tandem with each other. Planning includes user stories, stand-up meetings, and small releases. The design segment also stresses to not add functionality until it is needed. In the coding part, the user is always available for feedback, developers work in pairs, and the code is written to an agreed standard. In testing, the tests are written before the code. Extreme programming users are embedded into the development process. This technique is powerful because of the narrow communication gap between developers and users—it is a direct link. This saves valuable time and, again, continues to clarify needed (and unneeded) requirements.

One reason for XP's success is its stress on customer satisfaction. XP empowers developers to respond to changing customer and business requirements, even late in the systems development life cycle, and XP emphasizes teamwork. Managers, customers, and developers are all part of a team dedicated to delivering quality software. XP implements a simple, yet effective way to enable groupware-style development. Kent Beck, the father of XP, proposes conversation as the paradigm and suggests using index cards as a means to create dialog between business and technology. XP is a lot like a jigsaw puzzle; there are many small pieces. Individually the pieces make no sense, but when they are combined (again and again) an organization can gain visibility into the entire new system.

RATIONAL UNIFIED PROCESS (RUP) METHODOLOGY

The *rational unified process (RUP) methodology,* owned by IBM, provides a framework for breaking down the development of software into four gates. Each gate consists of executable iterations of the software in development. A project stays in a gate until the stakeholders are satisfied, and then it either moves to the next gate or is cancelled. The gates include:

- **Gate One: Inception.** This phase includes inception of the business case. This phase ensures all stakeholders have a shared understanding of the system.
- **Gate Two: Elaboration.** This phase provides a rough order of magnitude. Primary questions answered in this phase deal with agreed-upon details of the system including the ability to provide an architecture to support and build the system.
- **Gate Three: Construction.** This phase includes building and developing the product.
- **Gate Four: Transition.** Primary questions answered in this phase address ownership of the system and training of key personnel.

Because RUP is an iterative methodology, the user can reject the product and force the developers to go back to gate one. Approximately 500,000 developers have used RUP in software projects of varying sizes in the 20 years it has been available, according to IBM. RUP helps developers avoid reinventing the wheel and focuses on rapidly adding or removing reusable chunks of processes addressing common problems.

SCRUM METHODOLOGY

Another agile methodology, *Scrum methodology* uses small teams to produce small pieces of deliverable software using sprints, or 30-day intervals, to achieve an appointed goal. In rugby, a scrum is a team pack and everyone in the pack works together to move the ball down the field. Under this methodology, each day ends or begins with a stand-up meeting to monitor and control the development effort.

Primavera Systems, Inc., a software solutions company was finding it increasingly difficult to use the traditional waterfall methodology for development so it moved to an agile methodology. Scrum's insistence on delivering complete increments of business value in 30-day learning cycles helped the teams learn rapidly. It forced teams to test and integrate experiments and encouraged them to release them into production. Primavera's shift resulted in highly satisfied customers and a highly motivated, energetic development environment. Dick Faris, CTO of Primavera, said, "Agile programming is very different and new. It is a different feel to the way programming happens. Instead of mindlessly cranking out code, the process is one of team dialogue, negotiation around priorities and time and talents. The entire company commits to a 30-day sprint and delivery of finished, tested software. Maybe it is just one specific piece of functionality but it's the real thing, including delivery and client review against needs and requirements. Those needs and requirements, by the way, change. That is the strength we saw in the Scrum process."

IMPLEMENTING AGILE METHODOLOGIES

Amos Auringer, an executive adviser for the prestigious Gartner Group, said, "Concepts such as agile, RAD, and XP are all various approaches to the same model—idea, production, delivery. These models represent consolidated steps, skipped steps for project size, and compressed steps to achieve the same result—a delivered product. Emerging process engineering models tend to focus on eliminating or reducing steps. The SDLC phases do not change—we just learn how to do our jobs better and more efficiently."

If organizations choose to adopt agile methodologies, it is important to educate those involved. For an agile process to work, it must be simple and quick. The Agile Alliance is a group of software developers whose mission is to improve software development processes; the group's manifesto is displayed in Figure 17.7. Decisions must be made quickly without analysis paralysis. The best way to do this is to involve stakeholders, develop excellent communication processes, and implement strong project management skills. Understanding that communication is the most crucial aspect of a project is the core of collaborative development. Standish Group reports that projects in which users or user groups have a good understanding of their true needs have a better rate of return and lower risk. Strong project management is key to building successful enterprise applications and is covered in detail in the following section.

Developing Successful Software

Gartner Research estimates that 65 percent of agile projects are successful. This success rate is extraordinary compared to the 10 percent success rate of waterfall projects. The following are the primary principles an organization should follow for successful agile software development.

SLASH THE BUDGET

Small budgets force developers and users to focus on the essentials. Small budgets also make it easier to kill a failing project. For example, imagine that a project that has already cost $20 million is going down the tubes. With that much invested, it is tempting to invest another $5 million to rescue it rather than take a huge loss. All too often, the system fails and the company ends up with an even bigger loss.

The Agile Alliance Manifesto
Early and continuous delivery of valuable software will satisfy the customer.
Changing requirements, even late in development, are welcome.
Businesspeople and developers must work together daily throughout the project.
Projects should be built around motivated individuals. Give them the environment and support they need, and trust them to get the job done.
The best architectures, requirements, and designs emerge from self-organizing teams.
At regular intervals, the team should reflect on how to become more effective, then tune and adjust its behavior accordingly.

FIGURE 17.7

The Agile Alliance Manifesto

Jim Johnson, chairman of the Standish Group, says he forced the CIO of one Fortune 500 company to set a $100,000 ceiling on all software development projects. There were no exceptions to this business rule without approval from the CIO and CEO. Johnson claims the company's project success rate went from 0 percent to 50 percent.

IF IT DOESN'T WORK, KILL IT

Bring all key stakeholders together at the beginning of a project and as it progresses bring them together again to evaluate the software. Is it doing what the business wants and, more important, requires? Eliminate any software that is not meeting business expectations. This is called triage, and it's "the perfect place to kill a software project," said Pat Morgan, senior program manager at Compaq's Enterprise Storage Group. He holds monthly triage sessions and says they can be brutal. "At one [meeting], engineering talked about a cool process they were working on to transfer information between GUIs. No one in the room needed it. We killed it right there. In our environment, you can burn a couple of million dollars in a month only to realize what you're doing isn't useful."

KEEP REQUIREMENTS TO A MINIMUM

Start each project with what the software must absolutely do. Do not start with a list of everything the software should do. Every software project traditionally starts with a requirements document that will often have hundreds or thousands of business requirements. The Standish Group estimates that only 7 percent of the business requirements are needed for any given application. Keeping requirements to a minimum also means that scope creep and feature creep must be closely monitored. *Scope creep* occurs when the scope of the project increases. *Feature creep* occurs when developers add extra features that were not part of the initial requirements. Both scope creep and feature creep are major reasons software development fails.

TEST AND DELIVER FREQUENTLY

As often as once a week, and not less than once a month, complete a part of the project or a piece of software. The part must be working and it must be bug-free. Then have the customers test and approve it. This is the agile methodology's most radical departure from traditional development. In some traditional software projects, the customers did not see any working parts or pieces for years.

ASSIGN NON-IT EXECUTIVES TO SOFTWARE PROJECTS

Non-IT executives should coordinate with the technical project manager, test iterations to make sure they are meeting user needs, and act as liaisons between executives and IT. Having the business side involved full-time will bring project ownership and a desire to succeed to all parties involved. SpreeRide, a Salt Lake City market research outfit, used the agile methodology to set up its company's website. The project required several business executives designated full-time. The company believes this is one of the primary reasons that the project was successfully deployed in less than three months.

Software Problems Are Business Problems

Only 28 percent of projects are developed within budget and delivered on time and as promised, says a report from the Standish Group, a Massachusetts-based consultancy. The primary reasons for project failure are:

- Unclear or missing business requirements.
- Skipping SDLC phases.
- Failure to manage project scope.

- Failure to manage project plan.
- Changing technology.

UNCLEAR OR MISSING BUSINESS REQUIREMENTS

The most common reason systems fail is because the business requirements are either missing or incorrectly gathered during the analysis phase. The business requirements drive the entire system. If they are not accurate or complete, the system will not be successful.

It is important to discuss the relationship between the SDLC and the cost for the organization to fix errors. An error found during the analysis and design phase is relatively inexpensive to fix. All that is typically required is a change to a Word document. However, exactly the same error found during the testing or implementation phase is going to cost the organization an enormous amount to fix because it has to change the actual system. Figure 17.8 displays how the cost to fix an error grows exponentially the later the error is found in the SDLC.

SKIPPING SDLC PHASES

The first thing individuals tend to do when a project falls behind schedule is to start skipping phases in the SDLC. For example, if a project is three weeks behind in the development phase, the project manager might decide to cut testing down from six weeks to three weeks. Obviously, it is impossible to perform all the testing in half the time. Failing to test the system will lead to unfound errors, and chances are high that the system will fail. It is critical that an organization perform all phases in the SDLC during every project. Skipping any of the phases is sure to lead to system failure.

FAILURE TO MANAGE PROJECT SCOPE

As the project progresses, the project manager must track the status of each activity and adjust the project plan if an activity is added or taking longer than expected. Scope creep and feature creep are difficult to manage and can easily cause a project to fall behind schedule.

FAILURE TO MANAGE PROJECT PLAN

Managing the project plan is one of the biggest challenges during systems development. The project plan is the road map the organization follows during the development of the system. Developing the initial project plan is the easiest part of the

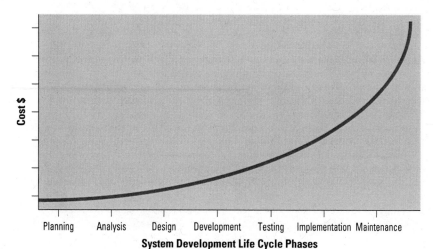

FIGURE 17.8

The Cost of Finding Errors

project manager's job. Managing and revising the project plan is the hard part. The project plan is a living document since it changes almost daily on any project. Failing to monitor, revise, and update the project plan can lead to project failure.

CHANGING TECHNOLOGY

Many real-world projects have hundreds of business requirements, take years to complete, and cost millions of dollars. Gordon Moore, co-founder of Intel Corporation, observed in 1965 that chip density doubles every 18 months. This observation, known as Moore's law, simply means that memory sizes, processor power, and so on, all follow the same pattern and roughly double in capacity every 18 months. As Moore's law states, technology changes at an incredibly fast pace; therefore, it is possible to have to revise an entire project plan in the middle of a project as a result of a change in technology. Technology changes so fast that it is almost impossible to deliver an information system without feeling the pain of changing technology.

OPENING CASE STUDY QUESTIONS

1. Identify the benefits associated with successful software development.
2. Which of the seven phases of the systems development life cycle is the most critical to the development of an e-espionage application?
3. Which of the seven phases of the systems development life cycle is the least critical to the development of an e-espionage application?
4. If you were consulting to the government on building an e-espionage application, which development methodology would you recommend and why?

Chapter Seventeen Case: Software Developing Androids

Android, the Google-developed open mobile phone platform, is a "software stack" development operating system for mobile phones—designed to compete head-to-head with Apple's iPhone. According to Google, a software stack is comprised of the operating system (the platform on which everything runs), the middleware (the programming that allows applications to talk to a network and to one another), and the applications (the actual programs that the phones will run). In short, the Android software stack is all the software that will make an Android phone an Android phone.

It is also important to note that Android is based on the Linux operating system, and all of its applications will be written using Java. This represents a significant risk to Microsoft and its operations systems. Microsoft states that it is unworried by the prospect of increased competition from Android, based on Linux, a software whose code is freely available via the Internet and developed by programmers the world over. Virtually anyone can download an Android software development kit from Google and write an application for Android. Google and its partners first unveiled plans for the Android operating system as software that would run mobile phones, or Android-enabled handsets, but soon, customers will be seeing Android in a number of other electronic devices. Just ask Mark Hamblin, designer of the original touchscreen for the Apple iPhone, who is now the CEO of Touch Revolution and is tinkering with Android so it can work in a slew of gadgets other than wireless phones including:

- A remote control and a touchscreen land-line home phone that will be powered by Android.
- Touchscreen menus for restaurants.
- Android-based medical devices.
- A 15-inch kitchen computer where family members can leave messages for one another.

Additional Android Applications

Seeing Android applications developed by the thousands would be excellent news for Google and chipmakers such as Qualcomm and Texas Instruments that have invested in its development and would welcome the chance to sell semiconductors in new markets. But Android ubiquity could cause headaches for Microsoft, which would rather see its own software on a wider range of electronic devices. Currently, there are a handful of electronics manufacturers developing Android-based mobile Internet devices (MIDs).

Designed to Run on Any Device

Android applications may have a unique first-mover advantage as they show up in devices such as netbooks or digital photo frames where Microsoft has yet to establish a beachhead. Manufacturers that work with Texas Instruments have already built Android into video and audio players and picture frames. Rival semiconductor manufacturer Qualcomm is helping vendors ready more than 20 Android-based products, including video players and small tablet PCs.

Google has not announced plans to market Android for use in nonphone gadgets. While Google did not discuss nonwireless devices when they first started talking about Android, they designed Android to run on any device—from a smart phone to a server—as they had the foresight to design it with bigger screens and chips in mind. Unlike many cell-phone and PC-based operating systems, Android can run on devices powered by a variety of semiconductors with minimal modifications needed.

Competition from Linux

With flexibility comes economy. Manufacturers can keep costs low by being able to choose from a wider range of chips. Android software is also free to use, while Microsoft charges licensing fees. And just in case consumers fret that they will not be able to use their favorite Microsoft applications on an Android device, a company called DataViz will soon unveil software that it says will let people open, edit, and send Word, Excel, and Microsoft PowerPoint files. The software will also allow synching between Android and Outlook email.

As potent as it may be, Android faces competition from Microsoft and Linux. One of Android's creators, Intel recently introduced its own Linux software, Moblin, for use with MIDs and netbooks running its Atom processors. It will be interesting to watch the future of Android.

Questions

1. List and describe the seven phases in the systems development life cycle and determine which phase you think is most important to an individual developing an application for Android.
2. Identify the primary difference between the different software development methodologies. Which methodology would you recommend an individual developing an application for Android use and why?
3. What are the common reasons why software projects fail and how can an Android developer mitigate these risks?
4. If you could develop software for Android what would it be and what business purpose would it serve? How could you ensure the successful development of the software?

CHAPTER **19** Outsourcing in the 21st Century

19.1. Describe the advantages and disadvantages of insourcing, outsourcing, and offshore outsourcing.

19.2. Describe why outsourcing is a critical business decision.

Outsourcing Projects

In the high-speed global business environment, an organization needs to maximize its profits, enlarge its market share, and restrain its ever-increasing costs. Businesses need to make every effort to rethink and adopt new processes, especially the prospective resources regarding insourcing and outsourcing. Two basic options are available to organizations wishing to develop and maintain their information systems—insourcing or outsourcing.

Insourcing (*in-house development*) is a common approach using the professional expertise within an organization to develop and maintain the organization's information technology systems. Insourcing has been instrumental in creating a viable supply of IT professionals and in creating a better quality workforce combining both technical and business skills.

Outsourcing is an arrangement by which one organization provides a service or services for another organization that chooses not to perform them in-house. In some cases, the entire information technology department is outsourced, including planning and business analysis as well as the installation, management, and servicing of the network and workstations. Outsourcing can range from a large contract under which an organization such as IBM manages IT services for a company such as Xerox to the practice of hiring contractors and temporary office workers on an individual basis. Figure 19.1 compares the functions companies have outsourced, and Figure 19.2 displays the primary reasons companies outsource.

FIGURE 19.1

Common Departments Outsourced by Organizations

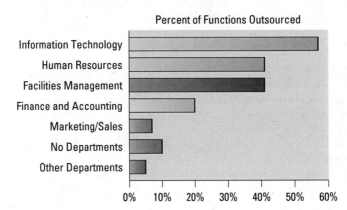

Percent of Functions Outsourced

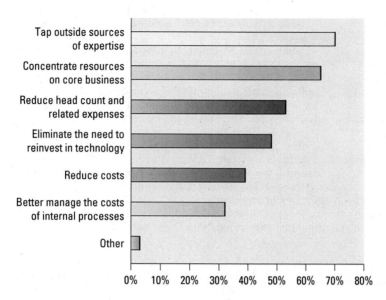

FIGURE 19.2

Reasons Companies
Outsource

British Petroleum (BP) began looking at IT outsourcing as a way to radically reduce costs and gain more flexible and higher-quality IT resources that directly improve the overall business. Over the past decade, all companies within the global BP Group have incorporated outsourcing initiatives in their business plans. BP's information technology costs were reduced by 40 percent globally over the first three years of the outsourcing engagement and have continued at a 10 percent reduction year after year, leading to hundreds of millions of dollars in savings to BP.

Information technology outsourcing enables organizations to keep up with market and technology advances—with less strain on human and financial resources and more assurance that the IT infrastructure will keep pace with evolving business priorities (see Figure 19.3). Planning, deploying, and managing IT environments is both a tactical and a strategic challenge that must take into account a company's organizational, industrial, and technological concerns. The three different forms of outsourcing options a project must consider are:

1. **Onshore outsourcing**—engaging another company within the same country for services.

2. **Nearshore outsourcing**—contracting an outsourcing arrangement with a company in a nearby country. Often this country will share a border with the native country.

3. **Offshore outsourcing**—using organizations from developing countries to write code and develop systems. In offshore outsourcing the country is geographically far away.

FIGURE 19.3

Outsourcing Models and
Cost Savings

Since the mid-1990s, major U.S. companies have been sending significant portions of their software development work offshore—primarily to vendors in India, but also to vendors in China, Eastern Europe (including Russia), Ireland, Israel, and the Philippines. The big selling point for offshore outsourcing is inexpensive good work. A programmer who earns as much as $63,000 per year in the United States is paid as little as $5,000 per year overseas (see Figure 19.4). Companies can easily realize cost savings of 30 to 50 percent through offshore outsourcing and still get the same, if not better, quality of service.

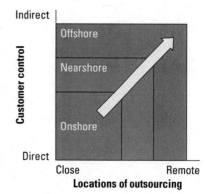

Country	Salary Range Per Year
China	$5,000–$9,000
India	6,000–10,000
Philippines	6,500–11,000
Russia	7,000–13,000
Ireland	21,000–28,000
Canada	25,000–50,000
United States	60,000–90,000

FIGURE 19.4

Typical Salary Ranges for Computer Programmers

Developed and developing countries throughout Europe and Asia offer some IT outsourcing services, but most are hampered to some degree by language, telecommunications infrastructure, or regulatory barriers. The first and largest offshore marketplace is India, whose English-speaking and technologically advanced population has built its IT services business into a $4 billion industry. Infosys, NIIT, Satyam, TCS, and Wipro are among the biggest Indian outsourcing service providers, each with a significant presence in the United States.

Ever since Eastman Kodak announced it was outsourcing its information systems function to IBM, large organizations have found it acceptable to transfer their IT assets, leases, and staff to outsourcers. In view of the changes in sourcing, the key question now is not "Should we outsource IT?" but rather "Where and how can we take advantage of the rapidly developing market of IT services providers?" Some of the influential drivers affecting the growth of the outsourcing market include:

- **Core competencies.** Many companies have recently begun to consider outsourcing as a means to fuel revenue growth rather than just a cost-cutting measure. Outsourcing enables an organization to maintain an up-to-date technology infrastructure while freeing it to focus on revenue growth goals by reinvesting cash and human capital in areas offering the greatest return on investment.

- **Financial savings.** It is typically cheaper to hire workers in China and India than similar workers in the United States. Technology is advancing at such an accelerated rate that companies often lack the resources, workforce, or expertise to keep up. It is close to impossible for an IT department to maintain a "best-of-breed" status, especially for small and medium-sized enterprises where cost is a critical factor.

- **Rapid growth.** A company's sustainability depends on both speed to market and ability to react quickly to changes in market conditions. By taking advantage of outsourcing, an organization is able to acquire best-practices process expertise. This facilitates the design, building, training, and deployment of business processes or functions.

- **Industry changes.** High levels of reorganization across industries have increased demand for outsourcing to better focus on core competencies. The significant increase in merger and acquisition activity created a sudden need to integrate multiple core and noncore business functions into one business, while the deregulation of the utilities and telecom industries created a need to ensure compliance with government rules and regulations. Companies in either situation turned to outsourcing so they could better focus on industry changes at hand.

- **The Internet.** The pervasive nature of the Internet as an effective sales channel has allowed clients to become more comfortable with outsourcing. Barriers to entry, such as lack of capital, are dramatically reduced in the world of ebusiness due to the Internet. New competitors enter the market daily.

- **Globalization.** As markets open worldwide, competition heats up. Companies may engage outsourcing service providers to deliver international services.

Best Buy Co. Inc. is the number one U.S. specialty retailer for consumer electronics, personal computers, entertainment software, and appliances. Best Buy needed to find a strategic IT partner that could help the company leverage its IT functions to meet its business objectives. Best Buy also wanted to integrate its disparate enterprise systems and minimize its operating expenses. Best Buy outsourced these functions to Accenture, a global management consulting, technology services, and outsourcing company. The comprehensive outsourcing relationship that drove Best Buy's transformation produced spectacular results that were measurable in every key area of its business, such as a 20 percent increase in key category revenue that translated into a $25 million profit improvement.

According to PricewaterhouseCoopers' survey of CEOs from 452 of the fastest growing U.S. companies, "Businesses that outsource are growing faster, larger, and more profitably than those that do not. In addition, most of those involved in outsourcing say they are saving money and are highly satisfied with their outsourcing service providers." Figure 19.5 lists common areas for outsourcing opportunities across industries.

OUTSOURCING BENEFITS

The many benefits associated with outsourcing include:

- Increased quality and efficiency of a process, service, or function.
- Reduced operating expenses.
- Resources focused on core profit-generating competencies.
- Reduced exposure to risks involved with large capital investments.
- Access to outsourcing service provider's economies of scale.
- Access to outsourcing services provider's expertise and best-in-class practices.
- Access to advanced technologies.
- Increased flexibility with the ability to respond quickly to changing market demands.
- No costly outlay of capital funds.
- Reduced head count and associated overhead expense.
- Reduced frustration and expense related to hiring and retaining employees in an exceptionally tight job market.
- Reduced time to market for products or services.

OUTSOURCING CHALLENGES

Outsourcing comes with several challenges. These arguments are valid and should be considered when a company is thinking about outsourcing. Many challenges can be avoided with proper research. The challenges include:

- **Contract length.** Most of the outsourced IT contracts are for a relatively long time period (several years). This is because of the high cost of transferring assets

Industry	Outsourcing Opportunities
Banking and finance	Check and electronic payment processing, credit report issuance, delinquency management, securities, and trades processing
Insurance	Claims reporting and investigation, policy administration, check processing, risk assessment
Telecommunications	Invoice and bill production, transaction processing
Health care	Electronic data interchange, database management, accounting
Transportation	Ticket and order processing
Government	Loan processing, Medicaid processing
Retail	Electronic payment processing

FIGURE 19.5

Outsourcing Opportunities

and employees as well as maintaining technological investment. The long contract causes three particular issues:

1. Difficulties in getting out of a contract if the outsourcing service provider turns out to be unsuitable.

2. Problems in foreseeing what the business will need over the next 5 or 10 years (typical contract lengths), hence creating difficulties in establishing an appropriate contract.

3. Problems in reforming an internal IT department after the contract period is finished.

- **Competitive edge.** Effective and innovative use of IT can give an organization a competitive edge over its rivals. A competitive business advantage provided by an internal IT department that understands the organization and is committed to its goals can be lost in an outsourced arrangement. In an outsourced arrangement, IT staff are striving to achieve the goals and objectives of the outsourcing service provider, which may conflict with those of the organization.

- **Confidentiality.** In some organizations, the information stored in the computer systems is central to the enterprise's success or survival, such as information about pricing policies, product mixing formulas, or sales analysis. Some companies decide against outsourcing for fear of placing confidential information in the hands of the provider, particularly if the outsourcing service provider offers services to companies competing in the same marketplace. Although the organization usually dismisses this threat, claiming it is covered by confidentiality clauses in a contract, the organization must assess the potential risk and costs of a confidentiality breach in determining the net benefits of an outsourcing agreement.

- **Scope definition.** Most IT projects suffer from problems associated with defining the scope of the system. The same problem afflicts outsourcing arrangements. Many difficulties result from contractual misunderstandings between the organization and the outsourcing service provider. In such circumstances, the organization believes that the service required is within the contract scope while the service provider is sure it is outside the scope and so is subject to extra fees.

OPENING CASE STUDY QUESTIONS

1. What are the benefits and risks associated with outsourcing?

2. What are the ethical issues associated with outsourcing government applications?

3. What are the security issues associated with outsourcing government applications?

Chapter Nineteen Case: UPS in the Computer Repair Business

When people think of UPS they usually think of brown delivery trucks and employees in shorts dropping off and picking up packages. This image is about to change. UPS has now entered the laptop repair business. Toshiba is handing over its entire laptop repair operation to UPS Supply Chain Solutions, the shipper's $2.4 billion logistics outsourcing division. Toshiba's decision to allow a shipping company to fix its laptops might appear odd. However, when you understand that the primary challenge of computer repair is more logistical than technical,

Toshiba's business decision seems brilliant. "Moving a unit around and getting replacement parts consumes most of the time," explained Mark Simons, general manager at Toshiba's digital products division. "The actual service only takes about an hour."

UPS sends broken Toshiba laptops to its facility in Louisville, Kentucky, where UPS engineers diagnose and repair defects. In the past, repairs could take weeks, depending on whether Toshiba needed components from Japan. Since the UPS repair site is adjacent to its air hub, customers should get their machines back, as good as new, in just a matter of days. UPS has been servicing Lexmark and Hewlett-Packard printers since 1996 and has been performing initial inspections on laptops being returned to Toshiba since 1999.

The expanded Toshiba relationship is another step in UPS's strategy to broaden its business beyond package delivery into commerce services. The company works with clients to manage inventory, ordering, and custom processes. It recently introduced a service to dispose of unwanted electrical devices. To take on laptop repair, UPS put 50 technicians through a Toshiba-certified training course.

Questions

1. Do you think UPS's entrance into the laptop repair business was a good business decision? Why or why not?

2. Explain why Toshiba decided to outsource its computer repair business to UPS.

3. What are some advantages UPS can offer Toshiba in the outsourcing arrangement?

4. Explain the advantages of forming an outsourcing relationship with a parcel delivery company such as UPS.

Business Plug-Ins

B3

Hardware and Software

LEARNING OUTCOMES

1. Describe the six major categories of hardware and provide an example of each.
2. Identify the different computer categories and explain their potential business uses.
3. Explain the difference between primary and secondary storage.
4. List the common input, output, storage, and communication devices.
5. Describe the eight categories of computers by size.
6. Define the relationship between operating system software and utility software.

Introduction

Managers need to determine what types of hardware and software will satisfy their current and future business needs, the right time to buy the equipment, and how to protect their IT investments. This does not imply that managers need to be experts in all areas of technology; however, building a basic understanding of hardware and software can help them make the right IT investment choices.

Information technology (IT) is a field concerned with the use of technology in managing and processing information. Information technology can be composed of the Internet, a personal computer, a cell phone that can access the web, a personal digital assistant, or presentation software. All of these technologies help to perform specific information processing tasks. There are two basic categories of information technology: hardware and software. *Hardware* consists of the physical devices associated with a computer system. *Software* is the set of instructions that the hardware executes to carry out specific tasks. Software, such as Microsoft Excel, and various hardware devices, such as a keyboard and a monitor, interact to create a spreadsheet or a graph. This plug-in covers the basics of computer hardware and software including terminology, business uses, and common characteristics.

Hardware Basics

In many industries, exploiting computer hardware is key to gaining a competitive advantage. Frito-Lay gained a competitive advantage by using handheld devices to track the strategic placement and sale of items in convenience stores. Sales

Six Hardware Components	
Central processing unit (CPU)	The actual hardware that interprets and executes the program (software) instructions and coordinates how all the other hardware devices work together.
Primary storage	The computer's main memory, which consists of the random access memory (RAM), the cache memory, and the read-only memory (ROM) that is directly accessible to the central processing unit (CPU).
Secondary storage	The equipment designed to store large volumes of data for long-term storage (e.g., diskette, hard drive, memory card, CD).
Input devices	The equipment used to capture information and commands (e.g., keyboard, scanner).
Output devices	The equipment used to see, hear, or otherwise accept the results of information processing requests (e.g., monitor, printer).
Communication devices	The equipment used to send information and receive it from one location to another (e.g., modem).

FIGURE B3.1

Hardware Components of a Computer System

representatives could track sale price, competitor information, the number of items sold, and item location in the store all from their handheld device.

A *computer* is an electronic device operating under the control of instructions stored in its own memory that can accept, manipulate, and store data. A computer system consists of six hardware components (see Figure B3.1). Figure B3.2 displays how these components work together to form a computer system.

CENTRAL PROCESSING UNIT

The dominant manufacturers of CPUs today include Intel (with its Celeron and Pentium lines for personal computers) and Advanced Micro Devices (AMD) (with its Athlon series). AMD was initially dismissed as a company that simply cloned current chips, producing processors that mimic the features and capabilities of those from industry leader Intel. However, over the past few years, AMD has begun introducing innovative CPUs that are forcing Intel into the unfamiliar position of reacting to competition. AMD led the way in transforming the processor market by creating chips that handle 64 bits of data at a time, up from

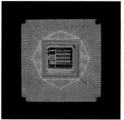 

32 bits. It also broke new territory when it became the first provider of dual-core processors for the server market. Hector Ruiz, chairman and CEO of AMD, stated, "In our position there is only one thing we can do: Stay close to our customers and end users, understand what they need and want, and then simply out-innovate the competition. Innovation is at the center of our ability to succeed. We cannot win by just copying the competition."

The *central processing unit (CPU)* (or *microprocessor*) is the actual hardware that interprets and executes the program (software) instructions and coordinates how all the other hardware devices work together. The CPU is built on a small flake of silicon and can contain the equivalent of several million transistors. CPUs are unquestionably one of the 20th century's greatest technological advances.

A CPU contains two primary parts: control unit and arithmetic/logic unit. The *control unit* interprets software instructions and literally tells the other hardware devices what to do, based on the software instructions. The *arithmetic-logic unit*

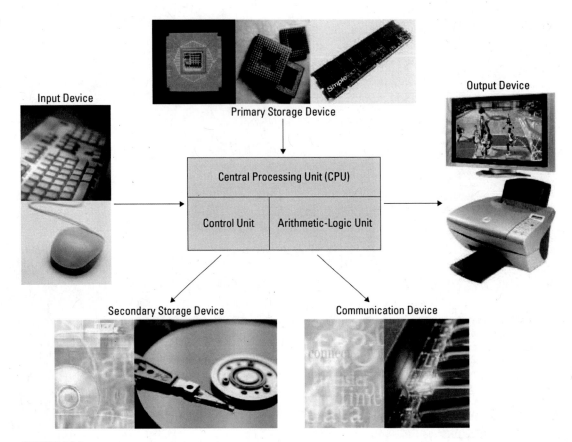

Input Device

Output Device

Primary Storage Device

Central Processing Unit (CPU)

Control Unit | Arithmetic-Logic Unit

Secondary Storage Device

Communication Device

FIGURE B3.2

How the Hardware Components Work Together

(ALU) performs all arithmetic operations (for example, addition and subtraction) and all logic operations (such as sorting and comparing numbers). The control unit and ALU perform different functions. The control unit obtains instructions from the software. It then interprets the instructions, decides which tasks other devices perform, and finally tells each device to perform the task. The ALU responds to the control unit and does whatever it dictates, performing either arithmetic or logic operations.

The number of CPU cycles per second determines how fast a CPU carries out the software instructions; more cycles per second means faster processing, and faster CPUs cost more than their slower counterparts. CPU speed is usually quoted in megahertz and gigahertz. *Megahertz (MHz)* is the number of millions of CPU cycles per second. *Gigahertz (GHz)* is the number of billions of CPU cycles per second. Figure B3.3 displays the factors that determine CPU speed.

Advances in CPU Design

Chip makers are pressing more functionality into CPU technology. Most CPUs are *complex instruction set computer (CISC) chips,* which is a type of CPU that can recognize as many as 100 or more instructions, enough to carry out most computations directly. *Reduced instruction set computer (RISC) chips* limit the number of instructions the CPU can execute to increase processing speed. The idea of RISC is to reduce the instruction set to the bare minimum, emphasizing the instructions used most of the time and optimizing them for the fastest possible execution. A RISC processor runs faster than a CISC processor.

FIGURE B3.3

Factors That Determine
CPU Speed

CPU Speed Factors
Clock speed—the speed of the internal clock of a CPU that sets the pace at which operations proceed within the computer's internal processing circuitry. Clock speed is measured in megahertz (MHz) and gigahertz (GHz). Faster clock speeds bring noticeable gains in microprocessor-intensive tasks, such as recalculating a spreadsheet.
Word length—number of bits (0s and 1s) that can be processed by the CPU at any one time. Computers work in terms of bits and bytes using electrical pulses that have two states: on and off. A *binary digit (bit)* is the smallest unit of information that a computer can process. A bit can be either a 1 (on) or a 0 (off). A group of eight bits represents one natural language character and is called a *byte*.
Bus width—the size of the internal electrical pathway along which signals are sent from one part of the computer to another. A wider bus can move more data, hence faster processing.
Chip line width—the distance between transistors on a chip. The shorter the chip line width the faster the chip since more transistors can be placed on a chip and the data and instructions travel short distances during processing.

FIGURE B3.3

Factors That Determine
CPU Speed

In the next few years, better performance, systems management capabilities, virtualization, security, and features to help track computer assets will be built directly into the CPU (see Figure B3.4). *Virtualization* is a protected memory space created by the CPU allowing the computer to create virtual machines. Each virtual machine can run its own programs isolated from other machines.

PRIMARY STORAGE

Primary storage is the computer's main memory, which consists of the random access memory (RAM), cache memory, and the read-only memory (ROM) that is directly accessible to the CPU.

Random Access Memory

Random access memory (RAM) is the computer's primary working memory, in which program instructions and data are stored so that they can be accessed directly by the CPU via the processor's high-speed external data bus.

RAM is often called read/write memory. In RAM, the CPU can write and read data. Most programs set aside a portion of RAM as a temporary work space for data so that one can modify (rewrite) as needed until the data are ready for printing or storage on secondary storage media, such as a hard drive or memory key. RAM does not retain its contents when the power to the computer is switched off, hence individuals should save their work frequently. When the computer is turned off, everything in RAM is wiped clean. *Volatility* refers to RAM's

FIGURE B3.4

Chip Advancements by
Manufacturer

Chip Advancements
AMD: Security, virtualization, and advanced power-management technology.
IBM: Cryptography for additional security and floating point capability for faster graphics processing.
Intel: Cryptography for additional security, hardware-assisted virtualization, and Active Management Technology for asset tracking, patching, and software updates.
Sun Microsystems: Cryptography for additional security, increased speed for data transmission and receipt, and ability to run 32 computations simultaneously.

complete loss of stored information if power is interrupted. RAM is volatile and its contents are lost when the computer's electric supply fails.

Cache Memory

Cache memory is a small unit of ultra-fast memory that is used to store recently accessed or frequently accessed data so that the CPU does not have to retrieve this data from slower memory circuits such as RAM. Cache memory that is built directly into the CPU's circuits is called primary cache. Cache memory contained on an external circuit is called secondary cache.

Read Only Memory (ROM)

Read-only memory (ROM) is the portion of a computer's primary storage that does not lose its contents when one switches off the power. ROM contains essential system programs that neither the user nor the computer can erase. Since the computer's internal memory is blank during start-up, the computer cannot perform any functions unless given start-up instructions. These instructions are stored in ROM.

Flash memory is a special type of rewriteable read-only memory (ROM) that is compact and portable. ***Memory cards*** contain high-capacity storage that holds data such as captured images, music, or text files. Memory cards are removable; when one is full the user can insert an additional card. Subsequently, the data can be downloaded from the card to a computer. The card can then be erased and used again. Memory cards are typically used in digital devices such as cameras, cellular phones, and personal digital assistants (PDA). ***Memory sticks*** provide nonvolatile memory for a range of portable devices including computers, digital cameras, MP3 players, and PDAs.

SECONDARY STORAGE

Storage is a hot area in the business arena as organizations struggle to make sense of exploding volumes of data. Storage sales grew more than 16 percent to nearly $8 billion in 2004, according to IDC market research. ***Secondary storage*** consists of equipment designed to store large volumes of data for long-term storage. Secondary storage devices are nonvolatile and do not lose their contents when the computer is turned off. Some storage devices, such as a hard disk, offer easy update capabilities and a large storage capacity. Others, such as CD-ROMs, offer limited update capabilities but possess large storage capacities.

Storage capacity is expressed in bytes, with megabytes being the most common. A ***megabyte (MB or M or Meg)*** is roughly 1 million bytes. Therefore, a computer with 256 MB of RAM translates into the RAM being able to hold roughly 256 million characters of data and software instructions. A ***gigabyte (GB)*** is roughly 1 billion bytes. A ***terabyte (TB)*** is roughly 1 trillion bytes (refer to Figure B3.5).

Most standard desktops have a hard drive with storage capacity in excess of 80 GB. Hard drives for large organizational computer systems can hold in excess of 100 TB of information. For example, a typical double-spaced page of pure text is roughly 2,000 characters. Therefore, a 40 GB (40 gigabyte or 40 billion characters) hard drive can hold approximately 20 million pages of text.

Common storage devices include:

- Magnetic medium
- Optical medium

Term	Size
Kilobyte (KB)	1,024 Bytes
Megabyte (MB)	1,024 KB 1,048,576 Bytes
Gigabyte (GB)	1,024 MB (10^9 bytes)
Terabyte (TB)	1,024 GB (10^{12} bytes) 1 TB = Printing of 1 TB would require 50,000 trees to be made into paper
Petabyte (PB)	1,024 TB (10^{15} bytes) 200 PB = All production of digital magnetic tape in 1995
Exabyte (EB)	1,024 PB (10^{18} bytes) 2 EB = total volume of information generated worldwide annually 5 EB = all words ever spoken by human beings

FIGURE B3.5

Binary Terms

Magnetic Medium

Magnetic medium is a secondary storage medium that uses magnetic techniques to store and retrieve data on disks or tapes coated with magnetically sensitive materials. Like iron filings on a sheet of waxed paper, these materials are reoriented when a magnetic field passes over them. During write operations, the read/write heads emit a magnetic field that orients the magnetic materials on the disk or tape to represent encoded data. During read operations, the read/write heads sense the encoded data on the medium.

One of the first forms of magnetic medium developed was magnetic tape. *Magnetic tape* is an older secondary storage medium that uses a strip of thin plastic coated with a magnetically sensitive recording medium. The most popular type of magnetic medium is a hard drive. A *hard drive* is a secondary storage medium that uses several rigid disks coated with a magnetically sensitive material and housed together with the recording heads in a hermetically sealed mechanism. Hard drive performance is measured in terms of access time, seek time, rotational speed, and data transfer rate.

Optical Medium

Optical medium is a secondary storage medium for computers on which information is stored at extremely high density in the form of tiny pits. The presence or absence of pits is read by a tightly focused laser beam. Optical medium types include:

- **Compact disk-read-only memory (CD-ROM) drive**—an optical drive designed to read the data encoded on CD-ROMs and to transfer this data to a computer.
- **Compact disk-read-write (CD-RW) drive**—an optical drive that enables users to erase existing data and to write new data repeatedly to a CD-RW.
- **Digital video disk (DVD)**—a CD-ROM format capable of storing up to a maximum of 17 GB of data; enough for a full-length feature movie.
- **DVD-ROM drive**—a read-only drive designed to read the data encoded on a DVD and transfer the data to a computer.
- **Digital video disk-read/write (DVD-RW)**—a standard for DVD discs and player/recorder mechanisms that enables users to record in the DVD format.

CD-ROMs and DVDs offer an increasingly economical medium for storing data and programs. The overall trend in secondary storage is toward more direct-access methods, higher capacity with lower costs, and increased portability.

INPUT DEVICES

An ***input device*** is equipment used to capture information and commands. A keyboard is used to type in information, and a mouse is used to point and click on buttons and icons. Numerous input devices are available in many different environments, some of which have applications that are more suitable in a personal setting than a business setting. A keyboard, mouse, and scanner are the most common forms of input devices (see Figures B3.6 and B3.7).

New forms of input devices allow people to exercise and play video games at the same time. The Kilowatt Sport from Powergrid Fitness lets people combine strength training with their favorite video games. Players can choose any PlayStation or Xbox game that uses a joystick to run the elliptical trainer. After loading the game, participants stand on a platform while pushing and pulling a resistance rod in all directions to control what happens in the game. The varied movement targets muscle groups on the chest, arms, shoulders, abdomen, and back. The machine's display shows information such as pounds lifted and current resistance level, and players can use one-touch adjustment to vary the degree of difficulty.

Another new input device is a stationary bicycle. A computer design team of graduate and undergraduate students at MIT built the Cyclescore, an integrated video game and bicycle. The MIT students tested current games on the market but found users would stop pedaling to concentrate on the game. To engage users, the team is designing games that interact with the experience of exercise itself, for example, monitoring heart rate and adjusting the difficulty of the game according to the user's bicycling capabilities. In one game, the player must pedal to make a hot-air balloon float over mountains, while collecting coins and shooting at random targets.

OUTPUT DEVICES

An ***output device*** is equipment used to see, hear, or otherwise accept the results of information processing requests. Among output devices, printers and monitors are the most common; however, speakers and plotters (special printers that draw output on a page) are widely used (see Figure B3.8). In addition, output devices are responsible for converting computer-stored information into a form that can be understood.

Manual Input Devices
Joystick—widely used as an alternative to the keyboard for computer games and some professional applications, such as computer-aided design
Keyboard—provides a set of alphabetic, numeric, punctuation, symbol, and control keys
Microphone—captures sounds such as a voice for voice recognition software
Mouse—one or more control buttons housed in a palm-sized case and designed so that one can move it about on the table next to the keyboard
Pointing stick—causes the pointer to move on the screen by applying directional pressure (popular on notebooks and PDAs)
Touch screen—allows the use of a finger to point at and touch a particular function to perform
Touch pad—a form of a stationary mouse on which the movement of a finger causes the pointer on the screen to move

FIGURE B3.6

Manual Input Devices

Automated Input Devices
Bar code scanner—captures information that exists in the form of vertical bars whose width and distance apart determine a number
Digital camera—captures still images or video as a series of 1s and 0s
Magnetic ink character reader—reads magnetic ink numbers printed on checks that identify the bank, checking account, and check number
Optical-character recognition—converts text into digital format for computer input
Optical-mark recognition (OMR)—detects the presence or absence of a mark in a predetermined place (popular for multiple-choice exams)
Point-of-sale (POS)—captures information at the point of a transaction, typically in a retail environment
Radio frequency identification (RFID)—uses active or passive tags in the form of chips or smart labels that can store unique identifiers and relay this information to electronic readers

FIGURE B3.7

Automated Input Devices

Output Devices
Cathode-ray tube (CRT)—a vacuum tube that uses an electron gun (cathode) to emit a beam of electrons that illuminates phosphors on a screen as the beam sweeps across the screen repeatedly; a monitor is often called a CRT
Liquid crystal display (LCDs)—a low-powered display technology used in laptop computers where rod-shaped crystal molecules change their orientation when an electrical current flows through them
Laser printer—a printer that forms images using an electrostatic process, the same way a photocopier works
Ink-jet printer—a printer that makes images by forcing ink droplets through nozzles
Plotter—a printer that uses computer-directed pens for creating high-quality images, blueprints, schematics, etc.

FIGURE B3.8

Output Devices

A new output device based on sensor technology aims to translate American Sign Language (ASL) into speech, enabling the millions of people who use ASL to better communicate with those who do not know the rapid gesturing system. The AcceleGlove is a glove lined on the inside with sensors embedded in rings. The sensors, called accelerometers, measure acceleration and can categorize and translate finger and hand movements. Additional, interconnected attachments for the elbow and shoulder capture ASL signs that are made with full arm motion. When users wear the glove while signing ASL, algorithms in the glove's software translate the hand gestures into words. The translations can be relayed through speech synthesizers or read on a PDA-size computer screen. Inventor Jose L. Hernandez-Rebollar started with a single glove that could translate only the ASL alphabet. Now, the device employs two gloves that contain a 1,000-word vocabulary.

Other new output devices are being developed every day. Needapresent.com, a British company, has developed a vibrating USB massage ball, which plugs into a computer's USB port to generate a warm massage for sore body parts during those long evenings spent coding software or writing papers. Needapresent.com also makes a coffee cup warmer that plugs into the USB port.

COMMUNICATION DEVICES

A *communication device* is equipment used to send information from one location and receive it at another. A telephone modem connects a computer to a phone line in order to access another computer. The computer works in terms of digital signals, while a standard telephone line works with analog signals. Each digital signal represents a bit (either 0 or 1). The modem must convert the digital signals of a computer into analog signals so they can be sent across the telephone line. At the other end, another modem translates the analog signals into digital signals, which can then be used by the other computer. Figure B3.9 displays the different types of modems.

Computer Categories

Supercomputers today can hit processing capabilities of well over 200 teraflops—the equivalent of everyone on earth performing 35,000 calculations per second (see Figure B3.10). For the past 20 years, federally funded supercomputing research has given birth to some of the computer industry's most significant technology breakthroughs including:

- Clustering, which allows companies to chain together thousands of PCs to build mass-market systems.
- Parallel processing, which provides the ability to run two or more tasks simultaneously and is viewed as the chip industry's future.
- Mosaic browser, which morphed into Netscape and made the web a household name.

Federally funded supercomputers have also advanced some of the country's most dynamic industries, including advanced manufacturing, gene research in the life sciences, and real-time financial-market modeling.

Computers come in different shapes, sizes, and colors. Some are small enough to carry around, while others are the size of a telephone booth. Size does not always correlate to power, speed, and price (see Figure B3.11).

Carrier Technology	Description	Speed	Comments
Dial-up Access	On demand access using a modem and regular telephone line (POT).	2400 bps to 56 Kbps	■ Cheap but slow.
Cable	Special cable modem and cable line required.	512 Kbps to 20 Mbps	■ Must have existing cable access in area. ■ Bandwidth is shared.
DSL Digital Subscriber Line	This technology uses the unused digital portion of a regular copper telephone line to transmit and receive information. A special modem and adapter card are required.	128 Kbps to 8 Mbps	■ Doesn't interfere with normal telephone use. ■ Bandwidth is dedicated. ■ Must be within 5 km (3.1 miles) of telephone company switch.
Wireless (LMCS)	Access is gained by connection to a high-speed cellular like local multipoint communications system (LMCS) network via wireless transmitter/receiver.	30 Mbps or more	■ Can be used for high-speed data, broadcast TV, and wireless telephone service.
Satellite	Newer versions have two-way satellite access, removing need for phone line.	6 Mbps or more	■ Bandwidth is not shared. ■ Some connections require an existing Internet service account. ■ Setup fees can range from $500 to $1,000.

FIGURE B3.9

Comparing Modems

MIT's Media Lab is developing a laptop that it will sell for $100 each to government agencies around the world for distribution to millions of underprivileged schoolchildren. Using a simplified sales model and some reengineering of the device helped MIT reach the $100 price point. Almost half the price of a current laptop comprises marketing, sales, distribution, and profit. Of the remaining costs, the display panel and backlight account for roughly half while the rest covers the operating system. The low-cost laptop will use a display system that costs less than $25, a 500 MHz processor from AMD, a wireless LAN connection, 1 GB of storage, and

FIGURE B3.10

Supercomputer

Computer Category	Description	Size
Personal digital assistant (PDA)	A small handheld computer that performs simple tasks such as taking notes, scheduling appointments, and maintaining an address book and a calendar. The PDA screen is touch-sensitive, allowing a user to write directly on the screen, capturing what is written.	Fits in a person's hand
Laptop	A fully functional computer designed to be carried around and run on battery power. Laptops come equipped with all of the technology that a personal desktop computer has, yet weigh as little as two pounds.	Similar to a textbook
Tablet	A pen-based computer that provides the screen capabilities of a PDA with the functional capabilities of a laptop or desktop computer. Similar to PDAs, tablet PCs use a writing pen or stylus to write notes on the screen and touch the screen to perform functions such as clicking on a link while visiting a website.	Similar to a textbook
Desktop	Available with a horizontal system box (the box is where the CPU, RAM, and storage devices are held) with a monitor on top, or a vertical system box (called a tower) usually placed on the floor within a work area.	Fits on a desk
Workstation	Similar to a desktop but has more powerful mathematical and graphics processing capabilities and can perform more complicated tasks in less time. Typically used for software development, web development, engineering, and ebusiness tools.	Fits on a desk
Minicomputer (midrange computer)	Designed to meet the computing needs of several people simultaneously in a small to medium-size business environment. A common type of minicomputer is a server and is used for managing internal company networks and websites. Minicomputers are more powerful than desktop computers but also cost more, ranging in price from $5,000 to several hundred thousand dollars.	Ranges from fitting on a desk to the size of a filing cabinet
Mainframe computer	Designed to meet the computing needs of hundreds of people in a large business environment. Mainframe computers are a step up in size, power, capability, and cost from minicomputers. Mainframes can cost in excess of $1 million. With processing speeds greater than 1 trillion instructions per second (compared to a typical desktop that can process about 2.5 billion instructions per second), mainframes can easily handle the processing requests of hundreds of people simultaneously.	Similar to a refrigerator
Supercomputer	The fastest, most powerful, and most expensive type of computer. Organizations such as NASA that are heavily involved in research and number crunching employ supercomputers because of the speed with which they can process information. Other large, customer-oriented businesses such as General Motors and AT&T employ supercomputers just to handle customer information and transaction processing.	Similar to a car

FIGURE B3.11

Computer Categories

the Linux operating system. The machine will automatically connect with others. China and Brazil have already ordered 3 million and 1 million laptops, respectively. MIT's goal is to produce around 150 million laptops per year.

Software Basics

Hardware is only as good as the software that runs it. Over the years, the cost of hardware has decreased while the complexity and cost of software have increased. Some large software applications, such as customer relationship management systems, contain millions of lines of code, take years to develop, and cost millions of dollars. The two main types of software are system software and application software.

SYSTEM SOFTWARE

System software controls how the various technology tools work together along with the application software. System software includes both operating system software and utility software.

Operating System Software

Linus Torvalds, a shy Finnish programmer, may seem an unlikely choice to be one of the world's top managers. However, Linux, the software project he created while a university student, is now one of the most powerful influences on the computer world. Linux is an operating system built by volunteers and distributed for free and has become one of the primary competitors to Microsoft. Torvalds coordinates Linux development with a few dozen volunteer assistants and more than 1,000 programmers scattered around the globe. They contribute code for the kernel—or core piece—of Linux. He also sets the rules for dozens of technology companies that have lined up behind Linux, including IBM, Dell, Hewlett-Packard, and Intel.

Operating system software controls the application software and manages how the hardware devices work together. When using Excel to create and print a graph, the operating system software controls the process, ensures that a printer is attached and has paper, and sends the graph to the printer along with instructions on how to print it.

Operating system software also supports a variety of useful features, one of which is multitasking. *Multitasking* allows more than one piece of software to be used at a time. Multitasking is used when creating a graph in Excel and simultaneously printing a word processing document. With multitasking, both pieces of application software are operating at the same time. There are different types of operating system software for personal environments and for organizational environments (see Figure B3.12).

Utility Software

Utility software provides additional functionality to the operating system. Utility software includes antivirus software, screen savers, and anti-spam software. Figure B3.13 displays a few types of available utility software.

APPLICATION SOFTWARE

Application software is used for specific information processing needs, including payroll, customer relationship management, project management, training, and many others. Application software is used to solve specific problems or perform specific tasks. From an organizational perspective, payroll software, collaborative software such as videoconferencing (within groupware), and inventory management software are all examples of application software (see Figure B3.14).

FIGURE B3.12

Operating System
Software

Operating System Software	
Linux	An open source operating system that provides a rich environment for high-end workstations and network servers. Open source refers to any program whose source code is made available for use or modification as users or other developers see fit.
Mac OS X	The operating system of Macintosh computers.
Microsoft Windows	Generic name for the various operating systems in the Microsoft Windows family, including Microsoft Windows CE, Microsoft Windows 98, Microsoft Windows ME, Microsoft Windows 2000, Microsoft Windows XP, Microsoft Windows NT, and Microsoft Windows Server 2003.
MS-DOS	The standard, single-user operating system of IBM and IBM-compatible computers, introduced in 1981. MS-DOS is a command-line operating system that requires the user to enter commands, arguments, and syntax.
UNIX	A 32-bit multitasking and multiuser operating system that originated at AT&T's Bell Laboratories and is now used on a wide variety of computers, from mainframes to PDAs.

FIGURE B3.13

Utility Software

Types of Utility Software	
Crash-proof	Helps save information if a computer crashes.
Disk image for data recovery	Relieves the burden of reinstalling and tweaking scores of applications if a hard drive crashes or becomes irretrievably corrupted.
Disk optimization	Organizes information on a hard disk in the most efficient way.
Encrypt data	Protects confidential information from unauthorized eyes. Programs such as BestCrypt simply and effectively apply one of several powerful encryption schemes to hard drive information. Users unlock the information by entering a password in the BestCrypt control panel. The program can also secure information on rewritable optical disks or any other storage media that is assigned a drive letter.
File and data recovery	Retrieves accidental deletion of photos or documents in Windows XP by utilities such as Free Undelete, which searches designated hard drive deletion areas for recognizable data.
Text protect	In Microsoft Word, prevents users from typing over existing text after accidentally hitting the Insert key. Launch the Insert Toggle Key program, and the PC will beep whenever a user presses the Insert key.
Preventative security	Through programs such as Window Washer, erases file histories, browser cookies, cache contents, and other crumbs that applications and Windows leave on a hard drive.
Spyware	Removes any software that employs a user's Internet connection in the background without the user's knowledge or explicit permission.
Uninstaller	Can remove software that is no longer needed.

Types of Application Software	
Browser	Enables the user to navigate the World Wide Web. The two leading browsers are Netscape Navigator and Microsoft Internet Explorer.
Communication	Turns a computer into a terminal for transmitting data to and receiving data from distant computers through the telephone system.
Data management	Provides the tools for data retrieval, modification, deletion, and insertion; for example, Access, MySQL, and Oracle.
Desktop publishing	Transforms a computer into a desktop publishing workstation. Leading packages include Adobe FrameMaker, Adobe PageMaker, and QuarkXpress.
Email	Provides email services for computer users, including receiving mail, sending mail, and storing messages. Leading email software includes Microsoft Outlook, Microsoft Outlook Express, and Eudora.
Groupware	Increases the cooperation and joint productivity of small groups of co-workers.
Presentation graphics	Creates and enhances charts and graphs so that they are visually appealing and easily understood by an audience. A full-features presentation graphics package such as Lotus Freelance Graphics or Microsoft PowerPoint includes facilities for making a wide variety of charts and graphs and for adding titles, legends, and explanatory text anywhere in the chart or graph.
Programming	Possesses an artificial language consisting of a fixed vocabulary and a set of rules (called syntax) that programmers use to write computer programs. Leading programming languages include Java, C + +, C#, and .NET.
Spreadsheet	Simulates an accountant's worksheet onscreen and lets users embed hidden formulas that perform calculations on the visible data. Many spreadsheet programs also include powerful graphics and presentation capabilities to create attractive products. The leading spreadsheet application is Microsoft Excel.
Word processing	Transforms a computer into a tool for creating, editing, proofreading, formatting, and printing documents. Leading word processing applications include Microsoft Word and WordPerfect.

FIGURE B3.14

Application Software

✳ PLUG-IN SUMMARY

Information technology (IT) is a field concerned with the use of technology in managing and processing information. IT includes cell phones, PDAs, software such as spreadsheet software, and printers. There are two categories of IT: hardware and software. The six hardware components include CPU, primary storage, secondary storage, input devices, output devices, and communication devices. Computer categories include PDAs, laptops, tablets, desktops, workstations, minicomputers, mainframe computers, and supercomputers.

Software includes system software and application software. Operating system software and utility software are the two primary types of system software. There are many forms of application software from word processing to databases.

✳ KEY TERMS

Application software, B3.13
Arithmetic-logic unit (ALU), B3.3
Binary digit (bit), B3.5
Byte, B3.5
Cache memory, B3.6
Central processing unit (CPU)
  (or microprocessor), B3.3
Communication device, B3.10
Complex instruction set
  computer (CISC) chip, B3.4
Computer, B3.3
Control unit, B3.3
Flash memory, B3.6
Gigabyte (GB), B3.6
Gigahertz (GHz), B3.4

Hard drive, B3.7
Hardware, B3.2
Information technology
  (IT), B3.2
Input device, B3.8
Magnetic medium, B3.7
Magnetic tape, B3.7
Megabyte (MB, M, or
  Meg), B3.6
Megahertz (MHz), B3.4
Memory card, B3.6
Memory stick, B3.6
Multitasking, B3.13
Operating system
  software, B3.13

Output device, B3.8
Primary storage, B3.5
Random access memory
  (RAM), B3.5
Read-only memory
  (ROM), B3.6
Reduced instruction set
  computer (RISC) chip, B3.4
Secondary storage, B3.6
Software, B3.2
System software, B3.13
Terabyte (TB), B3.6
Utility software, B3.13
Virtualization, B3.5
Volatility, B3.5

✳ CLOSING CASE ONE

Changing Circuits at Circuit City

When Circuit City expanded the big-box warehouse format to consumer electronics retailing in the 1980s, the company was on its way to becoming the place to go for TVs and stereos. By the late 1980s, it had sidestepped its then top competitor, Silo, and it soon put the squeeze on the likes of Tweeter and RadioShack. Circuit City was doing so well in the 1990s that business consultant Jim Collins, in his best seller *Good to Great,* wrote: "From 1982 to 1999, Circuit City generated cumulative stock returns 22 times better than the market, handily beating Intel, Wal-Mart, GE, Hewlett-Packard and Coca-Cola."

Today, Circuit City is in a markedly different position. By 2001, Best Buy had raced past the Richmond, Virginia-based chain, usurping its position as the number one consumer electronics

retailer. Best Buy now has 608 stores compared with Circuit City's 599 and nearly $25 billion in revenue to Circuit City's $9.7 billion. Circuit City is ranked by consultancy Retail Forward as the number three seller of consumer electronics, behind Best Buy and Wal-Mart. "Circuit City was the 800-pound gorilla," said Joseph Feldman, a research analyst with the investment bank SG Cowen & Co. However, "they woke up one morning and Best Buy had doubled its size with the same number of stores."

Catching Best Buy

Circuit City has been trying to catch up to Best Buy, or at least cement its position as a serious contender in consumer electronics retailing. Its top executives announced plans to turn the company into a customer-focused business that delivers a personalized experience to all customers across all its channels (stores, web, and call centers). Michael Jones, who took over as Circuit City's CIO in January 2004, speaks passionately about the high-profile role technology will play in delivering personalized customer experiences. However, before he can achieve his vision of store associates recognizing customers through their loyalty cards as soon as they enter the store, he has a lot of unglamorous groundwork to lay. Circuit City's strategy hinges on a robust IT infrastructure that makes information readily accessible to decision makers. Everything the company is doing to improve its business—from developing more effective promotions to deciding which products should be displayed at the ends of aisles in stores—hinges on data. "This is heavy analytical work. It's fact-based, data-driven," said Philip Schoonover, Circuit City's new president who was hired in October 2004 from Best Buy.

Circuit City is just starting to invest heavily in the technology needed to act on this strategy. It is upgrading its mostly proprietary point-of-sale (POS) system and building an enterprise data warehouse to replace siloed databases. However, some analysts say Circuit City's turnaround effort has been hampered by a stodgy, overly complacent leadership that lacks vision. Top executives saw the Best Buy locomotive coming but failed to react as it steamed past them. Indeed, some analysts say they doubt Circuit City will ever catch up.

Bottom-Up Changes

As part of its turnaround effort over the past few years, Circuit City has sold all of its non-core businesses to focus on its core: consumer electronics. It also has changed the pay structure for in-store employees, begun relocating stores (it closed 19), and hired new management. In addition, the company is finally starting to hone its customer-centric strategy. Circuit City is already improving the customer experience in its stores by, among other things, locating accessories and services close to big-ticket items so that customers can see more quickly what they might need to furnish their home office or outfit a home theater. For example, when a customer is looking at a high-definition television, nearby is a selection of furniture to hold the TV, the cables needed to hook it up, and DirectTV or digital cable service products. Circuit City is also making merchandising decisions based on what is important to the customer. For example, its stores are beginning to feature products deemed most important to customers on the displays at the ends of aisles. The company is trying to nail the basics of customer service by making sure that items are not out of stock.

Questions

1. How would anticipating Best Buy's growth have helped Circuit City remain as an industry leader?
2. Why is keeping up with technology critical to a global company such as Circuit City?
3. Highlight some of the potential risks facing Circuit City's new business model.
4. Why is Circuit City benefiting from implementing strategic product placement techniques?

★ CLOSING CASE TWO

Electronic Breaking Points

What happens when someone accidentally spills a cup of hot coffee on a laptop, puts a USB memory key in a washing machine, or drops an iPod in the sand? How much abuse can electronic products take and keep on working? *PC World* tested several products to determine their breaking points.

Laptop

A Gateway laptop was placed in a shoulder bag and smashed into several doors and walls. It was also dropped off a six-foot-high bookcase to simulate a drop from an airplane's overhead bin. Finally, it was knocked off a desk onto a carpeted floor without the bag. After all the abuse, the Gateway consistently rebooted and recognized the wireless network; however, the battery did become slightly dislodged and the optical drive opened.

Severe physical damage was caused when the laptop was dropped onto a hardwood floor. The laptop's screen cracked, and the black plastic molding above the keyboard cracked. Plastic splinters littered the floor, and the optical drive refused to open.

Spilling coffee in a travel-size mug onto the keyboard caused a slight sizzle, after which the Gateway's blue light winked out. The machine was quickly turned off, the battery removed, the liquid drained, the keys mopped, and the unit set aside. Unfortunately, the laptop never recovered.

Smart Phone

The PalmOne Treo 600 smart phone was stepped on, buried in the sand, bounced around in a car, and dropped off a desk onto carpeted and hardwood floors. Even though the Treo 600 was not protected by a shock-absorbent case or plastic screen cover, there were no signs of failure. Repeatedly knocking it off the desk onto a carpeted floor also left it undamaged, although the unit did turn off on several occasions.

The desk-to-hardwood-floor test produced scratches but nothing else. If dropped when in phone mode, the Treo automatically turned off. If an application was running—the calculator, for example—the device stayed on and the data remained on the screen, though a mysterious extra numeral nine appeared every time it was dropped.

MP3 Player

A 6 GB silver iPod Mini went for a bouncy car ride, was dropped on wet grass and dry pavement, was knocked off a desk onto carpeted and hardwood floors, and was finally dropped in dry sand. Bouncing inside the car caused a couple of skips. Drops on soft wet grass and carpet had no ill effect. Dropping it from the car seat to the curb and off a desk onto a hardwood floor produced a few nicks and caused songs to skip and the device to shut down repeatedly. Still, all the unit's features continued to work after the abuse, and songs played.

However, the Mini did not like the beach. Without the benefit of a protective case or plastic display covering on the unit, sand wedged under the scroll wheel, affecting all controls. Feature settings could be seen and highlighted, but the crunching sand prevented the Mini from launching them. The unit turned on but could not turn off until the iPod's automatic shutdown feature took over.

Memory Stick

Lexar claims that its JumpDrive Sport 256 MB USB 2.0 Flash Drive is "built for the rugged life." A rubber cap protects the device, absorbing shock from any drops. For these experiments, the

Protecting Electronic Products
Bag it. Place your product in a cushioned case or shock-absorbent travel bag. The secret is to make sure it has plenty of padding.
Get protection. Almost every technology manufacturer offers some type of warranty and equipment-replacement program. For example, Sprint provides the PCS Total Equipment Protection service, which costs $5 per month and covers loss, theft, and accidental damage to a cell phone.
Clean up spills. Try these tips to bring a laptop and data back from the dead after a spill.
1. **Disconnect the battery.** The faster the battery is disconnected the less likely components will burn out.
2. **Empty it.** Turn over the device and pour out as much liquid as possible.
3. **Open it up.** Remove the optical drive and keyboard. This can be tricky, so check the user manual for instructions. Once open, use a towel to soak up as much liquid as possible. According to Herman De Hoop, HP's technical marketing manager, you can even use a hair dryer set on cool (not hot) to dry the liquid.
4. **Leave it alone.** Let the device sit for at least 12 to 24 hours. Robert Enochs, IBM's worldwide product manager for the ThinkPad Series, warns that you should not turn the device on until all the liquid is gone and it is completely dry.
5. **Plug and pray.** Reassemble the device, and if it powers up, copy off important data, and then call the manufacturer. Even if the unit works, a professional cleaning is recommended.
6. **Enter a recovery program.** For an average price of $900, enlist the help of data recovery services like DriveSavers to rescue data from drowned hard disks.

FIGURE B3.15

How to Protect
Electronic Products

device was used without its cap. It was dropped, stepped on, buried in the sand, and knocked off a desk onto a hardwood floor. It also took a spin through the washing machine and dryer and was even run over by a car.

There is truth in advertising. Neither water, heat, sand, nor car could keep the memory stick from its appointed storage rounds. The car did squeeze the metal USB connector tip a tad tighter, but the device was still able to make contact with the USB port, and it worked perfectly.

Memory Card

The SanDisk SD 64 MB memory card is easy to misplace, but not easy to break. It was swatted off a desk onto a hardwood floor, dropped, stepped on, and buried in the sand. It also underwent a two-rinse cycle in the wash in a jeans pocket and then tumbled in the dryer for an hour on a high-heat setting. The SanDisk memory card aced every torture test.

For tips on how to protect electronic products, review Figure B3.15.

Questions

1. Identify the six hardware categories and place each product listed in the case in its appropriate category.
2. Describe the CPU and identify which products would use a CPU.
3. Describe the relationship between memory sticks and laptops. How can a user employ one to help protect information loss from the other?
4. Identify the different types of software each of the products listed in the case might use.

✱ **MAKING BUSINESS DECISIONS**

1. Purchasing a Computer

Dell is considered the fastest company on earth and specializes in computer customization. Connect to Dell's web site at www.dell.com. Go to the portion of Dell's site that allows you to customize either a laptop or a desktop computer. First, choose an already prepared system and note its price and capability in terms of CPU speed, RAM size, monitor quality, and storage capacity. Now, customize that system to increase CPU speed, add more RAM, increase monitor size and quality, and add more storage capacity. What is the difference in price between the two? Which system is more in your price range? Which system has the speed and capacity you need?

2. Web-Enabled Cell Phones

When categorizing computers by size for personal needs, we focused on PDAs, laptops, and desktop computers. Other variations include web-enabled cell phones that include instant text messaging and web computers. For this project, you will need a group of four people, which you will then split into two groups of two. Have the first group research web-enabled cell phones, their capabilities and costs. Have that group make a purchase recommendation based on price and capability. Have the second group do the same for web computers. What is your vision of the future? Will we ever get rid of clunky laptops and desktops in favor of more portable and cheaper devices such as web-enabled cell phones and web computers? Why or why not?

3. Small Business Computers

Many different types of computers are available for small businesses. Use the Internet to find three different vendors of laptops or notebooks that are good for small businesses. Find the most expensive and the least expensive that the vendor offers and create a table comparing the different computers based on the following:

- CPU
- Memory
- Hard drive
- Optical drive
- Operating system
- Utility software
- Application software
- Support plan

Determine which computer you would recommend for a small business looking for an inexpensive laptop. Determine which computer you would recommend for a small business looking for an expensive laptop.

4. PDA Software

The personal digital assistant (PDA) market is ferocious, dynamic, and uncertain. One of the uncertainties is which operating system for PDAs will become dominant. Today, Microsoft operating systems dominate the laptop and desktop market. Research the more popular PDAs available today. What are the different operating systems? What different functionality do they offer? Are they compatible with each other? Determine which one will dominate in the future.

PLUG-IN

B4

Enterprise Architectures

LEARNING OUTCOMES

1. Explain the three components of an enterprise architecture.
2. Describe how an organization can implement a solid information architecture.
3. List and describe the five qualities of an infrastructure architecture.
4. Compare web services and open systems.

Enterprise Architectures

A 66-hour failure of an FBI database that performed background checks on gun buyers was long enough to allow criminals to buy guns. The database failed at 1:00 p.m. on a Thursday and was not restored until 7:30 a.m. Sunday. The FBI must complete a gun check within three days; if it fails to do so, a merchant is free to make the sale. During this outage, any gun checks that were in progress were not finished, allowing merchants to complete those gun sales at their own discretion.

To support the volume and complexity of today's user and application requirements, information technology needs to take a fresh approach to enterprise architectures by constructing smarter, more flexible environments that protect from system failures and crashes. *Enterprise architectures* include the plans for how an organization will build, deploy, use, and share its data, processes, and IT assets. A unified enterprise architecture will standardize enterprisewide hardware and software systems, with tighter links to the business strategy. A solid enterprise architecture can decrease costs, increase standardization, promote reuse of IT assets, and speed development of new systems. The end result is that the right enterprise architecture can make IT cheaper, strategic, and more responsive. The primary business goals of enterprise architectures are displayed in Figure B4.1.

Enterprise architectures are never static; they continually change. Organizations use enterprise architects to help manage change. An *enterprise architect (EA)* is a person grounded in technology, fluent in business, a patient diplomat, who provides the important bridge between IT and the business. An EA is expensive and

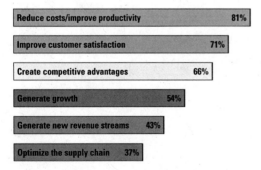

Reduce costs/improve productivity	81%
Improve customer satisfaction	71%
Create competitive advantages	66%
Generate growth	54%
Generate new revenue streams	43%
Optimize the supply chain	37%

FIGURE B4.1

Primary Business Goals of Enterprise Architectures

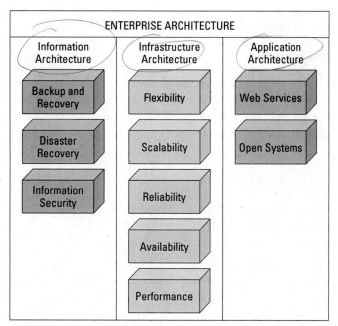

FIGURE B4.2

Three Components of Enterprise Architecture

generally receives a salary upward of $150,000 per year. T-Mobile International's enterprise architects review projects to ensure they are soundly designed, meet the business objectives, and fit in with the overall enterprise architecture. One T-Mobile project was to create software that would let subscribers customize the ring sounds on their cell phones. The project group assumed it would have to create most of the software from scratch. However, T-Mobile's EAs found software already written elsewhere at T-Mobile that could be reused to create the new application. The reuse reduced the development cycle time by eight months, and the new application was available in less than six weeks.

Companies that have created solid enterprise architectures, such as T-Mobile, are reaping huge rewards in savings, flexibility, and business alignment. Basic enterprise architectures contain three components (see Figure B4.2).

1. *Information architecture* identifies where and how important information, like customer records, is maintained and secured.
2. *Infrastructure architecture* includes the hardware, software, and telecommunications equipment that, when combined, provide the underlying foundation to support the organization's goals.
3. *Application architecture* determines how applications integrate and relate to each other.

Information Architecture

Information architecture identifies where and how important information, like customer records, is maintained and secured. A single backup or restore failure can cost an organization more than time and money; some data cannot be re-created, and the business intelligence lost from that data can be tremendous. Chief information officers should have enough confidence that they could walk around and randomly pull out cables to prove that the systems are safe. The CIO should also be secure enough to perform this test during peak business hours. If the thought of this test makes the CIO cringe, then the organization's customers should be cringing also. Figure B4.3 depicts the three primary areas an enterprise information architecture should focus on:

1. Backup and recovery
2. Disaster recovery
3. Information security

BACKUP AND RECOVERY

Each year businesses lose time and money because of system crashes and failures. One way to minimize the damage of a system crash is to have a backup and recovery strategy in place. A ***backup*** is an exact copy of a system's information. ***Recovery*** is the ability to get a system up and running in the event of a system crash or failure and includes restoring the information backup. Many different types of backup and recovery media are available, including redundant storage servers, tapes, disks, and even CDs and DVDs. All the different types of backup and recovery media are reliable; their primary differences are the speed and associated costs.

A chain of more than 4,000 franchise locations, 7-Eleven Taiwan uploads backup and recovery information from its central location to all its chain locations daily. The company implemented a new technology solution by Digital Fountain that could quickly and reliably download and upload backup and recovery information to all its stores. In addition, when a connection fails during the download or upload, the technology automatically resumes the download without having to start over, saving valuable time.

Organizations should choose a backup and recovery strategy that is in line with business goals. If the organization deals with large volumes of critical information, it will require daily backups, perhaps even hourly backups, to storage servers. If the organization deals with small amounts of noncritical information, then it might require only weekly backups to tapes, CDs, or DVDs. Deciding how often to back up information and what media to use is a critical business decision. If an organization decides to back up on a weekly basis, then it is taking the risk that, if a total system crash occurs, it could lose a week's worth of work. If this risk is acceptable, then a weekly backup strategy will work. If this risk is unacceptable, then the organization needs to move to a daily backup strategy. Some organizations find the risk of losing a day's worth of work too high and move to an hourly backup strategy.

Two techniques used to help in case of system failure are fault tolerance and failover. ***Fault tolerance*** is a computer system designed that in the event a component fails, a backup component or procedure can immediately take its place with no loss of service. Fault tolerance can be provided with software, or embedded

FIGURE B4.3

The Three Areas Enterprise Information Architecture Should Focus On

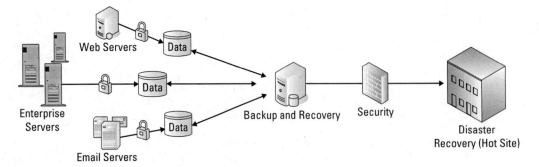

in hardware, or provided by some combination. ***Failover*** is a backup operational mode in which the functions of a computer component (such as a processor, server, network, or database) are assumed by secondary system components when the primary component becomes unavailable through either failure or scheduled down time. A failover procedure involves automatically offloading tasks to a standby system component so that the procedure is as seamless as possible to the end user. Used to make systems more fault tolerant, failover is typically an integral part of mission-critical systems that must be constantly available.

DISASTER RECOVERY

A northern Ohio power company, FirstEnergy, missed signs that there were potential problems in its portion of North America's electrical grid. The events that followed left an estimated 50 million people in the Northeast and Canada in the dark. The failings are laid out in the widely reported findings of a joint U.S./Canada task force that investigated the causes of the blackout and recommended what to do to avoid big-scale outages in the future. The report detailed many procedures or best practices including:

- Mind the enterprise architectures.
- Monitor the quality of computer networks that provide data on power suppliers and demand.
- Make sure the networks can be restored quickly in the case of downtime.
- Set up disaster recovery plans.
- Provide adequate staff training, including verbal communication protocols "so that operators are aware of any IT-related problems that may be affecting their situational awareness of the power grid."

Disasters such as power outages, floods, and even harmful hacking strike businesses every day. Organizations must develop a disaster recovery plan to prepare for such occurrences. A ***disaster recovery plan*** is a detailed process for recovering information or an IT system in the event of a catastrophic disaster such as a fire or flood. Spending on disaster recovery is rising worldwide among financial institutions (see Figure B4.4).

A comprehensive disaster recovery plan takes into consideration the location of the backup information. Many organizations store backup information in an off-site facility. StorageTek specializes in providing off-site information storage and disaster recovery solutions. A comprehensive disaster recovery plan also foresees the possibility that not only the computer equipment but also the building where employees work may be destroyed. A ***hot site*** is a separate and fully equipped facility where the company can move immediately after a disaster and resume business. A ***cold site*** is a separate facility that does not have any computer equipment, but is a place where employees can move after a disaster.

A ***disaster recovery cost curve*** charts (1) the cost to the organization of the unavailability of information and technology and (2) the cost to the organization of recovering from a disaster over time. Figure B4.5 displays a disaster recovery cost curve and shows that where the two lines intersect is the best recovery plan in terms of cost and time. Creating an organization's disaster recovery cost curve is no small task. It must consider the cost of losing information and technology within each department or functional area, and the cost of losing information and technology across the whole enterprise. During the first few hours of a disaster, those costs will be low but become increasingly higher over time. With those costs in hand, an organization must then determine the costs of recovery. Cost of recovery during the first few hours of a disaster is exceedingly high and diminishes over time.

FIGURE B4.4

Financial Institutions Worldwide Spending on Disaster Recovery

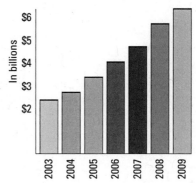

FIGURE B4.5

The Disaster Recovery
Cost Curve

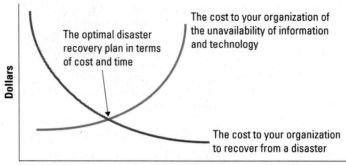

On April 18, 1906, San Francisco was rocked by an earthquake that destroyed large swathes of the city and claimed the lives of more than 3,000 inhabitants of the Bay Area. More than a century later, a bigger, bolder, rebuilt, and more resilient San Francisco is more important than ever. Now it serves as the heart of the global IT industry and a major world financial center. However, San Francisco remains well aware of the terrible potential danger that exists along the San Andreas fault.

The vast skyscrapers downtown may now be built to withstand huge pressures, but what about the infrastructure and the systems that keep modern business ticking—and the people who must be able to access them? ***Business continuity planning (BCP)*** is planning for how an organization will recover and restore partially or completely interrupted critical function(s) within a predetermined time after a disaster or extended disruption. Business continuity and disaster recovery are serious issues for all organizations in the Bay Area, including the Union Bank of California, which is based in the heart of downtown San Francisco.

Barry Cardoza, head of business continuity planning and disaster recovery at Union Bank of California, said, "You have disasters that you can see coming and you've got disasters that you can't see coming and an earthquake is an example of [the latter]. And you don't know how bad it's going to be until it hits."

Clearly, the bank must have processes in place ahead of such an event to mitigate the threat. Simply reacting is not a strategy. The continuity department must also understand every aspect of the business and weigh downtime for each in terms of financial and reputational damage. Union Bank of California has created a disaster recovery plan that includes multiple data centers in diverse locations, mirrored sites that can take over at the flick of a switch, hot sites where staff can walk in and start working exactly as they would if they were in their normal location, and a vast amount of redundancy. In addition, the bank has created real-time mirroring between data centers. It is now a matter of minutes not hours for Union Bank of California to be up and running in the event of a disaster.

INFORMATION SECURITY

Security professionals are under increasing pressure to do the job right and cost-effectively as networks extend beyond organizations to remote users, partners, and customers, and to cell phones, PDAs, and other mobile devices. Regulatory requirements to safeguard data have increased. Concerns about identity theft are at an all-time high. Hacking and other unauthorized access contribute to the approximately 10 million instances of identity theft each year, according to the Federal Trade Commission. A good information architecture includes a strong information security plan, along with managing user access and up-to-date antivirus software and patches.

Managing User Access

Managing user access to information is a critical piece of the information architecture. Passwords may still be the weakest link in the security chain. At Vitas Healthcare Corporation, with a workforce of 6,000 and operations across 15 states, authorized employees enter as many as a half-dozen passwords a day to access multiple systems. While it is important to maintain password discipline to secure customers' health care data, maintaining and managing the situation creates a drag on the IT department. "Our help desk spends 30 percent of their time on password management and provisioning," says John Sandbrook, senior IT director.

The company began using Fischer International Corporation's Identity Management Suite to manage passwords and comply with data-access regulations such as the Sarbanes-Oxley Act. The ID-management product includes automated audit, reporting, and compliance capabilities, plus a common platform for password management, provisioning, and self-service. With the software, Vitas can enforce stronger passwords with seven, eight, or nine characters, numbers, and capital letters that frequently change. The company anticipates curbing help-desk password time by 50 percent.

Up-to-Date Antivirus Software and Patches

Security is a top priority for business managers, regardless of the size of their company. Among Fortune 500 companies, more than 80 percent of those surveyed described updating security procedures, tools, and services as a key business priority. The same holds true for all small, midsize, or large companies and all IT managers and corporate managers.

The main focus for most managers is preventing hackers, spammers, and other malcontents from entering their networks, and nearly two-thirds are looking to enhance their network-security-management, intrusion-detection, content-filtering, and antispam software. More than half also plan to upgrade their encryption software.

Microsoft issues patches for its software on the second Tuesday of every month. These patches must be downloaded and installed on all systems across the entire enterprise if the company wants to keep its systems protected. At OMD, a media buying and planning subsidiary of Omnicom Group Inc., the network administrator had to manually install critical patches on all 100 servers, taking more than a week to deploy the patch across the company. Now, OMD uses automated installation software for patches and upgrades. The company purchased Altiris Management Suite for Dell servers, which let it move ahead with applying patches without taking down entire systems and balancing patch-deployment timing among servers so that all departments were not down at once during a patch install. Given everything else that security professionals need to think about, automated installation software is a welcome relief.

Infrastructure Architecture

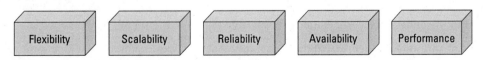

Gartner Inc. estimates that the typical web application goes down 170 hours per year. At Illinois-based online brokerage OptionsXpress, application performance problems can have a serious impact on livelihoods. Nearly 7,000 options traders visit the OptionsXpress website at any given time, completing nearly 20,000 transactions a day. With all this online traffic, the brokerage's IT administrators were always up against the clock when re-creating troublesome applications offline in the development environment. The company struggled to unlock the mystery behind a troublesome trading application that was forcing traders to resubmit orders. Sometimes the application would just die and then restart itself for no apparent reason.

Infrastructure architecture includes the hardware, software, and telecommunications equipment that, when combined, provide the underlying foundation to support the organization's goals (see Figure B4.6). As an organization changes, its systems must be able to change to support its operations. If an organization grows by 50 percent in a single year, its systems must be able to handle a 50 percent growth rate. Systems that cannot adapt to organizational changes can severely hinder the organization's ability to operate. The future of an organization depends on its ability to meet its partners and customers on their terms, at their pace, any time of the day, in any geographic location. The following are the five primary characteristics of a solid infrastructure architecture:

1. Flexibility
2. Scalability
3. Reliability
4. Availability
5. Performance

FLEXIBILITY   Multi currencies

Organizations must watch today's business, as well as tomorrow's, when designing and building systems. Systems must be flexible enough to meet all types of business changes. For example, a system might be designed to include the ability to handle multiple currencies and languages, even though the company is not currently performing business in other countries. When the company starts growing and performing business in new countries, the system will already have the flexibility to handle multiple currencies and languages. If the company failed to recognize that its business would someday be global, it would need to redesign all its systems to handle multiple currencies and languages, not easy once systems are up and running.

FIGURE B4.6

Infrastructure Architecture
Characteristics

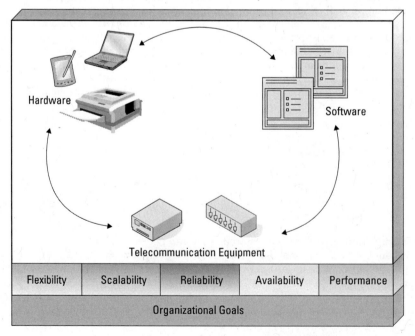

SCALABILITY   *4 demand.*

Estimating organizational growth is a challenging task. Growth can occur in a number of different forms including more customers and product lines and expansion into new markets. *Scalability* refers to how well a system can adapt to increased demands. A number of factors can create organizational growth including market, industry, and economy factors. If an organization grows faster than anticipated, it might experience all types of performance degradations, ranging from running out of disk space to a slowdown in transaction speeds. Anticipating expected—and unexpected—growth is key to building scalable systems that can support that growth.

MSNBC's website typically received moderate traffic. On September 11, 2001, the site was inundated with more than 91 million page views as its customers were trying to find out information about the terrorist attacks. Fortunately, MSNBC had anticipated this type of surging demand and built adaptable systems accordingly, allowing it to handle the increased page view requests.

Capacity planning determines the future IT infrastructure requirements for new equipment and additional network capacity. Performing a capacity plan is one way to ensure the IT infrastructure is scalable. It is cheaper for an organization to implement an IT infrastructure that considers capacity growth at the beginning of a system launch than to try to upgrade equipment and networks after the system has been implemented. Not having enough capacity leads to performance issues and hinders the ability of knowledge workers to perform their jobs. If 100 workers are using the Internet to perform their jobs and the company purchases bandwidth that is too small and the network capacity is too small, the workers will spend a great deal of time just waiting to get information from the Internet. Waiting for an Internet site to return information is not very productive.

Web 2.0 is driving demand for capacity planning. Delivering entertainment-grade video over the Internet poses significant challenges as service providers scale solutions to manage millions of users, withstand periods of peak demand, and deliver a superior quality of experience while balancing network capacity and efficient capital investment. Given the success of YouTube and the likelihood of similar video experiences, the bandwidth required to transport video services will continue to increase and the possibility of video degradation will become more challenging. Since video cannot tolerate packet loss (e.g., blocks of data lost), congestion due to overuse is not acceptable—admitting just one more stream to a network near peak capacity could degrade the video and broadcast quality for all users.

RELIABILITY

Reliability ensures all systems are functioning correctly and providing accurate information. Reliability is another term for accuracy when discussing the correctness of systems within the context of efficiency IT metrics. Inaccurate information processing occurs for many reasons, from the incorrect entry of data to information corruption. Unreliable information puts the organization at risk when making decisions based on the information.

AVAILABILITY

Availability (an efficiency IT metric) addresses when systems can be accessed by employees, customers, and partners. *High availability* refers to a system or component that is continuously operational for a desirably long length of time. Availability is typically measured relative to "100 percent operational" or "never failing." A widely held but difficult-to-achieve standard of availability for a system or product is known as "five 9s" (99.999 percent) availability.

Some companies have systems available 24x7 to support business operations and global customer and employee needs. With the emergence of the web, companies expect systems to operate around the clock. A customer who finds that a website closes at 9:00 p.m. is not going to be a customer long.

Systems, however, must come down for maintenance, upgrades, and fixes. One challenge organizations face is determining when to schedule system downtime if the system is expected to operate continually. Exacerbating the negative impact of scheduled system downtime is the global nature of business. Scheduling maintenance during the evening might seem like a great idea, but the evening in one city is the morning somewhere else in the world, and global employees may not be able to perform their jobs if the system is down. Many organizations overcome this problem by having redundant systems, allowing the organization to take one system down by switching over to a redundant, or duplicate, system.

PERFORMANCE

Performance measures how quickly a system performs a certain process or transaction (in terms of efficiency IT metrics of both speed and throughput). Not having enough performance capacity can have a devastating, negative impact on a business. A customer will wait only a few seconds for a website to return a request before giving up and moving on to another website. To ensure adaptable systems performance, capacity planning helps an organization determine future IT infrastructure requirements for new equipment and additional network capacity. It is cheaper for an organization to design and implement an IT infrastructure that envisions performance capacity growth than to update all the equipment after the system is already operational.

Abercrombie & Fitch (A&F) uses the Internet to market its distinctive image of being a fashion trendsetter to one of its largest customer segments, college students. The company designed its enterprise architecture with the help of IBM, which ensured www.abercrombie.com paralleled the same sleek but simple design of *A&F Quarterly*, the company's flagship magazine. Abercrombie & Fitch knew that its website had to be accessible, available, reliable, and scalable to meet the demands of its young customers. Young customers tend to be Internet savvy, and their purchasing habits vary from customers who only shop for sale items at midnight to customers who know exactly what they want immediately. The highly successful website gives customers not only an opportunity to shop online, but also a taste of the Abercrombie & Fitch lifestyle through downloadable MP3s, calendars, and desktop accessories.

Application Architecture

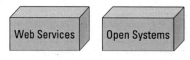

Gartner Inc. research indicates that application problems are the single largest source of downtime, causing 40 percent of annual downtime hours and 32 percent of average downtime costs. **Application architecture** determines how applications integrate and relate to each other. Advances in integration technology—primarily web services and open systems—are providing new ways for designing more agile, more responsive enterprise architectures that provide the kind of value businesses need. With these new architectures, IT can build new business capabilities faster, cheaper, and in a vocabulary the business can understand.

WEB SERVICES

Web services promise to be the next major frontier in computing. **Web services** contain a repertoire of web-based data and procedural resources that use shared protocols and standards permitting different applications to share data and services. The major application of web services is the integration among different applications (refer to Figure B4.7). Before web services, organizations had trouble with

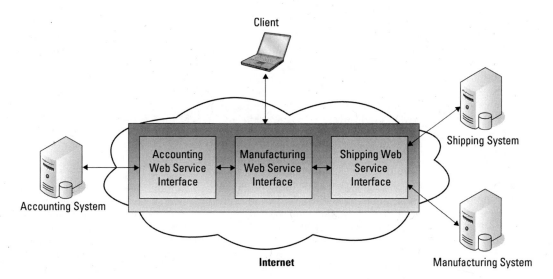

Client

Accounting
Web Service
Interface

Manufacturing
Web Service
Interface

Shipping Web
Service
Interface

Accounting System

Shipping System

Manufacturing System

Internet

FIGURE B4.7

Web Service Architecture

interoperability. ***Interoperability*** is the capability of two or more computer systems to share data and resources, even though they are made by different manufacturers. If a supply chain management (SCM) system can talk to (share information with) a customer relationship management (CRM) system, interoperability exists between the two systems. The traditional way that organizations achieved interoperability was to build integrations. Now, an organization can use web services to perform the same task.

Verizon's massive enterprise architecture includes three different companies GTE, Bell Atlantic, and Nynex, each with its own complex systems. To find a customer record in any of the three companies' systems, Verizon turns to its search engine, called Spider. Spider is Verizon's version of Google, and it's helping Verizon's business to thrive.

Spider contains a vital customer information web service that encapsulates Verizon's business rules, which help it to access the correct data repository when looking for customer information. Whenever a new system is built that needs to link to customer information, all the developer has to do is reuse the web service that will link to the customer records. Because Verizon has the web service in place as part of its enterprise architecture, development teams can build new applications within a month, as opposed to six months.

Web services encompass all the technologies that are used to transmit and process information on and across a network, most specifically the Internet. It is easiest to think of an individual web service as software that performs a specific task, with that task being made available to any user who needs its service. For example, a "Deposit" web service for a banking system might allow customers to perform the task of depositing money to their accounts. The web service could be used by a bank teller, by the customer at an ATM, and/or by the customer performing an online transaction through a web browser.

The "Deposit" web service demonstrates one of the great advantages of using the web service model to develop applications. Developers do not have to reinvent the wheel every time they need to incorporate new functionality. A web service is really a piece of reusable software code. A software developer can quickly build a new application by using many of these pieces of reusable code. The two primary parts of web services are events and services.

Events

Events are the eyes and ears of the business expressed in technology—they detect threats and opportunities and alert those who can act on the information. Pioneered by telecommunication and financial services companies, this involves using IT systems to monitor a business process for events that matter—a stock-out in the warehouse or an especially large charge on a consumer's credit card—and automatically alert the people best equipped to handle the issue. For example, a credit monitoring system automatically alerts a credit supervisor and shuts down an account when the system processes a $7,000 charge on a credit card with a $6,000 limit.

Services

Services are more like software products than they are coding projects. They must appeal to a broad audience, and they need to be reusable if they are going to have an impact on productivity. Early forms of services were defined at too low a level in the architecture to interest the business, such as simple "Print" and "Save" services. The new services are being defined at a higher level; they describe such things as "Credit Check," "Customer Information," and "Process Payment." These services describe a valuable business process. For example, "Credit Check" has value not just for programmers who want to use that code in another application, but also for businesspeople who want to use it across multiple products—say, auto loans and mortgages—or across multiple businesses.

The trick to building services is finding the right level of granularity. T-Mobile builds services starting at the highest level and then works its way down to lower levels, helping to ensure it does not build services that no one uses. The company first built a "Send Message" web service and then built a "Send SMS Message" web service that sends messages in special formats to different devices such as cell phones and pagers.

Lydian Trust's enterprise architects designed a web service called "Get Credit" that is used by several different business units for loan applications. "Get Credit" seeks out credit ratings over the Internet from the major credit bureaus. One day, one of the credit bureaus' web servers crashed, and Lydian Trust's "Get Credit" web service could not make a connection. Since the connection to the server was loosely linked, the system did not know what to do. "Get Credit" was not built to make more than one call. So, while it waited for a response, hundreds of loan applications sat idle.

Lydian Trust's loan officers had to work overnight to ensure that all of the applications were completed within 24 hours as promised by the company. Fortunately, Lydian Trust's customers never felt the pain; however, its employees did. Systems must be designed to deal with the existence of certain events, or the lack of an event, in a way that does not interrupt the overall business. The "Get Credit" web service has been modified to include an automatic email alert to a supervisor whenever the web service encounters a delay.

OPEN SYSTEMS

Microsoft Internet Explorer's share of the web browser market has dipped below 90 percent because of Mozilla's Firefox, an open source web browser. According to WebSideStory, which has been tracking the Firefox versus Internet Explorer numbers, the Mozilla-made open source browser had captured 5 percent of the U.S. market in January 2005, an increase of almost a full percentage point in a month. Firefox claimed more than 25 million copies of the browser had been downloaded in its first 15 weeks of release.

An *open system* is a broad, general term that describes nonproprietary IT hardware and software made available by the standards and procedures by which their products work, making it easier to integrate them. Amazon.com embraced open source technology converting from Sun's proprietary operating system to Linux. The switch to an open source operating system, such as Linux, is simplifying the process by which Amazon.com associates can build links to Amazon.com applications into their websites.

The designs of open systems allow for information sharing. In the past, different systems were independent of each other and operated as individual islands of control. The sharing of information was accomplished through software drivers and devices that routed data allowing information to be translated and shared between systems. Although this method is still widely used, its limited capability and added cost are not an effective solution for most organizations. Another drawback to the stand-alone system is it can communicate only with components developed by a single manufacturer. The proprietary nature of these systems usually results in costly repair, maintenance, and expansion because of a lack of competitive forces. On the other hand, open system integration is designed to:

- Allow systems to seamlessly share information. The sharing of information reduces the total number of devices, resulting in an overall decrease in cost.

- Capitalize on enterprise architectures. This avoids installing several independent systems, which creates duplication of devices.

- Eliminate proprietary systems and promote competitive pricing. Often a sole-source vendor can demand its price and may even provide the customer with less than satisfactory service. Utilization of open systems allows users to purchase systems competitively.

✳ PLUG-IN SUMMARY

Companies that have created solid enterprise architectures are reaping huge rewards in savings, flexibility, and business alignment. Basic enterprise architectures contain three components:

1. Information architecture identifies where and how important information, like customer records, is maintained and secured.

2. Infrastructure architecture includes the hardware, software, and telecommunications equipment that, when combined, provide the underlying foundation to support the organization's goals.

3. Application architecture determines how applications integrate and relate to each other.

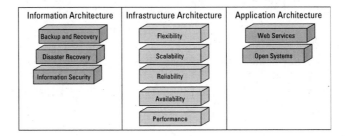

✳ KEY TERMS

Application architecture, B4.3, B4.10
Availability, B4.9
Backup, B4.4
Business continuity planning, B4.6
Capacity planning, B4.9
Cold site, B4.5
Disaster recovery cost curve, B4.5

Disaster recovery plan, B4.5
Enterprise architect (EA), B4.2
Enterprise architecture, B4.2
Failover, B4.5
Fault tolerance, B4.4
High availability, B4.9
Hot site, B4.5
Information architecture, B4.3
Infrastructure architecture, B4.3, B4.8

Interoperability, B4.11
Open system, B4.12
Performance, B4.10
Recovery, B4.4
Reliability, B4.9
Scalability, B4.9
Web service, B4.10

✳ CLOSING CASE ONE

Chicago Tribune's Server Consolidation a Success

The *Chicago Tribune* is the seventh-largest newspaper in the country. Overhauling its data center and consolidating servers was a difficult task; however, the payoff was tremendous. The *Chicago Tribune* successfully moved its critical applications from a mishmash of mainframes and older Sun Microsystems servers to a new dual-site enterprise architecture, which has resulted in lower costs and increased reliability throughout the company.

The paper's new enterprise architecture clustered its servers over a two-mile distance, lighting up a 1Gbps dark-fiber link—an optical fiber that is in place but not yet being used—between two data centers. This architecture lets the newspaper spread the processing load between the servers while improving redundancy and options for disaster recovery.

The transfer to the new architecture was not smooth. A small piece of software written for the transition contained a coding error that caused the *Tribune*'s editorial applications to experience intermittent processing failures. As a result, the paper was forced to delay delivery to about 40 percent of its 680,000 readers and cut 24 pages from a Monday edition, costing the newspaper nearly $1 million in advertising revenue.

After editorial applications were stabilized, the *Tribune* proceeded to migrate applications for operations—the physical production and printing of the newspaper—and circulation to the new enterprise architecture. "As we gradually took applications off the mainframe, we realized that we were incurring very high costs in maintaining underutilized mainframes at two different locations," says Darko Dejanovic, vice president and CTO of the Tribune Co., which owned the *Chicago Tribune,* the *Los Angeles Times,* Long Island's *Newsday,* and about a dozen other metropolitan newspapers. "By moving from two locations to one, we've achieved several million dollars in cost savings. There's no question that server consolidation was the right move for us."

The company is excited about its new enterprise architecture and is looking to consolidate software across its newspapers. Currently, each newspaper maintains its own applications for classified advertising and billing, which means the parent company must support about 10 billing packages and the same number of classified-ad programs. Most of the business processes can be standardized. So far, the company has standardized about 95 percent of classified-ad processes and about 90 percent of advertising-sales processes. Over three years, the company will replace the disparate billing and ad applications with a single package that will be used by all business units. The different newspapers will not necessarily share the same data, but they will have the same processes and the same systems for accessing them. Over time, that will allow some of the call centers to handle calls for multiple newspapers; East Coast centers will handle the early-morning calls and West Coast centers the late-day and evening calls.

The company is looking at a few additional projects including the implementation of hardware that will allow its individual applications to run on partial CPUs, freeing up processor power and making more efficient use of disk space.

Questions

1. Review the five characteristics of infrastructure architecture and rank them in order of their potential impact on the Tribune Co.'s business.
2. What is the disaster recovery cost curve? Where should the Tribune Co. operate on the curve?
3. Define backups and recovery. What are the risks to the Tribune's business if it fails to implement an adequate backup plan?
4. Why is a scalable and highly available enterprise architecture critical to current operations and future growth?
5. Identify the need for information security at the Tribune Co.
6. How could the Tribune Co. use a classified ad web service across its different businesses?

★ CLOSING CASE TWO

Fear the Penguin

Linux has proved itself the most revolutionary software of the past decade. Spending on Linux was reported to reach $280 million by 2006. Linus Torvalds, who wrote the kernel (the core) of the Linux operating system at age 21, posted the operating system on the Internet and invited other programmers to improve his code and users to download his operating system for free. Since then, tens of thousands of people have, making Linux perhaps the single largest collaborative project in the planet's history.

Today, Linux, if not its penguin mascot, is everywhere. You can find Linux inside a boggling array of computers, machines, and devices. Linux is robust enough to run the world's most powerful supercomputers, yet sleek and versatile enough to run inside consumer items like TiVo, cell phones, and handheld portable devices. Even more impressive than Linux's increasing prevalence in living rooms and pockets is its growth in the market for corporate computers.

Since its introduction in 1991, no other operating system in history has spread as quickly across such a broad range of systems as Linux, and it has finally achieved critical mass. According to studies by market research firm IDC, Linux is the fastest-growing server operating system, with shipments expected to grow by 34 percent per year over the next four years. With its innovative open source approach, strong security, reliability, and scalability, Linux can help companies achieve the agility they need to respond to changing consumer needs and stay ahead of the game.

Thanks to its unique open source development process, Linux is reliable and secure. A "meritocracy," a team specifically selected for their competence by the technical developer community, governs the entire development process. Each line of code that makes up the Linux kernel is extensively tested and maintained for a variety of different platforms and application scenarios.

This open collaborative approach means the Linux code base continually hardens and improves itself. If vulnerabilities appear, they get the immediate attention of experts from around the world, who quickly resolve the problems. According to Security Portal, which tracks vendor response times, it takes an average of 12 days to patch a Linux bug compared to an average of three months for some proprietary platforms. With the core resilience and reliability of Linux, businesses can minimize downtime, which directly increases their bottom line.

The Spread of Open Systems

Businesses and governments are opting for open source operating systems like Linux instead of Windows. One attendee at the Linux Desktop Consortium in 2004 was Dr. Martin Echt, a cardiologist from Albany, New York. Dr. Echt, chief operating officer of Capital Cardiology Associates, an eight-office practice, discussed his decision to shift his business from Microsoft's Windows to Linux. Dr. Echt is not your typical computer geek or Linux supporter, and he is not the only one switching to Linux.

The State Council in China has mandated that all ministries install the local flavor of Linux, dubbed Red Flag, on their PCs. In Spain, the government has installed a Linux operating system that incorporates the regional dialect. The city of Munich, despite a personal visit from Microsoft CEO Steve Ballmer, is converting its 14,000 PCs from Windows to Linux.

"It's open season for open source," declared Walter Raizner, general manager of IBM Germany. One of the biggest corporate backers of Linux, IBM has more than 75 government customers worldwide, including agencies in France, Spain, Britain, Australia, Mexico, the United States, and Japan.

The move toward Linux varies for each country or company. For Dr. Echt, it was a question of lower price and long-term flexibility. In China, the government claimed national security as a reason to move to open source code because it permitted engineers to make sure there were no security leaks and no spyware installed on its computers. In Munich, the move was largely political. Regardless of the reason, the market is shifting toward Linux.

Microsoft versus Linux

Bill Gates has openly stated that Linux is not a threat to Microsoft. According to IDC analysts, Microsoft's operating systems ship with 93.8 percent of all desktops worldwide. Ted Schadler, IDC research principal analyst, states that despite the push of lower cost Linux players into the market, Microsoft will maintain its desktop market share for the following three reasons:

1. Linux adds features to its applications that most computer users have already come to expect.

2. Linux applications might not be compatible with Microsoft applications such as Microsoft Word or Microsoft Excel.

3. Microsoft continues to innovate, and the latest version of Office is beginning to integrate word processing and spreadsheet software to corporate databases and other applications.

The Future of Linux

IDC analyst Al Gillen predicts that an open source operating system will not enjoy explosive growth on the desktop for at least six or eight years. Still, even Gillen cannot deny that Linux's penetration continues to rise, with an estimated 18 million users. Linux's market share increased from 1.5 percent at the end of 2000 to 4.2 percent at the beginning of 2004. According to IDC, by the end of 2005 it surpassed Apple's Mac OS, which has 2.9 percent of the market, as the second most popular operating system. Gartner Dataquest estimates Linux's server market share will grow seven times faster than Windows.

Questions

1. How does Linux differ from traditional software?
2. Should Microsoft consider Linux a threat? Why or why not?
3. How is open source software a potential trend shaping organizations?
4. How can you use Linux as an emerging technology to gain a competitive advantage?
5. Research the Internet and discover potential ways that open source software might revolutionize business in the future.

✳ MAKING BUSINESS DECISIONS

1. Planning for Disaster Recovery

You are the new senior analyst in the IT department at Beltz, a large snack food manufacturing company. The company is located on the beautiful shoreline in Charleston, North Carolina. The company's location is one of its best and also worst features. The weather and surroundings are beautiful, but the threat of hurricanes and other natural disasters is high. Compile a disaster recovery plan that will minimize any risks involved with a natural disaster.

2. Comparing Backup and Recovery Systems

Research the Internet to find three different vendors of backup and recovery systems. Compare and contrast the three systems and determine which one you would recommend if you were installing a backup and recovery system for a medium-sized business with 3,500 employees that maintains information on the stock market. Compile your findings in a presentation that you can give to your class that details the three systems' strengths and weaknesses, along with your recommendation.

3. Ranking the -ilities

In a group, review the following list of IT infrastructure qualities and rank them in order of their impact on an organization's success. Use a rating system of 1 to 7, where 1 indicates the biggest impact and 7 indicates the least impact.

4. Designing an Enterprise Architecture

Components of a solid enterprise architecture include everything from documentation to business concepts to software and hardware. Deciding which components to implement and how to implement them can be a challenge. New IT components are released

IT Infrastructure Qualities	Business Impact
Availability	
Accessibility	
Reliability	
Scalability	
Flexibility	
Performance	
Capacity Planning	

daily, and business needs continually change. An enterprise architecture that meets your organization's needs today may not meet those needs tomorrow. Building an enterprise architecture that is scalable, flexible, available, accessible, and reliable is key to your organization's success.

You are the enterprise architect (EA) for a large clothing company called Xedous. You are responsible for developing the initial enterprise architecture. Create a list of questions you will need answered to develop your architecture. Below is an example of a few of the questions you might ask.

- What are the company's growth expectations?
- Will systems be able to handle additional users?
- How long will information be stored in the systems?
- How much customer history must be stored?
- What are the organization's business hours?
- What are the organization's backup requirements?

PLUG-IN B5

Networks and Telecommunications

1. Compare LANs, WANs, and MANs.
2. List and describe the four components that differentiate networks.
3. Compare the two types of network architectures.
4. Explain topology and the different types found in networks.
5. Describe TCP/IP along with its primary purpose.
6. Identify the different media types found in networks.
7. Describe the business benefits associated with VoIP.
8. Explain the difference between a VPN and a VAN.
9. Identify the advantages and disadvantages of broadband technology.
10. List and describe many of the network security problems.

Networks and Telecommunications

Change is everywhere in the information technology domain, but nowhere is change more evident and more dramatic than in the realm of telecommunications and networking. Most information systems today rely on digital networks to communicate information in the form of data, graphics, video, and voice.

Companies large and small from all over the world use networked systems and the Internet to locate suppliers and buyers, to negotiate contracts with them, and to provide bigger, better, and faster services than ever before.

Telecommunication systems enable the transmission of data over public or private networks. A *network* is a communications, data exchange, and resource-sharing system created by linking two or more computers and establishing standards, or protocols, so that they can work together. Telecommunication systems and networks are traditionally complicated and historically inefficient. However, businesses can benefit from today's modern network infrastructures that provide reliable global reach to employees and customers. Businesses around the world are moving to network infrastructure solutions that allow greater choice in how they go to market—solutions with global reach. Plug-In B5 takes a detailed look at key network and telecommunication technologies being integrated into businesses around the world.

Network Basics

Networks range from small two-computer networks to the biggest network of all, the Internet. A network provides two principal benefits: the ability to communicate and the ability to share. Music is the hot product line at coffee retailer Starbucks. In Starbucks stores, customers can shop for music wirelessly through iTunes free, thanks to the company's own increasingly sophisticated in-store network.

Today's corporate digital networks include a combination of local area networks and the Internet. A ***local area network (LAN)*** is designed to connect a group of computers in close proximity to each other such as in an office building, a school, or a home. A LAN is useful for sharing resources like files, printers, games, or other applications. A LAN in turn often connects to other LANs, and to the Internet or wide area networks. A ***wide area network (WAN)*** spans a large geographic area, such as a state, province, or country. WANs often connect multiple smaller networks, such as local area networks or metropolitan area networks (MANs). A ***metropolitan area network (MAN)*** is a large computer network usually spanning a city. Email is the most popular form of network communication. Figure B5.1 illustrates each network type.

Networks are differentiated by the following:

- Architecture—peer-to-peer, client/server.
- Topology—bus, star, ring, hybrid, wireless.
- Protocols—Ethernet, Transmission Control Protocol/Internet Protocol (TCP/IP).
- Media—coaxial, twisted-pair, fiber-optic.

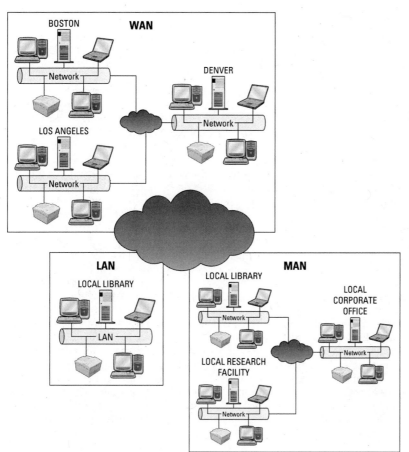

FIGURE B5.1

LAN, WAN, and MAN

Architecture

The two primary types of network architectures are: peer-to-peer networks and client/server networks.

PEER-TO-PEER NETWORKS

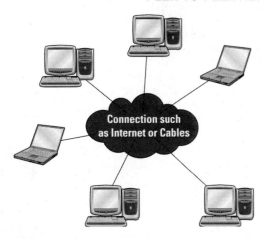

Connection such as Internet or Cables

A *peer-to-peer (P2P) network* is any network without a central file server and in which all computers in the network have access to the public files located on all other workstations, as illustrated in Figure B5.2. Each networked computer can allow other computers to access its files and use connected printers while it is in use as a workstation without the aid of a server.

While Napster may be the most widely known example of a P2P implementation, it may also be one of the most narrowly focused since the Napster model takes advantage of only one of the many capabilities of P2P computing: file sharing. The technology has far broader capabilities, including the sharing of processing, memory, and storage, and the supporting of collaboration among vast numbers of distributed computers. Peer-to-peer computing enables immediate interaction among people and computer systems.

FIGURE B5.2

Peer-to-Peer (P2P) Networks

CLIENT/SERVER NETWORKS

A *client* is a computer that is designed to request information from a server. A *server* is a computer that is dedicated to providing information in response to external requests. A *client/server network* is a model for applications in which the bulk of the back-end processing, such as performing a physical search of a database, takes place on a server, while the front-end processing, which involves communicating with the users, is handled by the clients (see Figure B5.3). A *network operating system (NOS)* is the operating system that runs a network, steering information between computers and managing security and users. The client/server model has become one of the central ideas of network computing. Most business applications written today use the client/server model.

A fundamental part of client/server architecture is packet-switching. *Packet-switching* occurs when the sending computer divides a message into a number of efficiently sized units called packets, each of which contains the address of the destination computer. Each packet is sent on the network and intercepted by routers. A *router* is an intelligent connecting device that examines each packet of data it receives and then decides which way to send it onward toward its destination. The packets arrive at their intended destination, although some may have actually traveled by different physical paths, and the receiving computer assembles the packets and delivers the message to the appropriate application. The number of network routers being installed by businesses worldwide is booming (see Figure B5.4).

Eva Chen, CIO at Trend Micro, built a router that helps prevent worms and viruses from entering networks. The problem with most existing antivirus software is that it starts working after a destructive sequence of code is identified, meaning it starts doing its job only after the virus or worm has been unleashed inside the network. Chen's router, the Network VirusWall, sits on the edge of a corporate network, scanning data packets and detaining those that might contain viruses or worms. Any suspicious packets are compared with up-to-the-second information from Trend Micro's virus-tracking command center. Viruses and worms are then deleted and refused entry to the network, allowing the company to perform a preemptive strike.

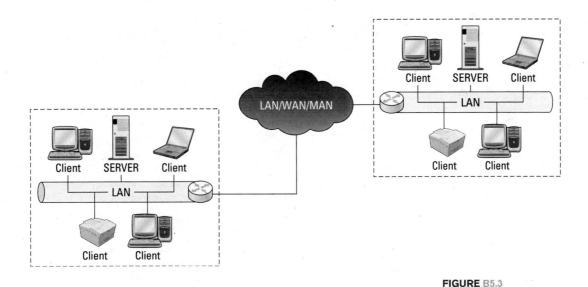

FIGURE B5.3

Client/Server Network

Topology

Networks are assembled according to certain rules. Cables, for example, have to be a certain length; each cable strand can support only a certain amount of network traffic. A *network topology* refers to the geometric arrangement of the actual physical organization of the computers (and other network devices) in a network. Topologies vary depending on cost and functionality. Figure B5.5 highlights the five common topologies used in networks, and Figure B5.6 displays each topology.

Protocols

A *protocol* is a standard that specifies the format of data as well as the rules to be followed during transmission. Simply put, for one computer (or computer program) to talk to another computer (or computer program) they must both be talking the same language, and this language is called a protocol.

A protocol is based on an agreed-upon and established standard, and this way all manufacturers of hardware and software that are using the protocol do so in a similar fashion to allow for interoperability. *Interoperability* is the capability of two or more computer systems to share data and resources, even though they are made by different manufacturers. The most popular network protocols used are Ethernet and Transmission Control Protocol/Internet Protocol (TCP/IP).

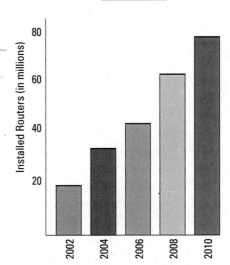

FIGURE B5.4

Worldwide Router Growth

ETHERNET

Ethernet is a physical and data layer technology for LAN networking (see Figure B5.7). Ethernet is the most widely installed LAN access method, originally developed by Xerox and then developed further by Xerox, Digital Equipment Corporation, and Intel. When it first began to be widely deployed in the 1980s, Ethernet supported a maximum theoretical data transfer rate of 10 megabits per second (Mbps). More recently, Fast Ethernet has extended traditional Ethernet technology to 100 Mbps peak, and Gigabit Ethernet technology extends performance up to 1,000 Mbps.

FIGURE B5.5

Five Network Topologies

Network Topologies	
Bus	All devices are connected to a central cable, called the bus or backbone. Bus networks are relatively inexpensive and easy to install for small networks.
Star	All devices are connected to a central device, called a hub. Star networks are relatively easy to install and manage, but bottlenecks can occur because all data must pass through the hub.
Ring	All devices are connected to one another in the shape of a closed loop, so that each device is connected directly to two other devices, one on either side of it. Ring topologies are relatively expensive and difficult to install, but they offer high bandwidth and can span large distances.
Hybrid	Groups of star-configured workstations are connected to a linear bus backbone cable, combining the characteristics of the bus and star topologies.
Wireless	Devices are connected by a receiver/transmitter to a special network interface card that transmits signals between a computer and a server, all within an acceptable transmission range.

Ethernet has survived as the major LAN technology—it is currently used for approximately 85 percent of the world's LAN-connected PCs and workstations—because its protocol has the following characteristics:

- Is easy to understand, implement, manage, and maintain.
- Allows low-cost network implementations.
- Provides extensive flexibility for network installation.
- Guarantees successful interconnection and operation of standards-compliant products, regardless of manufacturer.

FIGURE B5.6

Network Topologies

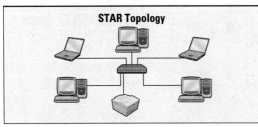

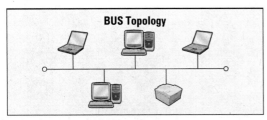

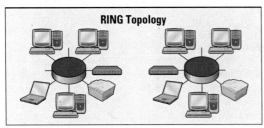

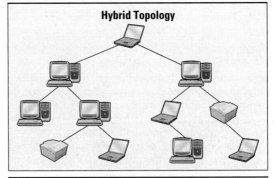

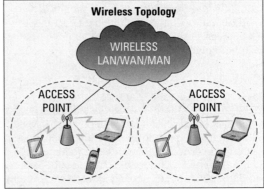

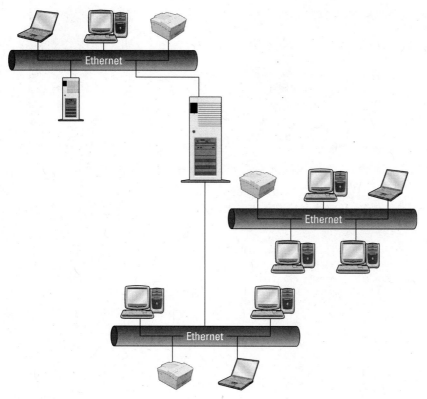

FIGURE B5.7

Ethernet Protocol

TRANSMISSION CONTROL PROTOCOL/INTERNET PROTOCOL

The most common telecommunication protocol is Transmission Control Protocol/Internet Protocol (TCP/IP), which was originally developed by the Department of Defense to connect a system of computer networks that became known as the Internet. *Transmission Control Protocol/Internet Protocol (TCP/ IP)* provides the technical foundation for the public Internet as well as for large numbers of private networks. The key achievement of TCP/IP is its flexibility with respect to lower-level protocols. TCP/IP uses a special transmission method that maximizes data transfer and automatically adjusts to slower devices and other delays encountered on a network. Although more than 100 protocols make up the entire TCP/IP protocol suite, the two most important of these are TCP and IP. **TCP** provides transport functions, ensuring, among other things, that the amount of data received is the same as the amount transmitted. **IP** provides the addressing and routing mechanism that acts as a postmaster. Figure B5.8 displays TCP/IP's four-layer reference model:

- Application layer—serves as the window for users and application processes to access network services.
- Transport layer—handles end-to-end packet transportation.
- Internet layer—formats the data into packets, adds a header containing the packet sequence and the address of the receiving device, and specifies the services required from the network.
- Network interface layer—places data packets on the network for transmission.

FIGURE B5.8

TCP/IP Four-Layer
Reference Model

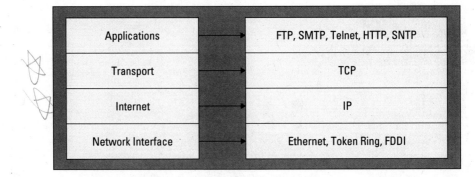

TCP/IP Applications	
File Transfer Protocol (FTP)	Allows files containing text, programs, graphics, numerical data, and so on to be downloaded off or uploaded onto a network.
Simple Mail Transfer Protocol (SMTP)	TCP/IP's own messaging system for email.
Telnet Protocol	Provides terminal emulation that allows a personal computer or workstation to act as a terminal, or access device, for a server.
Hypertext Transfer Protocol (HTTP)	Allows web browsers and servers to send and receive web pages.
Simple Network Management Protocol (SNMP)	Allows the management of networked nodes to be managed from a single point.

FIGURE B5.9

TCP/IP Applications

The TCP/IP suite of applications includes five protocols—file transfer, simple mail transfer, telnet, hypertext transfer, and simple network management (see Figure B5.9).

Another communication reference model is the seven-layer Open System Interconnection (OSI) reference model. Figure B5.10 shows the OSI model's seven layers.

The lower layers (1 to 3) represent local communications, while the upper layers (4 to 7) represent end-to-end communications. Each layer contributes protocol functions that are necessary to establish and maintain the error-free exchange of information between network users.

For many years, users thought the OSI model would replace TCP/IP as the preferred technique for connecting multivendor networks. But the slow pace of OSI standards as well as the expense of implementing complex OSI software and having products certified for OSI interoperability will preclude this from happening.

FIGURE B5.10

Open System
Interconnection Model

OSI Model
7. Application
6. Presentation
5. Session
4. Transport
3. Network
2. Data Link
1. Physical

Media

Network transmission media refers to the various types of media used to carry the signal between computers. When information is sent across the network, it is converted into electrical signals. These signals are generated as electromagnetic waves (analog signaling) or as a sequence of voltage pulses (digital signaling). To be sent from one location to another, a signal must travel along a physical path. The physical path that is used to carry a signal between a signal transmitter and a signal receiver is called the transmission media. The two types of transmission media are wire (guided) and wireless (unguided).

WIRE MEDIA

Wire media are transmission material manufactured so that signals will be confined to a narrow path and will behave predictably. The three most commonly used types of guided media are (see Figure B5.11):

- Twisted-pair wiring
- Coaxial cable
- Fiber-optic cable

Twisted-Pair Wiring

Twisted-pair wiring refers to a type of cable composed of four (or more) copper wires twisted around each other within a plastic sheath. The wires are twisted to reduce outside electrical interference. Twisted-pair cables come in shielded and unshielded varieties. Shielded cables have a metal shield encasing the wires that acts as a ground for electromagnetic interference. Unshielded twisted-pair (UTP) is the most popular and is generally the best option for LAN networks. The quality of UTP may vary from telephone-grade wire to high-speed cable. The cable has four pairs of wires inside the jacket. Each pair is twisted with a different number of twists per inch to help eliminate interference from adjacent pairs and other electrical devices. The RJ-45 connectors on twisted-pair cables resemble large telephone connectors.

Coaxial Cable

Coaxial cable is cable that can carry a wide range of frequencies with low signal loss. It consists of a metallic shield with a single wire placed along the center of a shield and isolated from the shield by an insulator. This type of cable is referred to as coaxial because it contains one copper wire (or physical data channel) that carries the signal and is surrounded by another concentric physical channel consisting of a wire mesh. The outer channel serves as a ground for electrical interference. Because of this grounding feature, several coaxial cables can be placed within a single conduit or sheath without significant loss of data integrity.

Fiber-Optic Cable

Fiber optic (or *optical fiber*) refers to the technology associated with the transmission of information as light impulses along a glass wire or fiber. The 10Base-FL and 100Base-FX optical fiber cable are the same types of cable used by most telephone companies for long-distance service. Optical fiber cable can transmit data over long distances with little loss in data integrity. In addition, because data are transferred as a pulse of light, optical fiber is not subject to interference. The light pulses travel through a glass wire or fiber encased in an insulating sheath.

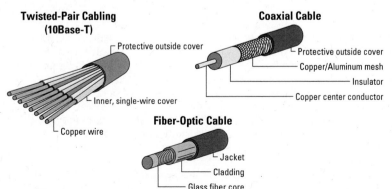

Twisted-Pair Cabling (10Base-T)
- Protective outside cover
- Inner, single-wire cover
- Copper wire

Coaxial Cable
- Protective outside cover
- Copper/Aluminum mesh
- Insulator
- Copper center conductor

Fiber-Optic Cable
- Jacket
- Cladding
- Glass fiber core

FIGURE B5.11

Twisted-Pair, Coaxial Cable, and Fiber-Optic

Optical fiber's increased maximum effective distance comes at a price. Optical fiber is more fragile than wire, difficult to split, and labor intensive to install. For these reasons, optical fiber is used primarily to transmit data over extended distances where the hardware required to relay the data signal on less expensive media would exceed the cost of optical fiber installation. It is also used where large amounts of data need to be transmitted on a regular basis.

WIRELESS MEDIA

Wireless media are natural parts of the Earth's environment that can be used as physical paths to carry electrical signals. The atmosphere and outer space are examples of wireless media that are commonly used to carry signals. These media can carry such electromagnetic signals as microwave, infrared light waves, and radio waves.

Network signals are transmitted through all media as a type of waveform. When transmitted through wire and cable, the signal is an electrical waveform. When transmitted through fiber-optic cable, the signal is a light wave, either visible or infrared light. When transmitted through the Earth's atmosphere, the signal can take the form of waves in the radio spectrum, including microwaves, infrared, or visible light.

Recent advances in radio hardware technology have produced significant advancements in wireless networking devices: the cellular telephone, wireless modems, and wireless LANs. These devices use technology that in some cases has been around for decades but until recently was too impractical or expensive for widespread use.

Using Networks and Telecommunications for Business Advantages

After gaining an understanding of networking and telecommunication fundamentals, it is easy to apply these to competitive advantages for any business including:

- Voice over IP.
- Networking businesses.
- Increasing the speed of business.
- Securing business networks.

VOICE OVER IP

Originally, phone calls made over the Internet had a reputation of offering poor call quality, lame user interfaces, and low call-completion rates. With new and improved technology and IT infrastructures, Internet phone calls now offer similar quality to traditional landline and cellular telephone calls. Today, many consumers are making phone calls over the Internet by using voice over Internet protocol (VoIP). *Voice over IP (VoIP)* uses TCP/IP technology to transmit voice calls over long-distance telephone lines. VoIP transmits over 10 percent of all phone calls in the United States and this number is growing exponentially.

The telecom industry is experiencing great benefits from combining VoIP with emerging standards that allow for easier development, interoperability among systems, and application integration. This is a big change for an industry that had relied on proprietary systems to keep customers paying for upgrades and new features. The VoIP and open standards combination has produced more choices, lower prices, and new applications.

Many VoIP companies, including Vonage, 8 × 8, and AT&T (CallVantage), typically offer calling within the United States for a fixed fee and a low per-minute charge for international calls. Broadband Internet access (broadband is described in detail later in this chapter) is required, and regular house phones plug in to an analog telephone adapter provided by the company or purchased from a third party (such as DLink or Linksys) as displayed in Figure B5.12.

Since VoIP uses existing network and Internet infrastructure to route telephone calls more efficiently and inexpensively than traditional telephone service, VoIP offers businesses significant cost savings, productivity gains, and service enhancements.

Unfortunately, VoIP routes calls through the same paths used by network and Internet traffic; therefore it has the same vulnerabilities and is subject to the same Internet threats. Much like data, VoIP traffic can be intercepted, captured, or modified. Any threat that slows or degrades service even slightly will disrupt business. As a result, VoIP traffic must be secured.

Skype has long been one of the most popular VoIP options for consumers—largely because of its low cost (free for calls between Skype users and only a few dollars per month to call landlines). Now, it is gaining popularity in the business world as well.

The company has been adding features that make it more business-friendly. Two examples are the Windows Installer/MSI package that makes it easy to roll out the application to multiple machines and the Skype for Business Control Panel that allows administrators to manage all of a company's Skype accounts from a centralized interface. The small-business market is especially amenable to Skype's budget-friendly and feature-rich service.

Rip Curl is one of the greatest surf and snow brands in the world. With more than 1,200 staff members and a retail presence in more than 60 countries, the company faces communications challenges in keeping abreast of global industry trends, sharing global marketing plans, coordinating events, and collaborating on design initiatives across many regions.

Rip Curl's finance and marketing divisions have been using Skype's free instant messaging and video calls for more than two years to track communications with international colleagues. Recently, Rip Curl's head of IT directed all staff to use Skype as their preferred method of communication.

Skype already includes many features that make it attractive to business users, including call forwarding and the ability to filter and block unwanted calls. In addition, Skype's conference calling feature lets users have conversations with multiple

FIGURE B5.12

Diagram of VoIP Connection

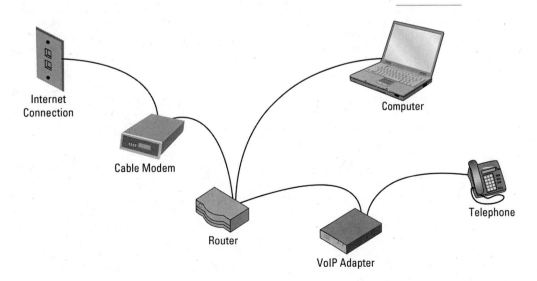

people (up to 10 participants), mixing participants who are using Skype, regular landline phones, and mobile phones.

Skype allows users to do more than just place voice calls. For instance, users with computers equipped with web cams can make video calls to get "face time" with coworkers or clients—without the hassle or expense of traveling. In addition to features built into the Skype software, many useful add-in programs are available to download that add functionality and enhance productivity (see Figure B5.13).

Skype also uses a file transfer feature that makes it easier to collaborate with colleagues over the phone; users can send copies of reports, pictures, or other files they need to share—with no limits on file size. This feature can be disabled if an administrator does not want users to be able to transfer files due to security or privacy issues.

Some features available using VoIP solutions include:

- Business application integration (for instance, tying IP telephony to a customer database).
- Calendar integration.
- Call waiting.
- Caller ID.
- Click-of-a-mouse simplicity—employees make or transfer calls right on their computer.

FIGURE B5.13

Skype Add-In Programs

Add-in	Function
Skype Office Toolbar	This add-on makes calls to names or phone numbers in a Word document, Excel spreadsheet, or PowerPoint presentation. After installing the add-in, users can use it to turn phone numbers in the document into links, which can be clicked to make a voice call or send an SMS message. Users can send the file they are working on in the Office application to a Skype contact.
Skylook	This add-on is an extension to Outlook that records calls and voice-mail to MP3 files and accesses them from Outlook. Users can call Outlook contacts over Skype and have emails read over the phone.
HotRecorder for VoIP	This add-on records Skype calls automatically using a third-party program, such as HotRecorder for VoIP (HR4VoIP). It works with Skype 3.0, as well as other VoIP applications such as Net2Phone, Google Talk, and Yahoo Messenger.
Universal Chat Translator	Today's business world is increasingly international in nature. If a user needs to communicate with people who speak another language, install the Universal Chat Translator to translate Skype chat conversations and read them. The add-on translator supports Arabic, Chinese (simplified and traditional), Dutch, French, German, Greek, Japanese, Italian, Korean, Portuguese, Russian, and Spanish. It translates the messages sent to the other language and translates the received messages to English. The translation takes place in real time for active chats or conversations can be stored in a chat history.
uSeeToo	This add-on shares photos, drawings, maps, and other graphical images. Users can add text captions and other content. It includes a drawing board, and it allows users to create, show, and save multiple boards.
PresenterNet	This add-in conducts interactive web meetings, sales presentations, "webinars," and more, using PowerPoint and Skype teleconferencing. It works with Windows, Windows Mobile, Linux, and Macintosh, and with Internet Explorer, Firefox, and Safari browsers.
Unyte	This add-in shares desktop applications with Skype contacts and others, and will share with multiple users.
TalkandWrite Extra for Skype 3.0	This add-on is a document collaboration program that allows two users to remotely work on the same document and annotate it, add text, and more, with the changes made by either party immediately made available to both.
RemoteCall	This add-in connects to remote desktops during a Skype call by clicking an icon added to the Skype Contacts and Tools menus.

- Conference call capabilities with on-screen document sharing.
- Comprehensive information about each caller.
- Desktop application (i.e., Microsoft Outlook) integration.
- Dial-by-name capability.
- Easy navigation.
- Four- or five-digit dialing to anyone, regardless of location.
- Mobility—users can work from anywhere.
- Three-way calling.

NETWORKING BUSINESSES

Retailer REI reports that one-third of all customers who buy online and pick up at the store make another purchase while there, spending an average of $90. From a technology perspective, in-store pickup needs to have some level of inventory integration to work effectively. The integration of data is critical in being able to display to the consumer the availability of products at the closest geographic store.

To set up an ebusiness even a decade ago would have required an individual organization to assume the burden of developing the entire network infrastructure. Today, industry-leading companies have developed Internet-based products and services to handle many aspects of customer and supplier interactions. "In today's retail market, you cannot be a credible national retailer without having a robust website," says Dennis Bowman, senior vice president and CIO of Circuit City, who adds that customers now expect seamless retailing between online and in-store just as they expect stores that are clean and well stocked. For this reason, retailers are working furiously to integrate their ebusiness sites with their inventory and point-of-sale (POS) systems so that they can accept in-store returns of merchandise bought online and allow customers to buy on the web and pick up in the store.

Some companies, such as Best Buy, Circuit City, Office Depot, and Sears, already have their physical and online stores integrated. These companies have been the fast movers because they already had an area in their stores for merchandise pickup (usually for big, bulky items such as TVs and appliances), and because long before the web they had systems and processes in place that facilitated the transfer of a sale from one store to another. To take on the challenge of business integration, an organization needs a secure and reliable network for mission-critical systems (see Figure B5.14).

A *virtual private network (VPN)* is a way to use the public telecommunication infrastructure (e.g., Internet) to provide secure access to an organization's network (see Figure B5.15). A *valued-added network (VAN)* is a private network, provided by a third party, for exchanging information through a high-capacity connection.

FIGURE B5.14

Business Network Characteristics

- Provide for the transparent exchange of information with suppliers, trading partners, and customers.
- Reliably and securely exchange information internally and externally via the Internet or other networks.
- Allow end-to-end integration and provide message delivery across multiple systems, in particular, databases, clients, and servers.
- Respond to high demands with scalable processing power and networking capacity.
- Serve as the integrator and transaction framework for both digital businesses and traditional brick-and-mortar businesses that want to leverage the Internet for any type of business.

FIGURE B5.15

Virtual Private Network
Overview

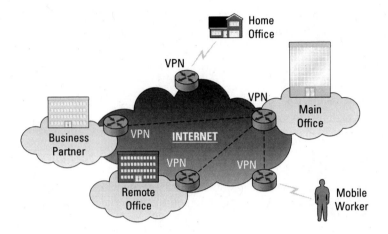

Organizations engaging in ebusiness have relied largely on VPNs, VANs, and other dedicated links handling electronic data interchange transactions. These traditional solutions are still deployed in the market, and for many companies will likely hold a strategic role for years to come. However, these conventional technologies present significant challenges:

- By handling only limited kinds of business information, these contribute little to a reporting structure intended to provide a comprehensive view of business operations.

- They offer little support for the real-time business process integration that will be essential in the digital marketplace.

- Relatively expensive and complex to implement, conventional technologies make it difficult to expand or change networks in response to market shifts.

INCREASING THE SPEED OF BUSINESS

Transmission can occur at different speeds. By speed we do not mean how fast the signal travels in terms such as miles per hour, but rather the volume of data that can be transmitted per unit of time. Terms such as bandwidth, hertz (Hz), and baud are used to describe transmission speeds, whereas a measure such as bits transmitted per second (bits per second, or bps) would be more understandable. **Bandwidth** is the difference between the highest and the lowest frequencies that can be transmitted on a single medium, and it is a measure of the medium's capacity. *Hertz* is cycles per second, and *baud* is the number of signals sent per second. If each cycle sends one signal that transmits exactly one bit of data, which is often the case, then all these terms are identical.

In information technology publications, baud was formerly used for relatively slow speeds such as 2,400 baud (2,400 bits per second) or 14,400 baud (14,400 bps), while hertz (with an appropriate prefix) was used for higher speeds such as 500 megahertz (500 million bps) or 2 gigahertz (2 billion bps). More recently, the term *baud* has fallen into disfavor, but hertz is still widely used. For clarity, we will stick with bps in this chapter.

The notion of bandwidth, or capacity, is important for telecommunications. For example, approximately 50,000 bits (0s and 1s) are required to represent one page of data. To transmit this page over a 128,000 bps (128 Kbps) digital subscriber line (DSL) would take only four-tenths of a second. Graphics require approximately 1 million bits for one page. This would require about 8 seconds over a 128 Kbps DSL. Full-motion video transmission requires the enormous bandwidth

Transmission Medium	Typical Speeds
Twisted pair—voice telephone	14.4 Kbps–56 Kbps
Twisted pair—digital telephone	128 Kbps–1.544 Mbps
Twisted pair—LAN	10 Mbps–100 Mbps
Coaxial cable—LAN	10 Mbps–1 Gbps
Wireless—LAN	6 Mbps–54 Mbps
Microwave—WAN	50 Kbps–100 Mbps
Satellite—WAN	50 Kbps–100 Mbps
Fiber-optic cable—WAN	100 Mbps–100 Gbps

KEY: bps = bits per second
Kbps = thousand bits per second
Mbps = million bits per second
Gbps = billion bits per second

FIGURE B5.16

Telecommunications
Transmission Speeds

of 12 million bps, and thus data compression techniques must be employed to be able to send video over the existing telephone network. The bandwidth determines what types of communication—voice, data, graphics, full-motion video—can reasonably be transmitted over a particular medium. Figure B5.16 outlines the typical transmission speeds found in business today (a few of the technologies mentioned in Figure B5.16 will be discussed in detail in the next section). Figure B5.17 gives an overview of the average time required to download specific Internet functions.

High-speed Internet, once an exotic and expensive service used only by larger companies, is now an inexpensive mainstream offering. The term ***broadband*** generally refers to high-speed Internet connections transmitting data at speeds greater than 200 kilobytes per second (Kbps), compared to the 56 Kbps maximum speed offered by traditional dial-up connections. While traditional dial-up access (using normal voice telephone line technology) suffices for some consumers, many need or want the much faster connections that technological advances now allow. The right option for Internet access will depend on a company's needs and which services are available. Figure B5.18 lists some of the advantages and disadvantages of current conventional broadband technology available.

SECURING BUSINESS NETWORKS

Networks are a tempting target for mischief and fraud. An organization has to be concerned about proper identification of users and authorization of network access, the control of access, and the protection of data integrity. A firm must identify users before they are granted access to a corporate network, and that access

Internet Function	Dial-up (56K)	Satellite (512K)	DSL (1M)	Cable (1M)	Wireless (5M)
An email	1 sec.	<1 sec.			
A basic web page (25K)	10 sec.	<1 sec.			
One five-minute song (5M)	15 min.	2 min.	1 min.		40 sec.
One two-hour movie (500M)	20 hrs.	4 hrs.	2 hrs.		70 min.

FIGURE B5.17

Internet Function Average
Download Time

Technology	Typical Download Speed (Mbps)	Typical Uplink Speed (Mbps)	Advantages	Disadvantages
Digital subscriber line (DSL)	.5–3	1.0	– Good upload rates – Uses existing telephone lines	– Speeds vary depending on distance from telephone company's central office – Slower downloads than less expensive alternatives
Cable	.5–4	.5–1	– Uses existing cable infrastructure – Low-cost equipment	– Shared connections can overload system, slowing upload times
TI/T3 dedicated line	1.5–3	1.5–3	– Uses existing phone wiring	– Performance drops significantly with range – Susceptible to cross talk
Fiber-to-the-home	4.5	10.2	– Fast data speeds – Infrastructure has long life expectancy – Low maintenance – Low power costs	– Not widely available – Significant deployment cost (for company)
Fixed wireless	.5–12	.5	– Typically inexpensive to install, no underground digging	– Weather, topography, buildings, and electronics can cause interference
Satellite	.5–2	.05	– Nearly universal coverage – Available in otherwise inaccessible areas	– Expensive service/equipment – Upload/download delays

FIGURE B5.18

Advantages and Disadvantages of Broadband Technology

should be appropriate for the given user. For example, an organization may allow outside suppliers access to its internal network to learn about production plans, but the firm must prevent them from accessing other information such as financial records. In addition, the organization should preserve the integrity of its data; users should be allowed to change and update only well-specified data. These problems are exacerbated on the Internet where individuals must be very concerned about fraud, invalid purchases, and misappropriation of credit card information.

Providing network security is a difficult challenge. Almost all networks require some kind of log-on, including user name and password. Many people are casual with their passwords, making them easy to guess. A good password has both letters and numbers along with a few punctuation marks for added security. Most corporate security goes far beyond passwords, however. One common approach is a firewall, a computer that sits between an internal network and the Internet. The firewall allows access to internal data from specified incoming sites but tries to detect unauthorized access attempts and prevent them from occurring.

For highly secure communications, a sender can encrypt data, that is, encode the data so that someone without the "key" to decode them cannot read the message. There are a number of encryption approaches, and controversy exists over how strong the encryption should be. The most secure approaches use longer keys, making it much more difficult for an intruder to compute the key. The U.S. government is concerned about terrorists and criminals who might have access to strong encryption that is beyond the capabilities of law enforcement authorities to decrypt. There are export restrictions on encryption programs.

For Internet commerce, various schemes have been proposed for sending credit card or other payments over the network in a secure manner. Some involve encryption and others various forms of digital certificates or digital cash. Many firms worry that customers will not want to complete transactions on the Internet because of the fear their credit card numbers might be stolen. However, a law limits individual liability for credit card misuse to $50.

Data Sharing

Even more important than the sharing of technology resources is the sharing of data. Either a LAN or a WAN permits users on the network to get data (if they are authorized to do so) from other points on the network. It is very important, for example, for managers to be able to retrieve overall corporate sales forecasts from corporate databases to use in developing spreadsheets (or any other program used for business analysis) to project future activity. To satisfy customers, automobile dealers need to be able to locate particular vehicle models and colors with specific equipment installed. Managers at various points in a supply chain need to have accurate, up-to-date data on inventory levels and locations. Accountants at corporate headquarters need to be able to retrieve summary data on sales and expenses from each of the company's divisional computer centers. The chief executive officer, using an executive information system, needs to be able to access up-to-the-minute data on business trends from the corporate network.

✳ PLUG-IN SUMMARY

Networks come in all sizes, from two computers connected to share a printer, to the Internet, which is the largest network of all, joining millions of computers of all types all over the world. In between are business networks, which vary in size from a dozen or fewer computers to many thousands. There are three primary types of networks: local area network (LAN), wide area network (WAN), and metropolitan area network (MAN). The following differentiate networks:

- Architecture—peer-to-peer, client/server.
- Topology—bus, star, ring, hybrid, wireless.
- Protocols—Ethernet, Transmission Control Protocol/Internet Protocol (TCP/IP).
- Media—coaxial, twisted-pair, fiber-optic.

Networking and telecommunications offer competitive advantages for any business including:

- Voice over IP.
- Networking businesses.
- Increasing the speed of business.
- Securing business networks.

✳ KEY TERMS

Bandwidth, B5.14
Broadband, B5.15
Client, B5.4
Client/server network, B5.4
Coaxial cable, B5.9
Ethernet, B5.5
Fiber optic (or optical fiber), B5.9
Interoperability, B5.5
Local area network (LAN), B5.3
Metropolitan area network (MAN), B5.3
Network, B5.2

Network operating system (NOS), B5.4
Network topology, B5.5
Network transmission media, B5.8
Packet-switching, B5.4
Peer-to-peer (P2P) network, B5.4
Protocol, B5.5
Router, B5.4
Server, B5.4
Telecommunication system, B5.2

Transmission Control Protocol/Internet Protocol (TCP/IP), B5.7
Twisted-pair wiring, B5.9
Valued-added network (VAN), B5.13
Virtual private network (VPN), B5.13
Voice over Internet Protocol (VoIP), B5.10
Wide area network (WAN), B5.3
Wire media, B5.9
Wireless media, B5.10

✳ CLOSING CASE ONE

Watching Where You Step—Prada

Prada estimates its sales per year at $22 million. The luxury retailer recently spent millions on IT for its futuristic "epicenter" store—but the flashy technology turned into a high-priced hassle. The company needed to generate annual sales of $75 million by 2007 to turn a profit on its new high-tech investment.

When Prada opened its $40 million Manhattan flagship, hotshot architect Rem Koolhaas promised a radically new shopping experience. And he kept the promise—though not quite according to plan. Customers were soon enduring hordes of tourists, neglected technology, and the occasional thrill of getting stuck in experimental dressing rooms. A few of the problems associated with the store:

1. **Fickle fitting rooms**—Doors that turn from clear to opaque confuse shoppers and frequently fail to open on cue.
2. **Failed RFID**—Touch screens meant to spring to life when items are placed in the RFID "closets" are often just blank.
3. **Pointless PDAs**—Salesclerks let the handheld devices gather dust and instead check the stockroom for inventory.
4. **Neglected network**—A lag between sales and inventory systems makes the wireless network nearly irrelevant.

This was not exactly the vision for the high-end boutique when it debuted in December 2001. Instead, the 22,000-square-foot SoHo shop was to be the first of four "epicenter" stores around the world that would combine cutting-edge architecture and 21st century technology to revolutionize the luxury shopping experience. Prada poured roughly 25 percent of the store's budget into IT, including a wireless network to link every item to an Oracle inventory database in real-time using radio frequency identification (RFID) tags on the clothes. The staff would roam the floor armed with PDAs to check whether items were in stock, and customers could do the same through touch screens in the dressing rooms.

But most of the flashy technology today sits idle, abandoned by employees who never quite embraced computing chic and are now too overwhelmed by large crowds to assist shoppers with handhelds. On top of that, many gadgets, such as automated dressing-room doors and touch screens, are either malfunctioning or ignored. Packed with experimental technology, the clear-glass dressing-room doors were designed to open and close automatically at the tap of a foot pedal, then turn opaque when a second pedal sent an electric current through the glass. Inside, an RFID-aware rack would recognize a customer's selections and display them on a touch screen linked to the inventory system.

In practice, the process was hardly that smooth. Many shoppers never quite understood the pedals and disrobed in full view, thinking the door had turned opaque. That is no longer a problem, since staff members usually leave the glass opaque, but often the doors get stuck. Some of the chambers are open only to VIP customers during peak traffic times.

With the smart closets and handhelds out of commission, the wireless network in the store is nearly irrelevant, despite its considerable expense. As Prada's debt reportedly climbed to around $1 billion in late 2001, the company shelved plans for the fourth epicenter store, in San Francisco. A second store opened in Tokyo to great acclaim, albeit with different architects in a different market. Though that store incorporates similar cutting-edge concepts, architect Jacques Herzog emphasized that avant-garde retail plays well only in Japan. "This building is clearly a building for Tokyo," he told *The New York Times*. "It couldn't be somewhere else."

The multimillion-dollar technology is starting to look more like technology for technology's sake than an enhancement of the shopping experience, and the store's failings have prompted Prada to reevaluate its epicenter strategy.

Questions

1. Explain how Prada was anticipating using its wireless network to help its stores operate more efficiently. What prevented the system from working correctly?
2. What could Prada have done to help its employees embrace the wireless network?
3. Would Prada have experienced the same issues if it had used a wire (guided) network instead of a wireless (unguided) network?
4. What security issues would Prada need to be aware of concerning its wireless network?
5. What should Prada do differently when designing its fourth store to ensure its success?

Banks Banking on Network Security

Bank of America, Commerce Bancorp, PNC Financial Services Group, and Wachovia were victims of a crime involving a person trying to obtain customer data and sell it to law firms and debt-collection agencies. New Jersey police seized 13 computers from the alleged mastermind with 670,000 account numbers and balances. There is no indication the data were used for identity theft, but it highlights how increasingly difficult it is to protect information against such schemes as the market value of personal information grows. In the past, banks were wary of the cost or customer backlash from adopting network security technologies. Today, banks are beefing up network security as more customers begin to view security as a key factor when choosing a bank.

Bank of America

Bank of America is moving toward a stronger authentication process for its 13 million online customers. Bank of America's new SiteKey service is designed to thwart scams in which customers think they are entering data on the bank's website, when they are actually on a thief's site built to steal data. This occurs when a worm tells a computer to reroute the bank's URL into a browser to another site that looks exactly like the bank's.

SiteKey offers two-factor authentication. When enrolling in SiteKey, a customer picks an image from a library and writes a brief phrase. Each time the customer signs on, the image and phrase are displayed, indicating that the bank recognizes the computer the customer is using and letting the customer know that he or she is at the bank's official website. The customer then enters a password and proceeds. When signing on from a different computer than usual, the customer must answer one of three prearranged questions.

Wells Fargo & Company

"Out-of-wallet" questions contain information that is not found on a driver's license or ATM card. Wells Fargo is implementing a security strategy that operates based on "out-of-wallet" questions as a second factor for network password enrollment and maintenance. It is also offering network security hardware such as key fobs that change passwords every 60 seconds. Last fall, it launched a two-factor authentication pilot in which small businesses making electronic funds transfers need a key fob to complete transactions.

E*Trade Financial Corporation

E*Trade Financial Corporation provides customers holding account balances of more than $50,000 with a free Digital Security ID for network authentication. The device displays a new six-digit code every 60 seconds, which the customer must use to log on. Accounts under $50,000 can purchase the Digital Security ID device for $25.

Barclays Bank

Barclays Bank instituted online-transfer delays of between several hours and one day. The delays, which apply the first time a transfer is attempted between two accounts, are intended to give the bank time to detect suspicious activity, such as a large number of transfers from multiple accounts into a single account. The online-transfer delay was adopted in response to a wave of phishing incidents in which thieves transferred funds from victims' bank accounts into accounts owned by "mules." Mules are people who open bank accounts based on email solicitations, usually under the guise of a business proposal. From the mule accounts, the thieves withdraw cash, open credit cards, or otherwise loot the account.

Barclays also offers account monitoring of customers' actions to compare them with historical profile data to detect unusual behavior. For instance, the service would alert the bank to contact the customer if the customer normally logs on from England and suddenly logs on from New York and performs 20 transactions.

Questions

1. What reason would a bank have for not wanting to adopt an online-transfer delay policy?
2. Why is network security critical to financial institutions?
3. Explain the differences between the types of network security offered by the banks in the case. Which bank would you open an account with and why?
4. What additional types of network security, not mentioned in the case, would you recommend a bank implement?
5. Identity three policies a bank should implement to help it improve network information security.

★ MAKING BUSINESS DECISIONS

1. Secure Access

Organizations that have traditionally maintained private, closed systems have begun to look at the potential of the Internet as a ready-made network resource. The Internet is inexpensive and globally pervasive: Every phone jack is a potential connection. However, the Internet lacks security. What obstacles must organizations overcome to allow secure network connections?

2. Rolling Out with Networks

As organizations begin to realize the benefits of adding a wireless component to their network, they must understand how to leverage this emerging technology. Wireless solutions have come to the forefront for many organizations with the rollout of more standard, cost-effective, and secure wireless protocols. With wireless networks, increased business agility may be realized by continuous data access and synchronization. However, with the increased flexibility comes many challenges. Develop a report detailing the benefits an organization could obtain by implementing wireless technology. Also, include the challenges that a wireless network presents along with recommendations for any solutions.

3. Wireless Fitness

Sandifer's Fitness Club is located in beautiful South Carolina. Rosie Sandifer has owned and operated the club for 20 years. The club has three outdoor pools, two indoor pools, 10 racquetball courts, 10 tennis courts, an indoor and outdoor track, along with a four-story exercise equipment and massage therapy building. Rosie has hired you as a summer intern specializing in information technology. The extent of Rosie's current technology includes a few PCs in the accounting department and two PCs with Internet access for the rest of the staff. Your first assignment is to create a report detailing networks and wireless technologies. The report should explain how the club could gain a business advantage by implementing a wireless network. If Rosie likes your report, she will hire you as the full-time employee in charge of information technology. Be sure to include all of the different uses for wireless devices the club could implement to improve its operations.

B11

Ebusiness

LEARNING OUTCOMES

1. Describe the four common tools an organization can use to access Internet information.
2. Compare ISPs, OSPs, and ASPs. Be sure to include an overview of common services offered by each.
3. Describe how marketing, sales, financial services, and customer service departments can use ebusiness to increase revenues or reduce costs.
4. Explain why an organization would use metrics to determine a website's success.
5. Identify the different types of egovernment business models.
6. Define mcommerce and explain how an egovernment could use it to increase its efficiency and effectiveness.

Introduction

As organizations, governments, and academia embrace the Internet to conduct business, new approaches in the way they reach their target customers have resulted in numerous ebusiness opportunities. A ***pure play (virtual) business*** is a business that operates on the Internet only without a physical store, such as Expedia.com and Amazon.com. New technologies, competition, and cost savings along with the global nature of the Internet have significantly transformed traditional businesses into ebusinesses. The core units introduced the concepts of ebusiness as well as ebusiness models. This plug-in will build on the units' discussion, providing specific details on the functions of ebusiness as well as current and future trends.

Accessing Internet Information

Many restaurant and franchise experts believe that Cold Stone Creamery's franchisee intranet is what keeps the company on the fast track. Franchisee owners communicate with other owners through Creamery Talk, the company's intranet-based chat room. Since it launched, Creamery Talk has turned into a franchisee's black book, with tips on everything from storefront design to equipment repair. When one owner's freezer broke recently, a post to the chat room turned up an easy fix involving a $21 motor fan.

Four common tools for accessing Internet information include:

- Intranet
- Extranet
- Portal
- Kiosk

INTRANET

An *intranet* is an internalized portion of the Internet, protected from outside access, that allows an organization to provide access to information and application software to only its employees. An intranet is an invaluable tool for presenting organizational information as it provides a central location where employees can find information. It can host all kinds of company-related information such as benefits, schedules, strategic directions, and employee directories. At many companies, each department has its own web page on the intranet for departmental information sharing. An intranet is not necessarily open to the external Internet and enables organizations to make internal resources available using familiar Internet clients, such as web browsers, newsreaders, and email.

Intranet publishing is the ultimate in electronic publishing. Companies realize significant returns on investment (ROI) simply by publishing information, such as employee manuals or telephone directories, on intranets rather than printed media.

Citigroup's Global Corporate and Investment Banking division uses an intranet to provide its entire IT department with access to all IT projects including information on project owners, delivery dates, key resources, budget information, and project metrics. Providing this information via an intranet, or one convenient location, has enabled Citigroup to gain a 15 percent improvement in IT project delivery.

EXTRANET

An *extranet* is an intranet that is available to strategic allies (such as customers, suppliers, and partners). Many companies are building extranets as they begin to realize the benefit of offering individuals outside the organization access to intranet-based information and application software such as order processing. Having a common area where employees, partners, vendors, and customers access information can be a major competitive advantage for an organization.

Wal-Mart created an extranet for its suppliers, which can view detailed product information at all Wal-Mart locations. Suppliers log on to Wal-Mart's extranet and view metrics on products such as current inventory, orders, forecasts, and marketing campaigns. This helps Wal-Mart's suppliers maintain their supply chains and ensure Wal-Mart never runs out of products.

PORTAL

Portal is a very generic term for what is in essence a technology that provides access to information. A *portal* is a website that offers a broad array of resources and services, such as email, online discussion groups, search engines, and online shopping malls. There are general portals and specialized or niche portals. Leading general portals include Yahoo!, Netscape, Microsoft, and America Online. Examples of niche portals include Garden.com (for gardeners), Fool.com (for investors), and SearchNetworking.com (for network administrators).

Pratt & Whitney, one of the largest aircraft-engine manufacturers in the world, has saved millions of dollars with its field service portal initiative. Pratt & Whitney's sales and service field offices are geographically scattered around the globe and were connected via expensive dedicated lines. The company saved $2.6 million annually by replacing the dedicated lines with high-speed Internet access to its

field service portal. Field staff can find information they need in a fraction of the time it took before. The company estimates this change will save another $8 million per year in "process and opportunity" savings.

KIOSK

A *kiosk* is a publicly accessible computer system that has been set up to allow interactive information browsing. In a kiosk, the computer's operating system has been hidden from view, and the program runs in a full-screen mode, which provides a few simple tools for navigation.

Jason Suker walked into the Mazda showroom in Bountiful, Utah, and quickly found what he was looking for in a car dealership—a web kiosk, one of six stationed around the showroom. Using the web kiosk, he could track down the latest pricing information from sites like Kelley Blue Book and Edmunds.com. Suker, eyeing a four-year-old limited-edition Miata in mint condition, quickly pulled up the average retail price on Kelley Blue Book. At $16,000, it was $500 more than the dealer's price. Then, on eBay, Suker checked bids for similar models and found they were going for far less. With a sales representative looking over his shoulder to confirm his findings, the skeptical Suker made a lowball offer and expected the worst: endless haggling over price. However, the sales representative, after commending Suker for his research talent, eventually compromised and offered up the Miata for $13,300.

It was an even better deal for Bountiful Mazda. By using a kiosk to help Suker find the bargain price he wanted, the dealership moved a used car (with a higher profit margin than a new model) and opened the door to the unexpected up-sell with a $1,300, 36,000-mile service warranty.

Providing Internet Information

British Airways, the $11.9 billion airline, outsourced the automation of its FAQ (frequently asked questions) web pages. The airline needed to automatically develop, manage, and post different sets of FAQs for British Airway's loyalty program customers, allowing the company to offer special promotions based on the customer's loyalty program status (gold, silver, bronze). The company outsourced the project to application service provider RightNow Technologies. The new system is helping British Airways create the right marketing programs for the appropriate customer tier.

There are three common forms of service providers including:

1. Internet service provider (ISP).
2. Online service provider (OSP).
3. Application service provider (ASP).

INTERNET SERVICE PROVIDER

An *Internet service provider (ISP)* is a company that provides individuals and other companies access to the Internet along with additional related services, such as website building. An ISP has the equipment and the telecommunication line access required to have a point of presence on the Internet for different geographic areas. Larger ISPs have their own high-speed leased lines so they are less dependent on telecommunication providers and can deliver better service to their customers. Among the largest national and regional ISPs are AT&T WorldNet, IBM Global Network, MCI, Netcom, UUNet, and PSINet.

Navigating the different options for an ISP can be daunting and confusing. There are more than 7,000 ISPs in the United States; some are large with household names, and others are literally one-person operations. Although Internet access is

FIGURE B11.1

Common ISP Services

Common ISP Services
■ **Web hosting**. Housing, serving, and maintaining files for one or more websites is a widespread offering.
■ **Hard-disk storage space**. Smaller sites may need only 300 to 500 MB (megabytes) of website storage space, whereas other ebusiness sites may need at least 10 GB (gigabytes) of space or their own dedicated web server.
■ **Availability**. To run an ebusiness, a site must be accessible to customers 24×7. ISPs maximize the availability of the sites they host using techniques such as load balancing and clustering many servers to reach 100 percent availability.
■ **Support**. A big part of turning to an ISP is that there is limited worry about keeping the web server running. Most ISPs offer 24×7 customer service.

viewed as a commodity service, in reality features and performance can differ tremendously among ISPs. Figure B11.1 highlights common ISP features.

Another member of the ISP family is the ***wireless Internet service provider (WISP),*** an ISP that allows subscribers to connect to a server at designated hotspots or access points using a wireless connection. This type of ISP offers access to the Internet and the web from anywhere within the zone of coverage provided by an antenna. This is usually a region with a radius of one mile. Figure B11.2 displays a brief overview of how this technology works.

One example of a WISP is T-Mobile International, a company that provides access to wireless laptop users in more than 2,000 locations including airports, airline clubs, Starbucks coffeehouses, and Borders Books. A wireless service called T-Mobile HotSpot allows customers to access the Internet and T-Mobile's corporate intranet via a wireless network from convenient locations away from their home or office. T-Mobile International is the first mobile communications company to extend service on both sides of the Atlantic, offering customers the advantage of using their wireless services when traveling worldwide.

ONLINE SERVICE PROVIDER

An ***online service provider (OSP)*** offers an extensive array of unique services such as its own version of a web browser. The term *online service provider* helps to distinguish ISPs that offer Internet access and their own online content, such as America

FIGURE B11.2

Wireless Access Diagram

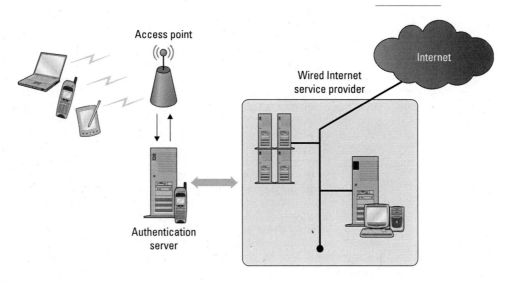

Online (AOL), from ISPs that simply connect users directly with the Internet, such as EarthLink. Connecting to the Internet through an OSP is an alternative to connecting through one of the national ISPs, such as AT&T or MCI, or a regional or local ISP.

APPLICATION SERVICE PROVIDER

An *application service provider (ASP)* is a company that offers an organization access over the Internet to systems and related services that would otherwise have to be located in personal or organizational computers. Employing the services of an ASP is essentially outsourcing part of a company's business logic. Hiring an ASP to manage a company's software allows the company to hand over the operation, maintenance, and upgrade responsibilities for a system to the ASP.

One of the most important agreements between the customer and the ASP is the service level agreement. *Service level agreements (SLAs)* define the specific responsibilities of the service provider and set the customer expectations. SLAs include such items as availability, accessibility, performance, maintenance, backup/recovery, upgrades, equipment ownership, software ownership, security, and confidentiality. For example, an SLA might state that the ASP must have the software available and accessible from 7:00 a.m. to 7:00 p.m. Monday through Friday. It might also state that if the system is down for more than 60 minutes, there will be no charge for that day. Most industry analysts agree that the ASP market is growing rapidly. International Data Corporation (IDC) estimates the worldwide ASP market will grow from around $25 billion by 2008 to $40 billion by 2011. Figure B11.3 displays the top ISPs, OSPs, and ASPs.

Organizational Strategies for Ebusiness

To be successful in ebusiness, an organization must master the art of electronic relationships. Traditional means of customer acquisition such as advertising, promotions, and public relations are just as important with a website. Primary business areas taking advantage of ebusiness include:

- Marketing/sales
- Financial services
- Procurement
- Customer service
- Intermediaries

MARKETING/SALES

Direct selling was the earliest type of ebusiness and has proven to be a stepping-stone to more complex commerce operations. Successes such as eBay, Barnes and Noble, Dell Inc., and Travelocity have sparked the growth of this segment, proving customer acceptance of ebusiness direct selling. Marketing and sales departments are initiating some of the most exciting ebusiness innovations (see Figure B11.4).

Cincinnati's WCPO-TV once was a ratings blip and is now the number three ABC affiliate in the nation. WCPO-TV credits its success largely to digital billboards that promote different programming depending on the time of day. The billboards are updated directly from a website. The station quickly noticed that when current events for the early-evening news were plugged during the afternoon, ratings spiked.

The digital billboards let several companies share one space and can change messages directly from the company's computer. In the morning, a department store can advertise a sale, and in the afternoon, a restaurant can advertise its specials. Eventually customers will be able to buy billboard sign time in hour or minute increments. Current costs to share a digital billboard are $40,000 a month, compared with $10,000 for one standard billboard.

Company	Description	Specialty
Appshop www.appshop.com	Application Service Provider	Oracle 11i ebusiness suite applications
BlueStar Solutions www.bluestarsolutions.com	Application Service Provider	Managing ERP solutions with a focus on SAP
Concur www.concur.com	Internet Service Provider	Integrates B2B procurement
Corio www.corio.com	Application Service Provider	Specializes in Oracle applications
Employease www.employease.com	Online service provider	Human resource application services
Intacct www.intacct.com	Online service provider	Online general ledger service
LivePerson www.liveperson.com	Online service provider	Real-time chat provider
NetLedger www.netledger.com	Online service provider	Web-based accounting platform
Outtask www.outtask.com	Application Service Provider	Integration of budgeting, customer service, sales management, and human resources applications
RightNow www.rightnow.com	Online service provider, Internet Service Provider	Suite of customer service applications
Salesforce.com www.salesforce.com	Online service provider	Suite of customer service applications
Salesnet www.salesnet.com	Online service provider	Suite of sales force automation products and services
Surebridge www.surebridge.com	Application Service Provider	High-tech manufacturing, distribution, health care applications
UpShot www.upshot.com	Online service provider	Sales force automation products and services
USi www.usinternetworking.com	Application Service Provider	Ariba, Siebel, Microsoft, and Oracle customer base

FIGURE B11.3

Top ISPs, OSPs, and ASPs

Ebusiness provides an easy way to penetrate a new geographic territory and extend global reach. Large, small, or specialized businesses can use their online sales sites to sell on a worldwide basis with little extra cost. This ability to tap into expanded domestic or even international markets can be an immediate revenue boost to artists, jewelry makers, wineries, and the like, for initial orders and especially for reorders.

FINANCIAL SERVICES

Financial services websites are enjoying rapid growth as they help consumers, businesses, and financial institutions distribute information with greater convenience and richness than is available in other channels. Consumers in ebusiness markets pay for products and services using a credit card or one of the methods outlined

FIGURE B11.4

Generating Revenue on the Internet through Marketing and Sales Departments

Marketing and Sales Ebusiness Innovations
■ An *online ad* is a box running across a web page that is often used to contain advertisements. The banner generally contains a link to the advertiser's website. Web-based advertising services can track the number of times users click the banner, generating statistics that enable advertisers to judge whether the advertising fees are worth paying. Online ads are like living, breathing classified ads.
■ A *pop-up ad* is a small web page containing an advertisement that appears on the web page outside of the current website loaded in the web browser. A *pop-under ad* is a form of a pop-up ad that users do not see until they close the current web browser screen.
■ *Associate programs (affiliate programs)* allow businesses to generate commissions or royalties from an Internet site. For example, a business can sign up as an associate of a major commercial site such as Amazon. The business then sends potential buyers to the Amazon site using a code or banner ad. The business receives a commission when the referred customer makes a purchase on Amazon.
■ *Viral marketing* is a technique that induces websites or users to pass on a marketing message to other websites or users, creating exponential growth in the message's visibility and effect. One example of successful viral marketing is Hotmail, which promotes its service and its own advertisers' messages in every user's email notes. Viral marketing encourages users of a product or service supplied by an ebusiness to encourage friends to join. Viral marketing is a word-of-mouth type advertising program.
■ *Mass customization* is the ability of an organization to give its customers the opportunity to tailor its products or services to the customers' specifications. For example, customers can order M&M's with customized sayings such as "Marry Me."
■ *Personalization* occurs when a website can know enough about a person's likes and dislikes that it can fashion offers that are more likely to appeal to that person. Personalization involves tailoring a presentation of an ebusiness website to individuals or groups of customers based on profile information, demographics, or prior transactions. Amazon uses personalization to create a unique portal for each of its customers.
■ A *blog* (the contraction of the phrase "web log") is a website in which items are posted on a regular basis and displayed in reverse chronological order. Like other media, blogs often focus on a particular subject, such as food, politics, or local news. Some blogs function as online diaries. A typical blog combines text, images, and links to other blogs, web pages, and other media related to its topic. Since its appearance in 1995, blogging has emerged as a popular means of communication, affecting public opinion and mass media around the world.
■ *Real simple syndications (RSS)* is a family of web feed formats used for web syndication of programs and content. RSS is used by (among other things) news websites, blogs, and podcasting, which allows consumers and journalists to have news constantly fed to them instead of searching for it. In addition to facilitating syndication, RSS allows a website's frequent readers to track updates on the site.
■ *Podcasting* is the distribution of audio or video files, such as radio programs or music videos, over the Internet to play on mobile devices and personal computers. Podcasting's essence is about creating content (audio or video) for an audience that wants to listen when they want, where they want, and how they want. Podcasters' websites also may offer direct download of their files, but the subscription feed of automatically delivered new content is what distinguishes a podcast from a simple download or real-time streaming. Usually, the podcast features one type of show with new episodes either sporadically or at planned intervals such as daily, weekly, etc.
■ *Search engine optimization (SEO)* is a set of methods aimed at improving the ranking of a website in search engine listings. Search engines display different kinds of listings in the search engine results pages (SERPs), including: pay-per-click advertisements, paid inclusion listings, and organic search results. SEO is primarily concerned with advancing the goals of websites by improving the number and position of organic search results for a wide variety of relevant keywords. SEO strategies can increase the number of visitors and the quality of visitors, where quality means visitors who complete the action the site intends (e.g., purchase, sign up, learn something). SEO, or "white hat SEO," is distinguished from "black hat SEO," or spamdexing by methods and objectives. *Spamdexing* uses a variety of deceptive techniques in an attempt to manipulate search engine rankings, whereas legitimate SEO focuses on building better sites and using honest methods of promotion. What constitutes an honest, or ethical, method is an issue that has been the subject of numerous debates.

FIGURE B11.5

Types of Online Consumer
Payments

Online Consumer Payments	
Financial cybermediary	A *financial cybermediary* is an Internet-based company that facilitates payments over the Internet. PayPal is the best-known example of a financial cybermediary.
Electronic check	An *electronic check* is a mechanism for sending a payment from a checking or savings account. There are many implementations of electronic checks, with the most prominent being online banking.
Electronic bill presentment and payment (EBPP)	An *electronic bill presentment and payment (EBPP)* is a system that sends bills over the Internet and provides an easy-to-use mechanism (such as clicking on a button) to pay the bill. EBPP systems are available through local banks or online services such as Checkfree and Quicken.
Digital wallet	A *digital wallet* is both software and information—the software provides security for the transaction and the information includes payment and delivery information (for example, the credit card number and expiration date).

in Figure B11.5. Online business payments differ from online consumer payments because businesses tend to make large purchases (from thousands to millions of dollars) and typically do not pay with a credit card. Businesses make online payments using electronic data interchange (EDI) (see Figure B11.6). Transactions between businesses are complex and typically require a level of system integration between the businesses.

Many organizations are now turning to providers of electronic trading networks for enhanced Internet-based network and messaging services. Electronic trading networks are service providers that manage network services. They support business-to-business integration information exchanges, improved security, guaranteed service levels, and command center support (see Figure B11.7). As electronic trading networks expand their reach and the number of Internet businesses continues to grow, so will the need for managed trading services. Using these services allows organizations to reduce time to market and the overall development, deployment, and maintenance costs associated with their integration infrastructures.

Traders at Vanguard Petroleum Corporation spent most days on the phone, patrolling the market for pricing and volume information in order to strike the best possible deal. The process was slow and tied up traders on one negotiation at a time, making it inherently difficult to stay on top of quickly changing prices. One winter, for example, the weather got cold and stayed cold, causing propane prices to increase dramatically. The price was moving so fast that Vanguard was missing opportunities to buy, sell, and execute deals since it was able to complete only one deal at a time.

FIGURE B11.6

Types of Online Business
Payments

Online Business Payments
Electronic data interchange (EDI) is a standard format for exchanging business data. One way an organization can use EDI is through a value-added network. A *value-added network (VAN)* is a private network, provided by a third party, for exchanging information through a high-capacity connection. VANs support electronic catalogs (from which orders are placed), EDI-based transactions (the actual orders), security measures such as encryption, and EDI mailboxes.
Financial EDI (financial electronic data interchange) is a standard electronic process for B2B market purchase payments. National Cash Management System is an automated clearinghouse that supports the reconciliation of the payments.

FIGURE B11.7

Diagram of an Electronic
Trading Network

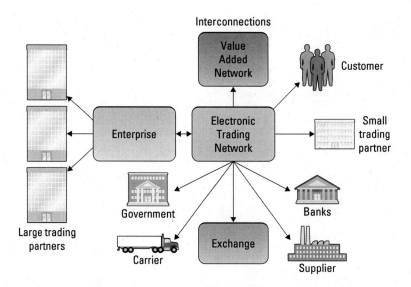

To bridge these shortcomings and speed the process, Vanguard became one of the first users of Chalkboard, a commodity markets electronic trading network that is now part of ChemConnect, a B2B emarketplace. Vanguard uses Chalkboard to put bids and offers in front of hundreds of traders and complete various trades at multiple delivery points simultaneously. Vanguard now completes deals in real time and is able to access a broader audience of buyers and sellers.

PROCUREMENT

Web-based procurement of maintenance, repair, and operations (MRO) supplies is expected to reach more than $200 billion worldwide by the year 2009. *Maintenance, repair, and operations (MRO) materials* (also called *indirect materials*) are materials necessary for running an organization but do not relate to the company's primary business activities. Typical MRO goods include office supplies (such as pens and paper), equipment, furniture, computers, and replacement parts. In the traditional approach to MRO purchasing, a purchasing manager would receive a paper-based request for materials. The purchasing manager would need to search a variety of paper catalogs to find the right product at the right price. Not surprisingly, the administrative cost for purchasing indirect supplies often exceeded the unit value of the product itself. According to the Organization for Economic Cooperation and Development (OECD), companies with more than $500 million in revenue spend an estimated $75 to $150 to process a single purchase order for MRO supplies.

Eprocurement

Eprocurement is the B2B purchase and sale of supplies and services over the Internet. The goal of many eprocurement applications is to link organizations directly to preapproved suppliers' catalogs and to process the entire purchasing transaction online. Linking to electronic catalogs significantly reduces the need to check the timeliness and accuracy of supplier information.

An *electronic catalog* presents customers with information about goods and services offered for sale, bid, or auction on the Internet. Some electronic catalogs manage large numbers of individual items, and search capabilities help buyers navigate quickly to the items they want to purchase. Other electronic catalogs emphasize merchandise presentation and special offers, much as a retail store is laid out to encourage impulse or add-on buying. As with other aspects of ebusiness, it is important to match electronic catalog design and functionality to a company's business goals.

CUSTOMER SERVICE

Ebusiness enables customers to help themselves by combining the communications capability of a traditional customer response system with the content richness only the web can provide—all available and operating 24 × 7. As a result, conducting business via the web offers customers the convenience they want while freeing key support staff to tackle more complex problems. The web also allows an organization to provide better customer service through email, special messages, and private password-web access to special areas for top customers.

Issues for Consumer Protection
■ Unsolicited goods and communication
■ Illegal or harmful goods, services, and content
■ Insufficient information about goods or their suppliers
■ Invasion of privacy
■ Cyberfraud

FIGURE B11.8

Consumer Protection

Vanguard manages $690 billion in assets and charges the lowest fees in the industry: 0.26 percent of assets versus an industry average of 0.81 percent. Vanguard keeps fees down by teaching its investors how to better use its website. For good reason: A web log-on costs Vanguard mere pennies, while each call to a service rep is a $9 expense.

Customer service is the business process where the most human contact occurs between a buyer and a seller. Not surprisingly, ebusiness strategists are finding that customer service via the web is one of the most challenging and potentially lucrative areas of ebusiness. The primary issue facing customer service departments using ebusiness is consumer protection.

Consumer Protection

An organization that wants to dominate by using superior customer service as a competitive advantage must not only consider how to service its customers, but also how to protect its customers. Organizations must recognize that many consumers are unfamiliar with their digital choices, and some ebusinesses are well aware of these vulnerabilities. For example, 17-year-old Miami high school senior Francis Cornworth offered his "Young Man's Virginity" for sale on eBay. The offer attracted a $10 million phony bid. Diana Duyser of Hollywood, Florida, sold half of a grilled cheese sandwich that resembles the Virgin Mary to the owners of an online casino for $28,000 on eBay. Figure B11.8 highlights the different protection areas for consumers.

Regardless of whether the customers are other businesses or end consumers, one of their greatest concerns is the security level of their financial transactions. This includes all aspects of electronic information, but focuses mainly on the information associated with payments (e.g., a credit card number) and the payments themselves, that is, the "electronic money." An organization must consider such issues as encryption, secure socket layers (SSL), and secure electronic transactions (SET), as explained in Figure B11.9.

FIGURE B11.9

Ebusiness Security

Ebusiness Security
Encryption scrambles information into an alternative form that requires a key or password to decrypt the information. Encryption is achieved by scrambling letters, replacing letters, replacing letters with numbers, and other ways.
A *secure socket layer (SSL)* (1) creates a secure and private connection between a client and server computer, (2) encrypts the information, and (3) sends the information over the Internet. SSL is identified by a website address that includes an "s" at the end—https.
A *secure electronic transaction (SET)* is a transmission security method that ensures transactions are secure and legitimate. Similar to SSL, SET encrypts information before sending it over the Internet. However, SET also enables customer authentication for credit card transaction. SETs are endorsed by major ecommerce players including MasterCard, American Express, Visa, Netscape, and Microsoft.

INTERMEDIARIES

Intermediaries are agents, software, or businesses that bring buyers and sellers together that provide a trading infrastructure to enhance ebusiness. With the introduction of ecommerce there was much discussion about disintermediation of middle people/organizations; however, recent developments in ebusiness have seen more reintermediation. *Reintermediation* refers to using the Internet to reassemble buyers, sellers, and other partners in a traditional supply chain in new ways. Examples include New York-based e-Steel Corp. and Philadelphia-based PetroChemNet Inc. bringing together producers, traders, distributors, and buyers of steel and chemicals, respectively, in web-based marketplaces. Figure B11.10 lists intermediaries and their functions, including the more commonly applied, such as the following:

- *Content providers* are companies that use the Internet to distribute copyrighted content, including news, music, games, books, movies, and many other types of information. Retrieving and paying for content is the second largest revenue source for B2C ebusiness.

- *Online brokers* act as intermediaries between buyers and sellers of goods and services. Online brokers, who usually work for commission, provide many services. For example, travel agents are information brokers who pass information from product suppliers to customers. They also take and process orders, collect money, and provide travel assistance, including obtaining visas.

FIGURE B11.10

Types of Intermediaries

Type of Intermediary	Description	Example
Internet service providers	Make money selling a service, not a product	Earthlink.com Comcast.com AOL.com
Portals	Central hubs for online content	Yahoo!.com MSN.com Google.com
Content providers	Use the Internet to distribute copyrighted content	wsj.com cnn.com espn.com
Online brokers	Intermediaries between buyers and sellers of goods and services	charlesschwab.com fidelity.com datek.com
Market makers	Aggregate three services for market participants: a place, rules, and infrastructure	amazon.com ebay.com priceline.com
Online service providers	Extensive online array of services	xdrive.com lawinfo.com
Intelligent agents	Software applications that follow instructions and learn independently	Sidestep.com WebSeeker.com iSpyNOW.com
Application service providers	Sell access to Internet-based software applications to other companies	ariba.com commerceone.com ibm.com
Infomediaries	Provide specialized information on behalf of producers of goods and services and their potential customers	autobytel.com BizRate.com

- *Market makers* are intermediaries that aggregate three services for market participants: (1) a place to trade, (2) rules to govern trading, and (3) an infrastructure to support trading. For example, eBay's ebusiness model focuses on creating a digital electronic environment for buyers and sellers to meet, agree on a price, and conduct a transaction.

Measuring Ebusiness Success

Traffic on the Internet retail site for Wal-Mart has grown 66 percent in the last year. The site receives over 500,000 visitors daily (6.5 million per week), downloads 2 million web pages daily, and averages 60,000 users logged on simultaneously. Wal-Mart's primary concern is maintaining optimal performance for online transactions. A disruption to the website directly affects the company's bottom line and customer loyalty. The company monitors and tracks the hardware, software, and network running the company's website to ensure high quality of service.

The Yankee Group reports that 66 percent of companies determine website success solely by measuring the amount of traffic. Unfortunately, heavy website traffic does not necessarily indicate large sales. Many websites with lots of traffic have minimal sales. The best way to measure a website's success is to measure such things as the revenue generated by web traffic, the number of new customers acquired by web traffic, or any reductions in customer service calls resulting from web traffic.

WEBSITE METRICS

Figure B11.11 displays a few metrics an organization can use to measure website effectiveness.

To help understand advertising effectiveness, interactivity measures are tracked and monitored. *Interactivity* measures the visitor interactions with the target ad. Such interaction measures include the duration of time the visitor spends viewing the ad, the number of pages viewed, and even the number of repeat visits to the target ad. Interactivity measures are a giant step forward for advertisers, since traditional methods of advertising—newspapers, magazines, radio, and television—provide few ways to track effectiveness metrics. Interactivity metrics measure actual consumer activities, something that was impossible to do in the past, and provides advertisers with tremendous amounts of business intelligence.

Effectiveness Website Metrics
■ *Cookie*—a small file deposited on a hard drive by a website containing information about customers and their web activities. Cookies allow websites to record the comings and goings of customers, usually without their knowledge or consent.
■ *Click-through*—a count of the number of people who visit one site and click on an advertisement that takes them to the site of the advertiser. Tracking effectiveness based on click-throughs guarantees exposure to target ads; however, it does not guarantee that the visitor liked the ad, spent any substantial time viewing the ad, or was satisfied with the information contained in the ad.
■ *Online ad*—a box running across a web page that is often used to contain advertisements. An online ad advertises the products and services of another business, usually another dot-com business. Advertisers can track how often customers click on online ads resulting in a click-through to their website. Often the cost of the online ad depends on the number of customers who click on the online ad. Tracking the number of online ad clicks is one way to understand the effectiveness of the ad on its target audience.

FIGURE B11.11

Website Effectiveness Metrics

The ultimate outcome of any advertisement is a purchase. Tying purchase amounts to website visits makes it easy to communicate the business value of the website. Organizations use metrics to tie revenue amounts and new customer creation numbers directly back to the websites or banner ads. Organizations can observe through *clickstream data* the exact pattern of a consumer's navigation through a site. Clickstream data can reveal a number of basic data points on how consumers interact with websites. Figure B11.12 displays different types of clickstream metrics.

Marc Barach is the co-inventor and chief marketing officer of Ingenio, a start-up company that specializes in connecting people in real time. When the Internet first emerged, banner ads were the prevalent marketing tools. Next came pay-per-click where the company pays the search engine each time its website is accessed from a search. Today 35 percent of online spending occurs through pay-per-clicks. Unfortunately, pay-per-clicks are not suitable for all businesses. Roofers, plumbers, auto repair people, and cosmetic surgeons rarely have websites and do not generate business via pay-per-clicks. Barach believes that the next line of Internet advertising will be pay-per-call, and Ingenio has invested five years and $50 million in building the platform to run the business. Here is how pay-per-call works:

- The user types a keyword into a search engine.
- The search engine passes the keyword to Ingenio.
- Ingenio determines the category and sends back the appropriate merchant's unique, traceable 800 telephone number.
- The 800 number routes through Ingenio's switches, and Ingenio charges the merchant when a customer calls.

A Jupiter Research study discovered that businesses were willing to pay between $2 and $35 for each call lead.

Figure B11.13 provides definitions of common metrics based on clickstream data. To interpret such data properly, managers try to benchmark against other companies. For instance, consumers seem to visit their preferred websites regularly, even checking back to the website multiple times during a given session. Consumers tend to become loyal to a small number of websites, and they tend to revisit those websites a number of times during a particular session.

FIGURE B11.12

Clickstream Data Metrics

Clickstream Data Metrics
■ The number of page views (i.e., the number of times a particular page has been presented to a visitor).
■ The pattern of websites visited, including most frequent exit page and most frequent prior website.
■ Length of stay on the website.
■ Dates and times of visits.
■ Number of registrations filled out per 100 visitors.
■ Number of abandoned registrations.
■ Demographics of registered visitors.
■ Number of customers with shopping carts.
■ Number of abandoned shopping carts.

Visitor	Visitor Metrics
Unidentified visitor	A visitor is an individual who visits a website. An "unidentified visitor" means that no information about that visitor is available.
Unique visitor	A unique visitor is one who can be recognized and counted only once within a given period of time. An accurate count of unique visitors is not possible without some form of identification, registration, or authentication.
Session visitor	A session ID is available (e.g., cookie) or inferred by incoming address plus browser type, which allows a visitor's responses to be tracked within a given visit to a website.
Tracked visitor	An ID (e.g., cookie) is available, which allows a user to be tracked across multiple visits to a website. No information, other than a unique identifier, is available for a tracked visitor.
Identified visitor	An ID is available (e.g., cookie or voluntary registration), which allows a user to be tracked across multiple visits to a website. Other information (name, demographics, possibly supplied voluntarily by the visitor) can be linked to this ID.
Exposure	**Exposure Metrics**
Page exposures (page-views)	The number of times a particular web page has been viewed by visitors in a given time period, without regard to duplication.
Site exposures	The number of visitor sessions at a website in a given time period, without regard to visitor duplication.
Visit	**Visit Metrics**
Stickiness (visit duration time)	The length of time a visitor spends on a website. Can be reported as an average in a given time period, without regard to visitor duplication.
Raw visit depth (total web pages exposure per session)	The total number of pages a visitor is exposed to during a single visit to a website. Can be reported as an average or distribution in a given time period, without regard to visitor duplication.
Visit depth (total unique web pages exposure per session)	The total number of unique pages a visitor is exposed to during a single visit to a website. Can be reported as an average or distribution in a given time period, without regard to visitor duplication.
Hit	**Hit Metrics**
Hits	When visitors reach a website, their computer sends a request to the site's computer server to begin displaying pages. Each element of a requested page (including graphics, text, interactive items) is recorded by the website's server log file as a "hit."
Qualified hits	Exclude less important information recorded in a log file (such as error messages, etc.).

FIGURE B11.13

Definitions of Website Metrics

New Trends in Ebusiness: Egovernment and Mcommerce

Recent business models that have arisen to enable organizations to take advantage of the Internet and create value are within egovernment. *Egovernment* involves the use of strategies and technologies to transform government(s) by improving the

FIGURE B11.14

Extended Ebusiness
Models

	Business	Consumer	Government
Business	B2B conisint.com	B2C dell.com	B2G lockheedmartin.com
Consumer	C2B priceline.com	C2C ebay.com	C2G eGov.com
Government	G2B export.gov	G2C medicare.gov	G2G disasterhelp.gov

delivery of services and enhancing the quality of interaction between the citizen-consumer within all branches of government (refer to Figure B11.14).

One example of an egovernment portal, FirstGov.gov, the official U.S. gateway to all government information, is the catalyst for a growing electronic government. Its powerful search engine and ever-growing collection of topical and customer-focused links connect users to millions of web pages, from the federal government, to local and tribal governments, to foreign nations around the world. Figure B11.15 highlights specific egovernment models.

FIGURE B11.15

Egovernment Models

Egovernment Models	
Consumer-to-government (C2G)	C2G will mainly constitute the areas where a consumer (or citizen) interacts with the government. It will include areas like elections, when citizens vote for government officials; census, where the consumer provides demographic information to the government; and taxation, where the consumer is paying taxes to the government.
Government-to-business (G2B)	This model includes all government interaction with business enterprises whether it is procurement of goods and services from suppliers or information regarding legal and business issues that is transmitted electronically.
Government-to-consumer (G2C)	Governments around the world are now dealing with consumers (or citizens) electronically, providing them with updated information. Governments are also processing applications for visas, renewal of passports and driver's licenses, advertising of tender notices, and other services online.
Government-to-government (G2G)	Governments around the world are now dealing with other governments electronically. Still at an inception stage, this ebusiness model will enhance international trade and information retrieval, for example, on criminal records of new migrants. At the state level, information exchange and processing of transactions online will enable enhanced efficiencies.

MCOMMERCE

In a few years, Internet-enabled mobile devices will outnumber PCs. ***Mobile commerce,*** or ***mcommerce,*** is the ability to purchase goods and services through a wireless Internet-enabled device. The emerging technology behind mcommerce is a mobile device equipped with a web-ready micro-browser. To take advantage of the mcommerce market potential, handset manufacturers Nokia, Ericsson, Motorola, and Qualcomm are working with telecommunication carriers AT&T Wireless and Sprint to develop smartphones. Using new forms of technology, smartphones offer fax, email, and phone capabilities all in one, paving the way for mcommerce to be accepted by an increasingly mobile workforce. Figure B11.16 gives a visual overview of mcommerce.

Amazon.com has collaborated with Nokia to pioneer a new territory. With the launch of its Amazon.com Anywhere service, it has become one of the first major online retailers to recognize and do something about the potential of Internet-enabled wireless devices. As content delivery over wireless devices becomes faster, more secure, and scalable, mcommerce will surpass landline ebusiness (traditional telephony) as the method of choice for digital commerce transactions. According to the research firm Strategy Analytics, the global mcommerce market was expected to be worth more than more than $400 million by 2010, with 800 million customers generating almost 30 billion transactions annually. Additionally, information activities like email, news, and stock quotes will progress to personalized transactions, "one-click" travel reservations, online auctions, and videoconferencing.

Organizations face changes more extensive and far reaching in their implications than anything since the modern industrial revolution occurred in the early 1900s. Technology is a primary force driving these changes. Organizations that want to survive must recognize the immense power of technology, carry out required organizational changes in the face of it, and learn to operate in an entirely different way.

FIGURE B11.16

Mcommerce Technology Overview

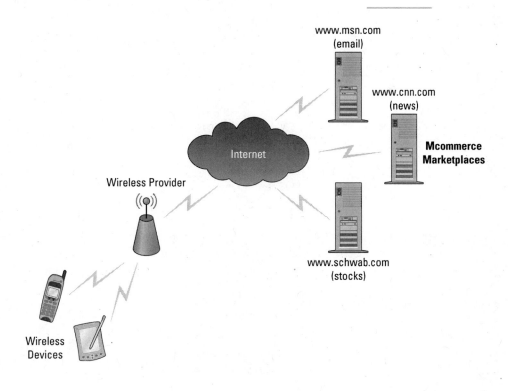

www.msn.com
(email)

www.cnn.com
(news)

Mcommerce Marketplaces

Internet

Wireless Provider

www.schwab.com
(stocks)

Wireless Devices

✳ PLUG-IN SUMMARY

With the advent of the Internet and ecommerce, ebusiness is booming. To capitalize on ebusiness and create new channels that cut expenses, speed delivery time, and open new markets, new strategic ebusinesses are emerging daily. To establish an environment conducive to ebusiness, companies are required to change their strategies, realign their organizations with emerging opportunities, and articulate the new strategies to partners.

Merely deciding to adopt a new ebusiness model does not guarantee success. Organizations must embrace ASPs, OSPs, intranets, extranets, online bill payments, and so on, all of which involve considerable disruption to current business processes. Technical adjustments, such as integration, debugging, software integration, and effective website management, are necessary. Effectively managing the changes associated with the implementation of a new ebusiness will help an organization find the path to electronic success.

✳ KEY TERMS

Application service provider (ASP), 382
Associate program (affiliate program), 384
Blog, 384
Clickstream data, 390
Click-through, 389
Content provider, 388
Cookie, 389
Digital wallet, 385
Egovernment, 391
Electronic bill presentment and payment (EBPP), 385
Electronic catalog, 386
Electronic check, 385
Electronic data interchange (EDI), 385
Encryption, 387
Eprocurement, 386
Extranet, 379
Financial cybermediary, 385

Financial EDI (financial electronic data interchange), 385
Interactivity, 389
Intermediary, 388
Internet service provider (ISP), 380
Intranet, 379
Kiosk, 380
Maintenance, repair, and operations (MRO) materials (also called indirect materials), 386
Market maker, 389
Mass customization, 384
Mobile commerce, or mcommerce, 393
Online ad, 384, 389
Online broker, 388
Online service provider (OSP), 381
Personalization, 384

Podcasting, 384
Pop-under ad, 384
Pop-up ad, 384
Portal, 379
Pure play (virtual) business, 378
Real simple syndication (RSS), 384
Reintermediation, 388
Search engine optimization (SEO), 384
Secure electronic transaction (SET), 387
Secure socket layer (SSL), 387
Service level agreements (SLA), 382
Spamdexing, 384
Value-added network (VAN), 385
Viral marketing, 384
Wireless Internet service provider (WISP), 381

✳ CLOSING CASE ONE

Mail with PostalOne

Despite billions of dollars invested in automation and information technology since the early 1970s, the 226-year-old United States Postal Service's (USPS) productivity grew by only 11 percent over the past three decades. The 800,000 employees at USPS faced a fiscal deficit of $2.4 billion in 2001. Factors in the shortfall included the slow economy, rising fuel costs, and electronic alternatives to paper mail.

Agency leaders maintain that technology is one of the keys to making the USPS more competitive, as they have started a heavy campaign to combat declining revenues using a series of web technology projects. One of the most significant projects for the USPS is a web front-end for PostalOne, a system that seeks to eliminate the administrative paperwork for bulk mail, which accounts for 70 percent of total mail volume and 50 percent of the agency's $65 billion in revenue. More than 770,000 businesses use the USPS to send bulk mail.

PostalOne is one of the main customer-facing portions of the USPS's plan to build the Information Platform, which comprises the core IT systems that receive, process, transport, and deliver the mail. A tremendous amount of paperwork is associated with verifying a mailing to receive a discounted postage rate and creating related documentation. Business customers will install a USPS application that will reside on their server and manage the online paperwork, validate and encrypt files, and handle communications with PostalOne servers.

The Information Platform will include a web interface to the agency's Processing Operations Information System (POIS), which collects, tracks, and ultimately delivers performance data on the agency's more than 350 processing and distribution facilities. These efforts follow several ebusiness projects:

- **NetPost Mailing Online** lets small businesses transmit documents, correspondence, newsletters, and other first-class, standard, and nonprofit mail over the web to the USPS. Electronic files are transmitted to printing contractors, which print the documents, insert them into addressed envelopes, sort the mail pieces, and then add postage. The finished pieces are taken to a local post office for processing and delivery. Customers get the automated first-class rate, which is a few cents less per piece than the first-class rate.

- **Post Electronic Courier Service, or PosteCS,** a secure messaging product, allows mailers to send documents by email or over the web to recipients via a secure communication session. PosteCS has an electronic postmark, an electronic time and date stamp developed by USPS, embedded for proof of delivery. PosteCS is used mainly to transfer large files, such as financial statements. Cost is based on the security option chosen and file size.

- **NetPost.Certified,** a secure messaging product, was developed to help federal agencies comply with the Government Paperwork Elimination Act. NetPost.Certified is used, for example, by the Social Security Administration to receive notification from prisons when inmates are no longer eligible for benefits. NetPost.Certified includes an electronic postmark. The service costs 50 cents per transaction.

- **EBillPay** lets customers receive, view, and pay their bills via the agency's website. The Postal Service partners with CheckFree, which offers its service on the USPS site and performs back-end processing. Some enhancements to this service are being developed, including an embedded electronic postmark, person-to-person payments, and the ability to receive and pay bills via email. The ability to offer businesses and consumers online bill payment options is vital for the Postal Service, which estimates that $17 billion in annual revenue is at risk from first-class mail going through electronic alternatives for bill payment and presentment.

Despite its problems, the USPS has been resilient over the years, in large part because of its enormous resources. It is the nation's second largest employer behind Wal-Mart, and its revenue would rank it eighth in the Fortune 500.

Questions

1. Do you think the steps by the USPS are far-reaching enough to ensure its relevance in ebusiness?
2. What other strategic alliances, akin to its partnership with CheckFree, can the USPS develop to stay competitive?
3. Why would the USPS compete in a market that private companies already serve well?
4. How can the USPS use portals to help grow its business?

5. How can the USPS use ebusiness sales and marketing techniques such as blogs, podcasts, and SEO to improve its business?

6. How can the USPS use ASPs to improve its business?

✶ CLOSING CASE TWO

Made-to-Order Businesses

In the past, customers had two choices for purchasing products: (1) purchase a mass-produced product like a pair of jeans or a candy bar, or (2) commission a custom-made item that was perfect but cost a lot more. Mass customization is a new trend in the retail business. Mass customization hits that sweet spot between harnessing the cost efficiencies of mass production and offering so many different options that customers feel the product has been designed just for them. Today, strategic information systems help many companies implement mass customization business strategies.

Lands' End

Lands' End built a decision support system that could pinpoint a person's body size by taking just a few of their measurements and running a series of algorithms. The process begins when the customer answers questions on Lands' End's website about everything from waist size to inseam. Lands' End saves the data in its customer relationship management system, which is used for reorders, promotions, and marketing campaigns. When a customer places an order, the order is sent to San Francisco where supply chain management software determines which one of five contracted manufacturers should receive the order. The chosen manufacturer then cuts and sews the material and ships the finished garment directly to the customer.

Over 40 percent of Lands' End shoppers prefer a customized garment to the standard-sized equivalent, even though each customized garment costs at least $20 more and takes four weeks to deliver. Customized clothes account for a growing percentage of Lands' End's $511 million online business. Reorder rates for Lands' End custom-clothing buyers are 34 percent higher than for buyers of its standard-sized clothing.

Nike

The original business model for Nike iD concentrated on connecting with consumers and creating customer loyalty. Nike iD's website allows customers to build their own running shoes. The process begins when customers choose from one of seven styles and a multitude of color combinations. Think dark-pink bottoms, red mesh, bright yellowing lining, purple laces, blue swoosh, and a eucalyptus green accent. Customers can even place eight-character personalized messages on the side of the shoe. The cost averages about $30 more than buying the regular shoes in a store.

Once Nike receives the custom order, its supply chain management system sends it to one of 15 plants depending on production availability. Customers receive their shoes within four weeks. The program has experienced triple-digit annual growth for two years.

Stamps.com

Stamps.com, which provides online stamp purchases, made an agreement with the U.S. Postal Service to sell customized stamps. Customers could put pictures of their choice on an actual U.S. postage stamp. Pictures ranged from dogs to fiancées. The response was phenomenal: Within seven weeks, Stamps.com processed and sold more than 2 million PhotoStamps at $1 each (37 cents for a regular stamp). Unfortunately, pranksters managed to slip controversial photos through the system, and the U.S. Postal Service temporarily canceled the agreement.

Making mass customization a goal changes the way businesses think about their customers. Using supply chain management and customer relationship management to implement mass customization can have a direct impact on a business's bottom line.

Questions

1. What role does ebusiness play in a mass customization business strategy?
2. How can Lands' End use additional sales and marketing ebusiness techniques to improve its business?
3. How can Nike use ebusiness financial services to improve its business?
4. How can Stamps.com use ASPs and electronic bill payment to improve its business?
5. Choose one of the examples above and analyze its ebusiness approach. Would you invest $20,000 in the company?
6. Choose one of the examples above and explain how the company is attempting to gain a competitive advantage with mass customization and personalization. How could this company use podcasts, blogs, and SEO to improve its business?

 MAKING BUSINESS DECISIONS

1. Analyzing Websites

Stars Inc. is a large clothing corporation that specializes in reselling clothes worn by celebrities. The company's four websites generate 75 percent of its sales. The remaining 25 percent of sales occur directly through the company's warehouse. You have recently been hired as the director of sales. The only information you can find on the success of the four websites follows:

Website	Classic	Contemporary	New Age	Traditional
Traffic analysis	5,000 hits/day	200 hits/day	10,000 hits/day	1,000 hits/day
Stickiness (average)	20 min.	1 hr.	20 min.	50 min.
Number of abandoned shopping carts	400/day	0/day	5,000/day	200/day
Number of unique visitors	2,000/day	100/day	8,000/day	200/day
Number of identified visitors	3,000/day	100/day	2,000/day	800/day
Average revenue per sale	$1,000	$1,000	$50	$1,300

You decide that maintaining four separate websites is expensive and adds little business value. You want to propose consolidating to one website. Create a report detailing the business value gained by consolidating to a single website, along with your recommendation for consolidation. Be sure to include your website profitability analysis.

2. A Portal into Saab

Saab Cars USA, a marketing and distribution arm for the Swedish automaker, knew it had to improve communication with dealerships. Specifically, Saab wanted to ensure that dealers could communicate more reliably and easily access all the business systems and tools they needed. That meant upgrading the current system so dealers could tap into several of the company's legacy systems without having to install any Saab-specific hardware or software onsite. In addition, the refined system had to be reliable and inexpensive to maintain, easily support future upgrades, work within existing network and hardware designs, and integrate with existing systems. The portal was designed to make it easy for dealers across the United States to instantly access remote inventory, order parts, conduct online training sessions or research, and submit warranty claims. Identify the specific technological services Saab is looking to integrate into its new portal.

3. Online Auction Sites

You are working for a new Internet start-up company, eMart.com, an online marketplace for the sale of goods and services. The company offers a wide variety of features and services that enable online members to buy and sell their goods and services quickly and conveniently. Its mission is to provide a global trading platform where anyone can trade practically anything. Suggest some ways that eMart.com can gain business efficiencies in its marketing, sales, customer service, financial service, and purchasing departments. Be sure to include intranets, extranets, portals, ASPs, and OSPs.

4. Brewing Marketplace

Founded in 2003, the Foothills Brewing Company, foothillsbrew.com, is a pure play Internet brewing master. In its first year, the brewery sold 1,500 barrels of beer online. Its lagers and ales are brewed in small batches, handcrafted by a team of dedicated workers with high ideals of quality. Identify the advantages and disadvantages foothillsbrew.com will experience if it continues to operate as a pure play in the midst of a highly competitive marketplace.

5. Ebusiness Metrics

The Razor is a revolutionary mountain bike with full-suspension and shock-adjustable forks that is being marketed via the Internet. The Razor needs an ebusiness solution that will easily enable internal staff to deliver fresh and relevant product information through its website. To support its large audience, it also needs the ability to present information in multiple languages and serve more than 1 million page-views per month to global visitors. Identify the many different website metrics Razor should be evaluating to ensure its ebusiness solution is as efficient and effective as possible.

PLUG-IN

B13

Strategic Outsourcing

LEARNING OUTCOMES

1. Summarize a list of leading offshore outsourcing countries.
2. Summarize a list of up-and-coming offshore outsourcing countries.
3. Summarize a list of rookie offshore outsourcing countries.
4. Describe the future trend of multisourcing and how it can support a business need for outsourcing.

Introduction

The core units introduced the concept of **outsourcing,** an arrangement by which one organization provides a service or services for another organization that chooses not to perform them in-house. Typically, the outsourced process or function is a noncore business activity; what is outsourced can range from high-volume, repetitive processes such as electronic transaction processing to more customized services such as a help desk. There are three different forms of outsourcing options:

1. **Onshore outsourcing** is the process of engaging another company within the same country for services.

2. **Nearshore outsourcing** refers to contracting an outsourcing arrangement with a company in a nearby country. Often this country will share a border with the native country.

3. **Offshore outsourcing** is using organizations from developing countries to write code and develop systems. In offshore outsourcing the country is geographically far away.

OFFSHORE OUTSOURCING

Since the mid-1990s, major U.S. companies have been sending significant portions of their software development work offshore— primarily to vendors in India, but also to vendors in China, Eastern Europe (including Russia), Ireland, Israel, and the Philippines. The big selling point for offshore outsourcing to these countries is "inexpensive good work." A programmer who earns as much as $63,000 per year in the United States is paid as little as $5,000 per year overseas (see Figure B13.1). Companies can easily realize cost savings of 30 percent to 50 percent through offshore outsourcing and still get the same, if not better, quality of service.

Developed and developing countries throughout Europe and Asia offer some IT outsourcing services, but most are hampered to some degree by language, telecommunications infrastructure, or regulatory barriers. The first and largest offshore marketplace is India, whose English-speaking and technologically advanced population have built its IT services business into a $4 billion industry. Infosys, NIIT, Satyam, TCS, and Wipro are among the biggest Indian outsourcing service providers, each with a significant presence in the United States. There are currently three categories of outsourcing countries (see Figure B13.2):

1. The leaders—countries that are leading the outsourcing industry.
2. The up-and-comers—countries that are beginning to emerge as solid outsourcing options.
3. The rookies—countries that are just entering the outsourcing industry.

Country	Salary Range Per Year
China	$ 5,000–$9,000
India	6,000–10,000
Philippines	6,500–11,000
Russia	7,000–13,000
Ireland	21,000–28,000
Canada	25,000–50,000
United States	60,000–90,000

FIGURE B13.1

Typical Salary Ranges for Computer Programmers

The Leaders

The following countries are leaders in the outsourcing industry:

- Canada
- India
- Ireland
- Israel
- Philippines

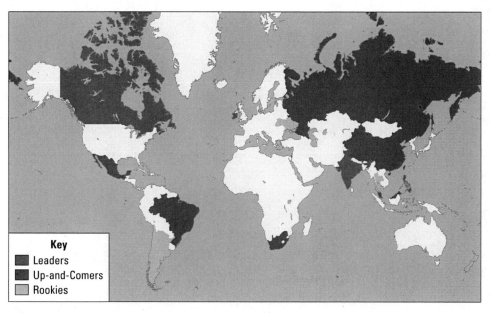

Key
- Leaders
- Up-and-Comers
- Rookies

FIGURE B13.2

Categories of Outsourcing Countries

CANADA

Expertise	■ Software development/maintenance, contact centers, technical support.
Major Customers	■ Allmerica, Agilent.
Advantages	■ Though labor costs are high, geographic proximity and cultural affinity with the United States make it highly desirable. ■ Contact center turnover is low.
Disadvantage	■ High cost of labor pool, but still less expensive than outsourcing in the United States.

INDIA

Expertise	■ Software development/maintenance, contact centers, financial processing.
Major Customers	■ Citigroup, GE Capital, American Express.
Advantages	■ India is the leader in business process and IT services outsourcing. ■ Two million English-proficient speakers graduate every year from more than 1,000 colleges that offer information technology education. ■ Strong history of software development. ■ Highly skilled labor pool. ■ Favorable cost structure.
Disadvantages	■ Political instability. ■ Labor costs are rising as demand for IT workers begins to exceed supply. ■ High turnover, particularly in contact centers, is becoming an issue.

IRELAND

Expertise	■ European shared-services centers, software development, contact centers.
Major Customers	■ Intel, Dell, Microsoft.
Advantages	■ Reputation for producing highly skilled IT professionals. ■ Strong cultural affinity with the United States. ■ Low political or financial risk. ■ Solid telecommunications infrastructure. ■ Strong educational system.
Disadvantage	■ High cost of IT salaries, however, labor costs are still lower than in the United States.

ISRAEL

Expertise	■ Software development/maintenance, packaged software implementation, application integration, security, ebusiness.
Major Customers	■ Merrill Lynch, Shaw Industries.
Advantages	■ Highly skilled workforce including scientists and engineers from Eastern Europe and Russia. ■ Excellent educational system. ■ Hotbed for IT innovation.
Disadvantages	■ Political instability. ■ Employee safety is a cause for concern. ■ High cost of IT salaries.

Expertise	■ Accounting, finance, contact centers, human resources.
Major Customers	■ Procter & Gamble, American International Group, Citigroup.
Advantages	■ The population boasts a high percentage of English speakers with American accents. ■ Culture dictates aim-to-please attitude. ■ Estimated 15,000 technology students graduate from universities annually.
Disadvantages	■ Filipinos are not nearly as strong in software development and maintenance as other outsourcing countries. ■ Political instability.

PHILIPPINES

The Up-and-Comers

The following countries are up-and-coming in the outsourcing industry:

- Brazil
- China
- Malaysia
- Mexico
- Russia
- South Africa

Expertise	■ Software development/maintenance.
Major Customers	■ General Electric, Goodyear, Xerox.
Advantages	■ Big cost savings from a large supply of IT labor. ■ Brazil is Latin America's largest economy with a strong industrial base. ■ Brazil's national focus is on growing small and midsize businesses, including IT services. ■ Affinity with U.S. culture including minimal time zone differences.
Disadvantage	■ Remains on priority watch list of International Intellectual Property Alliance for copyright infractions.

BRAZIL

Expertise	■ Transaction processing, low-end software development/maintenance.
Major Customers	■ HSBC Bank, Microsoft.
Advantages	■ Large pool of educated IT workers with broad skill sets. ■ Government provides strong support for IT outsourcing industry. ■ Telecommunications infrastructure is improving. ■ Entry into World Trade Organization winning confidence of foreign investors. ■ Government has established 15 national software industrial parks.
Disadvantages	■ English proficiency low. ■ Workers lack knowledge of Western business culture. ■ Workers lack project management skills. ■ Intellectual property protections weak. ■ Piracy. ■ Red tape and corruption from a highly bureaucratic government.

CHINA

MALAYSIA

Expertise	■ Wireless applications.
Major Customers	■ IBM, Shell, DHL, Motorola, Electronic Data Systems Corporation.
Advantages	■ Good business environment with strong government support for IT and communications industries. ■ Workforce has strong global exposure. ■ World-class telecommunications infrastructure. ■ Over half of the 250,000 students in higher education major in scientific or technical disciplines.
Disadvantages	■ Labor costs higher than India. ■ Few suppliers, which limits business choices. ■ Shortage of skilled IT talent.

MEXICO

Expertise	■ Software development, contact centers.
Major Customers	■ AOL Time Warner, General Motors, IBM.
Advantages	■ Solid telecommunications infrastructure. ■ Shares cultural affinity and time zones with the United States. ■ Second-largest U.S. trading partner. ■ Programmers highly proficient on latest technologies.
Disadvantages	■ English proficiency low. ■ Government corruption.

RUSSIA

Expertise	■ Web design, complex software development, aerospace engineering.
Major Customer	■ Boeing.
Advantages	■ Large number of highly skilled workers with degrees in science, engineering, and math. ■ Strong venue for research and development. ■ Programmers have skills for both cutting-edge projects and working with legacy applications. ■ European-based companies benefit from historic cultural affinity and geographic proximity.
Disadvantages	■ English proficiency not as widespread as in India or the Philippines, making contact centers impractical. ■ Government corruption and red tape. ■ Copyright piracy. ■ Outsourcing industry is fragmented and many firms have 20 programmers or less, making them unattractive to companies with large IT projects. ■ Telecommunications infrastructure needs work.

SOUTH AFRICA

Expertise	■ Contact centers, ebusiness, software development, IT security.
Major Customers	■ AIG, Old Mutual, Sage Life, Swissair.
Advantages	■ Time zone compatibility with Europe. ■ English is a native language. ■ Solid telecommunications infrastructure.
Disadvantages	■ Small pool of IT skilled workers. ■ IT talent tends to emigrate. ■ Crime.

The Rookies

The following countries are just beginning to offer outsourcing and are considered rookies in the industry:

- Argentina
- Chile
- Costa Rica
- New Zealand
- Thailand
- Ukraine

ARGENTINA

Expertise	■ Software development/maintenance, contact centers.
Major Customers	■ BankOne, Citibank, Principal Financial Group.
Advantages	■ Low costs resulting from an economic collapse in 2001. ■ Economy began to rebound in 2003, growing more than 8 percent, but unemployment remains high. ■ Large labor pool, including solid base of engineering talent.
Disadvantages	■ Country has yet to reach agreement with creditors on restructuring debt. ■ Foreign investors are cautious.

CHILE

Expertise	■ Software development/maintenance.
Major Customer	■ Compaq.
Advantages	■ Large highly skilled pool of IT talent. ■ State-of-the-art telecommunications infrastructure. ■ Good satellite connectivity and digital network. ■ Government actively supports business process and software development sectors. ■ Government plans to begin offering English classes to technical workers.
Disadvantages	■ English proficiency lacking. ■ Slightly higher costs than neighboring countries.

COSTA RICA

Expertise	■ Contact centers, ebusiness.
Major Customer	■ Unisys.
Advantages	■ Business-friendly environment. ■ Highly skilled pool of engineering talent. ■ Well-educated workforce. ■ Favorable cost structure. ■ English and Spanish widely spoken.
Disadvantage	■ Relatively small labor supply.

NEW ZEALAND

Expertise	■ Contact centers, ebusiness, web hosting, web design.
Major Customers	■ IBM, Microsoft, Cisco.
Advantages	■ Stable political and economic environment. ■ Well-established telecommunications infrastructure. ■ Thriving contact center industry. ■ Limited supply of domestic labor. To meet demand, the government has eased visa restrictions allowing entry of workers from countries such as Bangladesh.
Disadvantage	■ New Zealand cannot compete on costs with India and the Philippines.

THAILAND

Expertise	■ Software development/maintenance.
Major Customers	■ Dell, Glovia, Sungard.
Advantages	■ Reasonable telecommunications infrastructure. ■ Cost structure is slightly lower than Malaysia.
Disadvantages	■ Demand for skilled IT labor exceeds supply. ■ Population is not as educated as in neighboring countries. ■ English is not widely spoken.

UKRAINE

Expertise	■ Software development, website development.
Major Customers	■ Sears, Roebuck and Company, Target Corporation.
Advantages	■ History of training highly educated scientists and engineers. (The Soviet Union based the majority of its space and aviation technology work here.) ■ Information technology outsourcing growth predicted to double over the next couple of years.
Disadvantages	■ Unstable political climate. ■ Fears that the country is drifting away from democracy and pro-Western stance.

In summary, many countries are racing to participate in the outsourcing phenomenon. When an organization outsources, it needs to analyze all of its options and weigh all of the advantages and disadvantages. When faced with an outsourcing decision, be sure to evaluate the countries on such things as geopolitical risk, English proficiency, and salary cost (see Figure B13.3).

Future Trends

Companies are getting smarter about outsourcing and about aligning efficiency with core business priorities. As businesses become increasingly networked (for instance, via the Internet)—global, commoditized, 24 × 7, and collaborative—outsourcing is becoming less of a cost-saving strategy and more an overall context for business.

THE LEADERS			
Country	**Geopolitical Risk**	**English Proficiency**	**Average Programmer Salary**
Canada	Low	Good	> $12K
India	Moderate	Good	$4K–$12K
Ireland	Low	Good	> $12K
Israel	Moderate	Good	> $12K
Philippines	Moderate	Good	$4K–12K
THE UP-AND-COMERS			
Country	**Geopolitical Risk**	**English Proficiency**	**Average Programmer Salary**
Brazil	Moderate	Poor	$4K–$12K
China	Low	Poor	$4K–$12K
Malaysia	Low	Fair	$4K–$12K
Mexico	Moderate	Poor	> $12K
Russia	Moderate	Poor	$4K–$12K
South Africa	Moderate	Good	> $12K
THE ROOKIES			
Country	**Geopolitical Risk**	**English Proficiency**	**Average Programmer Salary**
Argentina	Moderate	Fair	$4K–$12K
Chile	Low	Poor	< $4K
Costa Rice	Moderate	Good	$4K–$12K
New Zealand	Low	Good	> $12K
Thailand	Low	Poor	$4K–$12K
Ukraine	Moderate	Poor	$4K–$12K

FIGURE B13.3

Outsourcing Options

Outsourcing is rapidly approaching commodity status, and this will transform the outsourcing value equation from high margins and vendor control into a classic buyers' market with competition driving down margins, adding features and services, and increasing buyer choices. U.S. companies should consider Mexico and Canada for nearshore outsourcing since those countries often provide very competitive pricing. Vendors in these countries can be viable alternatives, such as IBM Global Services (Mexico and Canada), Softtek (Mexico), CGI (Canada), and Keane (Canada).

Companies should look for value-based pricing rather than the lowest possible price. The emerging trend of companies using reverse auction bidding to select offshore vendors is a dangerous one—it could result in low prices, but also low value and low customer satisfaction.

MULTISOURCING

For many years, outsourcing has predominantly been a means to manage and optimize businesses' ever-growing IT infrastructures and ensure return on IT investments—or at a minimum, more cost-effective operations. As businesses move to Internet-based models, speed and skill have become more important than cost efficiencies, giving way to a "utility" service provider model called multisourcing. *Multisourcing* is a combination of professional services, mission-critical support, remote management, and hosting services that are offered to customers in any combination needed. Like the general contractor model, multisourcing brings together a wide set of specialized IT service providers, or "subcontractors," under one point of accountability. The goal of multisourcing is to integrate a collection of IT services into one stable and cost-effective system. Therefore, multisourcing helps companies achieve the advantages of a best-of-breed strategy.

A multisourcing service provider can offer a seamless, inexpensive migration path to whatever delivery model makes sense at that time. For instance, HR processes are outsourced to one best-of-breed outsourcing service provider. Logistics are outsourced to another, and IT development and maintenance to another. Although multisourcing mitigates the risk of choosing a single outsourcing service provider, additional resources and time are required to manage multiple service providers.

✳ PLUG-IN SUMMARY

Outsourcing IT services and business functions is becoming an increasingly common global practice among organizations looking for competitive advantage. The guiding principle is that noncore and critical activities of an enterprise can be handed over to companies with expertise in those activities, thereby freeing internal resources to focus on enhancing the added-value of the organization's core business.

Outsourcing is no longer a simple matter of cutting costs and improving service levels. As more companies consider the benefits of outsourcing their IT functions and their business processes, they will find new ways to create business value. Companies that succeed will find innovative solutions to help drive costs down, select only the problem areas to outsource, and more important, learn to use outsourcing as a strategic weapon.

Companies continue to outsource at an increasing rate, despite reports of organizations disappointed and disillusioned by the process. The ultimate goal is multisourcing, combining professional services, mission-critical support, remote management, and hosting services.

✳ KEY TERMS

Multisourcing, B13.10   Offshore outsourcing, B13.2   Outsourcing, B13.2
Nearshore outsourcing, B13.2   Onshore outsourcing, B13.2

✳ CLOSING CASE ONE

Mobil Travel Guide

For the past 45 years, the *Mobil Travel Guide* has been providing information on destinations, route planning, resorts, accommodations, restaurant reviews, and other travel-related subjects for people traveling in the United States and Canada. Print versions of the *Mobil Travel Guide* are created and updated annually at the company's Park Ridge, Illinois, headquarters, and are sold at most major booksellers and other publishing outlets.

Mobil Travel Guide, a well-known name in the travel industry, wanted to leverage its brand recognition by providing a highly responsive, real-time online service for leisure travelers that include customized travel planning, an around-the-clock customer service center, and a variety of privileges and rewards at a linked network of hotels and restaurants.

Mobil's existing online solution offered only a limited amount of static web content that ran on just four servers, which were unable to process the site's considerable traffic, resulting in downtime for customers. Mobil needed a more robust solution that would provide real-time services such as route planning and fast access to the company's vast travel information database. The solution also had to be flexible and resilient enough to handle seasonal usage fluctuations, including anticipated spikes during the summertime and over major holidays. Mobil Travel Guide's internal goals also created a challenge for any solution. The site was expected to grow rapidly, but the company did not want to invest in an infrastructure capable of supporting its vision for the website.

Instead of using stand-alone web, application, and database servers, Mobil Travel Guide decided to outsource all these functions to IBM. Because IBM delivers ebusiness infrastructure capacity as a utility, Mobil Travel Guide pays only for the processing, storage, and networking capacity it needs and can scale its virtual infrastructure up to meet demand spikes.

By avoiding up-front capital investment without sacrificing scalability, reliability, or flexibility, Mobil Travel Guide is positioned for success. The company can optimize its spending by scaling its infrastructure dynamically to meet demands and channeling resources toward generating new business and revenue. "Otherwise, we would have to buy enough infrastructure to handle the biggest day we could imagine, but typically it would sit unused. Now, we can take advantage of any market sweet spot we find, because we can scale with minimal lead time and capital dollars," explained Paul Mercurio, chief information officer for Mobil Travel Guide.

What is more, this capability moves portions of the web-serving workload from Mobil Travel Guide's site onto servers located at strategic network points, so end users get faster responses even while Mobil Travel Guide lowers its per-transaction costs. "Because our service level ramps up or down dynamically in response to peaks and valleys in demand, we pay only for the capacity we need at any given moment in time," Mercurio said.

The on-demand delivery has already benefited Mobil Travel Guide in an unexpected way. After initially setting a committed capacity level that was too high, the company was able to leverage the flexibility of its IBM solution to "right-size" its capacity by reducing its contracted capacity level.

By outsourcing the solution to IBM, Mobil anticipates it will save about 35 percent in overall maintenance and software costs, while deploying an excellent ebusiness infrastructure solution that guarantees high availability, rapid scalability, and easy management of usage fluctuations.

Questions

1. What are the main reasons Mobil Travel Guide used an outsourcing option?
2. What other areas would you recommend Mobil Travel Guide outsource?
3. What advantages and disadvantages would offshore outsourcing or nearshore outsourcing have for Mobil Travel Guide?
4. List the countries where Mobil could outsource its *Travel Guide*.

★ CLOSING CASE TWO

Outsourcing Brew

Coors Brewing Company, the third-largest brewer in the United States, manufactures and markets more than a dozen varieties of beer and malt beverages in 30 markets around the world. In a rapidly consolidating industry, Coors had a choice: keep growing or be acquired. To create the optimal conditions for growth, the company needed to improve access to information, consolidate systems, and reduce costs.

In less than a decade, Coors Brewing Company had more than doubled in size. Managing that growth became increasingly difficult for the company's internal IT staff. The company wanted to maintain responsibility for the technologies directly related to making and selling beer. Therefore, Coors was looking for a partner with deep industry expertise, mature application experience, and global reach to help revitalize its technology to support its business goals—including bringing new acquisitions online quickly.

The company decided to outsource its day-to-day management of its technical operations, conversion of legacy applications, and systems. Coors outsourced these functions to EDS in order to create a globally integrated enterprise solution, helping to optimize the supply chain from beginning to end. EDS is an experienced outsourcing services company with more than 130,000 employees and 2003 revenues of $21.5 billion, ranked 80th on the Fortune 500.

EDS offered Coors an infrastructure "on demand." Coors avoids a huge up-front investment in infrastructure, but is able to access increased capacity when business volumes increase.

Now IT costs are predictable, and additional infrastructure is instantly available when the company needs it. Coors also controls costs by using EDS's Best ShoreSM Services, which enables Coors to reduce the cost of applications management by as much as 40 percent through a combination of offshore, nearshore, and local service centers and personnel.

EDS's solutions at Coors deliver much more than lower costs and increased reliability. As EDS assumed control of Coors's help desk, staff increased service levels while identifying patterns that let Coors focus training where it was most needed and kept the company aware of where potential problems lay. Standardizing the company's desktop environment has allowed Coors to get rid of many obsolete applications.

EDS is much more than an information technology outsourcing service provider; it is Coors's business partner. "They work with us on project management and root-cause analysis, which have helped us to add a lot of discipline in our organization," said CIO Virginia Guthrie. With a modernized and efficient information environment taking shape, EDS and Coors have ambitious plans for the future, from improving manufacturing processes to enhancing Coors's global presence. Guthrie said, "What we really want here is for this partnership to be a poster child for how outsourcing partnerships should work."

With the help of EDS, Coors was able to:

- Within just 60 days, reduce cost of application maintenance by 70 percent.
- Save more than $1.2 million on project resources related to SAP implementation.
- Reduce applications in use by 48 percent.
- Work to retire 70 percent of legacy systems.

Questions

1. Describe an alternative approach that Coors could have used instead of outsourcing to EDS.
2. What would be the advantages of offshore outsourcing the Coors IT department?
3. What are some other reasons Coors outsourced its information technology functions that were not mentioned in the case?
4. Describe some of the factors causing Coors to be "forced" to outsource its information technology functions.

★ MAKING BUSINESS DECISIONS

1. Sports Sourcing

Sierra Sports Network launched its website SierraSports.com in 2001. With a huge influx of new visitors expected this football season, it is critical that SierraSports.com attracts, retains, and handles its web traffic. It needs an overhaul of its existing website. Since Sierra Sports Network does not have the in-house skills to support the needed changes, it must look at outsourcing its web development. Some of the company's needs are working with an outsourcing service provider who is proficient in English, has a solid telecommunications infrastructure, and operates in a similar time zone. List the outsourcing countries that could assist Sierra Sports for web development needs, in addition to the advantages that each country could give to the company.

2. Ops.com

Contact center Ops.com provides information to those who are involved in real-time customer service. Contact centers have emerged as *the* critical link between a company and its customers. The growth in contact centers has resulted in a strong demand for Ops.com's services; so much that it now needs to outsource part of its operation. One main reason for the move to an outsourcing service provider is its need to develop a new service to collect information, such as account numbers, via an automated attendant and tie it back to a database. Ops.com can tap the database information to give callers automated access to more information, such as account balances, and create priority queuing for their most important customers. Describe the advantages that outsourcing would give Ops.com and list the outsourcing options along with a recommendation of prospective countries that have the resources available to be considered.

3. The Travel Store

In 2004, The Travel Store faced a dilemma. The retailer had tripled in size over a three-year period to $1 billion in sales, but it had done so despite operational deficiencies. The company's inability to evolve its business processes as it grew was causing problems. Within a year, sales and profits fell below expectations, and its stock price plummeted from approximately $10 a share to less than $2 a share. The Travel Store is determined to take quick and decisive action to restore profitability and improve its credibility in the marketplace. One of its top priorities is to overhaul its inventory management system in an effort to create optimal levels of inventory to support sales demand. This would prevent higher volume stores from running out of key sale items while also ensuring that lower sales stores would not be burdened with excess inventory that could only be moved at closeout prices. The company would like to outsource this function but is worried about the challenges of transferring the responsibility of this important business function, as well as the issues surrounding confidentiality, and scope definition. Make a list of the competitive advantages outsourcing could give to The Travel Store, along with recommendations for addressing the company's outsourcing concerns.

4. Software Solutions

Founded in 2003, Gabster Software provides innovative search software, website demographics, and testing software. All serve as part of its desktop and enterprise resource planning solutions for government, corporate, educational, and consumer markets. Website publishers, digital media publishers, content managers, document managers, business users, consumers, software companies, and consulting services companies use Gabster's solutions. The company is currently thinking about offshore outsourcing its call center functions, its ebusiness strategies, and its application development. Describe how Gabster could use multisourcing along with the potential advantages it might receive.

PLUG-IN

B14 Systems Development

1. Summarize the activities associated with the planning phase in the SDLC.
2. Summarize the activities associated with the analysis phase in the SDLC.
3. Summarize the activities associated with the design phase in the SDLC.
4. Summarize the activities associated with the development phase in the SDLC.
5. Summarize the activities associated with the testing phase in the SDLC.
6. Summarize the activities associated with the implementation phase in the SDLC.
7. Summarize the activities associated with the maintenance phase in the SDLC.

Introduction

Today, systems are so large and complex that teams of architects, analysts, developers, testers, and users must work together to create the millions of lines of custom-written code that drive enterprises. For this reason, developers have created a number of different system development methodologies including waterfall, prototyping, rapid application development (RAD), extreme programming, agile, and others. All these methodologies are based on the ***systems development life cycle (SDLC),*** which is the overall process for developing information systems from planning and analysis through implementation and maintenance (see Figure B14.1).

The systems development life cycle is the foundation for all systems development methodologies, and there are literally hundreds of different activities associated with each phase in the SDLC. Typical activities include determining budgets, gathering system requirements, and writing detailed user documentation. The activities performed during each systems development project will vary. This plug-in takes a detailed look at a few of the more common activities performed during the systems development life cycle, along with common issues facing software development projects (see Figure B14.2).

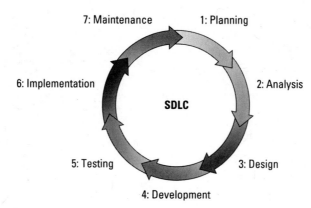

FIGURE B14.1

The Systems Development
Life Cycle (SDLC)

SDLC Phase	Activities
1. Planning	■ Identify and select the system for development ■ Assess project feasibility ■ Develop the project plan
2. Analysis	■ Gather business requirements ■ Create process diagrams ■ Perform a buy versus build analysis
3. Design	■ Design the IT infrastructure ■ Design system models
4. Development	■ Develop the IT infrastructure ■ Develop the database and programs
5. Testing	■ Write the test conditions ■ Perform the system testing
6. Implementation	■ Determine implementation method ■ Provide training for the system users ■ Write detailed user documentation
7. Maintenance	■ Build a help desk to support the system users ■ Perform system maintenance ■ Provide an environment to support system changes

FIGURE B14.2

Common Activities
Performed During
Systems Development

Systems Development Life Cycle

PHASE 1: PLANNING

The ***planning phase*** involves establishing a high-level plan of the intended project and determining project goals. The three primary activities involved in the planning phase are:

1. Identify and select the system for development.
2. Assess project feasibility.
3. Develop the project plan.

FIGURE B14.3

Evaluation Criteria for
Determining Software
Development Projects

Evaluation Criteria	Description
Value chain analysis	The value chain determines the extent to which the new system will add value to the organization. Systems with greater value are given priority over systems with less value.
Strategic alignment	Projects that are in line with the organization's strategic goals and objectives are given priority over projects not in line with the organization's strategic goals and objectives.
Cost-benefit analysis	A cost-benefit analysis determines which projects offer the organization the greatest benefits with the least amount of cost.
Resource availability	Determine the amount and type of resources required to complete the project and determine if the organization has these resources available.
Project size, duration, and difficulty	Determine the number of individuals, amount of time, and technical difficulty of the project.

Identify and Select the System for Development

Systems are successful only when they solve the right problem or take advantage of the right opportunity. Systems development focuses on either solving a problem or taking advantage of an opportunity. Determining which systems are required to support the strategic goals of an organization is one of the primary activities performed during the planning phase. Typically, employees generate proposals to build new information systems when they are having a difficult time performing their jobs. Unfortunately, most organizations have limited resources and cannot afford to develop all proposed information systems. Therefore, they look to critical success factors to help determine which systems to build.

A *critical success factor (CSF)* is a factor that is critical to an organization's success. To determine which system to develop, an organization tracks all the proposed systems and prioritizes them by business impact or critical success factors. This allows the business to prioritize which problems require immediate attention and which problems can wait. Figure B14.3 displays possible evaluation criteria for determining which projects to develop.

Assess Project Feasibility

A *feasibility study* determines if the proposed solution is feasible and achievable from a financial, technical, and organizational standpoint. Typically, an organization will define several alternative solutions that it can pursue to solve a given problem. A feasibility study is used to determine if the proposed solution is achievable, given the organization's resources and constraints in regard to technology, economics, organizational factors, and legal and ethical considerations. Figure B14.4 displays the many different types of feasibility studies an organization can perform.

Develop the Project Plan

Developing a project plan is one of the final activities performed during the planning phase and it is one of the hardest and most important activities. The project plan is the guiding force behind on-time delivery of a complete and successful system. It logs and tracks every single activity performed during the project. If an activity is missed, or takes longer than expected to complete, the project plan must be updated to reflect these changes. Updating of the project plan must be performed in every subsequent phase during the systems development effort.

Types of Feasibility Studies	
Economic feasibility study (often called a **cost-benefit analysis**)	Identifies the financial benefits and costs associated with the systems development project.
Legal and contractual feasibility study	Examines all potential legal and contractual ramifications of the proposed system.
Operational feasibility study	Examines the likelihood that the project will attain its desired objectives.
Schedule feasibility study	Assesses the likelihood that all potential time frames and completion dates will be met.
Technical feasibility study	Determines the organization's ability to build and integrate the proposed system.

FIGURE B14.4

Types of Feasibility Studies

PHASE 2: ANALYSIS

The *analysis phase* involves analyzing end-user business requirements and refining project goals into defined functions and operations of the intended system. The three primary activities involved in the analysis phase are:

1. Gather business requirements.
2. Create process diagrams.
3. Perform a buy versus build analysis.

Gather Business Requirements

Business requirements are the detailed set of business requests that the system must meet to be successful. At this point, there is little or no concern with any implementation or reference to technical details. For example, the types of technology used to build the system, such as an Oracle database or the Java programming language, are not yet defined. The only focus is on gathering the true business requirements for the system. A sample business requirement might state, "The system must track all customer sales by product, region, and sales representative." This requirement states what the system must do from the business perspective, giving no details or information on how the system is going to meet this requirement.

Gathering business requirements is basically conducting an investigation in which users identify all the organization's business needs and take measurements of these needs. Figure B14.5 displays a number of ways to gather business requirements.

The *requirements definition document* contains the final set of business requirements, prioritized in order of business importance. The system users review the requirements definition document and determine if they will sign off on the business requirements. *Sign-off* is the system users' actual signatures indicating they approve all of the business requirements. One of the first major milestones on the project plan is usually the users' sign-off on business requirements.

A large data storage company implemented a project called Python whose purpose was to control all the company's information systems. Seven years, tens of millions of dollars, and 35 programmers later Python was canceled. At the end of the project, Python had over 1,800 business requirements of which 900 came from engineering and were written in order to make the other 900 customer requirements work. By the time the project was canceled, it was unclear what the primary goals, objectives, and needs of the project were. Management should have realized Python's issues when the project's requirements phase dragged on, bulged, and took years to complete. The sheer number of requirements should have raised a red flag.

Methods for Gathering Business Requirements
Perform a *joint application development (JAD)* session where employees meet, sometimes for several days, to define or review the business requirements for the system.
Interview individuals to determine current operations and current issues.
Compile questionnaires to survey employees to discover issues.
Make observations to determine how current operations are performed.
Review business documents to discover reports, policies, and how information is used throughout the organization.

Create Process Diagrams

Once a business analyst takes a detailed look at how an organization performs its work and its processes, the analyst can recommend ways to improve these processes to make them more efficient and effective. *Process modeling* involves graphically representing the processes that capture, manipulate, store, and distribute information between a system and its environment. One of the most common diagrams used in process modeling is the data flow diagram. A *data flow diagram (DFD)* illustrates the movement of information between external entities and the processes and data stores within the system (see Figure B14.6). Process models and data flow diagrams establish the specifications of the system. *Computer-aided software engineering (CASE)* tools are software suites that automate systems analysis, design, and development. Process models and data flow diagrams can provide the basis for the automatic generation of the system if they are developed using a CASE tool.

FIGURE B14.6

Sample Data Flow
Diagram

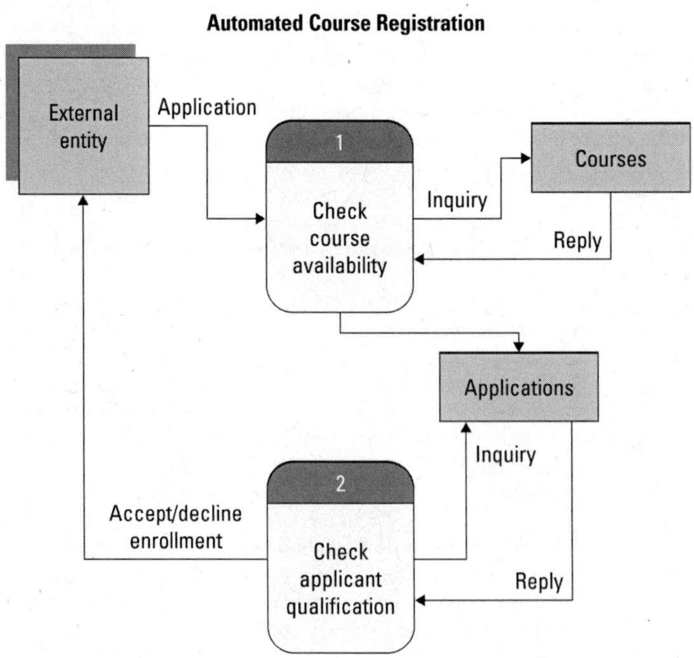

Automated Course Registration

Perform a Buy versus Build Analysis

An organization faces two primary choices when deciding to develop an information system: (1) it can *buy* the information system from a vendor or (2) it can *build* the system itself. ***Commercial off-the-shelf (COTS)*** software is a software package or solution that is purchased to support one or more business functions and information systems. Most customer relationship management, supply chain management, and enterprise resource planning solutions are COTS. Typically, a cost-benefit analysis forms the basis of the buy versus build decision. Organizations must consider the questions displayed in Figure B14.7 during the buy versus build decision.

Three key factors an organization should also consider when contemplating the buy versus build decision are: (1) time to market, (2) corporate resources, and (3) core competencies. Weighing the complex relationship between each of these three variables will help an organization make the right choice (see Figure B14.8).

When making the all-important buy versus build decision consider when the product must be available, how many resources are available, and how the organization's core competencies affect the product. If these questions can be definitely answered either yes or no, then the answer to the buy versus build question is easy. However, most organizations cannot answer these questions with a solid yes or no. Most organizations need to make a trade-off between the lower cost of buying a system and the need for a system that meets all of their requirements. Finding a system to buy that meets all an organization's unique business requirements is next to impossible.

Buy versus Build Decision Questions
Do any currently available products fit the organization's needs?
Are unavailable features important enough to warrant the expense of in-house development?
Can the organization customize or modify an existing COTS to fit its needs?
Is there a justification to purchase or develop based on the cost of acquisition?

FIGURE B14.7

Buy versus Build Decision Questions

Three Key Factors in Buy versus Build Decisions	
1. **Time to market**	If time to market is a priority, then purchasing a good base technology and potentially building on to it will likely yield results faster than starting from scratch.
2. **Availability of corporate resources**	The buy versus build decision is a bit more complex to make when considering the availability of corporate resources. Typically, the costs to an organization to buy systems such as SCM, CRM, and ERP are extremely high. These costs can be so high—in the multiple millions of dollars—that acquiring these technologies might make the entire concept economically unfeasible. Building these systems, however, can also be extremely expensive, take indefinite amounts of time, and constrain resources.
3. **Corporate core competencies**	The more an organization wants to build a technical core competency, the less likely it will want to buy.

FIGURE B14.8

Key Factors in Buy versus Build Decisions

PHASE 3: DESIGN

The **design phase** involves describing the desired features and operations of the system including screen layouts, business rules, process diagrams, pseudo code, and other documentation. The two primary activities involved in the design phase are:

1. Design the IT infrastructure.
2. Design system models.

Design the IT Infrastructure

The system must be supported by a solid IT infrastructure or chances are the system will crash, malfunction, or not perform as expected. The IT infrastructure must meet the organization's needs in terms of time, cost, technical feasibility, and flexibility. Most systems run on a computer network with each employee having a client and the application running on a server. During this phase, the IT specialists recommend what types of clients and servers to buy including memory and storage requirements, along with software recommendations. An organization typically explores several different IT infrastructures that must meet current as well as future system needs. For example, databases must be large enough to hold the current volume of customers plus all new customers that the organization expects to gain over the next several years (see Figure B14.9).

Design System Models

Modeling is the activity of drawing a graphical representation of a design. An organization should model everything it builds including reports, programs, and

FIGURE B14.9

Sample IT Infrastructure

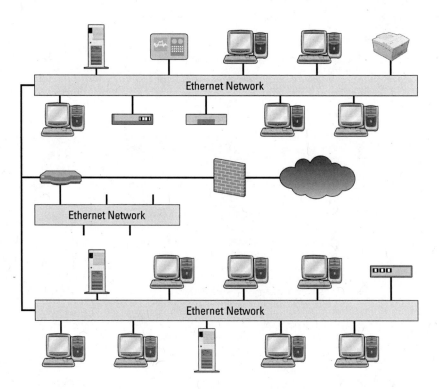

databases. Many different types of modeling activities are performed during the design phase, including:

- The **graphical user interface (GUI)** is the interface to an information system. **GUI screen design** is the ability to model the information system screens for an entire system using icons, buttons, menus, and submenus.

- **Data models** represent a formal way to express data relationships to a database management system (DBMS).

- **Entity relationship diagram (ERD)** is a technique for documenting the relationships between entities in a database environment (see Figure B14.10).

FIGURE B14.10

Sample Entity Relationship Diagram

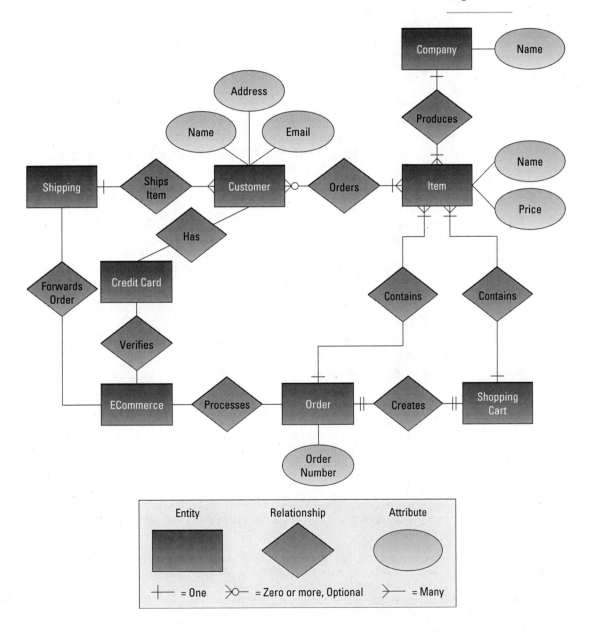

PHASE 4: DEVELOPMENT

The ***development phase*** involves taking all of the detailed design documents from the design phase and transforming them into the actual system. The two primary activities involved in the development phase are:

1. Develop the IT infrastructure.
2. Develop the database and programs.

Develop the IT Infrastructure

The platform upon which the system will operate must be built before building the actual system. In the design phase, an organization creates a blueprint of the proposed IT infrastructure displaying the design of the software, hardware, and telecommunication equipment. In the development phase, the organization purchases and implements the required equipment to support the IT infrastructure.

Most new systems require new hardware and software. It may be as simple as adding memory to a client or as complex as setting up a wide area network across several states.

Develop the Database and Programs

Once the IT infrastructure is built, the organization can begin to create the database and write the programs required for the system. IT specialists perform these functions and it may take months or even years to design and create all the needed elements to complete the system.

PHASE 5: TESTING

According to a report issued by the National Institute of Standards and Technology (NIST), defective software costs the U.S. economy an estimated $87.5 billion each year. Of that total, software users incurred 64 percent of the costs and software developers 36 percent. NIST suggests that improvements in testing could reduce this cost by about a third, or $30 billion, but that unfortunately testing improvements would not eliminate all software errors.

The ***testing phase*** involves bringing all the project pieces together into a special testing environment to test for errors, bugs, and interoperability, in order to verify that the system meets all the business requirements defined in the analysis phase. The two primary activities involved in the testing phase are:

1. Write the test conditions.
2. Perform the system testing.

Write the Test Conditions

Testing is critical. An organization must have excellent test conditions to perform an exhaustive test. ***Test conditions*** are the detailed steps the system must perform along with the expected results of each step. Figure B14.11 displays several test conditions for testing user log-on functionality in a system. The tester will execute each test condition and compare the expected results with the actual results in order to verify that the system functions correctly. Notice in Figure B14.11 how each test condition is extremely detailed and states the expected results that should occur when executing each test condition. Each time the actual result is different from the expected result, a "bug" is generated and the system goes back to development for a bug fix.

Test condition 6 in Figure B14.11 displays a different actual result than the expected result because the system failed to allow the user to log on. After this test condition fails, it is obvious that the system is not functioning correctly and it must be sent back to development for a bug fix.

Test Condition Number	Date Tested	Tested	Test Condition	Expected Result	Actual Result	Pass/ Fail
1	1/1/09	Emily Hickman	Click on System Start Button	Main Menu appears	Same as expected result	Pass
2	1/1/09	Emily Hickman	Click on Log-on Button in Main Menu	Log-on Screen appears asking for User name and Password	Same as expected result	Pass
3	1/1/09	Emily Hickman	Type Emily Hickman in the User Name Field	Emily Hickman appears in the User Name Field	Same as expected result	Pass
4	1/1/09	Emily Hickman	Type Zahara123 in the password field	XXXXXXXXX appears in the password field	Same as expected result	Pass
5	1/1/09	Emily Hickman	Click on O.K. button	User log-on request is sent to database and user name and password are verified	Same as expected result	Pass
6	1/1/09	Emily Hickman	Click on Start	User name and password are accepted and the system main menu appears	Screen appeared stating log-on failed and user name and password were incorrect	Fail

FIGURE B14.11

Sample Test Conditions

A typical system development effort has hundreds or thousands of test conditions. Every single test condition must be executed to verify that the system performs as expected. Writing all the test conditions and performing the actual testing of the software takes a tremendous amount of time and energy. Testing is critical to the successful development of any system.

Perform the System Testing

System developers must perform many different types of testing to ensure that the system works as expected. Figure B14.12 displays a few of the more common types of tests performed during this phase.

PHASE 6: IMPLEMENTATION

The *implementation phase* involves placing the system into production so users can begin to perform actual business operations with the system. The three primary activities involved in the implementation phase are:

1. Write detailed user documentation.
2. Determine implementation method.
3. Provide training for the system users.

Write Detailed User Documentation

System users require *user documentation* that highlights how to use the system. This is the type of documentation that is typically provided along with the new system. System users find it extremely frustrating to have a new system without documentation.

FIGURE B14.12

Types of Tests Performed
During the Testing Phase

Types of Tests Performed During the Testing Phase	
Application (or system) testing	Verifies that all units of code work together and the total system satisfies all of its functional and operational requirements.
Backup and recovery testing	Tests the ability of an application to be restarted after failure.
Documentation testing	Verifies that the instruction guides are helpful and accurate.
Integration testing	Exposes faults in the integration of software components or software units.
Regression testing	Determines if a functional improvement or repair to the system has affected the other functional aspects of the software.
Unit testing	Tests each unit of code as soon as the unit is complete to expose faults in the unit regardless of its interaction with other units.
User acceptance testing (UAT)	Determines whether a system satisfies its acceptance criteria, enabling the customer to decide whether or not to accept a system.

Determine Implementation Method

An organization must choose the right implementation method to ensure a successful system implementation. Figure B14.13 highlights the four primary implementation methods an organization can choose from.

Provide Training for the System Users

An organization must provide training for the system users. The two most popular types of training are online training and workshop training. *Online training* runs over the Internet or off a CD-ROM. System users perform the training at any time, on their own computers, at their own pace. This type of training is convenient for system users because they can set their own schedule for the training. *Workshop training* is set in a classroom-type environment and led by an instructor. Workshop training is recommended for difficult systems where the system users require one-on-one time with an individual instructor.

FIGURE B14.13

Primary Implementation
Methods

Primary Implementation Methods	
1. **Parallel implementation**	Using both the old and new systems until it is evident that the new system performs correctly.
2. **Phased implementation**	Implementing the new system in phases (e.g., accounts receivables then accounts payable) until it is evident that the new system performs correctly and then implementing the remaining phases of the new system.
3. **Pilot implementation**	Having only a small group of people use the new system until it is evident that the new system performs correctly and then adding the remaining people to the new system.
4. **Plunge implementation**	Discarding the old system completely and immediately using the new system.

PHASE 7: MAINTENANCE

The *maintenance phase* involves performing changes, corrections, additions, and upgrades to ensure the system continues to meet the business goals. Once a system is in place, it must change as the organization changes. The three primary activities involved in the maintenance phase are:

1. Build a help desk to support the system users.
2. Perform system maintenance.
3. Provide an environment to support system changes.

Build a Help Desk to Support the System Users

A *help desk* is a group of people who respond to internal system user questions. Typically, internal system users have a phone number for the help desk they call whenever they have issues or questions about the system. Staffing a help desk that answers internal user questions is an excellent way to provide comprehensive support for new systems.

Perform System Maintenance

Maintenance is fixing or enhancing an information system. Many different types of maintenance must be performed on the system to ensure it continues to operate as expected. These include:

- **Adaptive maintenance**—making changes to increase system functionality to meet new business requirements.
- **Corrective maintenance**—making changes to repair system defects.
- **Perfective maintenance**—making changes to enhance the system and improve such things as processing performance and usability.
- **Preventive maintenance**—making changes to reduce the chance of future system failures.

Provide an Environment to Support System Changes

As changes arise in the business environment, an organization must react to those changes by assessing the impact on the system. It might well be that the system needs to adjust to meet the ever-changing needs of the business environment. If so, an organization must modify its systems to support the business environment.

A *change management system* includes a collection of procedures to document a change request and define the steps necessary to consider the change based on the expected impact of the change. Most change management systems require that a change request form be initiated by one or more project stakeholders (users, customers, analysts, developers). Ideally, these change requests are reviewed by a *change control board (CCB)* responsible for approving or rejecting all change requests. The CCB's composition typically includes a representative for each business area that has a stake in the project. The CCB's decision to accept or reject each change is based on an impact analysis of the change. For example, if one department wants to implement a change to the software that will increase both deployment time and cost, then the other business owners need to agree that the change is valid and that it warrants the extended time frame and increased budget.

The systems development life cycle (SDLC) is the foundation for all systems development methodologies. Understanding the phases and activities involved in the systems development life cycle is critical when developing information systems regardless of which methodology is being used. The SDLC contains the following phases:

1. The *planning phase* involves establishing a high-level plan of the intended project and determining project goals.

2. The *analysis phase* involves analyzing end-user business requirements and refining project goals into defined functions and operations of the intended system.

3. The *design phase* involves describing the desired features and operations of the system including screen layouts, business rules, process diagrams, pseudo code, and other documentation.

4. The *development phase* involves taking all the detailed design documents from the design phase and transforming them into the actual system.

5. The *testing phase* involves bringing all the project pieces together into a special testing environment to test for errors, bugs, and interoperability, in order to verify that the system meets all the business requirements defined in the analysis phase.

6. The *implementation phase* involves placing the system into production so users can begin to perform actual business operations with the system.

7. The *maintenance phase* involves performing changes, corrections, additions, and upgrades to ensure the system continues to meet the business goals.

✱ **KEY TERMS**

Analysis phase, 403
Business requirement, 403
Change control board
(CCB), 411
Change management
system, 411
Commercial off-the-shelf
(COTS), 405
Computer-aided software
engineering (CASE), 404
Critical success factor
(CSF), 402
Data flow diagram (DFD), 404
Data model, 407

Design phase, 406
Development phase, 408
Entity relationship diagram
(ERD), 407
Feasibility study, 402
Graphical user interface
(GUI), 407
GUI screen design, 407
Help desk, 411
Implementation phase, 409
Joint application development
(JAD), 404
Maintenance, 411
Maintenance phase, 411

Modeling, 406
Online training, 410
Planning phase, 401
Process modeling, 404
Requirements definition
document, 403
Sign-off, 403
Systems development life cycle
(SDLC), 400
Test condition, 408
Testing phase, 408
User documentation, 409
Workshop training, 410

Disaster at Denver International Airport

One good way to learn how to develop successful systems is to review past failures. One of the most infamous system failures is Denver International Airport's (DIA) baggage system. When the automated baggage system design for DIA was introduced, it was hailed as the savior of modern airport design. The design relied on a network of 300 computers to route bags and 4,000 telecars to carry luggage across 21 miles of track. Laser scanners were to read bar-coded luggage tags, while advanced scanners tracked the movement of toboggan-like baggage carts.

When DIA finally opened its doors for reporters to witness its revolutionary baggage handling system the scene was rather unpleasant. Bags were chewed up, lost, and misrouted in what has since become a legendary systems nightmare.

One of the biggest mistakes made in the baggage handling system fiasco was that not enough time was allowed to properly develop the system. In the beginning of the project, DIA assumed it was the responsibility of individual airlines to find their own way of moving the baggage from the plane to the baggage claim area. The automated baggage system was not involved in the initial planning of the DIA project. By the time the developers of DIA decided to create an integrated baggage system, the time frame for designing and implementing such a complex and huge system was not possible.

Another common mistake that occurred during the project was that the airlines kept changing their business requirements. This caused numerous issues including the implementation of power supplies that were not properly updated for the revised system design, which caused overloaded motors and mechanical failures. Besides the power supplies design problem, the optical sensors did not read the bar codes correctly, causing issues with baggage routing.

Finally, BAE, the company that designed and implemented the automated baggage system for DIA, had never created a baggage system of this size before. BAE had created a similar system in an airport in Munich, Germany, where the scope was much smaller. Essentially, the baggage system had an inadequate IT infrastructure since it was designed for a much smaller system.

DIA simply could not open without a functional baggage system so the city had no choice but to delay the opening date for over 16 months, costing taxpayers roughly $1 million per day, which totaled around $500 million.

Questions

1. One of the problems with DIA's baggage system was inadequate testing. Describe the different types of tests DIA could have used to help ensure its baggage system's success.

2. Evaluate the different implementation approaches. Which one would have most significantly increased the chances of the project's success?

3. Explain the cost of finding errors. How could more time spent in the analysis and design phase have saved Colorado taxpayers hundreds of millions of dollars?

4. Why could BAE not take an existing IT infrastructure and simply increase its scale and expect it to work?

✳ **CLOSING CASE TWO**

Reducing Ambiguity in Business Requirements

The number one reason projects fail is bad business requirements. Business requirements are considered "bad" because of ambiguity or insufficient involvement of end users during analysis and design.

A requirement is unambiguous if it has the same interpretation for all parties. Different interpretations by different participants will usually result in unmet expectations. Here is an example of an ambiguous requirement and an example of an unambiguous requirement:

- **Ambiguous requirement:** The financial report must show profits in local and U.S. currencies.
- **Unambiguous requirement:** The financial report must show profits in local and U.S. currencies using the exchange rate printed in *The Wall Street Journal* for the last business day of the period being reported.

Ambiguity is impossible to prevent completely because it is introduced into requirements in natural ways. For example:

- Requirements can contain technical implications that are obvious to the IT developers but not to the customers.
- Requirements can contain business implications that are obvious to the customer but not to the IT developers.
- Requirements may contain everyday words whose meanings are "obvious" to everyone, yet different for everyone.
- Requirements are reflections of detailed explanations that may have included multiple events, multiple perspectives, verbal rephrasing, emotion, iterative refinement, selective emphasis, and body language—none of which are captured in the written statements.

Tips for Reviewing Business Requirements

When reviewing business requirements always look for the following words to help dramatically reduce ambiguity:

- **"And"** and **"or"** have well-defined meanings and ought to be completely unambiguous, yet they are often understood only informally and interpreted inconsistently. For example, consider the statement "The alarm must ring if button T is pressed and if button F is pressed." This statement may be intended to mean that to ring the alarm, both buttons must be pressed or it may be intended to mean that either one can be pressed. A statement like this should never appear in a requirement because the potential for misinterpretation is too great. A preferable approach is to be very explicit, for example, "The alarm must ring if both buttons T and F are pressed simultaneously. The alarm should not ring in any other circumstance."
- **"Always"** might really mean "most of the time," in which case it should be made more explicit. For example, the statement "We always run reports A and B together" could be challenged with "In other words, there is never any circumstance where you would run A without B and B without A?" If you build a system with an "always" requirement, then you are actually building the system to never run report A without report B. If a user suddenly wants report B without report A, you will need to make significant system changes.
- **"Never"** might mean "rarely," in which case it should be made more explicit. For example, the statement "We never run reports A and B in the same month" could be challenged with, "So that means that if I see that A has been run, I can be absolutely certain that

no one will want to run B." Again, if you build a system that supports a "never" requirement then the system users can never perform that requirement. For example, the system would never allow a user to run reports A and B in the same month, no matter what the circumstances.

- **Boundary conditions** are statements about the line between true and false and do and do not. These statements may or may not be meant to include end points. For example, "We want to use method X when there are up to 10 pages, but method Y otherwise." If you were building this system, would you include page 10 in method X or in method Y? The answer to this question will vary causing an ambiguous business requirement.

Questions

1. Why are ambiguous business requirements the leading cause of system development failures?
2. Why do the words *and* and *or* tend to lead to ambiguous requirements?
3. Research the web and determine other reasons for "bad" business requirements.
4. What is wrong with the following business requirement: "The system must support employee birthdays since every employee always has a birthday every year."

★ MAKING BUSINESS DECISIONS

1. Understanding Project Failure

You are the director of project management for Stello, a global manufacturer of high-end writing instruments. The company sells to primarily high-end customers, and the average price for one of its fine writing instruments is about $350. You are currently implementing a new customer relationship management system and you want to do everything you can to ensure a successful systems development effort. Create a document summarizing the five primary reasons this project could fail, along with your strategy to eliminate the possibility of system development failure on your project.

2. Missing Phases in the Systems Development Life Cycle

Hello Inc. is a large concierge service for executives operating in Chicago, San Francisco, and New York. The company performs all kinds of services from dog walking to airport transportation. Your manager, Dan Martello, wants to skip the testing phase during the company's financial ERP implementation. Dan feels that since the system came from a vendor it should work correctly. To meet the project's looming deadline he wants to skip the testing phase. Draft a memo explaining to Dan the importance of following the SDLC and the ramifications to the business if the financial system is not tested.

3. Saving Failing Systems

Crik Candle Company manufactures low-end candles for restaurants. The company generates over $40 million in annual revenues and has over 300 employees. You are in the middle of a large multimillion-dollar supply chain management implementation. Your project manager has just come to you with the information that the project might fail for the following reasons:

- Several business requirements were incorrect and the scope has to be doubled.
- Three developers recently quit.
- The deadline has been moved up a month.

Develop a list of options that your company can follow to ensure the project remains on schedule and within budget.

4. Refusing to Sign Off

You are the primary client on a large extranet development project. After carefully reviewing the requirements definition document, you are positive that there are missing, ambiguous, inaccurate, and unclear requirements. The project manager is pressuring you for your sign-off since he has already received sign-off from five of your co-workers. If you fail to sign off on the requirements, you are going to put the entire project at risk since the time frame is nonnegotiable. What would you do? Why?

5. Feasibility Studies

John Lancert is the new managing operations director for a large construction company, LMC. John is currently looking for an associate who can help him prioritize the 60 proposed company projects. You are interested in working with John and have decided to apply for the job. John has asked you to compile a report detailing why project prioritization is critical for LMC, along with the different types of feasibility studies you would recommend that LMC use when determining which projects to pursue.

GLOSSARY

A

acceptable use policy (AUP)   A policy that a user must agree to follow in order to be provided access to a network or to the Internet.

accounting   Analyzes the transactional information of the business so the owners and investors can make sound economic decisions.

accounting and finance ERP component   Manages accounting data and financial processes within the enterprise with functions such as general ledger, accounts payable, accounts receivable, budgeting, and asset management.

accounting department   Provides quantitative information about the finances of the business including recording, measuring, and describing financial information.

adware   Software that generates ads that install themselves on a computer when a person downloads some other program from the Internet.

affinity grouping   Determine which things go together.

agile methodology   Aims for customer satisfaction through early and continuous delivery of useful software components developed by an iterative process with a design point that uses the bare minimum requirements.

analysis latency   The time from which data are made available to the time when analysis is complete.

analysis phase   Analyzing end-user business requirements and refining project goals into defined functions and operations of the intended system.

analytical CRM   Supports back-office operations and strategic analysis and includes all systems that do not deal directly with the customers.

analytical information   Encompasses all organizational information, and its primary purpose is to support the performing of managerial analysis tasks.

anti-spam policy   States that email users will not send unsolicited emails (or spam).

application architecture   Determines how applications integrate and relate to each other.

application programming interface (API)   A set of routines, protocols, and tools for building software applications.

application service provider (ASP)   A company that offers an organization access over the Internet to systems and related services that would otherwise have to be located in personal or organizational computers.

application software   Used for specific information processing needs, including payroll, customer relationship management, project management, training, and many others.

arithmetic/logic unit (ALU)   Performs all arithmetic operations (for example, addition and subtraction) and all logic operations (such as sorting and comparing numbers).

artificial intelligence (AI)   Simulates human intelligence such as the ability to reason and learn.

As-Is process model   Represents the current state of the operation that has been mapped, without any specific improvements or changes to existing processes.

asset   Anything owned that has value or earning power.

associates program (affiliate program)   Businesses can generate commissions or royalties from an Internet site.

association detection   Reveals the degree to which variables are related and the nature and frequency of these relationships in the information.

attribute   Characteristics or properties of an entity class.

authentication   A method for confirming users' identities.

authorization   The process of giving someone permission to do or have something.

automatic call distribution   A phone switch routes inbound calls to available agents.

autonomic computing   A self-managing computing model named after, and patterned on, the human body's autonomic nervous system.

availability   Addresses when systems can be accessed by employees, customers, and partners.

B

backdoor program   Viruses that open a way into the network for future attacks.

backup   An exact copy of a system's information.

backward integration   Takes information entered into a given system and sends it automatically to all upstream systems and processes.

balance sheet   Gives an accounting picture of property owned by a company and of claims against the property on a specific date.

balanced scorecard   A management system that enables organizations to clarify their vision and strategy and translate them into action.

bandwidth   The difference between the highest and the lowest frequencies that can be transmitted on a single medium; a measure of the medium's capacity.

benchmark   Baseline values the system seeks to attain.

benchmarking   The process of continuously measuring system results, comparing those results to optimal system performance (benchmark values), and identifying steps and procedures to improve system performance.

binary digit (bit)   The smallest unit of information that a computer can process.

biometric   The identification of a user based on a physical characteristic, such as a fingerprint, iris, face, voice, or handwriting.

black-hat hacker   Breaks into other people's computer systems and may just look around or steal and destroy information.

blog   Website in which items are posted on a regular basis and displayed in reverse chronological order.

Bluetooth   An omnidirectional wireless technology that provides limited-range voice and data transmission over the unlicensed 2.4-GHz frequency band, allowing connections with a wide variety of fixed and portable devices that normally would have to be cabled together.

bookkeeping   The actual recording of the business's transactions, without any analysis of the information.

break-even point   The point at which revenues equal costs.

brick-and-mortar business   A business that operates in a physical store without an Internet presence.

broadband   High-speed Internet connections transmitting data at speeds greater than 200 kilobytes per second (Kbps), compared to the 56 Kbps maximum speed offered by traditional dial-up connections.

bullwhip effect   Occurs when distorted product demand information passes from one entity to the next throughout the supply chain.

business continuity planning (BCP)   A plan for how an organization will recover and restore partially or completely interrupted critical function(s) within a predetermined time after a disaster or extended disruption.

business-critical integrity constraint   Enforces business rules vital to an organization's success and often requires more insight and knowledge than relational integrity constraints.

business facing process   Invisible to the external customer but essential to the effective management of the business and includes goal setting, day-to-day planning, performance feedback, rewards, and resource allocation.

business intelligence   Refers to applications and technologies that are used to gather, provide access to, and analyze data and information to support decision-making efforts.

business process   A standardized set of activities that accomplish a specific task, such as processing a customer's order.

business process management (BPM)   Integrates all of an organization's business processes to make individual processes more efficient.

business process management tool   Used to create an application that is helpful in designing business process models and also helpful in simulating, optimizing, monitoring, and maintaining various processes that occur within an organization.

business process model   A graphic description of a process, showing the sequence of process tasks, which is developed for a specific purpose and from a selected viewpoint.

business process modeling (or mapping)   The activity of creating a detailed flow chart or process map of a work process showing its inputs, tasks, and activities, in a structured sequence.

business process reengineering (BPR)   The analysis and redesign of workflow within and between enterprises.

business requirement   The detailed set of business requests that the system must meet in order to be successful.

business-to-business (B2B)   Applies to businesses buying from and selling to each other over the Internet.

business-to-consumer (B2C)   Applies to any business that sells its products or services to consumers over the Internet.

business wiki   Collaborative web pages that allow users to edit documents, share ideas, or monitor the status of a project.

buyer power   Is assessed by analyzing the ability of buyers to directly impact the price they are willing to pay for an item.

byte   Group of eight bits represents one natural language character.

C

cache memory   A small unit of ultra-fast memory that is used to store recently accessed or frequently accessed data so that the CPU does not have to retrieve this data from slower memory circuits such as RAM.

call scripting system   Accesses organizational databases that track similar issues or questions and automatically generate the details for the CSR who can then relay them to the customer.

campaign management system   Guides users through marketing campaigns performing such tasks as campaign definition, planning, scheduling, segmentation, and success analysis.

capability maturity model integration method (CMMI)   A process improvement approach that contains 22 process areas.

capacity planning   Determines the future IT infrastructure requirements for new equipment and additional network capacity.

capital   Represents money whose purpose is to make more money, for example, the money used to buy a rental property or a business.

central processing unit (CPU) (or microprocessor)   The actual hardware that interprets and executes the program (software) instructions and coordinates how all the other hardware devices work together.

change control board (CCB)   Responsible for approving or rejecting all change requests.

change management   A set of techniques that aid in evolution, composition, and policy management of the design and implementation of a system.

change management system   Includes a collection of procedures to document a change request and define the steps necessary to consider the change based on the expected impact of the change.

chief information officer (CIO)   Responsible for (1) overseeing all uses of information technology and (2) ensuring the strategic alignment of IT with business goals and objectives.

chief knowledge officer (CKO)   Responsible for collecting, maintaining, and distributing the organization's knowledge.

chief privacy officer (CPO)   Responsible for ensuring the ethical and legal use of information within an organization.

chief security officer (CSO)   Responsible for ensuring the security of IT systems and developing strategies and IT safeguards against attacks from hackers and viruses.

chief technology officer (CTO) Responsible for ensuring the throughput, speed, accuracy, availability, and reliability of an organization's information technology.

classification Assigns records to one of a predefined set of classes.

click-and-mortar business A business that operates in a physical store and on the Internet.

clickstream Records information about a customer during a web surfing session such as what websites were visited, how long the visit was, what ads were viewed, and what was purchased.

clickstream data Exact pattern of a consumer's navigation through a site.

click-through A count of the number of people who visit one site and click on an advertisement that takes them to the site of the advertiser.

click-to-talk Buttons allow customers to click on a button and talk with a CSR via the Internet.

client Computer that is designed to request information from a server.

client/server network A model for applications in which the bulk of the back-end processing, such as performing a physical search of a database, takes place on a server, while the front-end processing, which involves communicating with the users, is handled by the clients.

cloud computing Refers to resources and applications hosted remotely as a shared service over the Internet.

cluster analysis A technique used to divide an information set into mutually exclusive groups such that the members of each group are as close together as possible to one another and the different groups are as far apart as possible.

clustering Segmenting a heterogeneous population of records into a number of more homogeneous subgroups.

coaxial cable Cable that can carry a wide range of frequencies with low signal loss.

cold site A separate facility that does not have any computer equipment, but is a place where employees can move after a disaster.

collaboration system An IT-based set of tools that supports the work of teams by facilitating the sharing and flow of information.

collaborative demand planning Helps organizations reduce their investment in inventory, while improving customer satisfaction through product availability.

collaborative engineering Allows an organization to reduce the cost and time required during the design process of a product.

commercial off-the-shelf (COTS) A software package or solution that is purchased to support one or more business functions and information systems.

Committee of Sponsoring Organizations (COSO) Key for evaluating internal controls such as human resources, logistics, information technology, risk, legal, marketing and sales, operations, financial functions, procurement, and reporting.

communication device Equipment used to send information and receive it from one location to another.

competitive advantage A product or service that an organization's customers place a greater value on than similar offerings from a competitor.

complex instruction set computer (CISC) chip Type of CPU that can recognize as many as 100 or more instructions, enough to carry out most computations directly.

compliance The act of conforming, acquiescing, or yielding.

computer Electronic device operating under the control of instructions stored in its own memory that can accept, manipulate, and store data.

computer-aided software engineering (CASE) Software suites that automate systems analysis, design, and development.

computer simulation Complex systems, such as the U.S. economy, can be modeled by means of mathematical equations and different scenarios can be run against the model to determine "what if" analysis.

confidentiality The assurance that messages and information are available only to those who are authorized to view them.

consolidation Involves the aggregation of information and features simple roll-ups to complex groupings of interrelated information.

consumer-to-business (C2B) Applies to any consumer that sells a product or service to a business over the Internet.

consumer-to-consumer (C2C) Applies to sites primarily offering goods and services to assist consumers interacting with each other over the Internet.

contact center (call center) Customer service representatives (CSRs) answer customer inquiries and respond to problems through a number of different customer touch points.

contact management CRM system Maintains customer contact information and identifies prospective customers for future sales.

content filtering Occurs when organizations use software that filters content to prevent the transmission of unauthorized information.

content management system Provides tools to manage the creation, storage, editing, and publication of information in a collaborative environment.

content provider Companies that use the Internet to distribute copyrighted content, including news, music, games, books, movies, and many other types of information.

continuous process improvement model Attempts to understand and measure the current process, and make performance improvements accordingly.

control unit Interprets software instructions and literally tells the other hardware devices what to do, based on the software instructions.

cookie A small file deposited on a hard drive by a website containing information about customers and their web activities.

copyright The legal protection afforded an expression of an idea, such as a song, video game, and some types of proprietary documents.

core competency An organization's key strength or business function that it does better than any of its competitors.

core competency strategy When an organization chooses to focus specifically on what it does best (its core competency) and forms partnerships and alliances with other specialist organizations to handle nonstrategic business processes.

core ERP component Traditional components included in most ERP systems and they primarily focus on internal operations.

corporate policy   A dimension of social responsibility that refers to the position a firm takes on social and political issues.

corporate responsibility   A dimension of social responsibility that includes everything from hiring minority workers to making safe products.

corporation (also called **organization, enterprise,** or **business**)   An artificially created legal entity that exists separate and apart from those individuals who created it and carry on its operations.

counterfeit software   Software that is manufactured to look like the real thing and sold as such.

cracker   A hacker with criminal intent.

critical path   A path from the start to the finish that passes through all the tasks that are critical to completing the project in the shortest amount of time.

critical success factor (CSF)   A factor that is critical to an organization's success.

CRM analysis technologies   Help organizations segment their customers into categories such as best and worst customers.

CRM predicting technologies   Help organizations make predictions regarding customer behavior such as which customers are at risk of leaving.

CRM reporting technologies   Help organizations identify their customers across other applications.

cross-selling   Selling additional products or services to a customer.

cube   The common term for the representation of multidimensional information.

customer facing process   Results in a product or service that is received by an organization's external customer.

customer metric   Assesses the management of customer relationships by the organization.

customer relationship management (CRM)   Involves managing all aspects of a customer's relationship with an organization to increase customer loyalty and retention and an organization's profitability.

cyberterrorist   Seeks to cause harm to people or to destroy critical systems or information and use the Internet as a weapon of mass destruction.

cycle inventory   The average amount of inventory held to satisfy customer demands between inventory deliveries.

D

data   Raw facts that describe the characteristics of an event.

database   Maintains information about various types of objects (inventory), events (transactions), people (employees), and places (warehouses).

database-based workflow system   Stores documents in a central location and automatically asks the team members to access the document when it is their turn to edit the document.

database management system (DBMS)   Software through which users and application programs interact with a database.

data-driven website   An interactive website kept constantly updated and relevant to the needs of its customers through the use of a database.

data flow diagram (DFD)   Illustrates the movement of information between external entities and the processes and data stores within the system.

data latency   The time duration to make data ready for analysis (i.e., the time for extracting, transforming, and cleansing the data) and loading the data into the database.

data mart   Contains a subset of data warehouse information.

data mining   The process of analyzing data to extract information not offered by the raw data alone.

data-mining tool   Uses a variety of techniques to find patterns and relationships in large volumes of information and infer rules from them that predict future behavior and guide decision making.

data model   A formal way to express data relationships to a database management system (DBMS).

data warehouse   A logical collection of information—gathered from many different operational databases—that supports business analysis activities and decision-making tasks.

decision latency   The time it takes a human to comprehend the analytic result and determine an appropriate action.

decision support system (DSS)   Models information to support managers and business professionals during the decision-making process.

demand planning software   Generates demand forecasts using statistical tools and forecasting techniques.

denial-of-service attack (DoS)   Floods a website with so many requests for service that it slows down or crashes the site.

dependency   A logical relationship that exists between the project tasks, or between a project task and a milestone.

deperimeterization   Occurs when an organization moves employees outside its firewall, a growing movement to change the way corporations address technology security.

design phase   Involves describing the desired features and operations of the system including screen layouts, business rules, process diagrams, pseudo code, and other documentation.

development phase   Involves taking all of the detailed design documents from the design phase and transforming them into the actual system.

digital asset management system (DAM)   Though similar to document management, DAM generally works with binary rather than text files, such as multimedia file types.

digital Darwinism   Organizations that cannot adapt to the new demands placed on them for surviving in the information age are doomed to extinction.

digital dashboard   Integrates information from multiple components and tailors the information to individual preferences.

digital divide   When those with access to technology have great advantages over those without access to technology.

digital ink (or **electronic ink**)   Technology that digitally represents handwriting in its natural form.

digital paper (or **electronic paper**)   Any paper that is optimized for any type of digital printing.

digital wallet   Both software and information—the software provides security for the transaction and the information includes payment and delivery information (for example, the credit card number and expiration date).

disaster recovery cost curve Charts (1) the cost to the organization of the unavailability of information and technology and (2) the cost to the organization of recovering from a disaster over time.

disaster recovery plan A detailed process for recovering information or an IT system in the event of a catastrophic disaster such as a fire or flood.

disruptive technology A new way of doing things that initially does not meet the needs of existing customers.

distributed denial-of-service attack (DDoS) Attacks from multiple computers that flood a website with so many requests for service that it slows down or crashes.

distribution management software Coordinates the process of transporting materials from a manufacturer to distribution centers to the final customer.

dividend A distribution of earnings to shareholders.

document management system (DMS) Supports the electronic capturing, storage, distribution, archival, and accessing of documents.

drill-down Enables users to get details, and details of details, of information.

E

ebusiness The conducting of business on the Internet, not only buying and selling, but also serving customers and collaborating with business partners.

ebusiness model An approach to conducting electronic business on the Internet.

ecommerce The buying and selling of goods and services over the Internet.

effectiveness IT metric Measures the impact IT has on business processes and activities including customer satisfaction, conversion rates, and sell-through increases.

efficiency IT metric Measures the performance of the IT system itself including throughput, speed, and availability.

egovernment Involves the use of strategies and technologies to transform government(s) by improving the delivery of services and enhancing the quality of interaction between the citizen-consumer within all branches of government.

electronic bill presentment and payment (EBPP) System that sends bills over the Internet and provides an easy-to-use mechanism (such as clicking on a button) to pay the bill.

electronic catalog Presents customers with information about goods and services offered for sale, bid, or auction on the Internet.

electronic check Mechanism for sending a payment from a checking or savings account.

electronic data interchange (EDI) A standard format for exchanging business data.

electronic marketplace (emarketplace) Interactive business communities providing a central market space where multiple buyers and suppliers can engage in ebusiness activities.

electronic tagging A technique for identifying and tracking assets and individuals via technologies such as radio frequency identification and smart cards.

elevation of privilege Process by which a user misleads a system into granting unauthorized rights, usually for the purpose of compromising or destroying the system.

elogistics Manages the transportation and storage of goods.

email privacy policy Details the extent to which email messages may be read by others.

emall Consists of a number of eshops; it serves as a gateway through which a visitor can access other eshops.

employee monitoring policy States how, when, and where the company monitors its employees.

employee relationship management (ERM) Provides employees with a subset of CRM applications available through a web browser.

encryption Scrambles information into an alternative form that requires a key or password to decrypt the information.

enterprise application integration (EAI) middleware Represents a new approach to middleware by packaging together commonly used functionality, such as providing prebuilt links to popular enterprise applications, which reduces the time necessary to develop solutions that integrate applications from multiple vendors.

enterprise architect (EA) Person grounded in technology, fluent in business, a patient diplomat, and provides the important bridge between IT and the business.

enterprise architecture Includes the plans for how an organization will build, deploy, use, and share its data, processes, and IT assets.

enterprise resource planning (ERP) Integrates all departments and functions throughout an organization into a single IT system (or integrated set of IT systems) so that employees can make decisions by viewing enterprisewide information on all business operations.

entity In the relational database model, a person, place, thing, transaction, or event about which information is stored.

entity-relationship diagram (ERD) A technique for documenting the relationships between entities in a database environment.

entry barrier A product or service feature that customers have come to expect from organizations in a particular industry and must be offered by an entering organization to compete and survive.

environmental scanning The acquisition and analysis of events and trends in the environment external to an organization.

ePolicies Policies and procedures that address the ethical use of computers and Internet usage in the business environment.

eprocurement The B2B purchase and sale of supplies and services over the Internet.

eshop (estore or etailer) A version of a retail store where customers can shop at any hour of the day without leaving their home or office.

estimation Determine values for an unknown continuous variable behavior or estimated future value.

ethernet A physical and data layer technology for LAN networking.

ethical computer use policy Contains general principles to guide computer user behavior.

ethics Principles and standards that guide our behavior toward other people.

ewaste Old computer equipment, does not end up in a landfill, where the toxic substances it contains can leach into groundwater, among other problems.

executive information system (EIS) A specialized DSS that supports senior level executives within the organization.

executive sponsor The person or group who provides the financial resources for the project.

expense Refers to the costs incurred in operating and maintaining a business.

expert system Computerized advisory programs that imitate the reasoning processes of experts in solving difficult problems.

explicit knowledge Consists of anything that can be documented, archived, and codified, often with the help of IT.

extended ERP component The extra components that meet the organizational needs not covered by the core components and primarily focus on external operations.

extensible markup language (XML) A markup language for documents containing structured information.

extraction, transformation, and loading (ETL) A process that extracts information from internal and external databases, transforms the information using a common set of enterprise definitions, and loads the information into a data warehouse.

extranet An intranet that is available to strategic allies (such as customers, suppliers, and partners).

extreme programming (XP) methodology Breaks a project into tiny phases, and developers cannot continue on to the next phase until the first phase is complete.

F

failover Backup operational mode in which the function of a computer component (such as a processor, server, network, or database) is assumed by secondary system components when the primary component becomes unavailable through either failure or scheduled down time.

fair use doctrine In certain situations, it is legal to use copyrighted material.

fault tolerance A computer system designed so that in the event a component fails, a backup component or procedure can immediately take its place with no loss of service.

feasibility study Determines if the proposed solution is feasible and achievable from a financial, technical, and organizational standpoint.

feature creep Occurs when developers add extra features that were not part of the initial requirements.

fiber optic (optical fiber) The technology associated with the transmission of information as light impulses along a glass wire or fiber.

finance Deals with the strategic financial issues associated with increasing the value of the business while observing applicable laws and social responsibilities.

financial accounting Involves preparing financial reports that provide information about the business's performance to external parties such as investors, creditors, and tax authorities.

financial cybermediary Internet-based company that facilitates payments over the Internet.

financial EDI (financial electronic data interchange) Standard electronic process for B2B market purchase payments.

financial quarter A three-month period (four quarters per year).

financial statement Written records of the financial status of the business that allow interested parties to evaluate the profitability and solvency of the business.

firewall Hardware and/or software that guards a private network by analyzing the information leaving and entering the network.

first-mover advantage An organization can significantly impact its market share by being first to market with a competitive advantage.

Five Forces model Helps determine the relative attractiveness of an industry.

flash memory A special type of rewriteable read-only memory (ROM) that is compact and portable.

for profit corporations Primarily focus on making money and all profits and losses are shared by the business owners.

forecast Predictions made on the basis of time-series information.

foreign key A primary key of one table that appears as an attribute in another table and acts to provide a logical relationship between the two tables.

forward integration Takes information entered into a given system and sends it automatically to all downstream systems and processes.

fuzzy logic A mathematical method of handling imprecise or subjective information.

G

Gantt chart A simple bar chart that depicts project tasks against a calendar.

genetic algorithm An artificial intelligence system that mimics the evolutionary, survival-of-the-fittest process to generate increasingly better solutions to a problem.

geoeconomic Refers to the effects of geography on the economic realities of international business activities.

geographic information system (GIS) Designed to work with information that can be shown on a map.

gigabyte (GB) Roughly 1 billion bytes.

gigahertz (GHz) The number of billions of CPU cycles per second.

global inventory management system Provides the ability to locate, track, and predict the movement of every component or material anywhere upstream or downstream in the supply chain.

global positioning system (GPS) A device that determines current latitude, longitude, speed, and direction of movement.

goal-seeking analysis Finds the inputs necessary to achieve a goal such as a desired level of output.

governance Method or system of government for management or control.

graphical user interface (GUI) The interface to an information system.

grid computing An aggregation of geographically dispersed computing, storage, and network resources, coordinated to deliver improved performance, higher quality of service, better utilization, and easier access to data.

groupware   Software that supports team interaction and dynamics including calendaring, scheduling, and videoconferencing.

GUI screen design   The ability to model the information system screens for an entire system using icons, buttons, menus, and submenus.

H

hacker   People very knowledgeable about computers who use their knowledge to invade other people's computers.

hactivist   Person with philosophical and political reasons for breaking into systems who will often deface website as a protest.

hard drive   Secondary storage medium that uses several rigid disks coated with a magnetically sensitive material and housed together with the recording heads in a hermetically sealed mechanism.

hardware   Consists of the physical devices associated with a computer system.

hardware key logger   A hardware device that captures keystrokes on their journey from the keyboard to the motherboard.

help desk   A group of people who respond to internal system user questions.

hierarchical database model   Information is organized into a tree-like structure that allows repeating information using parent/child relationships, in such a way that it cannot have too many relationships.

high availability   Refers to a system or component that is continuously operational for a desirably long length of time.

historical analysis   Historical events are studied to anticipate the outcome of current developments.

hoaxes   Attack computer systems by transmitting a virus hoax, with a real virus attached.

hot site   A separate and fully equipped facility where the company can move immediately after a disaster and resume business.

human resource ERP component   Tracks employee information including payroll, benefits, compensation, and performance assessment, and assures compliance with the legal requirements of multiple jurisdictions and tax authorities.

human resources (HR)   Includes the policies, plans, and procedures for the effective management of employees (human resources).

hypertext transfer protocol (HTTP)   The Internet standard that supports the exchange of information on the WWW.

I

identity theft   The forging of someone's identity for the purpose of fraud.

implementation phase   Involves placing the system into production so users can begin to perform actual business operations with the system.

income statement   (also referred to as **earnings report, operating statement,** and **profit-and-loss (P&L) statement**) Reports operating results (revenues minus expenses) for a given time period ending at a specified date.

information   Data converted into a meaningful and useful context.

information accuracy   Extent to which a system generates the correct results when executing the same transaction numerous times.

information architecture   Identifies where and how important information, like customer records, is maintained and secured.

information cleansing or scrubbing   A process that weeds out and fixes or discards inconsistent, incorrect, or incomplete information.

information granularity   Refers to the extent of detail within the information (fine and detailed or "coarse" and abstract information).

information integrity   A measure of the quality of information.

information partnership   Occurs when two or more organizations cooperate by integrating their IT systems, thereby providing customers with the best of what each can offer.

information privacy   Concerns the legal right or general expectation of individuals, groups, or institutions to determine for themselves when and to what extent information about them is communicated to others.

information privacy policy   Contains general principles regarding information privacy.

information reach   Refers to the number of people a business can communicate with, on a global basis.

information richness   Refers to the depth and breadth of information transferred between customers and businesses.

information security   A broad term encompassing the protection of information from accidental or intentional misuse by persons inside or outside an organization.

information security plan   Details how an organization will implement the information security policies.

information security policy   Identifies the rules required to maintain information security.

Information Systems Audit and Control Association (ISACA)   A set of guidelines and supporting tools for IT governance that is accepted worldwide and generally used by auditors and companies as a way to integrate technology to implement controls and meet specific business objectives.

information technology (IT)   The field concerned with the use of technology in managing and processing information.

Information Technology Infrastructure Library (ITIL)   A framework provided by the government of the United Kingdom that offers eight sets of management procedures.

information technology monitoring   Tracking people's activities by such measures as number of keystrokes, error rate, and number of transactions processed.

infrastructure architecture   Includes the hardware, software, and telecommunications equipment that, when combined, provide the underlying foundation to support the organization's goals.

innovation   The introduction of new equipment or methods.

input device   Equipment used to capture information and commands.

insider   Legitimate users who purposely or accidentally misuse their access to the environment and cause some kind of business-affecting incident.

insourcing (in-house development)   A common approach using the professional expertise within an organization to develop and maintain the organization's information technology systems.

instant messaging (IM or **IMing)**   A type of communications service that enables someone to create a kind of private chat room with another individual in order to communicate in real-time over the Internet.

integration   Allows separate systems to communicate directly with each other.

integrity constraint   The rules that help ensure the quality of information.

intellectual property   Intangible creative work that is embodied in physical form.

intelligent agent   A special-purpose knowledge-based information system that accomplishes specific tasks on behalf of its users.

intelligent system   Various commercial applications of artificial intelligence.

interactive voice response (IVR)   Directs customers to use touch-tone phones or keywords to navigate or provide information.

interactivity   Measures the visitor interactions with the target ad.

intermediary   Agent, software, or business that brings buyers and sellers together to provide a trading infrastructure to enhance ebusiness.

International Organization for Standardization (ISO)   A nongovernmental organization established in 1947 to promote the development of world standards to facilitate the international exchange of goods and services.

Internet   A global public network of computer networks that pass information from one to another using common computer protocols.

Internet service provider (ISP)   A company that provides individuals and other companies access to the Internet along with additional related services, such as website building.

Internet use policy   Contains general principles to guide the proper use of the Internet.

interoperability   Capability of two or more computer systems to share data and resources, even though they are made by different manufacturers.

intranet   An internalized portion of the Internet, protected from outside access, that allows an organization to provide access to information and application software to only its employees.

intrusion detection software (IDS)   Searches out patterns in information and network traffic to indicate attacks and quickly responds to prevent any harm.

inventory management and control software   Provides control and visibility to the status of individual items maintained in inventory.

iterative development   Consists of a series of tiny projects.

IT infrastructure   Includes the hardware, software, and telecommunications equipment that, when combined, provide the underlying foundation to support the organization's goals.

J

joint application development (JAD)   A session where employees meet, sometimes for several days, to define or review the business requirements for the system.

K

key logger, or **key trapper, software**   A program that, when installed on a computer, records every keystroke and mouse click.

key performance indicator (KPI)   Measures that are tied to business drivers.

kill switch   A trigger that enables a project manager to close the project prior to completion.

kiosk   Publicly accessible computer system that has been set up to allow interactive information browsing.

knowledge management (KM)   Involves capturing, classifying, evaluating, retrieving, and sharing information assets in a way that provides context for effective decisions and actions.

knowledge management system (KMS)   Supports the capturing, organization, and dissemination of knowledge (i.e., know-how) throughout an organization.

L

liability   An obligation to make financial payments.

limited liability   Means that the shareholders are not personally liable for the losses incurred by the corporation.

limited liability corporation (LLC)   A hybrid entity that has the legal protections of a corporation and the ability to be taxed (one time) as a partnership.

limited partnership   Much like a general partnership except for one important fundamental difference; the law protects the limited partner from being responsible for all of the partnership's losses.

list generator   Compiles customer information from a variety of sources and segments the information for different marketing campaigns.

local area network (LAN)   Computer network that uses cables or radio signals to link two or more computers within a geographically limited area, generally one building or a group of buildings.

location-based services (LBS)   Wireless mobile content services that provide location-specific information to mobile users moving from location to location.

logical view   Focuses on how users logically access information to meet their particular business needs.

logistics   The set of processes that plans for and controls the efficient and effective transportation and storage of supplies from suppliers to customers.

loose coupling   The capability of services to be joined together on demand to create composite services, or disassembled just as easily into their functional components.

loss   Occurs when businesses sell products or services for less than they cost to produce.

loyalty program   Rewards customers based on the amount of business they do with a particular organization.

M

magnetic medium   Secondary storage medium that uses magnetic techniques to store and retrieve data on disks or tapes coated with magnetically sensitive materials.

magnetic tape   Older secondary storage medium that uses a strip of thin plastic coated with a magnetically sensitive recording medium.

mail bomb   Sends a massive amount of email to a specific person or system resulting in filling up the recipient's disk space, which, in some cases, may be too much for the server to handle and may cause the server to stop functioning.

maintenance   The fixing or enhancing of an information system.

maintenance phase   Involves performing changes, corrections, additions, and upgrades to ensure the system continues to meet the business goals.

maintenance, repair, and operations (MRO) materials (also called **indirect materials**)   Materials necessary for running an organization but that do not relate to the company's primary business activities.

malicious code   Includes a variety of threats such as viruses, worms, and Trojan horses.

management information systems (MIS)   A general name for the business function and academic discipline covering the application of people, technologies, and procedures—collectively called information systems—to solve business problems.

managerial accounting   Involves analyzing business operations for internal decision making and does not have to follow any rules issued by standard-setting bodies such as GAAP.

market basket analysis   Analyzes such items as websites and checkout scanner information to detect customers' buying behavior and predict future behavior by identifying affinities among customers' choices of products and services.

marketing   The process associated with promoting the sale of goods or services.

marketing communication   Seeks to build product or service awareness and to educate potential consumers on the product or service.

marketing mix   Includes the variables that marketing managers can control in order to best satisfy customers in the target market.

market maker   Intermediaries that aggregate three services for market participants: (1) a place to trade, (2) rules to govern trading, and (3) an infrastructure to support trading.

market segmentation   The division of a market into similar groups of customers.

market share   Calculated by dividing the firm's sales by the total market sales for the entire industry.

mashup editor   WYSIWYGs (What You See Is What You Get) for mashups that provide a visual interface to build a mashup, often allowing the user to drag and drop data points into a web application.

mass customization   Ability of an organization to give its customers the opportunity to tailor its products or services to the customers' specifications.

materials requirement planning (MRP) system   Sales forecasts to make sure that needed parts and materials are available at the right time and place in a specific company.

megabyte (MB or **M** or **Meg)**   Roughly 1 million bytes.

megahertz (MHz)   The number of millions of CPU cycles per second.

memory card   Contains high-capacity storage that holds data such as captured images, music, or text files.

memory stick   Provides nonvolatile memory for a range of portable devices including computers, digital cameras, MP3 players, and PDAs.

messaging-based workflow system   Sends work assignments through an email system.

methodology   A set of policies, procedures, standards, processes, practices, tools, techniques, and tasks that people apply to technical and management challenges.

metropolitan area network (MAN)   A computer network that provides connectivity in a geographic area or region larger than that covered by a local area network, but smaller than the area covered by a wide area network.

microwave transmitter   Commonly used to transmit network signals over great distances.

middleware   Different types of software that sit in the middle of and provide connectivity between two or more software applications.

mobile commerce, or **mcommerce**   The ability to purchase goods and services through a wireless Internet-enabled device.

model   A simplified representation or abstraction of reality.

modeling   The activity of drawing a graphical representation of a design.

monopsony   A market in which there are many suppliers and only one buyer.

multisourcing   A combination of professional services, mission-critical support, remote management, and hosting services that are offered to customers in any combination needed.

multitasking   Allows more than one piece of software to be used at a time.

N

nearshore outsourcing   Contracting an outsourcing agreement with a company in a nearby country.

net income   The amount of money remaining after paying taxes.

network   A communications, data exchange, and resource-sharing system created by linking two or more computers and establishing standards, or protocols, so that they can work together.

network database model   A flexible way of representing objects and their relationships.

network operating system (NOS)   The operating system that runs a network, steering information between computers and managing security and users.

network topology   Refers to the geometric arrangement of the actual physical organization of the computers (and other network devices) in a network.

network transmission media   Various types of media used to carry the signal between computers.

neural network (an **artificial neural network**)   A category of AI that attempts to emulate the way the human brain works.

nonrepudiation   A contractual stipulation to ensure that ebusiness participants do not deny (repudiate) their online actions.

not for profit (or **nonprofit**) **corporation**   Usually exists to accomplish some charitable, humanitarian, or educational purpose, and the profits and losses are not shared by the business owners.

O

offshore outsourcing   Using organizations from developing countries to write code and develop systems.

online ad   Box running across a web page that is often used to contain advertisements.

online analytical processing (OLAP)   The manipulation of information to create business intelligence in support of strategic decision making.

online broker   Intermediaries between buyers and sellers of goods and services.

online service provider (OSP)   Offers an extensive array of unique services such as its own version of a web browser.

online training   Runs over the Internet or off a CD-ROM.

online transaction processing (OLTP)   The capturing of transaction and event information using technology to (1) process the information according to defined business rules, (2) store the information, and (3) update existing information to reflect the new information.

onshore outsourcing   The process of engaging another company within the same country for services.

open system   A broad term that describes nonproprietary IT hardware and software made available by the standards and procedures by which their products work, making it easier to integrate them.

operating system software   Controls the application software and manages how the hardware devices work together.

operational CRM   Supports traditional transactional processing for day-to-day front-office operations or systems that deal directly with the customers.

operational planning and control (OP&C)   Deals with the day-to-day procedures for performing work, including scheduling, inventory, and process management.

operations management   The management of systems or processes that convert or transform resources (including human resources) into goods and services.

opportunity management CRM system   Targets sales opportunities by finding new customers or companies for future sales.

opt-in   Indicates that a company will contact only the people who have agreed to receive promotions and marketing material via email.

output device   Equipment used to see, hear, or otherwise accept the results of information processing requests.

outsourcing   An arrangement by which one organization provides a service or services for another organization that chooses not to perform them in-house.

owner's equity   The portion of a company belonging to the owners.

P

packet-switching   Occurs when the sending computer divides a message into a number of efficiently sized units called packets, each of which contains the address of the destination computer.

packet tampering   Altering the contents of packets as they travel over the Internet or altering data on computer disks after penetrating a network.

partner relationship management (PRM)   Focuses on keeping vendors satisfied by managing alliance partner and reseller relationships that provide customers with the optimal sales channel.

partnership   Similar to sole proprietorships, except that this legal structure allows for more than one owner.

partnership agreement   A legal agreement between two or more business partners that outlines core business issues.

peer-to-peer (P2P) network   Any network without a central file server and in which all computers in the network have access to the public files located on all other workstations.

performance   Measures how quickly a system performs a certain process or transaction.

personalization   Occurs when a website can know enough about a person's likes and dislikes that it can fashion offers that are more likely to appeal to that person.

PERT (Program Evaluation and Review Technique) chart   A graphical network model that depicts a project's tasks and the relationships between those tasks.

phishing   Technique to gain personal information for the purpose of identity theft, usually by means of fraudulent email.

physical view   The physical storage of information on a storage device such as a hard disk.

pirated software   The unauthorized use, duplication, distribution, or sale of copyrighted software.

planning phase   Involves establishing a high-level plan of the intended project and determining project goals.

podcasting   Distribution of audio or video files, such as radio programs or music videos, over the Internet to play on mobile devices and personal computers.

polymorphic virus and worm   Change their form as they propagate.

pop-under ad   Form of a pop-up ad that users do not see until they close the current web browser screen.

pop-up ad   Small web page containing an advertisement that appears on the web page outside the current website loaded in the web browser.

portal   A website that offers a broad array of resources and services, such as email, online discussion groups, search engines, and online shopping malls.

predictive dialing   Automatically dials outbound calls and when someone answers, the call is forwarded to an available agent.

primary key   A field (or group of fields) that uniquely identifies a given entity in a table.

primary storage   Computer's main memory, which consists of the random access memory (RAM), cache memory, and read-only memory (ROM) that is directly accessible to the CPU.

privacy   The right to be left alone when you want to be, to have control over your own personal possessions, and not to be observed without your consent.

process modeling   Involves graphically representing the processes that capture, manipulate, store, and distribute information between a system and its environment.

product life cycle   Includes the four phases a product progresses through during its life cycle including introduction, growth, maturity, and decline.

production   The creation of goods and services using the factors of production: land, labor, capital, entrepreneurship, and knowledge.

production and materials management ERP component Handles the various aspects of production planning and execution such as demand forecasting, production scheduling, job cost accounting, and quality control.

production management Describes all the activities managers do to help companies create goods.

profit Occurs when businesses sell products or services for more than they cost to produce.

project A temporary endeavor undertaken to create a unique product or service.

project assumption Factor that is considered to be true, real, or certain without proof or demonstration.

project charter A document issued by the project initiator or sponsor that formally authorizes the existence of a project and provides the project manager with the authority to apply organizational resources to project activities.

project constraint Specific factor that can limit options.

project deliverable Any measurable, tangible, verifiable outcome, result, or item that is produced to complete a project or part of a project.

project management The application of knowledge, skills, tools, and techniques to project activities in order to meet or exceed stakeholder needs and expectations from a project.

project management institute Develops procedures and concepts necessary to support the profession of project management.

project management office An internal department that oversees all organizational projects.

project management software Supports the long-term and day-to-day management and execution of the steps in a project.

project manager An individual who is an expert in project planning and management, defines and develops the project plan, and tracks the plan to ensure all key project milestones are completed on time.

project milestone Represents key dates when a certain group of activities must be performed.

project objective Quantifiable criteria that must be met for the project to be considered a success.

project plan A formal, approved document that manages and controls project execution.

project risk An uncertain event or condition that, if it occurs, has a positive or negative effect on a project objective(s).

project scope Defines the work that must be completed to deliver a product with the specified features and functions.

project stakeholders Individuals and organizations actively involved in the project or whose interests might be affected as a result of project execution or project completion.

protocol A standard that specifies the format of data as well as the rules to be followed during transmission.

prototype A smaller-scale representation or working model of the user's requirements or a proposed design for an information system.

public key encryption (PKE) Encryption system that uses two keys: a public key that everyone can have and a private key for only the recipient.

pull technology Organizations receive or request information.

pure-play (virtual) business A business that operates on the Internet only without a physical store.

push technology Organizations send information.

R

radio frequency identification (RFID) Technologies using active or passive tags in the form of chips or smart labels that can store unique identifiers and relay this information to electronic readers.

RadioPaper A dynamic high-resolution electronic display that combines a paper-like reading experience with the ability to access information anytime, anywhere.

random access memory (RAM) The computer's primary working memory, in which program instructions and data are stored so that they can be accessed directly by the CPU via the processor's high-speed external data bus.

rapid application development (RAD) (also called rapid prototyping) methodology Emphasizes extensive user involvement in the rapid and evolutionary construction of working prototypes of a system to accelerate the systems development process.

rational unified process (RUP) methodology Provides a framework for breaking down the development of software into four gates.

read-only memory (ROM) The portion of a computer's primary storage that does not lose its contents when one switches off the power.

real simple syndication (RSS) Family of web feed formats used for web syndication of programs and content.

real-time information Immediate, up-to-date information.

real-time system Provides real-time information in response to query requests.

recovery The ability to get a system up and running in the event of a system crash or failure and includes restoring the information backup.

reduced instruction set computer (RISC) chip Limits the number of instructions the CPU can execute to increase processing speed.

redundancy The duplication of information or storing the same information in multiple places.

reintermediation Using the Internet to reassemble buyers, sellers, and other partners in a traditional supply chain in new ways.

relational database model A type of database that stores information in the form of logically related two-dimensional tables.

relational integrity constraint The rules that enforce basic and fundamental information-based constraints.

reliability Ensures all systems are functioning correctly and providing accurate information.

report generator Allows users to define formats for reports along with what information they want to see in the report.

requirements definition document Contains the final set of business requirements, prioritized in order of business importance.

response time The time it takes to respond to user interactions such as a mouse click.

revenue Refers to the amount earned resulting from the delivery or manufacture of a product or from the rendering of a service.

RFID tag Contains a microchip and an antenna, and typically works by transmitting a serial number via radio waves to an electronic reader, which confirms the identity of a person or object bearing the tag.

risk management The process of proactive and ongoing identification, analysis, and response to risk factors.

rivalry among existing competitors High when competition is fierce in a market and low when competition is more complacent.

router An intelligent connecting device that examines each packet of data it receives and then decides which way to send it onward toward its destination.

S

safety inventory Includes extra inventory held in the event demand exceeds supply.

sales The function of selling a good or service that focuses on increasing customer sales, which increases company revenues.

sales force automation (SFA) A system that automatically tracks all of the steps in the sales process.

sales management CRM system Automates each phase of the sales process, helping individual sales representatives coordinate and organize all of their accounts.

satellite A big microwave repeater in the sky; it contains one or more transponders that listen to a particular portion of the electromagnetic spectrum, amplifying incoming signals, and retransmitting them back to Earth.

scalability Refers to how well a system can adapt to increased demands.

scope creep Occurs when the scope of the project increases.

script kiddies or **script bunnies** Find hacking code on the Internet and click-and-point their way into systems to cause damage or spread viruses.

SCRUM methodology Uses small teams to produce small pieces of deliverable software using sprints, or 30-day intervals, to achieve an appointed goal.

search engine optimization (SEO) Set of methods aimed at improving the ranking of a website in search engine listings.

secondary storage Consists of equipment designed to store large volumes of data for long-term storage.

secure electronic transaction (SET) Transmission security method that ensures transactions are secure and legitimate.

secure socket layer (SSL) (1) Creates a secure and private connection between a client and server computer, (2) encrypts the information, and (3) sends the information over the Internet.

selling chain management Applies technology to the activities in the order life cycle from inquiry to sale.

semantic web An evolving extension of the World Wide Web in which web content can be expressed not only in natural language, but also in a format that can be read and used by software agents, thus permitting them to find, share, and integrate information more easily.

sensitivity analysis The study of the impact that changes in one (or more) parts of the model have on other parts of the model.

server Computer that is dedicated to providing information in response to external requests.

service A business task.

service level agreement (SLA) Defines the specific responsibilities of the service provider and sets the customer expectations.

service-oriented architecture (SOA) A collection of services that communicate with each other, for example, passing data from one service to another or coordinating an activity between one or more services.

shareholder Another term for business owners.

shopping bot Software that will search several retailer websites and provide a comparison of each retailer's offerings including price and availability.

sign-off The system users' actual signatures indicating they approve all of the business requirements.

slice-and-dice The ability to look at information from different perspectives.

smart card A device that is around the same size as a credit card, containing embedded technologies that can store information and small amounts of software to perform some limited processing.

smartphone Combines the functions of a cellular phone and a PDA in a single device.

sniffer A program or device that can monitor data traveling over a network.

social engineering Using one's social skills to trick people into revealing access credentials or other information valuable to the attacker.

social responsibility Implies that an entity whether it is a government, corporation, organization, or individual has a responsibility to society.

software The set of instructions that the hardware executes to carry out specific tasks.

Software as a Service (SaaS) A model of software deployment where an application is licensed for use as a service provided to customers on demand.

sole proprietorship A business form in which a single person is the sole owner and is personally responsible for all the profits and losses of the business.

solvency Represents the ability of the business to pay its bills and service its debt.

source document Describes the basic transaction data such as its date, purpose, and amount and includes cash receipts, canceled checks, invoices, customer refunds, employee time sheet, etc.

spam Unsolicited email.

spamdexing Uses a variety of deceptive techniques in an attempt to manipulate search engine rankings, whereas legitimate search engine optimization focuses on building better sites and using honest methods of promotion.

spoofing The forging of the return address on an email so that the email message appears to come from someone other than the actual sender.

spyware Software that comes hidden in free downloadable software and tracks online movements, mines the information stored on a computer, or uses a computer's CPU and storage for some task the user knows nothing about.

statement of cash flow   Summarizes sources and uses of cash, indicates whether enough cash is available to carry on routine operations, and offers an analysis of all business transactions, reporting where the firm obtained its cash and how it chose to allocate the cash.

statement of owner's equity (also called the **statement of retained earnings** or **equity statement**)   Tracks and communicates changes in the shareholder's earnings.

strategic business units (SBUs)   Consists of several stand-alone businesses.

strategic planning   Focuses on long-range planning such as plant size, location, and type of process to be used.

structured collaboration (or **process collaboration**)   Involves shared participation in business processes, such as workflow, in which knowledge is hard coded as rules.

supplier power   High when one supplier has concentrated power over an industry.

supplier relationship management (SRM)   Focuses on keeping suppliers satisfied by evaluating and categorizing suppliers for different projects, which optimizes supplier selection.

supply chain   Consists of all parties involved, directly or indirectly, in the procurement of a product or raw material.

supply chain event management (SCEM)   Enables an organization to react more quickly to resolve supply chain issues.

supply chain execution (SCE) software   Automates the different steps and stages of the supply chain.

supply chain management (SCM)   Involves the management of information flows between and among stages in a supply chain to maximize total supply chain effectiveness and profitability.

supply chain planning (SCP) software   Uses advanced mathematical algorithms to improve the flow and efficiency of the supply chain while reducing inventory.

supply chain visibility   The ability to view all areas up and down the supply chain.

sustainable, or "green," IT   Describes the manufacture, management, use, and disposal of information technology in a way that minimizes damage to the environment, which is a critical part of a corporation's responsibility.

sustainable IT disposal   Refers to the safe disposal of IT assets at the end of their life cycle.

sustaining technology   Produces an improved product customers are eager to buy, such as a faster car or larger hard drive.

switching cost   The costs that can make customers reluctant to switch to another product or service.

system availability   Number of hours a system is available for users.

systems development life cycle (SDLC)   The overall process for developing information systems from planning and analysis through implementation and maintenance.

system software   Controls how the various technology tools work together along with the application software.

system virtualization   The ability to present the resources of a single computer as if it is a collection of separate computers ("virtual machines"), each with its own virtual CPUs, network interfaces, storage, and operating system.

T

tacit knowledge   The knowledge contained in people's heads.

tactical planning   Focuses on producing goods and services as efficiently as possible within the strategic plan.

telecommunication system   Enables the transmission of data over public or private networks.

teleliving   Using information devices and the Internet to conduct all aspects of life seamlessly.

telematic   Blending computers and wireless telecommunications technologies with the goal of efficiently conveying information over vast networks to improve business operations.

terabyte (TB)   Roughly 1 trillion bytes.

test condition   The detailed steps the system must perform along with the expected results of each step.

testing phase   Involves bringing all the project pieces together into a special testing environment to test for errors, bugs, and interoperability and verify that the system meets all of the business requirements defined in the analysis phase.

threat of new entrants   High when it is easy for new competitors to enter a market and low when there are significant entry barriers to entering a market.

threat of substitute products or services   High when there are many alternatives to a product or service and low when there are few alternatives from which to choose.

throughput   The amount of information that can travel through a system at any point in time.

time-series information   Time-stamped information collected at a particular frequency.

To-Be process model   Shows the results of applying change improvement opportunities to the current (As-Is) process model.

token   Small electronic devices that change user passwords automatically.

transaction   Exchange or transfer of goods, services, or funds involving two or more people.

transaction processing system (TPS)   The basic business system that serves the operational level (analysts) in an organization.

transaction speed   Amount of time a system takes to perform a transaction.

transborder data flows (TDF)   When business data flows across international boundaries over the telecommunications networks of global information systems.

transactional information   Encompasses all of the information contained within a single business process or unit of work, and its primary purpose is to support the performing of daily operational tasks.

transformation process   The technical core, especially in manufacturing organizations; the actual conversion of inputs to outputs.

Transmission Control Protocol/Internet Protocol (TCP/IP)   Provides the technical foundation for the public Internet as well as for large numbers of private networks.

transportation planning software   Tracks and analyzes the movement of materials and products to ensure the delivery of materials and finished goods at the right time, the right place, and the lowest cost.

trend analysis   A trend is examined to identify its nature, causes, speed of development, and potential impacts.

trend monitoring Trends viewed as particularly important in a specific community, industry, or sector are carefully monitored, watched, and reported to key decision makers.

trend projection When numerical data are available, a trend can be plotted to display changes through time and into the future.

Trojan-horse virus Hides inside other software, usually as an attachment or a downloadable file.

twisted-pair wiring A type of cable composed of four (or more) copper wires twisted around each other within a plastic sheath.

U

unstructured collaboration (or information collaboration) Includes document exchange, shared whiteboards, discussion forums, and email.

up-selling Increasing the value of a sale.

user documentation Highlights how to use the system.

utility software Provides additional functionality to the operating system.

V

value-added The term used to describe the difference between the cost of inputs and the value of price of outputs.

value-added network (VAN) A private network, provided by a third party, for exchanging information through a high-capacity connection.

value chain Views an organization as a series of processes, each of which adds value to the product or service for each customer.

videoconference A set of interactive telecommunication technologies that allow two or more locations to interact via two-way video and audio transmissions simultaneously.

viral marketing Technique that induces websites or users to pass on a marketing message to other websites or users, creating exponential growth in the message's visibility and effect.

virtual assistant A small program stored on a PC or portable device that monitors emails, faxes, messages, and phone calls.

virtualization Protected memory space created by the CPU allowing the computer to create virtual machines.

virtual private network (VPN) A way to use the public telecommunication infrastructure (e.g., Internet) to provide secure access to an organization's network.

virus Software written with malicious intent to cause annoyance or damage.

voice over IP (VoIP) Uses TCP/IP technology to transmit voice calls over long-distance telephone lines.

volatility Refers to RAM's complete loss of stored information if power is interrupted.

W

waterfall methodology A sequential, activity-based process in which each phase in the SDLC is performed sequentially from planning through implementation and maintenance.

Web 2.0 A set of economic, social, and technology trends that collectively form the basis for the next generation of the Internet—a more mature, distinctive medium characterized by user participation, openness, and network effects.

web-based self-service system Allows customers to use the web to find answers to their questions or solutions to their problems.

web conference Blends audio, video, and document-sharing technologies to create virtual meeting rooms where people "gather" at a password-protected website.

web content management system (WCM) Adds an additional layer to document and digital asset management that enables publishing content both to intranets and to public websites.

web log Consists of one line of information for every visitor to a website and is usually stored on a web server.

web mashup A website or web application that uses content from more than one source to create a completely new service.

web service Contains a repertoire of web-based data and procedural resources that use shared protocols and standards permitting different applications to share data and services.

web traffic Includes a host of benchmarks such as the number of page views, the number of unique visitors, and the average time spent viewing a web page.

what-if analysis Checks the impact of a change in an assumption on the proposed solution.

white-hat hacker Works at the request of the system owners to find system vulnerabilities and plug the holes.

wide area network (WAN) Computer network that provides data communication services for business in geographically dispersed areas (such as across a country or around the world).

wiki Web-based tools that make it easy for users to add, remove, and change online content.

WiMAX The Worldwide Interoperability for Microwave Access is a telecommunications technology aimed at providing wireless data over long distances in a variety of ways, from point-to-point links to full mobile cellular type access.

wireless fidelity (wi-fi) A means of linking computers using infrared or radio signals.

wireless Internet service provider (WISP) An ISP that allows subscribers to connect to a server at designated hotspots or access points using a wireless connection.

wire media Transmission material manufactured so that signals will be confined to a narrow path and will behave predictably.

wireless media Natural parts of the Earth's environment that can be used as physical paths to carry electrical signals.

workflow Defines all the steps or business rules, from beginning to end, required for a business process.

workflow management system Facilitates the automation and management of business processes and controls the movement of work through the business process.

workshop training Set in a classroom-type environment and led by an instructor.

World Wide Web (WWW) A global hypertext system that uses the Internet as its transport mechanism.

worm A type of virus that spreads itself, not only from file to file, but also from computer to computer.

REFERENCES

Unit One

2005 CSI/FBI Computer Crime and Security Survey, www.usdoj.gov/criminal/cybercrime/FBI2005.pdf, accessed February 2005.

Adam Horowitz and the editors of *Business 2.0, The Dumbest Moments in Business History: Useless Products, Ruinous Deals, Clueless Bosses, and Other Signs of Unintelligent Life in the Workplace* (New York: Portfolio, 2004).

"Apple Profit Surges 95 Percent on iPod Sales," Yahoo! News, news.yahoo.com/s/afp/20060118/bs_afp/uscompanyearningsit_060118225009, accessed January 18, 2005.

"Apple's IPod Success Isn't Sweet Music for Record Company Sales," Bloomberg.com, quote.bloomberg.com/apps/news?pid=nifea&& sid=aHP5Ko1pozM0, accessed November 2, 2005.

Audra Ang , "China Court Upholds 5 Sentences in Milk Scandal," *BusinessWeek Online,* March 26, 2009, http://www.businessweek.com/ap/financialnews/D975PBH00.htm.

Barbara Ettorre, "Reengineering Tales from the Front," *Management Review,* January 1995, p. 13.

Ben Worthen, "ABC: An Introduction to SCM," www.cio.com/article/40940/ABC_An_Introduction_to_Supply_Chain_Management, accessed May 30, 2007.

Bittorrent, http://www.bittorrent.com/, accessed June 15, 2004.

Booze, Allen, Hamilton, *Information Sharing* (New York: HarperCollins, 2006).

Larry Bossidy and Ram Charan, *Execution* (New York: Random House, 2002).

Bruce Caldwell, "Missteps, Miscues-Business Reengineering Failures," *InformationWeek,* June 20, 1994, p. 50.

Business Dictionary, www.glossarist.com/glossaries/business/, accessed December 15, 2003.

Chi-Chu Tschang , "Contaminated Milk Sours China's Dairy Business," *BusinessWeek Online,* September 26, 2008, http://www.businessweek.com/globalbiz/content/sep2008/gb20080926_543133.htm.

Christopher Koch, "The ABC's of Supply Chain Management," www.cio.com, accessed October 12, 2003.

Cisco Press, www.ciscopress.com/index.asp?rl=1, accessed October 2003.

"CRM Enterprise," *CIO Magazine,* www.cio.com.au/index.php/secid;2, accessed May 28, 2007.

"Customer Success Stories—Charles Schwab," www.siebel.com, accessed November 12, 2003.

"Customer Success Stories—Saab," www.siebel.com, accessed November 12, 2005.

Dave Lindorff, "General Electric and Real Time," www.cioinsight.com/article2/0,3959,686147,00.asp, accessed October 2003.

Dexter Roberts, "Starbucks Caffeinates Its China Growth Plan," *BusinessWeek Online,* October 25, 2006, http://www.businessweek.com/globalbiz/content/oct2006/gb20061025_712453.htm.

eBay Financial News, Earnings and Dividend Release, January 15, 2002.

"Enron, Who's Accountable?" www.time.com/time/business/article/0,8599,193520,00.html, accessed June 7, 2005.

ERP White Paper, www.bitpipe.com/rlist/term/ERP.html, accessed July 3, 2007.

Exact Software, "ERP-II," www.exact.com, accessed April 17, 2007.

"Mastering Management," *Financial Times,* www.ft.com/pp/mfm, accessed December 15, 2003.

Thomas Friedman, www.thomaslfriedman.com, accessed September 14, 2005.

Gabriel Kahn and Cris Prystay, "'Charge It,' Your Cellphone Tells Your Bank," *The Wall Street Journal,* August 13, 2003.

Glossary of Business Terms, www.powerhomebiz.com/Glossary/glossary-A.htm, accessed December 15, 2003.

Glossary of Business Terms, www.smallbiz.nsw.gov.au/smallbusiness/, accessed December 15, 2003.

Glossary of Financial Terms, www.nytimes.com/library/financial/glossary/bfglosa.htm, accessed December 15, 2003.

Google Analytics, www.google.com/analytics, accessed July 13, 2007.

Health Information Management, www.gartner.com, accessed November 16, 2003.

Integrated Solutions, "The ABCs of CRM," www.integratedsolutionsmag.com, accessed November 12, 2003.

"Integrating Information at Children's Hospital," KMWorld, www.kmworld.com/Articles/ReadArticle.aspx?ArticleID=10253, accessed June 1, 2005.

IT Centrix, "Optimizing the Business Value of Information Technology," http://www.unisys.com/products/mainframes/insights/insights__compendium, accessed December 10, 2004.

"IT Master of the Senate," *CIO Magazine Online,* www.cio.com/archive/050104/tl_govt.html, accessed May 1, 2004.

Jay Yarow , "MLB's Real Competitive Advantage," *BusinessWeek Online,* August 29, 2008, http://www.businessweek.com/technology/content/aug2008/tc20080828_061722.htm.

John Heilmann, "What's Friendster Selling?" *Business 2.0,* March 2004, p. 46.

Jon Surmacz, "By the Numbers," *CIO Magazine,* www.cio.com, accessed October 2004.

Joshua Ramo, "Jeffrey Bezos," www.time.com/time/poy2000/archive/1999.html, accessed June 8, 2004.

Kaiser's Diabetic Initiative, www.businessweek.com, accessed November 15, 2003.

Robert Kaplan and David Norton, *The BSC: Translating Strategy into Action* (New York: Vintage Books, 1998).

Ken Blanchard, "Effectiveness vs. Efficiency," Wachovia Small Business, www.wachovia.com, accessed October 2003.

Kim Girard, "How Levi's Got Its Jeans into Wal-Mart," *CIO Magazine,* July 15, 2003.

Mark Eppler, *The Wright Way: 7 Problem-Solving Principles from the Wright Brothers That Can Make Your Business Soar,* Amacon (2003).

Maureen Weicher, "Business Process Reengineering: Analysis and Recommendation," www.netlib.com, accessed February 12, 2005.

Michael E. Porter, *Competitive Strategy: Techniques for Analyzing Industries and Competitors.* Free Press (1998)

Michael Hammer and James Champy, *Reengineering the Corporation* (New York: Harper Collins, 2003).

Michael Schrage, "Build the Business Case," *CIO Magazine Online,* www.cio.com, accessed November 17, 2003.

Michael Watkins, *The First 90 Days* (Boston: Harvard Business School Press, 2003).

news.com.com/NikeiPod+raises+RFID+privacy+concerns/2100-1029_3-6143606.html, accessed June 7, 2007.

Nicomachean Ethics: Aristotle, with an introduction by Hye-Kyung Kim, translated by F.H. Peters in Oxford, 1893 (Barnes & Noble, 2004).

Oracle Customer Study, "Trek Standardizes Worldwide Operations for Boost in Decision-Making Power Business Driver: Standardization for Cost and Process Efficiency," www.oracle.com/customers/snapshots/trek, accessed October 11, 2003,

Paul Ormerod, *Why Most Things Fail: Evolution, Extinction, and Economics* (Hoboken, NJ: John Wiley & Sons, 2005).

Peter Burrows, "How Apple Could Mess Up Again," *BusinessWeek Online,* yahoo.businessweek.com/technology/content/jan2006/tc20060109_432937.htm, accessed January 9, 2006.

Privacy.org, www.privacy.org/, accessed July 3, 2004.

"Q&A with Michael Porter," *BusinessWeek Online,* August 21, 2006, http://www.businessweek.com/magazine/content/06_34/b3998460.htm.

Saul Berman, "Strategic Direction: Don't Reengineer without It; Scanning the Horizon for Turbulence," *Planning Review,* November 1994, p. 18.

Scott Berianato, "Take the Pledge," *CIO Magazine Online,* www.cio.com, accessed November 17, 2003.

Sharon Gaudin, "Smokers Open the Door for Hackers," www.informationweek.com/news/articleID=9875367, accessed August 23, 2007.

"Shop Amazon.com with Your Voice," www.amazon.com/exec/obidos/subst/misc/anywhere/anywhere.html/ref=gw_hp_ls_1_2/002-7628940-9665649, accessed June 8, 2004.

Supply Chain Metrics.com, www.supplychainmetric.com/, accessed June 12, 2007.

The Balanced Scorecard Institute, www.balancedscorecard.org/, accessed May 15, 2007.

"The Business World According to Peter Drucker," www.peter-drucker.com, accessed May 25, 2007.

The New Real Minority Report, www.dailygalaxy.com/my_weblog/2007/08/project-hostile.html, accessed June 13, 2003.

Thomas H. Davenport, "Will Participative Makeovers of Business Processes Succeed Where Reengineering Failed?" *Planning Review,* January 1995, p. 24.

"Top 10 Bad Business Decisions," www.business20.com, accessed April 16, 2007.

"Trek Standardizes Worldwide Operations on J. D. Edwards," www.jdedwards.com, accessed November 15, 2003.

United Nations Division for Public Economics and Public Administration, www.un.com, accessed November 10, 2003.

"What Concerns CIOs the Most?" www.cio.com, accessed November 17, 2003.

www.apple.com/iphone, accessed June 7, 2007.

www.boozallen.com/publications/article/659327, accessed November, 10, 2003.

www.hipaa.org, accessed June 14, 2007.

www.norcrossgroup.com/casestudies.html, accessed October 2004.

Unit Two

"Alaska Fish and Game Yields a Bounty of High-Quality Information to Manage Natural Resources," www.oracle.com, accessed September 20, 2003.

Alice LaPante, "Big Things Come in Smaller Packages," *ComputerWorld,* June 24, 1996, pp. DW/6–7.

Barbara DePompa Reimers, "Too Much of a Good Thing," *ComputerWorld,* www.computerworld.com, April 14, 2003.

Bill Gates, *Business @ The Speed of Thought* (Grand Central Publishing, 1999).

Chicago Police Department, gis.chicagopolice.org/, accessed June 23, 2004.

Customer Success Stories, www.cognos.com, accessed January 2005.

"Cyber Bomb—Search Tampering," *BusinessWeek,* March 1, 2004.

Daniel Pink, "The Book Stops Here," *Wired,* March 2005, pp.125–39.

"Tapping the World's Brainpower with Wiki," *BusinessWeek,* October 11, 2004, p. 132.

"Data Mining: What General Managers Need to Know," *Harvard Management Update,* October 1999.

"Dr Pepper/Seven Up, Inc.," www.cognos.com, accessed September 10, 2003.

"Ford's Vision," donate.pewclimate.org/docUploads/Ford.pdf, accessed June 18, 2003.

Gary Loveman, "Diamonds in the Data Mine," *Harvard Business Review,* May 2003, p. 109.

Glossary of Business Terms, www.powerhomebiz.com/Glossary/glossary-A.htm, accessed December 15, 2003.

Glossary of Business Terms, www.smallbiz.nsw.gov.au/smallbusiness/, accessed December 15, 2003.

Glossary of Financial Terms, www.nytimes.com/library/financial/glossary/bfglosa.htm, accessed December 15, 2003.

"Google Knows Where You Are," *BusinessWeek,* February 2, 2004.

"Google Reveals High-Profile Users of Data Search Machine," *Reuters News Service,* August 13, 2003.

Julia Kiling, "OLAP Gains Fans among Data-Hungry Firms," *ComputerWorld,* January 8, 2001, p. 54.

Julie Schlosser, "Looking for Intelligence in Ice Cream," *Fortune,* March 17, 2003.

Kathleen Melymuka, "Premier 100: Turning the Tables at Applebee's," *ComputerWorld,* www.computerworld.com, accessed February 24, 2003.

Kim Nash, "Casinos Hit Jackpot with Customer Data," www.cnn.com, accessed October 14, 2003.

Leslie Goff, "Summertime Heats Up IT at Ben & Jerry's," *Computer World,* July 2001.

"Massachusetts Laws about Identity Theft," www.lawlib.state.ma.us/identity.html, accessed June 10, 2007.

Meridith Levinson, "Harrah's Knows What You Did Last Night," May 2001. http://www.cio.com.au/article/44514/harrah_knows_what_did_last_night

"Harrah's Entertainment Wins TDWI's 2000 DW Award," www.hpcwire.com, accessed October 10, 2003.

Michael S. Malone, "IPO Fever," *Wired*, March 2004.

Mitch Betts, "Unexpected Insights," *ComputerWorld*, April 14, 2003, www.computerworld.com, accessed September 4, 2003.

MSI Business Solutions, "Case Study: Westpac Financial Services," www.MSI.com, accessed August 4, 2003.

NCR, "Harrah's Entertainment, Inc.," www.ncr.com, accessed October 12, 2003.

"Cognos and Harrah's Entertainment Win Prestigious Data Warehousing Award," www.cognos.com, accessed October 14, 2003.

Nikhil Hutheesing, "Surfing with Sega," *Forbes*, November 4, 2002, p. 58.

Oracle Database, www.oracle.com/database/index.html, accessed May 17, 2007.

Robert Hoff, "Something Wiki This Way Comes," *BusinessWeek Online*, accessed June 7, 2004.

Serena Gordon, "Database Helps Assess Your Breast Cancer Risk", *BusinessWeek Online*, January 25, 2009, http://www.businessweek.com/lifestyle/content/healthday/618891.html.

Stephen Baker, "What Data Crunchers Did for Obama," January 23, 2009, *BusinessWeek Online*, http://www.businessweek.com/print/technology/content/jan2009/tc20090123_026100.htm.

"Sun Tzu on the Art of War," www.chinapage.com/sunzi-e.html, accessed September 15, 2007.

Sydney Finkelstein, *Why Smart Executives Fail*. Portfolio Hardcover, (2003)

Tommy Peterson, "Data Cleansing," *ComputerWorld*, www.computerworld.com, accessed February 10, 2003.

Webopedia.com, www.webopedia.comTERM/d/database.html, accessed May 15, 2007.

"Why Data Quality," www.trilliumsoft.com, accessed October 3, 2003.

www.chron.com, accessed September 3, 2003.

www.google.com, accessed September 13, 2003.

www.sitepoint.com/article/publishing-mysql-data-web, accessed May 16, 2007.

www.wikipedia.com, accessed November 2005.

www.wikipedia.org, accessed May, 22, 2007.

Unit Three

"1,000 Executives Best Skillset," *The Wall Street Journal*, July 15, 2003.

"1800 flowers.com," *Business 2.0*, February 2004.

"50 People Who Matter Now," money.cnn.com/magazines/business2/peoplewhomatter/, *Business 2.0*, accessed July 16, 2007.

Alison Overholt, "Smart Strategies: Putting Ideas to Work," *Fast Company*, April 2004, p. 63.

Andrew Binstock, "Virtual Enterprise Comes of Age," *InformationWeek*, November 6, 2004.

Michael A. Arbib (Ed.), *The Handbook of Brain Theory and Neural Networks* The MIT Press(1995).

Barclays, "Giving Voice to Customer-Centricity," crm.insightexec.com, accessed July 15, 2007

Beth Bacheldor, "Steady Supply," *InformationWeek*, November 24, 2003, www.informationweek.com, accessed June 6, 2003.

L. Biacino and G. Gerla, "Fuzzy logic, Continuity and Effectiveness," *Archive for Mathematical Logic* (2002).

Bill Breen, "Living in Dell Time," *Fast Company*, November 2004, p. 86.

"Boston Coach Aligns Service with Customer Demand in Real Time," www-1.ibm.com/services/us/index.wss, accessed November 4, 2003.

Bruce Caldwell, "Harley-Davidson Revs Up IT Horsepower," Internetweek.com, December 7, 2000.

"Bullwhips and Beer: Why Supply Chain Management Is So Difficult," forio.com/resources/bullwhips-and-beer/, accessed June 10, 2003.

cio.de/news/cio_worldnews/809030/index7.html, accessed May 4, 2005.

"Computerworld 100 Best Places to Work in IT 2003," *Computerworld*, June 9, 2003, pp. 36-48.

"Creating a Value Network," *Wired*, September 2003, p. S13.

"Customer First Awards," *Fast Company*, May, 2005.

"Customer Success—Brother," www.sap.com, accessed January 12, 2004.

"Customer Success—Cisco," www.sap.com, accessed April 5, 2003.

"Customer Success—PNC Retail Bank," www.siebel.com, accessed May 5, 2003.

"Customer Success—UPS," www.sap.com, accessed April 5, 2003.

"Customer Trust: Reviving Loyalty in a Challenging Economy," *Pivotal Webcast*, September 19, 2002.

"Darpa Grand Challenge," www.darpa.mil/grandchallenge/, accessed September 1, 2005.

"Del Monte Organic RFID," *BusinessWeek*, March 15, 2007.

Emanuel Rosen, *The Anatomy of Buzz* (New York: DoubleDay, 2000).

ERP Success, www.sap.com, accessed April 5, 2003, and March 15, 2007.

Exact Software, "ERP-II: Making ERP Deliver On Its Promise to the Enterprise," jobfunctions.bnet.com/whitepaper.aspx?docid=144338, accessed July 25, 2007.

"Finding the Best Buy," www.oracle.com, accessed April 4, 2003.

"Finding Value in the Real-Time Enterprise," *Business 2.0*, November 2003, pp. S1-S5.

"Forecasting Chocolate," www.sas.com, accessed October 3, 2003.

Fred Hapgood, "Smart Decisions," *CIO Magazine*, www.cio.com, August 15, 2001.

Frederick F. Reichheld, *Loyalty Rules* (Bain and Company, 2001).

Glossary of Business Terms, www.powerhomebiz.com/Glossary/glossary-A.htm, accessed December 15, 2003.

Glossary of Business Terms, www.smallbiz.nsw.gov.au/smallbusiness/, accessed December 15, 2003.

Glossary of Financial Terms, www.nytimes.com/library/financial/glossary/bfglosa.htm, accessed December 15, 2003.

Hagerty, "How Best to Measure Our Supply Chain."

James Harkin, "Get a (Second) Life," *Financial Times Online*, November 17, 2006, accessed June 15, 2007.

"Harley-Davidson Announces Go-Live: Continues to Expand Use of Manugistics Supplier Relationship Management Solutions," www.manugistics.com, May 7, 2002.

"How Creamy? How Crunchy?" www.sas.com, accessed October 3, 2003.

"Case Study: IBM Helps Shell Canada Fuel New Productivity with PeopleSoft EnterpriseOne," August 8, 2005, validated February 5, 2007, www-306 .ibm.com/software/success/cssdb.nsf.

"Industry Facts and Statistics," Insurance Information Institute, www.iii.org, accessed December 2005.

Internet Retailer, www.internetretailer.com, accessed February 17, 2005.

Jim Collins, *Built to Last* (Collins Business Essentials, 1994).

Jim Collins, *Good to Great* (Collins Business Essentials, 2001).

John Hagerty, "How Best to Measure Our Supply Chain," www. AMRresearch.com, March 3, 2005.

Keving Kelleher, "BudNet: 66,207,896 Bottles of Beer on the Wall," *Business 2.0,* February 2004.

Christopher Koch, "How Verizon Flies by Wire," *CIO Magazine,* November 1, 2004, and "Sleepless in Manhattan," CIO.com.

Leroy Zimdars, "Supply Chain Innovation at Harley-Davidson: An Interview with Leroy Zimdars," April 15, 2000. http://www.ascet .com/authors.asp?a_id=168

"Linden Lab to Open Source Second Life Software," Linden Lab, January 8, 2007, www.secondlife.org, accessed May 22, 2007.

"Maytag—Washing Away Maintenance," www.sas.com, accessed October 3, 2003.

Mitch Betts, "Kinks in the Chain," *ComputerWorld,* December 17, 2005.

Neil McManus, "Robots at Your Service," *Wired,* January 2003, p. O59.

Neil Raden, "Data, Data Everywhere," DSSResources.com, February 16, 2003.

"Neural Network Examples and Definitions," ece-www.colorado .edu/~ecen4831/lectures/NNdemo.html, accessed June 24, 2007.

"New York Knicks—Success," www.jdedwards.com, accessed January 15, 2004.

"Put Better, Faster Decision-Making in Your Sights," www.teradata.com, accessed July 7, 2003.

"REI Pegs Growth on Effective Multi-channel Strategy," *Internet Retailer,* www.internetretailer.com, accessed February 17, 2005,

Roger Villareal, "Docent Enterprise Increases Technician and Dealer Knowledge and Skills to Maximize Sales Results and Customer Service," www.docent.com, August 13, 2002.

S. Begley, "Software au Natural," *Newsweek,* May 8, 2005.

Santa Fe Institute, www.dis.anl.gov/abms/, accessed June 24, 2007.

Secondlife.com, accessed May 28, 2007.

secondlife.com/community/land-islands.php.

Irene Sege, "Leading a Double Life," *The Boston Globe Online,* October 25, 2006, accessed June 22, 2007.

"Smart Tools," *BusinessWeek,* March 24, 2003.

"Technology Terms," www.techterms.com/, accessed May 3, 2003.

"The 'New' *New York Times,*" *Business 2.0,* January 2004.

"The Corporate Portal Market 2005," BEA White Paper, www.bea .com, January 2005.

"The e-Biz Surprise," *BusinessWeek,* May 12, 2003, pp. 60–65.

"The Visionary Elite," *Business 2.0,* December 2003, pp. S1–S5.

"Verizon Executives," newscenter.verizon.com/leadership/ shaygan-kheradpir.html, accessed may 17, 2003.

Vinod Gupta, "Databases: Where the Customers Are," *BusinessWeek Online,* May 12, 2004, http://www.businessweek. com/smallbiz/content/may2004/sb20040512_9369.htm.

Walid Mougayar, "Old Dogs Learn New Tricks," *Business 2.0,* October 2000, www.Business2.com, accessed June 14, 2003.

Webopedia, www.webopedia.com, accessed May 14, 2003.

Whatis.com, whatis.techtarget.com, accessed May 4, 2003.

www.bae.com, accessed May 24, 2007.

www.dell.com, accessed September, 15, 2003.

www.investor.harley-davidson.com, accessed October 10, 2003.

www.netflix.com, accessed May 23, 2007.

www.secondlife.com, accessed May 25, 2007.

www.usps.com, accessed June 17, 2004.

www.wal-mart.com, accessed May 26, 2007.

Unit Four

"10 Tips for Wireless Home Security," compnetworking.about.com/ od/wirelesssecurity/tp/wifisecurity.htm, accessed September 15, 2006.

"Amazon Finds Profits in Outsourcing," *CIO Magazine,* October 15, 2002, www.cio.com/archive/101502/tl_ec.html, accessed November 14, 2003.

"A Site Stickier than a Barroom Floor," *Business 2.0,* June 2005, p. 741.

Adam Lashinsky, "Kodak's Developing Situation," *Fortune,* January 20, 2003, p. 176.

Adam Lashinsky, "The Disrupters," *Fortune,* August 11, 2003, pp. 62–65.

Anne Zelenka , "The Hype Machine, Best Mashup of Mashup Camp 3," gigaom.com/2007/01/18/the-hype-machine-bestmashup- of-mashup-camp-3/, accessed June 14, 2007.

"CenterCup Releases PDA Caddy to Leverage Legalized Golf GPS," www.golfgearreview.com/article-display/1665.html, accessed February 3, 2008.

Charles Waltner, "Florida Hospital Cuts Cord, Goes Wireless," newsroom.cisco.com, accessed February 1, 2008.

Chris Silva, Benjamin Gray, "Key Wireless Trends That Will Shape Enterprise Mobility in 2008," www.forrester.com, accessed February 12, 2008.

Cisco Press, www.ciscopress.com, accessed March 23, 2005.

"City of Logan, Utah," www.techrepublic.com, accessed February 2, 2008.

Clayton Christensen, *The Innovator's Dilemma* (Boston: Harvard Business School, 1997).

Coco Masters, "Bringing Wi-Fi to the Skies," www.time.com/time/ specials/2007/article/0,28804,1665220_1665225,00.html, accessed February 20, 2008.

Dan Nystedt, "Mobile Phones Grow Even More Popular," *PC World,* April 2006.

Deepak Pareek, "WiMAX: Taking Wireless to the MAX," *CRC Press,* 2006, pp. 150–51.

"D-FW Defense Contractors Show Mixed Fortunes since September 11," www.bizjournals.com/dallas/stories/2002/09/09/ focus2.htm, accessed June 8, 2004.

"Evolution of Wireless Networks," www.cisco.com, accessed September 15, 2007.

"GPS Innovation Gives Weather Bots a New Ride," www.cio.com/ article/108500/GPS, accessed September 15, 2007.

Gunjan Bagla, "Bringing IT to Rural India One Village at a Time," *CIO Magazine,* March 1, 2005.

Heather Harreld, "Lemon Aid," *CIO Magazine,* July 1, 2000.

"How Do Cellular Devices Work," www.cell-phone101.info/ devices.php, accessed February 9, 2008.

Internet Pioneers, www.ibiblio.org/pioneers/andreesen.html, accessed June 2004.

Internet World Statistics, www.internetworldstats.com, accessed January 2007.

Jim Rapoza, "First Movers That Flopped," etech.eweek.com/slideshow/index.php?directory _ first_movers, accessed June 26, 2007.

"Keeping Weeds in Check with Less Herbicide," www.ars.usda.gov/is/AR/archive/aug06/weeds0806.htm, accessed February 11, 2008.

Kevin Shult, "UPS vs. FedEx: Battle of the Brands," www.bloggingstocks.com/2007/04/09/ups-vs-fedex-battle-ofthe-brands/, accessed February 10, 2008.

Knowledge Management Research Center, *CIO Magazine,* www.cio.com/research/knowledge, December 2005.

Megan Santosus, "In The Know," *CIO Magazine,* January 2006.

Michael Dortch, "Winning RFID Strategies for 2008," *Benchmark Report,* December 31, 2007.

mobilementalism.com, accessed February 2, 2008.

Mohsen Attaran, "RFID: An Enabler of Supply Chain Operations," *Supply Chain Management: An International Journal* 12 (2007), pp. 249–57.

"Navigating the Mobility Wave," www.busmanagement.com, accessed February 2, 2008.

onstar.com, accessed February 10, 2008.

"RFID Privacy and You," www.theyaretrackingyou.com/rfid-privacy-and-you.html, accessed February 12, 2008.

"RFID Roundup," www.rfidgazette.org, accessed February 10, 2008.

"Security-Free Wireless Networks," www.wired.com, accessed February 11, 2008.

"Sprint Plans Launch of Commercial WiMAX Service in Q2 2008," www.intomobile.com, accessed February 10, 2008.

Steve Konicki, "Collaboration Is Cornerstone of $19B Defense Contract," www.business2.com/content/magazine/indepth/2000/07/11/17966, accessed June 8, 2004.

"Technology Terms," www.techterms.com/, accessed May 3, 2003.

"The 21st Century Meeting," February 27, 2007, www.businessweek.com/magazine/content/07_09/b4023059.htm, accessed June 2, 2007.

Thomas Claburn, "Law Professor Predicts Wikipedia's Demise," www.informationweek.com/showArticle.jhtml;jsessionid _ 2ZYHJY4LGVHBOQSNDLRSKHSCJUNN2JVN?articleID _ 196601766&queryText _ wikipedia, accessed June 8,2007.

"Toyota's One-Stop Information Shop," www.istart.co.nz/index/HM20/PC0/PV21873/EX236/CS25653, accessed June 8, 2004.

V. C. Gungor, F. C. Lambert, "A Survey on Communication Networks for Electric System Automation, Computer Networks," *The International Journal of Computer and Telecommunications Networking,* May 15, 2006, pp. 877–97.

"Video Conference," en.wikipedia.org/wiki/Video_conference, accessed June 1, 2007.

W. David Gardner, "McDonald's Targets Starbucks with Free Wi-Fi, Upscale Coffee Bars," *InformationWeek,* January 7, 2008.

Webmashup.com, www.webmashup.com/Insert New 25, accessed June 14, 2007.

Webopedia, www.webopedia.com, accessed May 14, 2003.

Whitfield Diffie, "Sun's Diffie AT&T Cyber Security Conference," accessed September 2, 2007. http://research.sun.com/people/diffie/accessed July 15, 2007

wimax.com, accessed February 9, 2008.

Whatis.com, whatis.techtarget.com, accessed May 4, 2003.

ww.emarketer.com, accessed January 2006.

www.amazon.com/Into-Leadership-Lessons-Westward-Expedition/dp/0814408168, accessed February 9, 2008.

www.drpepper.com, accessed February 1, 2008.

www.ebags.com, accessed June 21, 2007.

www.gis.rgs.org/10.html, accessed February 7, 2008.

www.ironman.com, accessed January 14, 2008.

www.lockheedmartin.com, accessed April 23, 2003.

www.mbia.com, accessed February 3, 2008.

www.powerofmobility.com, accessed February 9, 2008.

www.wired.com, accessed November 15, 2003.

Unit Five

"A New View," *Business 2.0,* November 10, 2003, pp. S1–S5.

Adam Lashinsky, "The Disrupters," *Fortune,* August 11, 2003, pp. 62–65.

"Agile Alliance Manifesto," www.agile.com, accessed November 1, 2003.

Art Jahnke, "Kodak Stays in the Digital Picture," www.cnn.com/TECH/computing/9908/06/kodak.ent.idg/, accessed June 8, 2004.

"Building Events," www.microsoft.com, accessed November 15, 2003.

"Building Software That Works," www.compaq.com, accessed November 14, 2003.

Charles Pelton, "How to Solve the IT Labor Shortage Problem," www.informationweek.com/author/eyeonit15.htm, accessed June 8, 2004.

Christopher Null, "How Netflix Is Fixing Hollywood," *Business 2.0,* July 2003, pp. 31–33.

"Customer Success Story—PHH," www.informatica.com, accessed December 12, 2003.

"Customer Success—Horizon," www.businessengine.com, accessed October 15, 2003.

"Defective Software Costs," National Institute of Standards and Technology (NIST), June 2002.

Edward Yourdon, *Death March: The Complete Software Developer's Guide to Surviving "Mission Impossible" Projects* (Upper Saddle River, NJ: Pearson Education, 1997).

"Future Three Partners with Ideal Technology Solutions, U.S. for Total Automotive Network Exchange (ANX) Capability," www.itsusnow.com/news_future3.htm, accessed June 8, 2004.

Gene Marks, "The Super User for Your Software Project," *BusinessWeek Online,* June 11, 2008, http://www.businessweek.com/print/technology/content/jun2008/tc20080610_363466.htm

Geoffrey James, "The Next Delivery? Computer Repair," CNNMoney.com, July 1, 2004.

Gini Graham Scott, *A Survival Guide for Working with Humans* (New York: AMACOM, 2004).

Glossary of Business Terms, www.powerhomebiz.com/Glossary/glossary-A.htm, accessed December 15, 2003

Glossary of Business Terms, www.smallbiz.nsw.gov.au/smallbusiness/, accessed December 15, 2003

Glossary of Financial Terms, www.nytimes.com/library/financial/glossary/bfglosa.htm, accessed December 15, 2003

"How Secure Is Digital Hospital," *Wired,* March 28, 2001.

Jaikumar Vijayan, "Companies Expected to Boost Offshore Outsourcing," www.computerworld.com/managementtopics/outsourcing/story/0,10801,78583,00.html, accessed June 8, 2004.

Jeffrey Hollender and Stephen Fenichell, *What Matters Most: The Future of Corporate Social Responsibility.* Basic Books (2006)

John Blau, "German Researchers Move Forward on Plastic RFID," *Computer World,* January 13, 2005.

Julia Scheeres, "Three R's: Reading, Writing, and RFID," *Wired,* October 14, 2003.

Kevin Kelleher, "The Wired 40," *Wired,* www.wired.com, accessed March 3, 2004.

Lynne Johnson, Ellen McGirt, and Sherri Smith, "The Most Influential Women in Technology", www.fastcompany.com, January 14, 2009, http://www.fastcompany.com/magazine/132/the-most-influential-women-in-technology.html.

"Merrill Lynch and Thomson Financial to Develop Wealth Management Workstation," www.advisorpage.com/modules.php?name=News&file=print&sid=666, accessed June 8, 2004.

Michael Kanellos, "IDC: PC Market on the Comeback Trail," news.com.com/2100-1001-976295. html?part=dtx&tag=ntop, accessed June 8, 2004.

Olga Kharif , "Android: One Multitasking Operating System," *BusinessWeek Online,* February 5, 2009, http://www.businessweek.com/print/technology/content/feb2009/tc2009024_366125.htm.

Peter F. Drucker Foundation, *The Leader of the Future: Visions, Practices, and Strategies for a New Era.* Jossey-Bass, (August 19, 1997)

Peter F. Drucker, *Management Challenges for the 21st Century.* Collins Business, (April 21, 1999)

"Sneaker Net," *CIO Magazine,* www.cio.com/archive/webbusiness/080199_nike.html, accessed June 8, 2004.

"Software Costs," *CIO Magazine,* www.cio.com, accessed December 5, 2003.

"Software Metrics," *CIO Magazine,* www.cio.com, accessed December 2, 2003.

Stephanie Overby, "In or Out?" *CIO Magazine,* www.cio.com/archive/081503/sourcing.html, accessed June 8, 2004.

"Technology Terms," www.techterms.com/, accessed May 3, 2003.

"The Web Smart 50," *BusinessWeek Online,* www.businessweek.com, accessed March 3, 2004.

Timothy Mullaney and Arlene Weintraub, "The Digital Hospital," *BusinessWeek,* March 28, 2005.

Tom Schultz, "PBS: A Clearer Picture," *Business 2.0,* January 2003.

"Top Reasons Why IT Projects Fail," *InformationWeek,* www.infoweek.com, accessed November 5, 2003.

Webopedia, www.webopedia.com, accessed May 14, 2003.

Whatis.com, whatis.techtarget.com, accessed May 4, 2003.

www.agile.com, accessed November 10, 2003.

www.businessweek.com, accessed November 1, 2005.

www.gartner.com, accessed November 3, 2003.

www.wired.com, accessed October 15, 2003.

Plug-In B1

Adrian Danescu, "Save $55,000," *CIO Magazine,* December 15, 2004, p. 70.

Alison Overholdt, "The Housewife Who Got Up Off the Couch," *Fast Company,* September 2004, p. 94.

Business Dictionary, www.glossarist.com/glossaries/business/, accessed December 15, 2003

"Can the Nordstroms Find the Right Style?" *BusinessWeek,* July 30, 2001.

"Mastering Management," *Financial Times,* www.ft.com/pp/mfm, accessed December 15, 2003.

"From the Bottom Up," *Fast Company,* June 2004, p. 54.

Geoff Keighley, "Will Sony's PSP Become the iPod of Gaming Devices?" *Business 2.0,* May 2004, p. 29.

Glossary of Business Terms, www.powerhomebiz.com/Glossary/glossary-A.htm, accessed December 15, 2003.

Glossary of Business Terms, www.smallbiz.nsw.gov.au/smallbusiness/, accessed December 15, 2003.

Glossary of Financial Terms, www.nytimes.com/library/financial/glossary/bfglosa.htm, accessed December 15, 2003.

"Harley-Davidson: Ride Your Heritage," *Fast Company,* August 2004, p. 44.

"Ford on Top," *Fast Company,* June 2004, p. 54.

"Innovative Managers," *BusinessWeek,* April 24, 2005.

Julie Schlosser, "Toys 'R'Us Braces for a Holiday Battle," *Money,* December 22, 2003.

Michael Hammer, *Beyond Reengineering: How the Process-Centered Organization Is Changing Our Work and Our Lives* (New York: HarperCollins Publishers, 1997).

"Progressive Insurance," *BusinessWeek,* March 13, 2004.

"Toy Wars," www.pbs.org, accessed December 23, 2003.

Plug-In B2

Bjorn Andersen, *Business Process Improvement Toolbox* (Milwaukee, WI: ASQ Quality Press, 1999).

"BPR Online," www.prosci.com/mod1.htm, accessed October 10, 2005.

"Business Process Reengineering Six Sigma," www .isixsigma.com/me/bpr/, accessed October 10, 2005.

"Customer Success Stories: Adidas," www.global360.com/collateral/Adidas_Case_History.pdf, accessed October 10, 2005.

Government Business Process Reengineering (BPR) Readiness Assessment Guide, General Services Administration (GSA), 1996.

H. James Harrington, *Business Process Improvement Workbook: Documentation, Analysis, Design, and Management of Business Process Improvement* (New York: McGraw-Hill, 1997).

H. James Harrington, *Business Process Improvement: The Breakthrough Strategy for Total Quality, Productivity, and Competitiveness* (New York: McGraw-Hill, 1991).

Michael Hammer and James Champy, "Reengineering the Corporation: A Manifest for Business Revolution," 1993. HarperBusiness (January 1, 1994)

Michael Hammer, *Beyond Reengineering: How the Process-Centered Organization Is Changing Our Work and Our Lives* (New York: HarperCollins, 1996).

Richard Chang, "Process Reengineering in Action: A Practical Guide to Achieving Breakthrough Results (Quality Improvement Series)," 1996.

"Savvion Helps 3Com Optimize Product Promotion Processes," www.savvion.com/customers/marketing_promotions.php, accessed October 10, 2005.

SmartDraw.com, www.smartdraw.com/, accessed October 11, 2005.

"What Is BPR?" searchcio.techtarget.com/sDefinition/0,,sid182_gci536451,00.html, accessed October 10, 2005.

Plug-In B3

Aaron Ricadela, "Seismic Shift," *InformationWeek,* March 14, 2005.

Denise Brehm, "Sloan Students Pedal Exercise," www.mit.edu, accessed May 5, 2003.

"Electronic Breaking Points," www.pcworld.com, accessed August 2005.

Hector Ruiz, "Advanced Micro Devices," *BusinessWeek,* January 10, 2005.

Margaret Locher, "Hands That Speak," *CIO Magazine,* June 1, 2005.

Meridith Levinson, "Circuit City Rewires," *CIO Magazine,* July 1, 2005.

"The Linux Counter," counter.li.org, accessed October 2005.

Tom Davenport, "Playing Catch-Up," *CIO Magazine,* May 1, 2001.

www.mit.com, accessed October 2005.

www.needapresent.com, accessed October 2005.

www.powergridfitness.com, accessed October 2005.

Plug-In B4

"Agile Enterprise," www.agiledata.org/essays/enterpriseArchitecture.html, accessed May 14, 2003.

"Can American Keep Flying?" *CIO Magazine,* www.cio.com, February 15, 2003.

Christine McGeever, "FBI Database Problem Halts Gun Checks," www.computerworld.com, accessed May 22, 2000.

Christopher Koch, "A New Blueprint for the Enterprise," *CIO Magazine,* March 1, 2005.

"Distribution of Software Updates of Thousands of Franchise Locations Was Slow and Unpredictable," www.fountain.com, accessed October 10, 2003.

Erick Schonfeld, "Linux Takes Flight," *Business 2.0,* January 2003, pp. 103–5.

Institute for Enterprise Architecture, www.enterprise-architecture.info/, May 2, 2003.

John Fontana, "Lydian Revs up with Web Services," *Network World,* March 10, 2004.

"Looking at the New," *InformationWeek,* May 2005.

Martin Garvey, "Manage Passwords," *InformationWeek,* May 20, 2005.

Martin Garvey, "Security Action Plans," *InformationWeek,* May 30, 2005.

Otis Port, "Will the Feud Choke the Life Out of Linux?" *BusinessWeek,* July 7, 2003, p. 81.

"Technology Terms," www.techterms.com/, accessed May 3, 2003.

Tim Wilson, "Server Consolidation Delivers," *InformationWeek,* May 30, 2005.

Webopedia, www.webopedia.com, accessed May 14, 2003.

"What Every Executive Needs to Know," www.akamai.com, accessed September 10, 2003.

Whatis.com, swhatis.techtarget.com, accessed May 4, 2003.

www.abercrombie&fitch.com, accessed November 2005.

www.gartner.com, accessed November 2005.

www.websidestory.com, accessed November 2005.

Plug-In B5

Enrique De Argaez, "What You Should Know about Internet Broadband Access," www.internetworldstats.com/articles/art096.htm, accessed January 29, 2004.

Eva Chen, "Shop Talk," *CIO Magazine,* October 15, 2004.

Networking.com, www.networking.com, accessed May 15, 2003.

"Overcoming Software Development Problems," www.samspublishing.com, October 7, 2002, accessed November 16, 2003.

"Rip Curl Turns to Skype for Global Communications," www.voipinbusiness.co.uk/rip_curl_turns_to_skype_for_gl.asp July 07, 2006, accessed January 21, 2008.

"Technology Terms," www.techterms.com/, accessed May 3, 2003.

"The Security Revolution," *CIO Magazine,* www.cio.com, accessed June 6, 2003.

"VoIP Business Solutions," www.vocalocity.com, accessed January 21, 2008.

Webopedia, www.webopedia.com, accessed May 14, 2003.

Whatis.com, whatis.techtarget.com, accessed May 4, 2003.

www.rei.com, accessed February 23, 2008.

www.skype.com, accessed February 15, 2008.

Plug-In B6

"2002 CSI/FBI Computer Crime and Security Survey," www.gocsi.com, accessed November 23, 2003.

"Hacker Hunters," *BusinessWeek,* May 30, 2005.

"Losses from Identity Theft to Total $221 Billion Worldwide," *CIO Magazine,* www.cio.com, May, 2005.

Mark Leon, "Keys to the Kingdom," www.computerworld.com, April 14, 2003, accessed August 8, 2003.

Scott Berinato and Sarah Scalet, "The ABCs of Information Security," *CIO Magazine,* www.cio.com, accessed July 7, 2003.

"Sony Fights Intrusion with 'Crystal Ball,'" *CIO Magazine,* www.cio.com, accessed August 9, 2003.

"Spam Losses to Grow to $198 Billion," *CIO Magazine,* www.cio.com, accessed August 9, 2003.

"Teen Arrested in Internet 'Blaster' Attack," www.cnn.com, August 29, 2003.

"The Security Revolution," *CIO Magazine,* www.cio.com, accessed June 6, 2003.

www.ey.com, accessed November 25, 2003.

Plug-In B7

Alice Dragon, "Be a Spam Slayer," *CIO Magazine,* November 1, 2003, www.cio.com, accessed March 9, 2004.

AMA Research, "Workplace Monitoring and Surveillance," www.amanet.org, April 2003, accessed March 1, 2004.

AnchorDeskStaff, "How to Spy on Your Employees and Why You May Not Want To," www.reviews-zdnet.com, August 21, 2003, accessed March 5, 2004.

"Computer Security Policy," www.computer-security-policies.com/, accessed March 24, 2007.

"FedLaw Computers and Information Technology," www.thecre.com/fedlaw/legal8.htm, accessed March 21, 2004

Information Security Policy World, www.information-security-policies-and-standards.com/, accessed March 23, 2004

Paul Roberts, "Report: Spam Costs $874 per Employee per Year," www.computerworld.com, July 2, 2003, accessed March 9, 2004.

Sarbanes-Oxley Act, www.workingvalues.com, accessed March 3, 2004.

Scott Berinato, "Take the Pledge—The CIO's Code of Ethical Data Management," *CIO Magazine,* July 1, 2002, www.cio.com, accessed March 7, 2004.

"Technology Terms," www.techterms.com/, accessed May 3, 2003.

Webopedia, www.webopedia.com, accessed May 14, 2003.

Whatis.com, whatis.techtarget.com, accessed May 4, 2003.

www.vault.com, accessed January 2006.

Plug-In B8

Bob Evans, "Business Technology: Sweet Home," *InformationWeek,* February 7, 2005.

Frank Quinn, "The Payoff Potential in Supply Chain Management," www.ascet.com, accessed June 15, 2003.

Jennifer Bresnahan, "The Incredible Journey," *CIO Enterprise,* August 15, 1998, www.cio.com, accessed March 12, 2004.

Justin Fox, "A Meditation on Risk," *Fortune,* October 3, 2005.

"Logistics and Supply Chain," logistics.about.com, accessed June 2, 2003.

Navi Radjou, "Manufacturing Sector IT Spending Profile for 2004," September 12, 2003, www.forrester.com, accessed March 15, 2004.

Parija Bhatnagar, "Wal-Mart Closes 123 Stores from Storm," www.cnnmoney.com, accessed August 2005.

William Copacino, "How to Become a Supply Chain Master," *Supply Chain Management Review,* September 1, 2001, www.manufacturing.net, accessed June 12, 2003.

Supply Chain Council, www.supply-chain.org/cs/root/home, accessed June 22, 2003.

"Technology Terms," www.techterms.com/, accessed May 3, 2003.

Walid Mougayar, "Old Dogs Learn New Tricks," *Business 2.0,* October 2000, www.Business2.com, accessed June 14, 2003.

Webopedia, www.webopedia.com, accessed May 14, 2003.

Whatis.com, whatis.techtarget.com, accessed May 4, 2003.

Plug-In B9

"3M Accelerates Revenue Growth Using Siebel eBusiness Applications," July 30, 2002, www.siebel.com, accessed July 10, 2003.

"Avnet Brings IM to Corporate America with Lotus Instant Messaging," websphereadvisor.com/doc/12196, accessed July 11, 2003.

"Barclays, Giving Voice to Customer-Centricity," crm.insightexec.com, accessed July 15, 2003.

Bob Evans, "Business Technology: Sweet Home," *InformationWeek,* February 7, 2005.

"California State Automobile Association Case Study," www.epiphany.com/customers/detail_csaa.html, accessed July 4, 2003.

"Customer Success," www.costco.com, accessed June 2005.

"Customer Success," www.rackspace.com, accessed June 2005.

"Customer Success—UPS," www.sap.com, accessed April 5, 2003.

"Documedics," www.siebel.com, accessed July 10, 2003.

"Partnering in the Fight against Cancer," www.siebel.com, accessed July 16, 2003.

"Sears: Redefining Business," *BusinessWeek,* www.businessweek.com, accessed April 15, 2003.

Supply Chain Planet, June 2003, newsweaver.co.uk/supplychainplanet/e_article000153342.cfm, accessed July 12, 2003.

"The Expanding Territory of Outsourcing," www.outsourcing.com, accessed August 15, 2003.

"Vail Resorts Implements FrontRange HEAT," *CRM Today,* October 16, 2003, www.crm2day.com/news/crm/EpyykllFyAqEUbqOhW.php, accessed December 2, 2003.

www.FedEx.com, accessed July 13, 2003.

www.nicesystems.com, accessed June 2005.

www.salesforce.com, accessed June 2005.

Plug-In B10

"Customer Success Stories," www.jdedwards.com, accessed October 15, 2003.

"Customer Success Story—Grupo Farmanova Intermed," www.jdedwards.com, accessed October 15, 2003.

"Customer Success Story—PepsiAmerica," www.peoplesoft.com, accessed October 22, 2003.

"Customer Success Story—Turner Industries," www.jdedwards.com, accessed October 15, 2003.

"Harley-Davidson on the Path to Success," www.peoplesoft.com/media/success, accessed October 12, 2003.

Michael Doane, "A Blueprint for ERP Implementation Readiness," www.metagroup.com, accessed October 17, 2003.

Thomas Wailgum, "Big Mess on Campus," *CIO Magazine,* May 1, 2005.

Plug-In B11

Amy Johnson, "A New Supply Chain Forged," *ComputerWorld,* September 30, 2002.

ColdStone Creamery Talk, www.creamerytalk.com/press/in_the_news_2005.html, accessed September 23, 2004.

Frank Quinn, "The Payoff Potential in Supply Chain Management," www.ascet.com, accessed June 15, 2003.

"Info on 3.9M Citigroup," *Money,* June 6, 2005.

Jack Welch, "What's Right about Wal-Mart," *CIO Magazine,* www.cio.com, accessed May 2005.

Joshua Ramo, "Jeffrey Bezos," www.time.com/time/poy2000/archive/1999.html, accessed June 8, 2004.

Laura Rohde, "British Airways Takes Off with Cisco," *Network World,* May 11, 2005.

"Let's Remake a Deal," *Business 2.0,* March 2004.

"Manage Your Mailing Experience Electronically, All in One Place," United States Postal Service, www.usps.com, accessed July 2005.

Penelope Patsuris, "Marketing Messages Made to Order," *Forbes,* August 2003.

Pratt & Whitney, *BusinessWeek,* June 2004.

Rachel Metz, "Changing at the Push of a Button," *Wired,* September 27, 2004.

"Watch Your Spending," *BusinessWeek,* May 23, 2004.

www.hotel-gatti.com, accessed June 2003.

www.idc.com, accessed June 2005.

www.ingenio.com, accessed July 2005.

www.oecd.org, accessed June 2005.

www.t-mobile.com, accessed June 2005.

www.vanguard.com, accessed June 2005.

www.yankeegroup.com, accessed May 2005.

Plug-In B12

Denise Dubie, "Tivoli Users Discuss Automation," *Network World,* April 14, 2003.

Marvin Cetron and Owen Davies, "50 Trends Shaping the Future," *2003 World Future Society Special Report,* April 2004.

Penelope Patsuris, "Marketing Messages Made to Order," *Forbes,* August 2003.

"Progressive Receives Applied Systems' 2003 Interface Best Practices Award," www.worksite.net/091203tech.htm, accessed June 18, 2004.

Stacy Crowley, "IBM, HP, MS Discuss Autonomic Computing Strategies," *Infoworld,* May 19, 2004.

"The Art of Foresight," *The Futurist,* May–June 2004, pp. 31–35.

William Halal, "The Top 10 Emerging Technologies," *The Futurist Special Report,* July 2004.

Plug-In B13

"BP: WebLearn," www.accenture.com/xd/xd.asp?it=enweb &xd=industries%5Cresources%5Cenergy%5Ccase%5Cener_bpweblearn.xml, accessed June 8, 2004.

"Call Center and CRM Statistics," www.cconvergence.com/shared/printableArticle. jhtml?articleID=7617915, accessed June 8, 2004.

"Coors Brewing Company," www.eds.com/case_studies/case_coors.shtml, accessed June 8, 2004.

Deni Connor, "IT Outlook Declines Due to Outsourcing, Offshoring," www.nwfusion.com/careers/2004/0531manside.html, accessed June 8, 2004.

IBM/Lotus Domino Server Hosting Service, www.macro.com.hk/solution_Outsourcing.htm, accessed June 8, 2004.

Stan Gibson, "Global Services Plays Pivotal Role," www.eweek.com/article2/0,1759,808984,00.asp, accessed June 8, 2004.

Todd Datz, "Outsourcing World Tour," CIO Magazine, July 15, 2004, pp. 42–48.

www.forrester.com, accessed June 8, 2004.

Plug-In B14

"Baggage Handling System Errors," www.flavors.com, accessed November 16, 2003.

Gary McGraw, "Making Essential Software Work," Software Quality Management, April 2003, www.sqmmagazine.com, accessed November 14, 2003.

Overcoming Software Development Problems," October 7, 2002, www.samspublishing.com, accessed November 16, 2003.

"Python Project Failure," www.systemsdev.com, accessed November 14, 2003.

www.microsoft.com, accessed November 16, 2003.

www.standishgroup.com, accessed November 14, 2003.

Plug-In B15

"Staying on Track at the Toronto Transit Commission," www.primavera.com, accessed December 16, 2003.

"Supply and Demand Chain," www.isourceonline.com, accessed December 14, 2003.

"Taking on Change," CIO Magazine, June 2005.

"The Project Manager in the IT Industry," www.si2.com, accessed December 15, 2003.

www.altria.com, accessed December 15, 2003.

www.calpine.com, accessed December 14, 2003.

www.change-management.org, accessed December 12, 2003.

www.microsoft.com, accessed December 13, 2003.

www.snapon.com, accessed December 13, 2003.

www.standishgroup.com, accessed December 12, 2003.

Plug-In B16

Aasron Bernstein, "Backlash: Behind the Anxiety of Globalization," BusinessWeek, April 24, 2006, pp. 36–42.

Terry Hill, Manufacturing Strategy: Text and Cases, 3rd ed. (New York: McGraw-Hill, 2000).

Andrew Binstock, "Virtual Enterprise Comes of Age," InformationWeek, November 6, 2004.

Bill Breen, "Living in Dell Time," Fast Company, November 2004, p. 86.

Christopher A. Bartlett and Sumantra Ghoshal, "Going Global: Lessons from Late Movers," Harvard Business Review, March–April 2000, pp. 132–34.

"Creating a Value Network," Wired, September 2003, p. S13.

Frank Quinn, "The Payoff Potential in Supply Chain Management," www.ascet.com, accessed June 15, 2003.

Fred Hapgood, "Smart Decisions," CIO Magazine, www.cio.com, accessed August 15, 2001.

Geoffrey Colvin, "Managing in the Info Era," Fortune, March 6, 2007, pp. F6–F9.

James Fitzsimmons and Mona Fitzsimmons, Service Management, 4th ed. (New York: McGraw-Hill Irwin, 2004).

James P. Womack, Daniel Jones, and Daniel Roos, The Machine That Changed the World (New York, Harper Perennial, 1991).

Jennifer Bresnahan, "The Incredible Journey," CIO Enterprise Magazine, August 15, 1998, www.cio.com, accessed March 12, 2004.

Jim Collins, Built to Last (Collins Business Essentials, 2004).

Jim Collins, Good to Great (Collins Business Essentials, 2001).

John Hagerty, "How Best to Measure Our Supply Chain," www.amrresearch.com, accessed March 3, 2005.

Kevin Kelleher, "BudNet: 66,207,896 Bottles of Beer on the Wall," Business 2.0, February 2004.

Kim Girard, "How Levi's Got Its Jeans into Wal-Mart," CIO Magazine, July 15, 2003.

Mitch Betts, "Kinks in the Chain," Computerworld, December 17, 2005.

Norman E. Bowie (Ed.), The Blackwell Guide to Business Ethics (Malden, MA: Blackwell, 2002).

William Copacino, "How to Become a Supply Chain Master," Supply Chain Management Review, September 1, 2001, www.manufacturing.net, accessed June 12, 2003.

Sharon Shinn, "What about the Widgets?" BizEd, November–December 2004, pp. 30–35.

Stuart Crainer, The Management Century (New York: Jossey-Bass, 2000).

"Success Story," www.perdue.com, accessed September 2003.

"The e-Biz Surprise," BusinessWeek, May 12, 2003, pp. 60–65.

Walid Mougayar, "Old Dogs Learn New Tricks," Business 2.0, October 2000, www.Business2.com, accessed June 14, 2003.

William J. Hopp and Mark Spearman, Factory Physics: Foundations of Manufacturing Management, 2nd ed. (Burr Ridge, IL: Irwin, 2001).

Plug-In B17

"Achieving a Single Customer View," www.sun.com, accessed January 12, 2008.

Alan Joch, "Grid Gets Down to Business," Network World, December 27, 2004.

Dirk Slama, Robert Paluch, "Key Concepts of Service-Oriented Architecture," www.csc.com/cscworld/012006/web/web002.html, accessed on January 4, 2008.

"EPA Report to Congress on Server and Data Center Energy Efficiency," www.energystar.gov/ia/partners/prod_development/downloads/EPA_Report_Exec_Summary_Final.pdf, accessed January 23, 2008.

Geoffrey Thomas, "Seeing Is Believing," Air Transport World, June 2007, p. 54.

"Google Groans under Data Strain," www.byteandswitch.com/document.asp?doc_id _ 85804, accessed January 30, 2008.

Grant Gross, "Grids Help eBay Do Big Business," www.infoworld.com/article/06/09/12/HNebaygarids_1.html?GRID%20COMPUTING, accessed January 23, 2008.

Julie Bort, "SOA Made Fast and Easy," Network World, October 22, 2007.

Julie Bort, "Subaru Takes a Virtual Drive," *Network World*, September 25, 2006.

Mark Morley, "Business Benefits of SaaS," www.gxs.com/insights/strategy_execution/0708_SaaS_02_MarkMorley.htm, accessed February 14, 2009.

Paul Krill, "Impending Death of Moore's Law Calls for Software Development Changes," *InfoWorld*, May 24, 2005.

Tim Wilson, "Don't Stop the Presses!" www.networkcomputing.com, accessed January 28, 2008.

"VMware—History of Virtualization," www.virtualizationworks.com/Virtualization-History.asp, accessed January 23, 2008.

www.usopen.org, accessed January 28, 2008.

Plug-In B18

Emanuel Rosen, *The Anatomy of Buzz* (New York:DoubleDay, 2000).

"Enterprise Business Intelligence," May 2006. Used with Permission: Dr. Claudia Imhoff, Intelligent Solutions, Inc.

Frederick F. Reichheld, *Loyalty Rules* (Bain and Company, 2001).

Meridith Levinson, "The Brain Behind the Big Bad Burger and Other Tales of Business Intelligence", www.cio.com, May 15, 2007, http://www.cio.com/article/109454/The_Brain_Behind_the_Big_Bad_Burger_and_Other_Tales_of_Business_Intelligence.

Second Life, www.secondlife.org, accessed March 2008.

Steve Hamm, "Business Intelligence Gets Smarter," *BusinessWeek*, May 15, 2006.

Jill Dyche, "The Business Case for Data Warehousing," 2005. Used with permission.

"The Critical Shift to Flexible Business Intelligence." Used with Permission: Dr. Claudia Imhoff, Intelligent Solutions, Inc.

"What Every Marketer Wants—And Needs—From Technology." Used with Permission: Dr. Claudia Imhoff, Intelligent Solutions, Inc.

Plug-In B19

Brian Grow, Keith Epstein, and Chi-Chu Tschang, "E-Spionage," *BusinessWeek*, April 10, 2008.

"Innovation," *BusinessWeek*, http://www.businessweek.com/innovate/, accessed February 15, 2008.

David Bornstein, *How to Change the World*. Oxford University Press, USA; Updated edition (September 17, 2007)

Harold Sirkin, "Tata's Nano: An Ingenious Coup," *BusinessWeek*, February 14, 2008.

Heather Green and Kerry Capell, "Carbon Confusion," *BusinessWeek*, March 6, 2008.

Jeffrey Hollender and Stephen Fenichell, *What Matters Most: The Future of Corporate Social Responsibility*. Basic Books (January 2, 2006)

Kerry Capell, "Building Expertise through Collective Innovation," *BusinessWeek*, March 5, 2008.

Peter F. Drucker Foundation, *The Leader of the Future: Visions, Practices, and Strategies for a New Era*.

Peter F. Drucker, *Management Challenges for the 21st Century*. Collins Business; (June 26, 2001)

William J. Holstein , "Corporate Governance in China and India," *BusinessWeek Online*, March 6, 2008, http://www.businessweek.com/managing/content/mar2008/ca2008036_282896.htm.

Plug-In B20

Brian Grow, Keith Epstein, and Chi-Chu Tschang, "E-Spionage," *BusinessWeek*, April 10, 2008.

"Innovation," *BusinessWeek*, http://www.businessweek.com/innovate/, accessed February 15, 2008.

David Bornstein, *How to Change the World*. Oxford University Press, USA; Updated edition (September 17, 2007)

Harold Sirkin, "Tata's Nano: An Ingenious Coup," *BusinessWeek*, February 14, 2008.

Heather Green and Kerry Capell, "Carbon Confusion," *BusinessWeek*, March 6, 2008.

Jeffrey Hollender and Stephen Fenichell, *What Matters Most: The Future of Corporate Social Responsibility*. Basic Books (January 2, 2006)

Kerry Capell, "Building Expertise through Collective Innovation," *BusinessWeek*, March 5, 2008.

Peter F. Drucker Foundation, *The Leader of the Future: Visions, Practices, and Strategies for a New Era*.

Peter F. Drucker, *Management Challenges for the 21st Century*. Collins Business; (June 26, 2001)

William J. Holstein , "Corporate Governance in China and India," *BusinessWeek Online*, March 6, 2008, http://www.businessweek.com/managing/content/mar2008/ca2008036_282896.htm.

Plug-In B21

"CenterCup Releases PDA Caddy to Leverage Legalized Golf GPS," www.golfgearreview.com/article-display/1665.html, accessed February 3, 2008.

clearwire.com, accessed January 27, 2009.

Coco Masters, "Bringing Wi-Fi to the Skies," www.time.com/time/specials/2007/article/0,28804,1665220_1665225,00.html, accessed February 20, 2008.

Dan Nystedt, "Mobile Phones Grow Even More Popular," *PC World*, April 2006.

Deepak Pareek, "WiMAX: Taking Wireless to the MAX," CRC Press, 2006, pp. 150–51.

"How Do Cellular Devices Work," www.cell-phone101.info/devices.php, accessed February 9, 2008.

"Keeping Weeds in Check with Less Herbicide," www.ars.usda.gov/is/AR/archive/aug06/weeds0806.htm, accessed February 11, 2008.

loopt.com, accessed January 29, 2009.

Michael Dortch, "Winning RFID Strategies for 2008," *Benchmark Report*, December 31, 2007.

mobilementalism.com, accessed February 2, 2008.

Mohsen Attaran, "RFID: an Enabler of Supply Chain Operations," *Supply Chain Management: An International Journal* 12 (2007), pp. 249–57.

onstar.com, accessed February 10, 2008.

"RFID Privacy and You," www.theyaretrackingyou.com/rfid-privacy-and-you.html, accessed February 12, 2008.

"RFID Roundup," www.rfidgazette.org, accessed February 10, 2008.

"Security-Free Wireless Networks," www.wired.com, accessed February 11, 2008.

"Sprint Plans Launch of Commercial WiMAX Service in Q2 2008," www.intomobile.com, accessed February 10, 2008.

V. C. Gungor, F. C. Lambert, "A Survey on Communication Networks for Electric System Automation, Computer Networks," *The International Journal of Computer and Telecommunications Networking*, May 15, 2006, pp. 877–897.

W. David Gardner, "McDonald's Targets Starbucks with Free Wi-Fi, Upscale Coffee Bars," *InformationWeek*, January 7, 2008.

wimax.com, accessed February 9, 2008.

www.gis.rgs.org/10.html, accessed February 7, 2008.

www.mbia.com, accessed February 3, 2008.

P 1.1A, page 3, ©McGraw-Hill Companies/Jill Braaten, photographer.

P 1.1B, page 3, The McGraw-Hill Companies, Inc./Lars A. Niki, photographer.

P 1.1C, page 3, The McGraw-Hill Companies, Inc./Christopher Kerrigan, photographer.

Figure 1.1, page 8, Paige Baltzan.

Figure 1.2, page 9, www.cio.com, accessed August 2005.

Figure 2.4a, page 21, Photo courtesy of Hyundai Motor America.

Figure 2.4b, page 21, Photo courtesy of Audi.

Figure 2.4c, page 21, Copyright © 2004 Kia Motors America, Inc. All Rights Reserved.

Figure 2.6, page 22, Porter, Michael E., Competitive Strategy: Techniques for Analyzing Industries and Competitors, The Free Press, 1998.

Figure 3.4, page 30, Caldwell, Bruce, "Missteps, Miscues—Business Reengineering Failures," *Information Week,* June 20, 1994, p. 50.

Figure 3.10, page 33, ERP White Paper, www.bitpipe.com/rlist/term/ERP.html, accessed July 3, 2007.

Figure 4.6, page 41, Google Analytics, www.google.com/analytics, accessed July 13, 2007.

Figure 4.7, page 41, Google Analytics, www.google.com/analytics, accessed July 13, 2007.

Figure 4.8, page 42, Supply Chain Metrics.com, www.supplychainmetric.com/, accessed June 12, 2007.

Figure 4.9, page 43, Kaplan, Robert, Norton, David, "The BSC: Translating Strategy into Action" (Vintage Books: 1998) The Balanced Scorecard Institute, http://www.balancedscorecard.org/BSCResources/AbouttheBalancedScorecard/tabid/55/Default.aspx. Adapted from **The Balanced Scorecard** by Kaplan & Norton, accessed May 15, 2007.

Figure 5.5, page 50, Scott Berimano, Take the Pledge, www.cio.com, accessed November 17, 2003.

Figure 5.8, page 53, Computer Security Institute.

Page 57 (left): Getty Images.

Page 57 (center): Royalty-Free/Corbis.

Page 57 (right): Royalty-Free/Corbis.

Page 59 (left): The McGraw-Hill Companies, Inc./John Flournoy, photographer.

Page 59 (center): Steven Brahms/Bloomberg News/Landov.

Page 59 (right): PRNewsFoto/Bank of America/AP/Wide World Photos.

P 2.1A, page 73, Digital Vision/Getty Images.

P 2.1B, page 73, BananaStock/PictureQuest.

P 2.1C, page 73, Jason Reed/Getty Images.

Figure 7.4, page 92, Webopedia.com, www.webopedia.comTERM/d/database.html, accessed May 15, 2007; Wikipedia, The Free Encyclopedia, en.wikipedia.org/wiki/Wiki, accessed May 22, 2007; Oracle Database, www.oracle.com/database/index.html, accessed May 17, 2007; www.sitepoint.com/article/publishing-mysql-data-web, accessed May 16, 2007.

P 2.2A, page 107, PhotoLink/Photodisc/Getty Images.

P 2.2B, page 107, Jack Star/PhotoLink/Getty Images.

P 2.2C, page 107, Oleg Svyatoslavsky/Life File/Getty Images.

P 2.3, page 109, Photo courtesy of Cray, Inc.

Page 119 (all): Courtesy of Linden Labs.

P 9.1, page 131, Alexander Heimann/AFP/Getty.

P 9.2, page 131, AP/Wide World Photos.

P 9.3, page 131, © Jeff Greenberg/Photo Edit.

Figure 12.3, page 159, Exact Software, "ERP-II: Making ERP Deliver On Its Promise to the Enterprise", jobfunctions.bnet.com/whitepaper.aspx?docid=144338, accessed July 25, 2007.

Figure 12.4, page 159, Exact Software, "ERP-II: Making ERP Deliver On Its Promise to the Enterprise", jobfunctions.bnet.com/whitepaper.aspx?docid=144338, accessed July 25, 2007.

P 3.2A, page 167, C. Sherburne/PhotoLink/Getty Images.

P 3.2B, page 167, Digital Vision/Getty Images.

P 3.2C, page 167, Ryan McVay/Getty Images.

P 3.2D, page 169, AP/Wide World Photos.

P 3.2E, page 169, Scott Olson/Getty Images.

P 3.2F, page 169, PRNewsFoto/Harley-Davidson/AP/Wide World Photos.

13.1A, page 181, Getty Images.

13.1B, page 181, Getty Images.

13.1C, page 181, Getty Images.

Figure 13.1, page 185, http://www.internetworldstats.com/stats.htm, accessed January 15, 2005.

Figure 13.8, page 189, Tim O'Reilly, "What Is Web 2.0: Design Patterns and Business Models for the Next Generation of Software", 9/30/2005.

Figure 13.9, page 189, Tim O'Reilly, "What Is Web 2.0: Design Patterns and Business Models for the Next Generation of Software", 9/30/2005.

Figure 14.9, page 197, Ecommerce Taxation, www.icsc.org/, accessed June 8, 2004.

Figure 15.10, page 212: Cartesia/PhotoDisc Imaging/Getty Images.

Figure 15.11, page 213: © Tom Grill/Corbis.

P 4.2A, page 224, Creatas/PunchStock.

P 4.2B, page 224, Dynamic Graphics/JupiterImages.

P 4.2C, page 224, PhotoLink/Getty Images.

P 4.2D, page 225, ThinkStock/SuperStock.

P 4.2E, page 225, The McGraw-Hill Companies, Inc./ John Flournoy, photographer.

P 4.2F, page 225, BananaStock/PictureQuest.

17.1A, page 241, Getty Images.

17.1B, page 241, Royalty-Free/CORBIS.

17.1C, page 241, Royalty-Free/CORBIS.

Figure 18.2, page 259, *Information Week.*

Figure 19.1, page 264, Common Outsourcing, www.cio.com, accessed June 15, 2004.

Figure 20.1, page 271, www.expedia.com, www.apple.com, www.dell.com, www.lendingtree.com, www.amazon.com, www.ebay.com, accessed October 13, 2004.

Figure 20.3, page 272, 2005 SCOnline.com, accessed January 2005.

P 5.2A, page 277, Tetra Images/Getty Images.

P 5.2B, page 277, Lars Niki.

P 5.2C, page 277, The McGraw-Hill Companies, Inc., Christopher Kerrigan, photographer.

P 5.2D, page 279, Getty Images/Blend Images.

P 5.2E, page 279, Stockbyte/Getty Images.

P 5.2F, page 279, Ingram Publishing/AGE Fotostock.

Figure B2.6, page B2.7, Michael Hammer. *Beyond Reengineering, How the Process-Centered Organization Is Changing Our Work and Our Lives, New York:* HarperCollins, Publisher, 1996.

P B3.1A, page B3.3, Royalty-Free/CORBIS.

P B3.1B, page B3.3, Stockbyte/Punchstock Images.

P B3.2, page B3.4, SimpleTech Inc.

P B3.3A, page B3.4, Getty Images.

P B3.3B, page B3.4, Daisuke Morita/Getty Images.

P B3.4A, page B3.4, © Stockbyte/PunchStock.

P B3.4B, page B3.4, © Stockbyte/PunchStock.

P B3.5A, page B3.4, Courtesy of Panasonic

P B3.5B, page B3.4, Courtesy of Dell Inc.

P B3.6A, page B3.4, Getty Images.

P B3.6B, page B3.4, Royalty-Free/CORBIS.

Figure B3.3, page B3.5, "Chip Wars," *PC World,* August 2005.

Figure B3.11, page B3.12, Ricadela, Aaron, "Seismic Shift," Information Week, March 14, 2005.

Figure B4.1, page B4.2, *Business Week,* January 10, 2005.

Figure B4.4, page B4.5, *Information Week,* August 9, 2004.

Figure B5.4, page B5.5, www.pcmagazine.com, accessed October 10, 2005.

Figure B6.3, page 303, www.ey.com, accessed November 25, 2003.

Figure B6.4, page 304, "The Security Revolution," www.cio.com, accessed June 6, 2003.

Figure B6.6, page 307, "Spam Losses to Grow to $198 Billion," www.cio.com, accessed August 9, 2003.

Figure B7.10, page 322, Paul Roberts, "Report Span Costs $874 per Employee per Year," www.computerworld.com, July 2, 2003, accessed March 9, 2004.

Figure B7.11, page 323, AMA Research, "Workplace Monitoring and Surveillance," www.amanet.org, April 2003, accessed March 1, 2004.

Figure B10.1, page 365, "ERP Knowledge Base," www.cio.com, accessed June 2005.

Figure B11.9, page 387, www.w3.org, W3C Security resources, accessed June 2005.

Figure B12.2, page B12.3, "50 Trends Shaping the Future," *2003 World Future Society Special Report,* April 2004.

Figure B12.3, page B12.4, Ibid.

Figure B12.4, page B12.5, Ibid.

Figure B13.1, page B13.3, Datz, Todd, "Outsourcing World Tour," *CIO Magazine,* July 15, 2004, pp. 42–48.

Figure B21.3, page 528, AP/World Wide.